Event- und Impaktforschung

Series Editors

Holger Preuß, Mainz, Germany

Markus Kurscheidt, Lehrstuhl Sportwissenschaft II, Universität Bayreuth, Bayreuth, Germany

Die Reihe bietet ein Forum für empirische Studien zur ökonomischen Wirkungsanalyse von Großveranstaltungen in Sport, Kultur und Tourismus. Die Bände beleuchten gleichermaßen die Effekte der Großereignisse auf ihr sozioökonomisches Umfeld als auch den Einfluss von Standortfaktoren auf die Wettbewerbsfähigkeit und Governance der Eventwirtschaft. Die Themenfelder umfassen alle Stakeholder von Events und reichen von Primärerhebungen zum Reise- und Konsumverhalten von Eventbesuchern sowie zu Werbe- und Imagewirkungen von Großveranstaltungen über den gesellschaftlichen Beitrag von Events, etwa zum Volunteering, bis zu Analysen der Eventinfrastruktur wie Stadien- und Ligenmärkte oder Finanzierungsquellen. Die Schriftenreihe richtet sich an Lehrende und Studierende der Wirtschafts-, Sport- oder Tourismuswissenschaft sowie an Praktiker und öffentliche Entscheidungsträger in eventbezogenen Handlungsfeldern.

Reihe herausgegeben von

Prof. Dr. Holger Preuß,
Universität Mainz, Deutschland

Prof. Dr. Markus Kurscheidt,
Universität Bayreuth, Deutschland

Weitere Bände in der Reihe http://www.springer.com/series/12513

Tobias Duffner

Strategic Equity Partnerships in Professional Football

Evidence on Stakeholder Attitudes for the Case of the German Bundesliga

Springer Gabler

Tobias Duffner
Bremen, Germany

Diese Arbeit wurde von Tobias Duffner unter folgendem Originaltitel als Dissertation an der Sportwissenschaftlichen Fakultät der Universität Leipzig eingereicht und angenommen: Strategic Equity Partnerships between Sponsors and Football Clubs in the German Bundesliga: A Grounded Theory about Motives, Success Factors, Processes, and Effects Generated by Corporate and Club Expert Interviews and a Fan Survey

ISSN 2662-9224 ISSN 2662-9232 (electronic)
Event- und Impaktforschung
ISBN 978-3-658-31300-5 ISBN 978-3-658-31301-2 (eBook)
https://doi.org/10.1007/978-3-658-31301-2

Responsible Editor: Carina Reibold
This Springer Gabler imprint is published by the registered company Springer Fachmedien Wiesbaden GmbH part of Springer Nature.
The registered company address is: Abraham-Lincoln-Str. 46, 65189 Wiesbaden, Germany

Geleitwort

Liebe Leserinnen, liebe Leser,

es war eine Revolution, die den deutschen Fußball von Grund auf veränderte: 1973 lief Eintracht Braunschweig in der Bundesliga als erster Klub mit einem Trikot-Sponsor auf. Die mediale Aufmerksamkeit war groß, der Sponsor in aller Munde, und für die Eintracht floss eine beträchtliche D-Mark-Summe. Eine gelungene Partnerschaft, eine gelungene Strategie beider Seiten.

Diese Premiere liegt nun fast 50 Jahre zurück. Seitdem ist viel passiert. Sponsoring ist noch immer eine wichtige finanzielle Säule der Clubs im Profifußball. Doch die Bedürfnisse der Partner haben sich enorm gewandelt. Trikot- und Bandenwerbung sind weiterhin unverzichtbar, aber schon seit langem schnüren die Clubs im Profifußball darüber hinaus immer individuellere Sponsoring-Pakete, abgestimmt auf die Wünsche der jeweiligen Partner.

Seit einiger Zeit hat auch das Thema „Strategische Partnerschaften" in Verbindung mit Sponsoring im Profifußball zunehmend an Bedeutung gewonnen. Und insbesondere wenn diese Partnerschaft mit dem Verkauf von Anteilen verbunden ist, wird darüber kontrovers diskutiert. Unstrittig ist: Strategische Investoren bieten dem Bundesliga-Fußball die Chance, einen erheblichen Kapitalbedarf zu akquirieren. Doch viele Fragen sind offen: Welcher Partner passt zu welchem Club? Welcher Grad der Einflussnahme, die mit dem Verkauf von Anteilen einhergeht, ist gewünscht? Wie steht es um die Akzeptanz eines strategischen Partners durch die Fans? Es sind Fragen, mit denen sich alle Verantwortlichen im Profifußball beschäftigen.

Und auch die Frage der Motivation von Unternehmen für ein strategisches Investment ist für die Clubs von großer Bedeutung: Warum sollte sich bei der bestehenden 50+1-Regel überhaupt ein strategischer Partner für eine Minderheitenbeteiligung an einem deutschen Profifußball-Club entscheiden? Und ist der deutsche Profifußball für strategische Partner doch erst dann wirklich interessant, wenn die 50+1-Regel fällt und somit auch Mehrheitsbeteiligungen möglich sind? Ich bin sicher, dass wir diesbezüglich in der Fußball-Bundesliga in den nächsten Jahren interessante und zum Teil rasante Entwicklungen erleben werden. Vielleicht keine Revolution wie 1973... Aber: Eine weitere Öffnung der Clubs für strategische Investoren, die mit den Vereinen etwas entwickeln und sie stärken wollen, ist nötig.

Eine detaillierte Auseinandersetzung mit diesem Thema und eine Beleuchtung aller Einflussgrößen ist somit von großer Bedeutung. Ich freue mich daher, dass Tobias Duffner sich diesem für den Profifußball wichtigen Thema angenommen hat und hier eine umfassende Untersuchung der komplexen Zusammenhänge vorlegt, die hinter der Frage stecken, warum sich Sponsoren am Eigenkapital von professionellen Fußballklubs in Deutschland beteiligen und warum Vereine diesen Schritt gehen. Die Ausführungen liefern konkrete Handlungsanweisungen. Die Lektüre kann daher jedem Verantwortlichen in deutschen Profi-Fußball-Clubs eindringlich empfohlen werden.

Klaus Filbry
Vorsitzender der Geschäftsführung/
Kaufmännischer Geschäftsführer
der SV Werder Bremen GmbH & Co KGaA

Abstract

Purpose: The purpose of this dissertation is to explore the underlying motives and processes why and how corporate sponsors and professional football clubs in Germany enter into an additional share deal given the contradictory nature of corporations (monetary driven) and football clubs (maximising sporting success while operating in economic equilibrium). While share deals at football clubs are a current trend in European football, a club sponsor shareholding is predominantly a phenomenon in German football due to the idiosyncratic governance structures of German clubs (e.g., the 50+1 rule). Since there is no empirical research on the issue to date, this dissertation aims to generate theory within the specific field of professional football and to provide recommendations for action.

Design and Methodology: This research is based on the grounded theory methodology. 24 face-to-face expert interviews were conducted with corporate and club authorities at a top management level. Those experts were chosen who actually take the decision (C-level) and those who are mainly involved in the management (higher management level) of partnerships in order to get first-hand insights. The perspective of the club members and fans were added by using an online survey (n= 1,589). Document analysis complemented the process. Theory was developed by a circular process of data collection and analysis (open, axial and selective coding, constant comparative method). The theory is presented through the storyline technique.

Findings: "A Management Theory of Strategic Equity Partnerships" was generated to explain the dynamic process of how a sponsorship develops into a strategic partnership (brand symbiosis). An additional shareholding is essentially based on a strategic intent. The study's core category "securing" explains the mutual motives of a share deal and refers to securing the club's competitiveness, planning security, deepening commitment, regional connectivity and appeal, and the deterring of competitors. Fans have a differential view on four shareholder types whereby a strategic partner (sponsor) is highly accepted (90.4%). Although fans and club members want to retain the 50+1 rule, 81.9% of fans support minority shareholdings.

Research Limitations and Implications: The theory is based on the subjective view of the research participants and applies to the particular research field. As the study focuses on equity partnerships with sponsors, the theory could be enriched by the views of other types of club investors. The findings may be of interest for scholars as they extend and challenge existing concepts and introduce new concepts for partnership management. This study also provides an orientation and guideline for managerial practice to those who want to enter into and effectively manage strategic (equity) partnerships.

Originality/Value: This study contributes to the management of football partnerships as it is the first empirical study to explain the motives and processes of strategic equity partnership development in the German football business. It illuminates equity partnerships holistically from the corporate, club, and fan perspective by presenting vital insights and guidance about critical success factors as well as indicating potential pitfalls. This study is also the first to investigate a differential view of football fans towards four types of football club investors.

Abstrakt

Ziel: Das Ziel dieser Dissertation ist die Untersuchung der zugrundeliegenden, beiderseitigen Motive und Prozesse, warum sich Sponsoren am Eigenkapital von professionellen Fußballklubs in Deutschland beteiligen und warum Vereine diesen Schritt gehen. Hintergrund sind die konträren Grundausrichtungen von Sponsoren (profitorientiert) und Klubs (Maximierung des sportlichen Erfolges unter Vermeidung der Insolvenz). Während Beteiligungen von Investoren an Fußballklubs ein aktueller Trend im Europäischen Fußball sind, erscheint das Phänomen, dass sich Sponsoren an Fußballklubs beteiligen, vorwiegend in Deutschland. Grund hierfür ist die spezifische Struktur deutscher Klubs (z. B. die 50+1 Regel). Da es bis heute noch keine empirische Untersuchung zu diesem Phänomen gibt, zielt diese Dissertation darauf ab, Theorie in dem speziellen Bereich Profifußball zu entwickeln und praktische Handlungsempfehlungen zu geben.

Design: Dieses Forschungsprojekt basiert auf der Grounded Theory Methodologie. 24 persönliche Experteninterviews wurden mit Vertretern von Sponsoren und Klubs auf einem Top-Management-Level geführt.

Es wurden jene Experten interviewt, die über eine Beteiligung entscheiden, maßgeblich daran beteiligt sind (insbesondere Vorstandsvorsitzende und Vorstandsmitglieder) und in dem Management solcher Partnerschaften involviert sind, um Einblicke aus erster Hand zu erhalten. Im Rahmen des theoretischen Samplings wurde mit Hilfe einer Online-Umfrage (n = 1,589) die Arbeit um die Perspektive der Fußballfans und Klubmitglieder erweitert. Die Auswertung von Dokumenten ergänzte den gesamten Prozess. Die Theorie wird anhand der Storyline-Technik dargestellt.

Ergebnisse: „A Management Theory of Strategic Equity Partnerships" wurde entwickelt. Diese Theorie erklärt den dynamischen Prozess, wie sich eine Sponsoring-Partnerschaft zu einer strategischen Partnerschaft entwickelt. Eine zusätzliche Beteiligung eines Sponsors am Klub basiert auf strategischen Zielen. Sie dient der Absicherung des Sponsorings für Sponsor und Klub und wandelt die Partnerschaft zu einer strategischen Beteiligungspartnerschaft um. Die Kernkategorie „Securing" erklärt die gegenseitigen Motive einer Beteiligung und bezieht sich auf die Wettbewerbsfähigkeit des Klubs, Planungssicherheit, vertiefende Verpflichtung und verbesserte Kooperationsbedingungen, regionale Konnektivität und die Absicherung gegenüber SponsoringKonkurrenten. Fans haben eine differenzierte Sichtweise von unterschiedlichen Investorentypen, wobei der strategische Partner eine sehr hohe Akzeptanz erfährt (90,4 %). Obwohl sich Fans und Klubmitglieder für die Beibehaltung der 50+1 Regel aussprechen, unterstützen 81,9 % Minderheitenbeteiligungen.

Limitationen und Auswirkungen: Die Theorie basiert auf der subjektiven Sichtweise der Forschungsteilnehmer und ist auf das spezifische Forschungsfeld begrenzt. Da sich die Studie auf Beteiligungen von Sponsoren fokussiert, wäre eine zusätzliche Betrachtung anderer Investorentypen interessant. Die Ergebnisse liefern einen Beitrag zum Forschungsfeld strategischer Partnerschaften, da sie nicht nur bestehende Konzepte erweitern und teilweise anfechten, sondern auch neue Konzepte hervorbringen. Die Studie liefert eine Orientierung und Hilfestellung für Manager, die eine strategische Beteiligung in Zukunft planen und eine strategische Partnerschaft im Fußball effektiv gestalten möchten.

Originalität/Nutzen: Dies ist die erste empirische Studie, die Motive und Prozesse strategischer Beteiligungspartnerschaften mit Sponsoren im Fußballbusiness erklärt. Strategische Beteiligungspartnerschaften werden ganzheitlich aus der Perspektive von Sponsoren, Klubs und Fans beleuchtet. Wichtige Einblicke und Anleitungen über kritische Erfolgsfaktoren, das Eingehen und Managen dieser Partnerschaften, als auch mögliche Tücken werden vermittelt. Diese Arbeit ist zudem die erste, die eine differenzierte Sichtweise der Akzeptanz von Fußballfans bezüglich vier unterschiedlicher Investorentypen untersucht.

Darstellung des wissenschaftlichen Werdegangs

01/2015 – 08/2020	Universität Leipzig, Sportwissenschaftliche Fakultät, Institut für Sportpsychologie und Sportpädagogik Promotion, Dr. phil.
10/2012 – 11/2014	Liverpool John Moores University (in Kooperation mit dem European College of Business and Management, London) Master of Business Administration (MBA)
09/2010 – 09/2012	University of Wales, Newport (in Kooperation mit dem European College of Business and Management, London) Bachelor of Arts in Business and Management
09/2008 – 09/2009	IST-Studieninstitut IHK-Sportfachwirt
09/2005 – 07/2007	IST-Studieninstitut Diplom Sportmanager (IST)
10/2004 – 08/2005	Christian-Albrechts-Universität Kiel Lehramt: Mathematik und Sport (nicht abgeschlossen)
10/2003 – 04/2004	Universität Bremen Lehramt: Mathematik und Sport (nicht abgeschlossen)

Bibliographische Beschreibung

Universität Leipzig, Sportwissenschaftliche Fakultät
Institut für Sportpsychologie und Sportpädagogik
Fachgebiet Sportmanagement

Dissertation

Strategic Equity Partnerships between Sponsors and Football Clubs in the German Bundesliga: A Grounded Theory about Motives, Success Factors, Processes, and Effects Generated by Corporate and Club Expert Interviews and a Fan Survey

Verfasser

	Name: Duffner	Vorname: Tobias
	Erscheinungsjahr: 2019	Abbildungen: 28
	Blattzahl: 401	Literaturangaben:607
	Anlagen: 8	Tabellen: 39

Versicherung (Declaration)

I declare that this thesis and the work reported herein was composed by and originated entirely from the author. Information derived from the published and unpublished work of others has been acknowledged in the text and references are given in the list of sources. No part of the thesis has been submitted as part of any other academic award.

Hiermit versichere ich, dass ich die vorliegende Arbeit ohne unzulässige Hilfe Dritter und ohne Benutzung anderer als der angegebenen Hilfsmittel angefertigt habe; die aus fremden Quellen direkt oder indirekt übernommenen Gedanken sind als solche kenntlich gemacht.

Bei der Auswahl und Auswertung des Materials sowie bei der Herstellung des Manuskripts habe ich Unterstützungsleistungen von folgenden Personen erhalten:

Weitere Personen waren an der geistigen Herstellung der Arbeit nicht beteiligt. Insbesondere habe ich nicht die Hilfe eines Promotionsberaters in Anspruch genommen. Dritte haben von mir weder unmittelbar noch mittelbar geldwerte

Leistungen für Arbeiten erhalten, die im Zusammenhang mit dem Inhalt der vorgelegten Dissertation stehen.

Die Arbeit wurde bisher weder im In- noch im Ausland in gleicher oder ähnlicher Form einer anderen Prüfungsbehörde vorgelegt und ist auch noch nicht veröffentlicht worden.

Tobias Duffner

Acknowledgements

First and foremost, I would like to thank my beloved family and fiancée for their moral support, encouragement and benevolence. In particular my fiancée was a steady motivator in tough times and throughout the study and coped with my frequent stress with humour and courage.

I would also like to thank my friends for understanding my personal situation and accepting the limited time I spent with them during the years of doctoral studies.

I wish to thank my supervisor Professor Gregor Hovemann for giving me the opportunity to work on a topic about which I am so enthusiastic. Likewise, I wish to express my thanks to Professor Gregor Hovemann and my second advisor Professor Robert Wilken for their constantly critical, supportive, motivating, and pleasant way of guiding and supporting me through this dissertation. Each stage of the project was informed by valuable discussions and advice, with regard to the content of the study but also in critical situations beyond the dissertation topic.

I would like to express my gratitude to the corporate and club managers who partook in my research study and shared their experiences with me in an intensive and stimulating way. They were amazingly positive towards my research and me as a person and provided a great deal of very valuable information and insights. From my perspective, such in-depth insights surpassed all my expectations and made a valuable contribution to the dissertation as well as my personal development.

I would also like to express my great gratitude and appreciation to Fiona Moore for her assistance, stamina and kindness in the proofreading of this dissertation.

Furthermore, I am grateful to those professors and scientific employees of Leipzig University who facilitated and supported me in the preparation to accomplish the additional modules required for the doctorate. A special thank you goes to Dr. Nadja Walter who was a supportive counterpart and assisted me with her advice and network.

Last but not least, I would like to thank Sebastian B. Bauers who facilitated my research journey in multiple ways; he initially introduced me to the major procedures as a doctoral student at Leipzig University and became a very cherished discussion partner and ultimately a good friend.

Tobias Duffner

Inhaltsverzeichnis

Abbreviations

B2B =	Business to business
B2C =	Business to customer
BVB =	Ballspielverein Borussia 09 Dortmund
CB =	Corporate brand
CR =	Critical realism
DFB =	Deutscher Fußball Bund
DFL =	Deutsche Fußball Liga
e.g. =	Exempli gratia
EPL =	English Premier League
et al. =	Et aliae
etc. =	Et cetera
FCB =	FC Bayern München
FIFA =	Fédération Internationale de Football Association
GT =	Grounded Theory
I.a. =	Inter alia
ibid. =	Ibidem
i.e. =	Id est
Inc. =	Incorporated
IT =	Information technology
Ltd. =	Limited
M&A =	Mergers and acquisitions
op. cit. =	Opere citato
RBV =	Resource-based view
RDT =	Resource dependence theory
RQ =	Research question
SC =	Supervisory committee

sect. =	Section
SQ =	Sub-question
SVW =	SV Werder Bremen
SI =	Symbolic interactionism
TCE =	Transaction cost economics
UEFA =	Union of European Football Associations
UVP =	Unique value proposition
VfB =	VfB Stuttgart
viz. =	Videlicet
vs. =	Versus

Abbildungsverzeichnis

Tabellenverzeichnis

Introduction

1

1.1 Increasing Emergence of Strategic Equity Partnerships in Germany

Strategic equity partnerships[1] in football are set to continue being a major part of football's development in the following years (Schuster & Unterhitzenberger, 2014), *"with further football club acquisitions across Europe seemingly inevitable"* (Boor et al., 2016; 2).

In recent years, football sponsorship[2] has transformed from a passive type of marketing to a strategic business building activity (Fahy et al., 2004; Dolphin, 2003), that is a legitimate part of the marketing communication mix, and has become a cornerstone in the corporate strategy of football clubs and corporate sponsors (Capasso & Rossi, 2013; Rudd, 2012).

Football clubs have progressed from the traditional approach of taking gate receipts during the 1990's to a much more multifaceted set of business and management activities, most notably sports sponsoring, in order to expand their value domain (Grundy, 1998). Due to global public interest, increased through technological advancements, in particular on the internet and in TV broadcasting, football—generally accepted as the number one sport in the world (Van der

[1]This term refers to a partnership between a corporate sponsor and a football club, in which the sponsor holds shares in the club in addition to the sponsorship. This will be explained in detail in Chapter 3.

[2]*"Sponsorship is the provision of assistance either financial or in kind to an activity by a commercial organisation for the purpose of achieving commercial objectives"* (Meenaghan, 1993; 9).

T. Duffner, *Strategic Equity Partnerships in Professional Football*, Event- und Impaktforschung, https://doi.org/10.1007/978-3-658-31301-2_1

Heijden, 2012; Nagy, 2011)—has evolved into a lucrative industry (Acero et al., 2017; Frick, 2007). As such, football is the highest-grossing sport in the sponsorship industry (Statista, 2016). For example, revenues from sponsorship and commercial sources total €6.3 billion in the financial year 2017 in European football (UEFA, 2017). Consequently, football as a sport is enormously fascinating to society, and as a business it is increasingly appealing to sponsors and corporate investors (Netzer et al., 2015; Capasso & Rossi, 2013). As Robinson (2013; Sect. 1) stated in the Financial Times: "*Companies continue to score with football sponsorship*".

Since football sponsorship has increasingly become intertwined with corporate strategy (Nufer & Bühler, 2011), this has given rise to a specific form of sponsorship in German football, namely strategic partnerships[3] (alliances), in which corporate sponsors buy additional club shares and thus become a shareholder of the club simultaneously (Boor et al., 2016; Prigge & Vöpel, 2014). Many academics such as Süßmilch (2004), Chemnitzer et al. (2015), Prigge and Vöpel (2014), and Henseler et al. (2007) view the roots of strategic partnerships in the German football business in the marketing discipline, because this form of "strategic equity partnership" has arisen from long-term sponsorship collaborations. Although the growing international nature of ownership (investor[4] presence in the form of patrons) of European football clubs is an enduring trend that is evident in professional leagues across Europe (Lammert et al., 2009; Müller, 2008), "strategic equity partnerships" have, first and foremost, become a phenomenon in German football.

The reason for this lies in the historically different tradition of governance structures in the various football associations in Europe and concomitant country specific regulations apply in each nation (Adam & Hovemann, 2018). Whereas clubs from the Big Five[5] of European top leagues are often controlled by a private party (e.g., all clubs in England, France, and Italy) (UEFA, 2017), in Germany club members and fans have traditionally been a central institution in

[3]There is a widespread understanding that the term strategic alliance can be transferred to the concept of strategic partnership, as both terms are largely used interchangeably (Vergauwen et al., 2010).

[4]An investor is a natural person or legal entity that holds a stake in the club shares.

[5]The Big Five of European football is known as the top (first) leagues of Germany, Italy, England, France, and Spain.

the club ("eingetragener Verein[6]") due to their co-determining role in the club's professional football unit (Merkel, 2012). In every other European league clubs are allowed to sell majority shares except for German clubs due to the 50+1 rule[7]. The 50+1 rule is to ensure that the club members keep overall control, prohibiting clubs to sell more than 49% of the club's shares (voting rights) and therefore defending them from the power of external investors/equity partners[8] (Lopatta et al., 2014; Bauers & Hovemann, 2019b).

1.2 Relevance of Strategic Equity Partnerships for German Clubs

For German clubs, selling shares as part of entering into an equity partnership with sponsors is an attractive financial option because it makes clubs wealthier, and their capacity for investing in player talents is accordingly greater (Rudd, 2012; Carmichael et al., 2010).

In today's football business, professional football clubs need to be considered in the context of international competition when fighting for players (Tome, 2003). The only way for a club to outperform competitors on the pitch is to have a better squad. The quality of the available players and the way they perform as a team are the main factors behind winning matches and maximising sporting success (Kuypers & Szymanski, 2012). This leads to a "War for Talent" (McNamara, 2013), in which clubs try to outspend their national and international rivals in order to attract highly talented players for the sake of winning (Tome, op. cit.). According to Bill Gerrad, professor of sport management at Leeds University Business School, *"the best playing talent goes to the highest wages"* (Gerrad cited by Bolgar, 2010; sect. 3).

[6]"*The Verein is a non-profit organisation whose members democratically elect representatives to take over management functions for specified election periods*" (Franck 2010a, 113).

[7]The "50+1 rule" is an informal term that refers to a regulation (§ 16C, digit 2 of DFB statute and § 8, digit 2 of DFL statue) of Deutscher Fußball Bund (DFB) and Deutsche Fußball-Liga (DFL). It states that a club must hold the majority (50+1) of its own voting rights in order to get a license to compete in professional football in Germany.

[8]In this dissertation the term "equity partner" refers to a general business partner (e.g., corporations or a private party) who acquires shares in the partner organisation (i.e., football club).

German football clubs financially trail behind competitors from other European top leagues due to lower TV broadcasting revenues (Chemnitzer et al., 2015). For instance, Schmitt (2015) speaks about a 'dramatic disadvantage' in terms of TV revenues and Rehm (2018) summarises that German clubs are only second-division with respect to international TV revenues. The financial advance of foreign clubs is further intensified due to the 'flood of investors' (majority acquisitions) in the past (Oediger, 2017b). Regarding this, the 50+1 rule restricts German clubs to generate additional funds by selling majority shares and therefore prevents equal opportunities in the European football business (Adam & Hovemann, 2018; Lammert et al., 2009).

In the light of the statistically proven correlation between financial power and sporting success (Kuypers & Szymanski, 2012; Wilkesmann, 2014; Hovemann & Wieschemann, 2009; Frick, 2005; Hall et al., 2002; Szymanski & Kuypers, 1999) and in order to stay competitive, German clubs try to close the (financial) gap by entering into strategic equity partnerships (Chemnitzer et al., 2015; Prigge & Vöpel, 2014). This trend has intensified within the last years given that between 2008 and 2018 seventeen strategic equity partnerships were announced by clubs in German professional football[9].

For example, in 2001 FC Bayern München (FCB) announced the first strategic equity partnership in German football (Groscuth, 2005) with its long-term sponsor Adidas, which invested €75 million for 10% stake of FCB (Adam & Hovemann, 2018; Groscuth, 2005). In the years that followed, FCB entered into further strategic equity partnerships with their sponsors Audi (€90 million for 9.09% stake in 2009) and Allianz (€110 million for 8.33% stake in 2014), each holding an 8.33%[10] stake in the club, generating a total of €275 million in the club's cash box. Similarly, many clubs in Germany (e.g., BVB Borussia Dortmund 09, Eintracht Frankfurt, VfB Stuttgart, FC Ingolstadt 04, etc.) entered into strategic equity partnerships with corporate sponsors, which are leading companies in their respective industries, such as Evonik (chemicals), Puma (sports articles), or Daimler AG (automotive), to name but a few.

[9]German professional football comprises the first three divisions of German football, namely the 1st Bundesliga, 2nd Bundesliga, and 3rd Liga.

[10]Via an increase in share capital the three corporations hold a stake of 8.33% each.

1.3 Conflicting Goals between Club and Corporation—Trophies vs. Profits

When a football club sells shares of stakes, the investment organisation has a share in the profits (property rights, e.g., dividends) or debts of the club, and gets voting (administrative rights, e.g., board of directors) and control power (Prigge & Vöpel, 2014). This leads to the following challenges: corporations (sponsors) usually operate within a hierarchy of diverse, interrelated business objectives. Whether financially (e.g., turnover, profit) or non-financially (e.g., image, growth), it is commonly accepted that increasing long-term shareholder value (generating profits) is the reason for their existence (Chemnitzer et al., 2015; Amis et al., 1997; Carroll, 1996) and all business strategies are linked to this overriding principle (Denning, 2011). According to Jones (2008; 7), "*businesses and their leaders must be evaluated based on their ability to deliver financial returns to investors*".

In contrast, football clubs in Germany originate from a non-profit nature (Verein). Even though German clubs are nowadays allowed to generate profits due to specific governance structures[11], are managed with economic criteria in mind (Adam & Hovemann, 2018; Quitzau, 2009), and match medium-sized companies with respect to annual turnover (Adam et al., 2017) and number of employees (Nufer & Bühler, 2011), it is widely acknowledged that the ultimate goal of European football clubs'[12] is not to make a profit, rather it is to maximise sporting success while trying to operate within economic equilibrium (Acero et al., 2017; Nagy, 2012; Rudd, 2012; Frick, 2007; Barros & Leach, 2006; Sloane, 1971). In other words, achieving the best possible sports performances and sustaining them is the highest priority for a football club (Chemnitzer et al., 2015; Von der Heijden, 2012; Pinnuck & Potter, 2006). If a club generates profits, these are largely reinvested in the team (Acero et al., 2017; Chemnitzer et al., 2015) or

[11]On the basis of the 1998 Resolution of the German Federal Parliament, football clubs in Germany are allowed to outsource their professional football department in the form of e.g., a limited liability company, limited partnership, share company, or a combination. The original management form of an association (eingetragener Verein, e. V.) must hold at least 51% of the outsourced department (50+1 rule) (Nagy, 2013).

[12]The European model of sports (football) is characterised by a hierarchical organisation of different leagues and a system of success-related promotion and relegation, whereas US sports is based on a franchise system in which profit is postulated as the overall goal of clubs (Neale, 1964).

utilised to enhance the club's infrastructure (Von der Heijden, 2012; Westberg et al., 2012). Consequently, paying dividends to shareholders is currently neither a mission nor a future strategic intent[13] (Rudd, 2012; Barros & Leach, 2006).

Against this background, the central question arises why sponsors (corporations) enter into strategic equity partnerships and invest[14] money to hold a stake in a football club. As Stefan Szymanski (Szymanski cited by Salz et al., 2015; sect. 6), a well-known English sport scientist, provokingly stated: "*I support the freedom of capitalists and investors to lose a huge amount of capital through the investment in football clubs*".

Furthermore, equity investments also have an impact on the club's members and fans (Bauers & Hovemann, 2019a; Pawlowski, 2013). Club members and fans often have reservations regarding equity partners (Bauers & Hovemann, 2019a; Herberger et al., 2013). This is rooted in the emotional attachment of football fans and as well as in the tradition of German football and its original governance structure (Beech, 2010). Selling minority shares to investors constitutes a change in the ownership structure of the club (Prigge & Vöpel, 2014). As a consequence, opportunities for co-determination and democratic decision-making for club members and fans are lessened (Roose & Schäfer, 2017; Giulianotti, 2002; Walsh & Giulianotti, 2001). Since investors normally have an interest in being able to determine how their investment is being used (Prigge & Vöpel, 2014), Ruf and Theweleit (2018) as well as Steinmann (2018) summarise that strategic equity partners and investors—from a club member and fan perspective—are often perceived as 'corporate raiders' who impinge on the club management with the overall aim of either trying to exert influence on the club's decisions or to exploit the club for their business goals. Therefore, in Germany the trend towards the increased presence of equity partnerships is perceived by fans as a "loss of identity" (Jacobs, 2014; Herberger et al., 2013) and a threat for the 50+1 rule (Bauers & Hovemann, 2019a). Since club members and fans are the critical factor why the club exists and continues to exist (Murphy, 2010), club authorities face the challenge of managing the discord between the interests of fans and other stake- and/or shareholders (Bauers & Hovemann, 2019b). The development of sponsorships towards strategic equity partnerships is, therefore, encompassed

[13]Strategic intent is classified as the long-term (future) business direction of the company (Johnston et al., 2011; Todeva & Knoke, 2005).

[14]In general, an investment entails an initial spending of money at a specific point of time (normally one large amount) and targets to yield economic benefits to the investor at some other point of time (a series of smaller amounts over a pre-defined period).

within a broader inter-organisational framework in which complex interactions emerge.

Research about strategic partnerships is found in a variety of contexts. There is a tremendous body of literature concerning strategic partnerships in a non-sports setting. For example, many studies concentrated on motives and the partnership creation process (e.g. DePamphilis, 2012; Lowensberg, 2010; Todeva & Knoke, 2005), other research focused on management processes (e.g. Christoffersen, 2013; Sluyts et al., 2011; Ireland, 2002), and many scholars have addressed knowledge (Park & Lee, 2012; Lui et al., 2010; Dyer & Singh, 1998) and the important role of trust (Costa e Silva et al., 2012; Parmigiani & Santos, 2011; Das & Teng, 2001).

The sport-related strategic partnership literature concentrates on partnership performance such as value creation and increasing brand equity (e.g., Tsiotsou et al., 2014; Alexander, 2009), focuses on partnership requirements (Morgan et al., 2014; Farrelly & Quester, 2005a), or examines strategic partnership failure (e.g., Westberg et al., 2011; Farrelly 2010).

In football, strategic partnerships in the form of share deals are mainly approached from a financial viewpoint. International studies have addressed the effects of 'cash injections' from patrons on earnings (e.g., Plumley et al., 2017) and profits (e.g., Oediger, 2017b), or the impact of club ownership and governance on financing opportunities (e.g., Adam & Hovemann, 2018) and sport performance (e.g., Rohde & Breuer, 2017). Dworak (2010) and Roy (2009) examined equity partnerships as a financing opportunity for clubs. Only a limited number of studies investigated strategic equity partnerships in German football from the perspective of the strategic equity partner (Welling & Westhoff, 2018; Chemnitzer et al., 2015; Prigge & Vöpel, 2014). However, these studies are of theoretical nature.

Another research area in German football addresses the impact of equity partnerships for club members and fans, specifically the fan view in terms of investor (equity partner) presence in general (Pawlowski, 2013) and the related debate about the retention or repeal of the 50+1 rule (e.g., Bauers & Hovemann, 2019a; Bühler, 2017; Pilz, 2011; Pfeiffer et al., 2007). While these scholars focus on the term investor, the results concur that the majority of fans are against investor presence in German football and in favour of the retention of the 50+1 rule. Yet, these studies have in common that they neglect to take different types of investors/equity partners (i.e., sponsors, financial investors, Maecenas, and oligarchs) into consideration. This raises the question as to whether fans are generally against all kinds of equity partner or whether fans have a differential view concerning diverse equity partner types.

On the basis of the rapid pace of this phenomenon's development in Germany and its economic significance empirical studies are urgently needed in order to comprehend the underlying motives, processes, success factors, and impact/effects.

The present empirical study is designed in order to holistically explore and understand the changing nature of corporate-football sponsorships towards strategic equity partnerships in German 1st Bundesliga from a strategic perspective. By taking a philosophical position consisting of critical realism (ontology) and symbolic interactionism (epistemology), the author uses a flexible research approach based on the grounded theory (GT) methodology, which considers all adequate and available methods to investigate the issue. Addressing the topic from the perspective of sponsors and clubs (24 personal expert interviews at top management level) as well as club members and fans (an online survey with football fans in Germany, n = 1,589) allows to enhance an understanding about motives, strategic demands, critical success factors, value generating processes, and impact/effects of the phenomenon.

Consequently, the overall goal of this dissertation is to develop theory[15] from the specific field of strategic equity partnerships in the German football business and to create recommendations for action (orientation towards practicability[16]; Franke, 2000).

1.4 Contribution of Research

The relevance of the subject has already been outlined in the previous sections. The ever-evolving football business occupies a cornerstone in generating revenue for the economy as a whole, and the interconnectedness with the business world is steadily intensifying (Nagy, 2011). Strategic equity partnerships between foot-

[15]The term 'theory' originates from the Greek word 'thorós', a spectator, and accents the feature that all theories are mental models of the perceived reality (Bradford, 2015). In this study the term is applied according to the definition of Strauss and Corbin (1994), and Franke (2002). Theory is a set of propositions, hypotheses, or accepted facts that tries to present a plausible explanation (comprehensive, coherent, and simple model to reduce the complexity of the empirical world) of a phenomenon under study (Franke, 2002; Strauss & Corbin, 1994).

[16]A pragmatic research objective focuses on generating guidance (recommendation for action), which is applicable and realisable in practice. In particular, this applies for the utility of study results (Franke, 2000).

ball clubs and corporate sponsors is a virtually unexplored area of sport management, marketing (sponsorship), and partnership literature. Therefore, this research study will contribute to the discipline of sport management and strategy in several ways.

First, the study has theoretical relevance as it is the first empirical study that investigates the motives and processes of why and how strategic equity partnerships in the football business are entered into. No empirical research study has been identified to date which investigates the formation of strategic equity partnerships. Therefore, this research study meets the call from Quitzau (2014) and Farrelly (2010) for empirical research on the topic. As a result, the findings may yield useful insights for future evaluations.

Second, the study enhances practical understanding. According to Bell et al. (2006), research can only be characterised as being of practical relevance if it integrates the interests of managers and enhances their decision-making. This dissertation attempts to develop theory from the insights of first-hand experts, from which an enhanced comprehension of the establishment (motives) and effective management processes of strategic equity partnerships can be derived. It combines theoretical insights from various disciplines (sport management, sponsoring, and partnership) with knowledge from business leaders and experts with a wide range of professional backgrounds and experiences.

Additionally, this is the first study that takes a differential view of football fans about four types of equity partners into account and therefore adds valuable insights to the current discussion about investor presence and the 50+1 rule in German football. The study also examines upon which aspects football fans base their opinion. This presents an overview for clubs as to which kind of equity partner is more or less accepted and which attributes an equity partner should possess in order to maximise fan acceptance.

A theory which is based on such a valuable range of data is likely to support corporate and club managers, marketing officers, and other practitioners in the sports field with their future work as it sheds light on strategic behaviour and managerial decision-making of football sponsors and clubs. The results will help to identify fundamental requirements when entering into strategic equity partnerships, present strategies/guidance to manage partnerships, and indicate failure and success factors. This practical relevance will become increasingly significant in German football due to the rising future importance of strategic equity partnerships for German football clubs (Boor et al., 2016; Schuster & Unterhitzenberger, 2014; Metrum[17], 2004).

Third, the study can make a methodological contribution since it utilises the grounded theory methodology that supports a flexible approach to data gathering but also encapsulates a highly systematic and rigorous strategy to data analysis. This not only allows the development of substantive theory[18], which is grounded in real-life data, but also provides the opportunity and basis for the development of formal theory[19] (Loonam, 2014; Glaser & Strauss, 1967). Grounded theory is rarely constructed to only produce new knowledge. Theories generated via grounded theory aspire to grant understanding of a phenomenon that will "*ultimately inform practice in a given discipline*" (Birks & Mills, 2015; 148), thus reinforcing its practical relevance.

Fourth, theory developed throughout this research could have the potential to change the view and management of long-term sport sponsorship partnerships due to its cross-disciplinary insights and knowledge. Hence, the research can contribute to several fields of study, in particular those of strategic partnerships and sponsorships, and can be the starting point for future research. For example, there is an opportunity to test the findings in other sport-related contexts. Moreover, the study provides a platform for lively discussions and can serve as a vehicle for implementing change in both clubs and corporations as regards the management of strategic sponsorship partnerships.

Finally, as prior research in the partnership field has often been focused on just a unilateral perspective (e.g., Lowensberg, 2010; Das & Teng, 2002; Barringer & Harrison, 2000; Gulati, 2000), this study uses a triple approach to investigate the topic from the perspectives of football clubs, football fans, and corporate sponsors. Taking a ternary view of the subject allows indispensable aspects to be more profoundly appreciated and variations considered with greater ease.

---

[17]Metrum is a company established in 1999 and concentrates on strategy and management consultancy.

[18]"*A substantive theory is grounded in research on a specific content area (e.g., sport development) and evolves from the study of a phenomenon situated in a particular context*" (Sotiriadou & Shilbury, 2008; 143).

[19]"*A formal theory pertains to a conceptual area (e.g., development) and therefore emerges from the study of a phenomenon examined under several different types of situations*" (Sotiriadou & Shilbury, 2008; 143).

1.5 Structure of the Dissertation

The study is structured as follows: Chapter 1 introduces the study's research topic, provides background information on the relevance of the issue, and succinctly outlines the research problem. Eventually, the study's theoretical and practical contributions are delineated and the value of the research is highlighted.

Chapter 2 presents a review of the sport-related strategic partnership literature allowing to unveil the research gaps in greater detail. The study's purpose is given and the central research question and sub-questions are elaborated.

In the array of the theoretical framework (Chapter 3), initially various theoretical backgrounds are outlined through which strategic partnerships can be understood and explanations are given as to which theoretical perspectives are incorporated. The reader is then familiarised with the study's underlying key terms, which are critically discussed, defined, and explained. Following on from this, the current state of the academic alliance/partnership literature is critically reviewed in order to provide a sound theoretical basis. Thereby, two aspects are emphasised: motives to enter into strategic alliances and critical success factors of strategic partnerships, as these are fundamental components upon which alliance success is based.

The application of the strategic partnership concept to the football business is presented in Chapter 4. Background information on the challenges/peculiarities of football clubs are provided and it is depicted how the concept of strategic partnership is understood in the football business. Additionally, the inherent characteristics of diverse equity partnerships and the various motives of four types of investors are discussed as presented in the football related literature. Next, the factors which attract corporations to enter into strategic equity partnerships with football clubs are delineated. Afterwards, the effects of strategic equity partnerships, in particular the fan perspective on strategic equity partnerships, are critically reviewed in detail.

Chapter 5 portrays a thorough overview of the research design, the underlying research philosophy, and research strategy. It is outlined and justified that the study is based on the grounded theory methodology for the main purpose of theory generation. The study's qualitative and quantitative data collection methods are explained. A detailed instruction of how data was analysed and theory generated is given in order to comprehend the research process, findings, and conclusions. A reflective part is included in order to consider the issue of theoretical sensitivity[20] and to acknowledge the researcher's preconceptions. Criteria for evaluation research and trustworthiness are discussed and research limitations in regard to the study's research design are acknowledged. Furthermore, ethical considerations are taken into account.

Chapter 6 depicts the core of the study, the study's empirical findings. "A Management Theory of Strategic Equity Partnerships" is presented using the storyline technique, a narrative form in which the theory is illustrated by reference to its core and main categories/concepts and their relationships.

Chapter 7 elucidates management implications and contributions and presents recommendations for action derived from the study results. Moreover, research limitations are discussed and an outlook for future research is given.

Chapter 8 summarises the study by responding to the research question and sub-questions. Finally, the study ends with a concluding statement.

[20]Theoretical sensitivity accepts that researchers enter a research site with a familiarity of the area but, significantly, without pre-conceived concepts and ideas about what they might discover (Weed, 2009).

Research Gaps and Research Questions 2

2.1 Status Quo of Strategic Partnership Research in the Sport Business

Strategic partnerships in the sport context are discussed from different theoretical views, most notably from a marketing/brand management, strategic management, strategic alliance, or financial perspective. Accordingly, different terminologies are used ranging from "co-branding partnerships" (e.g., Kahuni et al., 2009; Motion et al., 2003; Simonin & Ruth, 1998), "strategic partnerships" (e.g., Adam & Hovemann, 2018; Urriolagoitia & Planellas, 2007; Groscuth, 2005), "strategic relationships" (Farrelly, 2010), "strategic alliances" (e.g., Morgan et al., 2014; Hecox, 2007; Farrelly & Quester, 2005a), and "(strategic) investors" (e.g., Welling & Westhoff, 2018; Leister, 2017; Rentz, 2015). However, these terms are mostly used synonymously.

Even though sports sponsorship has the same characteristics as strategic partnerships since it encompasses the allocation of scarce resources with the intent of attaining specific organisational objectives, and has increasingly been delineated as a strategic activity (Fahy et al., 2004; Motion, 2003; Amis et al., 1999), it has mainly been neglected in the academic partnership literature. As such there are only limited studies which view and discuss the development from sponsorships towards strategic partnership (Urriolagoitia & Planellas, 2007; Hecox, 2007; Cousens et al., 2006; Farrelly & Quester, 2005a) and much less the development towards strategic equity partnership.

In 2003, Motion et al. illuminated sports sponsorship from a brand management perspective by investigating the "co-branding partnership" of Adidas and the All Blacks (the elite team of the New Zealand Rugby Union, NZRU) using a qualitative (single) case study approach. The authors explored the process of how

T. Duffner, *Strategic Equity Partnerships in Professional Football*, Event- und Impaktforschung, https://doi.org/10.1007/978-3-658-31301-2_2

to build a co-branded identity within sports sponsorship. In such a partnership, the concepts of co-brand and sports sponsorship are synthesised with the aim of creating and increasing brand equity[1] for both partners (Motion et al., 2003).

As key findings the study presents the success factors which are simultaneously articulated at strategic, tactical, ideological, and emotional stages and underpinned by a starting campaign with a focus on gaining acceptance by stakeholders (Motion et al., 2003). Thereby, brand equity is created by the way in which the partnership is experienced. Co-branding offers access to the partner's network and brand strategy and thus the chance to pursue new strategies assisted by an experienced associate. Brand equity was further generated via the alignment of corporate brand values. Sharing the same values might increase the credibility of the partnership (Kahuni et al., 2009; Motion et al., 2003) and might assign the values more efficiently to the co-brand, too (Andreas, 2009).

In a similar vein, Alexander (2009) also used a qualitative case study design for rugby, but this time in Wales. This study confirmed the aforementioned results of a fit (Alexander refers to a semantic fit) in brand values as the fundamental element in co-branding partnerships. However, Alexander (2009) adds that a co-branding partnership has not only the potential to identify and intensify, but also to redefine the brand values with the aid of the partner.

Kahuni and his allies (2009) considered the "co-branding partnership" between the Formula 1 team McLaren Mercedes and Vodafone. This paper, which is exclusively based on secondary research data, focuses on image transfer and its (negative) effects ("spillover") on corporate reputation due to a fraudulent conduct of the Formula One team (misuse of confidential data which belonged to Ferrari). Supporting evidence can be found that a fit of brand values and attitudes is the foundation for this co-branding relationship. It is indicated that in a strategic partnership, in which the images of two brands grow closer together and are marketed as one, both parties must be aware of the consequences of misbehaviour (ethical dilemma). Referring to Kahuni et al. (2009), the key to weathering difficult periods lies in effective crisis management. This finding is confirmed by Westberg et al. (2011), who also examined the impact of negative behaviour associated with a sponsored sport entity across a variety of sport contexts (football, rugby, and basketball) in Australia using in-depth interviews.

---

[1]Brand equity is defined as "*a set of assets and liabilities linked to a brand's name and symbols that adds to or subtracts from the value provided by a product or service to a firm and/or that firm's customers. The major asset categories are: brand name awareness, brand loyalty, perceived quality, and brand associations*" (Aaker, 1996; 78).

In particular, transparency, pro-activity, and media management appear to be fundamental aspects in lessening the degenerative episode[2]. In addition, the more trust, commitment, and open communication between partners the less the probability of termination (Westberg et al., 2011).

In more recent research, Tsiotsou et al. (2014) build on the results of Motion et al. (2003), Alexander (2009), and Kahuni et al. (2009) but include new insights by elucidating affective attitude formation and its underlying mechanisms. In contrast to the aforementioned papers, the authors used a quantitative approach with a conceptual framework. It includes two football clubs from Greece and data were collected via customer questionnaires (n = 280). The findings confirmed co-branding as an appropriate means in creating positive effects to both brands in terms of brand equity elements. It is illustrated that a strong emotional attachment to the sport brand makes up an essential prerequisite in creating brand equity for the sponsor brand. Previous research (Kahuni et al. 2009) did not consider the role of emotional bonds in co-branding. Tsiotsou et al. (2014; 316) determine that emotional attachment is *"the connecting chain that leads to attitude formation in co-branding"*.

The expectation of partners to invest in the partnership and produce value beyond stipulated content has already been emphasised by Farrelly et al. (2006). They conducted 28 expert interviews of sponsors and clubs in the sports field and come to the result that those involved require to apprehend the relationship as a form of co-marketing alliance and an opportunity for brand alignment including a shared sense of strategic intent. This finding is corroborated in a qualitative case study by Rennard and Sitz (2011) in the context of sailing.

Taken together, all these studies concur that, if managed as a co-branding partnership, sponsorship exceeds the purely traditional goals of increasing sponsors' exposure and awareness. Rather, it can develop into a strategic partnership that allows brand values to be extracted and transferred from the relationship at a variety of levels (Tsiotsou et al. 2014; Alexander, 2009).

The first scholars to address sport sponsorships from a strategic alliance perspective were Farrelly and Quester (2005a) by unveiling opportunities for sponsor and sport entities to invest jointly in order to attain their own strategic objectives. In their empirical qualitative study of Australian Football League, they ascertained that strategic compatibility, goal convergence, trust, and commitment

[2]Degenerative episode is defined as "*an episode having a negative effect on a relationship's state by decreasing cooperation, trust, mutual understanding and joint benefits*" (Schurr, 2007; 165).

are critical attributes that allow a sponsorship to act as a strategic alliance and to build a competitive advantage. Their seminal work is confirmed by Urriolagoitia and Planellas (2007), who extended this line of thought by incorporating a dynamic perspective. By approaching how sports sponsorships develop and change over time they suggest a life-cycle model including a formation, operation, and outcome stage. They use the partnership of USB and team Alinghi in the sailing business as a case example. The cornerstone in the formation stage is to formulate sponsorship objectives which are congruent with competitive strategy and engage in an open dialogue about role expectations.

The critical aspect of role expectations is revisited in subsequent studies by, e.g., Hecox (2007) and Morgan et al. (2014) among others. The key in the operation phase is to build trust and a compatible partnership environment by means of intense interactions. This can help to identify further synergies and additional value such as knowledge transfer during the outcome stage.

Another case analysis is the work of Hecox (2007), who uses the same theoretical background to illuminate the formation and management of the partnership between Reebok and the National Football League (NFL) in America. He corroborates the aforementioned results but puts greater emphasis on cross referencing to strategic alliances in other industries and tries to adopt these insights to the specific sport context. While Hecox (ibid.) argues a strategic alliance can lead to a competitive advantage, he also discusses the causes of alliance failure, most of all the failure to meet the partner's expectations, financial troubles, a shift in strategy, recognition that corporate cultures do not fit, or new leadership may re-determine strategic priorities. Due to these risks, he suggests to plan an exit strategy beforehand.

In contrast to Hecox (2007), Morgan et al. (2014) concentrate on value creation, stability, and factors for renewal of a sport sponsorship alliance between four sponsors and a sport event in Australia. The scholars consider the partnership from a dyadic perspective using semi-structured interviews. While the vital role of trust, transparency, open communication, and (role) expectations are sustained, the significance of informal processes, which create inter-partner confidence come to light. Ultimately, formal as well as informal processes should act in concert to generate mutual value, partner satisfaction, and renewal decisions (Morgan et al., 2014).

Farrelly (2010) offers a critical evaluation of sports sponsorship alliances by investigating relationship-related reasons of termination. 24 participants from League entities, clubs, and sponsors of major Australian sports (football, basketball, and rugby) were interviewed using a longitudinal study over four years. In line with the research focus, the interviews were conducted within a timeframe of three months of termination to make sure related experiences were still present in the minds of interviewees. The core finding is that partners need to have unified objectives.

To summarise, from an alliance perspective the underlying rationale of partnership formation has a strategic focus and aims to attain a sustainable competitive advantage.

Whilst the traditional form of strategic sponsoring still persists, the appearance of equity partnerships is set to take centre stage across football clubs in Europe (Boor et al., 2016). Even though there are different forms of equity partnerships, e.g., partnerships with patrons, Maecenas, financial investors, or corporate sponsors (Welling & Westhof, 2018; Leister, 2017; Prigge & Vöpel, 2014), research about equity partnerships has in common that it is mainly approached from a financial perspective by addressing investor presence as an attractive financial option for clubs. Based on this, if a club enters into an equity partnership (whether to sponsors, Maecenas, financial investor, or any other kind of organisation), the term "investor" is principally used but often also equated with "strategic partner" (Ruf & Theweleit, 2018; Welling & Westhof, 2018; Oediger, 2017b; Leister, 2017; Heun, 2016).

For the most part in European football leagues a shareholder approach predominates, in which private investors (called 'sugar daddies') hold the majority of club shares (Boor et al., 2016). Thus, research has largely concentrated on the impact of 'cash injections' (soft loans[3]) from 'sugar daddies' on sport performance, earnings, and profits (Rohde & Breuer, 2017; Plumley et al., 2017; Oediger, 2017b) or the influence of different forms of club governance on financing opportunities for clubs (e.g., Adam & Hovemann, 2018). Roy (2009) was one of the first to address the factors which influence the efficiency of equity partnerships for both the club and strategic partner. In his theoretical work, he illuminates the background of equity partnerships and identifies two main reasons for this trend: the increased financial means on the part of equity partners and the requirement for clubs to exploit new financial sources. Thereby, investors have the primary goal of increasing share value. Clubs are financially motivated, but are also in search of know-how. In his dissertation, Dworak (2010) investigates equity partnerships as a financial opportunity, but he focuses on clubs of 1st Bundesliga in the 2007/2008 season. Similarly, Hufnagel (2011) considers different equity investments but in the international sport business. Both studies have in common that they do not result in empirical data.

[3]A soft loan is an interest-free loan provided by a sugar daddy for his club (Franck & Lang, 2014).

The shareholding of a corporate sponsor at a club is rather a phenomenon of the German football landscape. Dworak (2010) as well as Chemnitzer et al. (2015) in a report about economic trends in football assume that an equity partnership with a sponsor allows the exploitation of "further synergies" due to a stronger bond between partners. In addition, an increase in share value is also named as a sponsor motive to buy stakes in a club.

Prigge and Vöpel (2014) descriptively constructed a typology of external investors ("return driven shareholder", i.e., financial investors; "strategic partner", i.e., club sponsors; and "Maecenas shareholder") for football clubs, discussing the pros and cons of equity partnerships from three perspectives: the club's, the investor's, and the implications for competition. The scholars underline the club's focus on generating additional money via an equity partnership but also mention that clubs are confronted with more investor influence and fan resistance. Referring to Prigge and Vöpel (ibid.), the Maecenas shareholder has no return related motives (social motives).

As opposed to this, from the perspective of the other two types of shareholders (financial investor and sponsor), the scholars contend there must be return-related objectives in the form of an increase in share value, dividends, or further synergies (due to their duty to justify their investment towards the own stakeholders). With respect to a strategic partner (a sponsor who buys additional club shares), the scholars assume "*advantages in other form*" or "*mutual reputation and image effects*" (Prigge & Vöpel, 2014; 3). They further presume exclusivity (in the form that the club loses the opportunity to enter better endowed sponsorship contracts) as another reason to buy club shares. As opposed to this, Prigge and Vöpel (ibid.) challenge whether the motives of the return driven shareholder are compatible with those of a football club. However, it remains obscure what is meant with "advantages in other form".

Recently, Welling and Westhoff (2018) conceptualised descriptively football investors at German clubs on the basis of their investment motive. Their investor matrix rests upon two dimensions (expectation and market aspects) which results in four investor types: the "goodwill investor" (Maecenasship or oligarch), the "classic investor" (which is equivalent to the agreement with private equity companies), the "safeguarding investor" (which is comparable to equity partnerships with sponsors), and the "strategic investor" (organisations or individuals that own several football clubs across the world).

They extend the work from Prigge and Vöpel (2014) by differentiating two forms of goodwill investors. While they agree with Prigge and Vöpel (ibid.) that a Maecenas has predominantly social motives (altruistic), Welling and Westhoff

(2018) add oligarchs as another type of goodwill investor. In contrast to Maecenas, oligarchs are rather geopolitical motivated. The "classic investor" is profit driven (dividend payments or selling shares profitably) while the "safeguarding" investor enters into an equity partnership in order to safeguard its sponsorship with the club as well as intensifies the sponsorship partnership. While Welling and Westhoff (2018) fail to explain how safeguarding takes place Fiedler (2017) remarks, that exclusivity (branch exclusivity in form of an exclusivity clause) is usually part of main sponsorship deals in the football business, too. The strategic investor (for example Red Bull) tries to extend its value-added chain. In this context, value-added chain means that the strategic investor has several stakes in different football clubs around the world. Value is generated as the investor is able to transfer players of "his" clubs easily, thus increases the players talent development and also adjusts the strength of his teams (via player transfers).

All of these studies argue that the decision made by equity partners to hold shares in football clubs is based on a combination of financial (e.g., increase of share value, dividends, profits), business (e.g., influence, safeguarding, exclusivity), and social interest which are grounded in exploiting the synergies that exist between the club and corporation (Nagy, 2012). Clubs choose equity partners mainly because these represents a fundamental source of income (one-off payment) (Prigge & Vöpel, 2014).

Several scholars also concentrate on the impact of different governance structures of football clubs and investor presence as a form of financing the clubs. For example, Franck (2010) discusses the variety of motives of patrons to invest in European football clubs by contrasting different club governance forms. He determines that German football clubs have a hostile governance structure due to the 50+1 rule and are hence not attractive for international sugar daddies. This view is recently supported by Adam and Hovemann (2018).

Other scholars addressed the impact of equity partnerships on (German) football by putting the fan perspective into the research focus. Following a survey of 1,700 football fans throughout Europe, Pawlowski (2013) found that the majority of fans questioned felt that investors lower the audience's enthusiasm for the sport. Pilz (2011), in a qualitative study, investigated the view of German fan club communities and initiatives of organised fans about football club investors and the 50+1 rule. He discovered the rule's social relevance in relation to fan identification, social integration, and participation. This finding is supported by several quantitative studies (fan surveys, e.g., Bauers & Hovemann, 2019a; Bühler, 2017; Pawlowski, 2013).

Bauers and Hovemann (2019a) published a comparative study from the years 2011 and 2017 about the interests of football fans regarding 50+1. In 2011, they polled 3,114 football fans. 91.3% of those favoured retention of the rule and 4.3% voted for its repeal. This outcome was confirmed in 2017 when Bauers and Hovemann repeated the survey. This time (n = 3,739) 90.1% voted for retention and 6.9% for the repeal of 50+1.

On behalf of FC Play Fair and as a part of a situational analysis, Bühler's (2017) findings strengthen those of Bauers and Hovemann from the years 2011 and 2017. In a survey of 17,330 football fans in Germany, it was found that 85.4% favour retention of the 50+1 rule whereas 14.6% are open-minded for investors in German professional football.

Bauers and Hovemann (2019a) also illuminated the background of fan opinions regarding the 50+1 rule (arguments for retention and arguments for repeal of the rule). The study, therefore, quantitatively verifies the findings from Pilz (2011) that 50+1 has a significant, symbolic meaning for fans in terms of protecting the social roots of football (fan's co-determination) and the fan's identification. Evidently, the discussion about 50+1 is shaped in particular by its relevance and impact in respect to the presence of investors in German football (Bauers et al., 2013, 2015; Schuster & Unterhitzenberger, 2014; Hovemann et al., 2010).

2.2 Identification of Research Gaps

The analysis of the sport-related strategic partnership research reveals a fragmented body of literature. Thus, Bell et al. (2006) already stressed the need for research studies that advance theoretical progress and integration, and offer practical advice for managers. Similarly, Demir and Söderman (2015) emphasised that the domain of strategic partnership is still in its infancy regarding conceptual rigor. Farrelly (2010; 332) also proclaimed that great value would be added to the partnership and sponsorship subject if prospective research studies were to investigate

> "sponsor property partnerships that have cultivated strategic collaborations with attention given to the planning process, formal and informal communications between partners and the nature of objectives set down for the relationship".

In the football business, Welling and Westhoff (2018), Chemnitzer et al. (2015), and Prigge and Vöpel (2014) are one of the few who investigated the motives of equity partners to buy shares in a football club. Chemnitzer et al. (2015) presumes "further synergies" as a motive for sponsors to buy club shares, but it remains vague how these synergies are created. Without presenting an explanation this also conveys that achieving further synergies could not be attained in (purely) contractual sponsorships. However, this contradicts to the findings by many academics (e.g., Rennard & Sitz, 2011; Urriolagoitia & Planellas, 2007; Farrelly & Quester, 2005a, etc.) who find support that sponsorship can be developed into strategic partnerships.

Moreover, Prigge and Vöpel (2014) neglect to specify what is meant by "advantages in other form" and Welling and Westhoff (2018) fail to explain how a strategic sponsorship partnership is "intensified" via equity. Therefore, their contributions to the subject lack depth. What these papers about strategic equity partnerships in German football have in common is that they use secondary data (Dworak, 2010; Roy, 2009) or are limited to descriptive analyses (e.g., Welling & Westhoff, 2018; Chemnitzer et al. 2015; Prigge & Vöpel, 2014). Hence, these studies remain hypothetically. Quitzau (2014, sect. 2) put it straight by stating that "*eventually, one cannot evaluate the intentions of investors appropriately from the outside*".

Those studies which focus on the impact of equity partnerships and put the fan perspective into the centre of research (e.g., Bauers & Hovemann, 2019a; Bühler, 2017; Pawlowski, 2013; Pilz, 2011) provide a current picture on the prevalent, basic view of club members and fans regarding investor presence and the 50+1 rule in German football. These scholars, however, base their research on the general term investor only. Consequently, it remains unexplored whether football fans in Germany have a differential view of various types of equity partners (investors).

Overall, why strategic equity partnerships are entered, how these relationships evolve, what are the managerial demands and success factors of the various steps through which equity partnerships pass, and what is the impact of this phenomenon will be a vital matter of investigation.

2.3 Research Purpose and Questions

Based on the identification of the aforementioned research gaps the purpose of this dissertation is to illustrate, conceptualise, and theorise actual procedures and practices of the formation and management of strategic equity partnerships. It is illustrated that in football country specific rules (specific governance structures) exist. This locates the research in the context of the German football business. The proposed study will concentrate explicitly on strategic partnerships in which corporate sponsors buy additional club shares. This clear distinction is essential as it prevents any confusion as regards the study results. Accordingly, the research topic is rooted in the inter-disciplinary field of sport management which addresses various theoretical facets, ranging from administrative, situational, and resource-related components right through to governance, supremacy, and personal aspects (Loonam, 2014).

Considering the conflicting nature of goals between football clubs and corporations, given the related high costs of football club shares, and giving the need for corporate sponsors to justify their engagement to their own stakeholders the central research question of this dissertation is as followed:

RQ: *Why do football clubs and corporations establish strategic equity partnerships?*

Beside this central question, the following research sub-questions (SQ) are derived and considered to be of major significance in terms of examining the research problem and answering the research question.

In 2004, Süßmilch already stated that strategic equity partnerships in German football evolve from prior sponsorship relationships. Consequently, sponsorships may act as lever to enter into a strategic equity partnership (Chemnitzer et al., 2015; Prigge & Vöpel, 2014). This was recently confirmed by Adam and Hovemann (2018) and is also underpinned by practical examples in various clubs in the German 1st Bundesliga (e.g., FC Bayern München, Borussia Dortmund, VfB Stuttgart, etc.). Therefore, in order to answer why strategic equity partnerships are established there needs to be an understanding about the critical success factors[4].

Discovering the critical success factors allows to get information about club characteristics which attracts corporations to enter into sponsorships in the first place and strategic equity partnerships after that. This may in particular support football clubs that are in search for a strategic (equity) partner to adjust their strategy accordingly in order to raise attractiveness. In addition, identifying the critical success factors of managing strategic partnerships is of further significance in order to understand the developmental process from sponsorships towards strategic equity partnerships and sheds also light on the basic requirements (preconditions) that need to be in place for clubs and sponsors in order to enter into a share deal. This results in research sub-question 1:

[4]Critical success factors are "*those characteristics, conditions, or variables that, when properly sustained, maintained, or managed, can have a significant impact on the success of a firm competing in a particular industry*" (Leidecker & Bruno, 1984; 24). In this study, critical success factors include those characteristics/aspects which attract corporations to enter into an equity partnership. These are referred to as 'attracting factors' comprise those conditions which need to be in place to enter into an equity partnership. These are referred to as 'basic requirements'.

SQ 1: *What are the critical success factors for entering into and managing strategic partnerships in the football business?*

In order to complement why a sponsor buys additional club shares it is also pivotal to discover why sponsors do not enter into a strategic equity partnership (impediments). The need to unveil the impediments is reinforced given that those authors (i.e., Welling & Westhoff, 2018; Chemnitzer et al., 2015; Prigge & Vöpel, 2014) who describe the motives of the various investor types for buying club shares fail to investigate the (potential) downside(s) of shareholding at a club from the equity partner's point of view (e.g., the downsides of safeguarding). Moreover, clubs might also have reservations against share deals. Prigge and Vöpel (2014), Diederich (2010), and Das and Teng (2001) argue that strategic control is of major importance for equity investors and they are interested in influencing the management of the target organisation (club). Referring to Dierig (2014b) and Bauers et al. (2013), the power of a strategic partner could become a challenge for clubs as these may fear a (financial) dependency on the equity partner and hence are worried about restricted decision-making. This leads to research sub-question 2:

SQ 2: *What are the impediments for corporate sponsors and football clubs to entering into strategic equity partnerships?*

Koza and Lewin (2000) observed that just as the strategy of a corporation develops over time so will the strategic intent[5] for a business partnership evolve. A variety of scholars (e.g., Ashelm & Horeni, 2015; Lin & Darnall, 2014; Prigge & Vöpel, 2014; Quimet, 2013) espouse that buying/selling equity shares is a strategic move which affects the future strategic direction of the partnership and the own organisation. In line with this, Ring (2000) states that the strategic intent for equity partnerships should be totally consistent with the organisation's overall strategic intent. This leads to research sub-question 3:

SQ 3: *How does an equity partnership affect the strategic intent of the partners (sponsoring corporation and football club)?*

While the aforementioned sub-questions clarified the formation (why and why not) of strategic equity partnerships there is a further need to explore the processes of how the dyad of contractual sponsorship and shareholding is managed.

[5]Strategic intent is classified as the long-term (future) business direction of the company (Johnston et al., 2011; Todeva & Knoke, 2005).

As a club shareholder the interest of the sponsor is shifting in maximising value for the club too instead of maximising value for the own organisation only (just as a sponsor). In other words, the interests and responsibility of the corporation might by different in the position of a sponsor with those of a shareholder. Exploring the processes of managing strategic equity partnerships becomes even more apparent since hitherto, no study addresses how football clubs in Germany manage the dyad of sponsorship and shareholding and concomitant the increased influence of strategic equity partners on clubs. Consequently, research sub-question 4 is as followed:

SQ 4: *How do football clubs and corporations manage strategic equity partnerships?*

In the course of the overlapping process of data collection and analysis (Birks & Mills, 2015) it appeared that football clubs and sponsors take the perspective of club members and fans into consideration during the decision-making process of a share deal. Since empirical data are in concert with existing findings from the literature that the club member and fan perspective is a crucial aspect in the shareholder decision-making process there is a fundamental necessity to incorporate the club member and fan perspective into the study. In line with the aforementioned research gap that existing studies (fan surveys) focus on the term investor only (e.g., Bauers & Hovemann, 2019a, 2018b, 2019c; Bühler, 2017; Pawlowski, 2013; Pilz, 2011) the following research sub-question is addressed within this study:

SQ 5: *How do club members and fans evaluate the four*[6] *types of equity partners at German football clubs?*

Based on this question valuable information are gathered about the acceptance of the four equity partner types from the fan perspective. Some scholars (e.g., Tsiotsou et al., 2014; Schade, 2012; Alexa, 2009) focus their research interest on how the brand personality of a club affects the attachment and behaviour of fans. In a similar vein, in order to allow valuable recommendations to be made for clubs and corporate partners (potential investors) as to how to adequately address fans' concerns and maximise fan acceptance it would be beneficial to know which aspects

[6]This question (fan survey) focuses on four types of equity partners identified in literature and qualitative data, namely: a sponsor, a financial investor, a Maecenas, and an oligarch.

(attributes of an equity partner) have an impact on the fans' opinion (in terms of "acceptance") and which arguments the fans' opinion is based on. This enables the fans' perspective to be considered in greater detail. Consequently, research sub-question 6 is:

SQ 6: *How do fans justify their opinion on the attributes of equity partners?*

Last but not least the study tries to examine the effects and impact on buying/selling equity to the partnership by classifying the added value of an additional shareholding. Knowledge about the added value would not only support how a shareholding may enrich an existing sponsorship partnership but also indicates on additional synergy effects between club and sponsor. This results in research sub-question 7:

SQ 7: *What is the added value of an additional shareholding to the sponsorship for both football clubs and corporations?*

The above-mentioned sub-questions are interrelated and should not be viewed in isolation. This is crucial as it may enable a better understanding of the mechanics of the partnership relationship generally and embrace the level of synergistic interplay between clubs (and fans) and corporations.

Theoretical Framework—General Partnership Literature

3

3.1 Introduction

This research project requires a comprehensive literature review of strategic partnerships as presented in academic writings in order to place the research question and sub-questions within the broader context of this literature. The insights provide a sound theoretical framework against which primary data can be contrasted.

First and foremost, different theoretical backgrounds are briefly explained and it is justified from which theoretical angle strategic partnerships are investigated in this study. In order to familiarise the reader with the key terms of the study, general definitions are provided next. The concept of strategic partnership is explained and various partnership types are delimited. Following from this, sponsorship as a specific form of strategic partnership is placed within the broader partnership context. Next, the general academic alliance and partnership literature is critically reviewed based on the various motives, success factors, and effects why corporations enter into strategic partnerships. Equity as a specific (governance) form of partnership is detailed and strategic considerations with respect to equity are discussed.

3.2 Justification of Theoretical Perspective

The 80's and 90's of the 20th century were regarded as the 'kick off' for researchers to investigate diverse forms of strategic partnerships in the field of strategic management (Mintzberg et al., 1998). Ever since, the number of studies has steadily increased and strategic partnerships have attracted the interest of various scholars from a broad spectrum of disciplines such as management and strategy

T. Duffner, *Strategic Equity Partnerships in Professional Football*, Event- und Impaktforschung, https://doi.org/10.1007/978-3-658-31301-2_3

(Contractor & Reuer, 2014; Kale & Singh, 2009; Jiang et al., 2008), marketing (Alexander, 2009; Farrelly & Quester, 2005a; Fahy et al., 2004), and recently sport management (Bauers et al., 2019a, 2019b, 2019c; Welling & Westhoff, 2018; Morgan et al., 2014; Prigge & Vöpel, 2014; Urriolagoitia & Planellas, 2007).

The topic has also been investigated from various theoretical angles, in particular the Resource-Based View (e.g., Ireland et al., 2002; Das & Teng, 2000; Amis et al., 1997) and Transaction Cost Economics[1] (e.g., Hennart, 1988; Williamson, 1991), but also Resource Dependence Theory (e.g., Barringer & Harrison, 2000; Das & Teng, 1998; Saxton, 1997), Knowledge Management (Knowledge-Based View; Park & Lee, 2012; Inkpen, 1998; Lei et al., 1997), Property Rights Theory (e.g., Lerner et al., 2003), Institutional Theory[2] (e.g., Berrett & Slack, 1999; Kraatz, 1998), and Game Theory[3] (e.g., Parkhe, 1993).

In respect to strategic alliances, Game Theory often assumes a co-existence of cooperation and competition between collaborating partners and has a narrow focus on the aspects of opportunistic behaviour of partners (Parkhe, 1993). Hence, it will not explicitly be referred to Game Theory in this study.

While Institutional Theory argues that economic activities from organisations are surrounded in normative and social contexts and these contexts motivate organisations to seek justification for their actions (Dacin et al., 2007), this framework is too slim to investigate the motives and success factors for entering into strategic equity partnerships in the corporate football business. However, insights from institutional theory might provide vital information in decision-making processes when clubs want to justify an equity partnership towards their community groups (in particular club members and fans). Therefore, elements of Institutional Theory may be touched upon.

---

[1]Transaction Costs Economics (TCE) or transaction cost theory is concerned with "*the minimization of an organisation's production and transaction costs*" (Lowensberg et al., 2010; 1093). According to TCE, alliances are considered the most transaction-cost-efficient organisational form (Geh, 2011).

[2]"*Institutional Theory proposes that institutional environments impose pressures on organisations to appear legitimate and conform to prevailing social norms*" (Barringer & Harrison, 2000; 370).

[3]Game Theory suggests that an investment signifies commitment to an alliance, implying good faith and trust (Parkhe, 1993a). Game theory appreciates the significance of reputation for organisations. Further, close interaction provides chances for the partners to develop mutual forbearance (Saxton, 1997).

Transaction Cost Economics (TCE) appears as a major theoretical approach in many partnership studies (Christoffersen, 2013; Jiang, 2012; Parkhe, 1993; Williamson, 1981) and has become a predominant theoretical perspective in the marketing literature too when analysing sponsorship partnerships. For example, Gronroos (1994) remarks that all business partnerships begin with a transactional exchange. Similarly, Wong and Sohal (2002; 34) state that co-operations are "*a series of transactions*". In addition, many scholars view the core of sponsorships in an exchange of services and services in response (e.g., Sam et al., 2005; Bruhn, 1987; Meenaghan, 1983). Whilst sponsorship indeed is an exchange relationship, these studies reduce partnerships to a "non-strategic" nature and capture only a limited aspect of partnerships by neglecting relational components (e.g., social exchange, synergy effects, etc.) (Chadwick, 2004). This perspective is also criticised by Barringer and Harrison (2000) as it does not take the human aspects of business partnerships into consideration, i.e., the assumption that various people and cultures will act together. It is acknowledged that there are transactional components in strategic business partnerships, however the TCE view will not be considered in detail due to the aforementioned reasons.

Instead of concentrating on single transactions, those sponsorship studies which focus on the strategic part of the partnership argue with a relational-focused paradigm in mind (e.g., Morgan et al., 2014; Cousens et al., 2006; Amis et al., 1999; Gronroos, 1994, 1989). These scholars underpin a relational exchange (relationship-based marketing) in which both parties have long-term partnership perspectives, make endeavours to maintain the partnership and engage in multi-dimensional roles (Bühler, 2006). However, a shift from a transactional view towards a relationship-oriented view is not only discernible in the marketing discipline but also in other contexts too, such as supply chain management (e.g., Sahay & Maini, 2002), the retail context (e.g., Rust & Zahoric, 1993) or B2B contexts (e.g., Ferreira et al., 2014; Woo & Ennew, 2004). As this research focuses on strategic, long-lasting equity partnerships with corporate sponsors in the football context, the relational aspect is of particular interest.

Concerning the alliance literature, this study will predominantly concentrate on three (four) theoretical perspectives, namely the Resource-Based View (RBV, including Knowledge-Based View), Resource Dependency Theory (RDT), and Property Rights Theory. The Resource-Based View, created by Barney (1991), regards organisations as bundles of resources. According to RBV, alliances emerge when a company needs additional resources that cannot be obtained via market transactions and cannot be built internally (Geh, 2011). Hence, the RBV emphasises that each partner will bring valuable resources to the partnership in order to get a sustainable competitive advantage (Das & Teng, 2000). Thereby, crucial resources can be of a different nature such as knowledge, money, or image. The RBV also gains support from scholars in the sponsorship literature (e.g., Davies et al., 2008; Fahy et al., 2004; Meenaghan, 1991), in which brand image is seen as a valuable resource for achieving a competitive advantage. Therefore, RBV engenders an interesting link to brand positioning[4] and highlights the strategic purpose of the partnership construct (to achieve/retain a competitive advantage).

In the context of resources, knowledge management has arisen as a main topic in the alliance literature. This theoretical perspective evolved as a combination of the RBV and Organisational Learning Theory[5]. As opposed to RBV, which accepts numerous kinds of resources (e.g., knowledge, image, money, etc.), the Knowledge-Based View focuses only on knowledge as a source of competitive advantage (Grant & Baden Fuller, 1995). Scholars such as Lei et al. (1997) and Grant and Baden-Fuller (1995) regard strategic partnerships as means to exchange and better utilise knowledge, others such as Inkpen (1998) and Hamel (1991) view alliances as a 'platform for learning'. Although the exclusive focus on knowledge seems to be narrow-minded, the Knowledge-Based View will still be embedded within this study as knowledge is perceived by many as the strategically most significant source of competitive advantage (Lui et al., 2010; Lei et al., 1997; Grant, 1996).

In contrast to the RBV, which focuses on resources owned by an organisation, Resource Dependence Theory, initiated by Pfeffer and Salancik (1978), classifies organisations as a system dependent on resources in the external surroundings (resources from other organisations) and therefore, considers the influence of external factors on organisational behaviour. Managers try to lessen environmental dependence and try to have control over vital resources (concept of power) (Hillman et al., 2009). It will be illustrated that professional football clubs are dependent on critical resources from their external environment (i.e., in particular financial sources, but also know-how) in order to be successful. Therefore, this theoretical framework—as recommended by Adam and Hovemann (2018)—can

---

[4]According to Kapferer (2012; 175) positioning a brand means "*emphasising the distinctive characteristics that make it different from its competitors and appealing to the public*". The concept is based on four questions: 1) A brand for what? 2) A brand for whom? 3) Reason? 4) A brand against whom?

[5]Organisational Learning Theory relates to all processes that lead to organisational learning. By increasing organisational competencies value should be added to the organisation (Barringer & Harrison, 2000).

be used to explain why football clubs enter into strategic equity partnerships with corporate sponsors.

According to the Property Rights Theory ownership of an asset (i.e., a property right) confers decision rights over it. Property rights is a theoretical framework which refers to the legal ownership of specific properties and the ability to determine how such properties are used (Alchian & Demsetz, 1973). While property rights can be dispersed, Property Rights Theory supposes that each asset owner (e.g., corporations) will choose that kind of partnership structure (ownership) that maximises its returns ex post facto (Elfenbein, 2017). Therefore, Property Rights Theory appears valuable in order to examine the needs and benefits of the various right holders (stakeholder groups) of an organisation such as the Verein (i.e., club members, club authorities), the economic-based football unit, corporate sponsors (and investors) and fans within the context of a football (Adam & Hovemann, 2018).

It has to be considered that each theoretical view alone seems to be insufficient in capturing the complex, cross-disciplinary nature of strategic (equity) partnerships. Moreover, the above-mentioned theoretical perspectives are correlated and should not be viewed in isolation. Barringer and Harrison (2000) and Lowensberg (2010) advocate this view and accentuate that researchers should implement a blend of paradigms in particular when alliance motives are the focus of investigation. For this reason, a combination of the aforementioned theoretical perspectives (relational paradigm, RBV, RDT, and Property Rights Theory) is used in this study to understand and explore the issue.

3.3 Definitions and Demarcation of the Strategic Partnership Concept

3.3.1 Origin and Definition

The concept of strategic partnership first became subject of the academic discussion in the work of Evan (1965) and Warren (1967) who focused on "theorising inter-organisational relationships" and "building alliance capability" respectively. Ever since, many scholars have focused on the topic but with differing use in terminology. Some discussions refer to "cooperative strategies" (Contractor & Lorange, 1988), others to "strategic networks" (Gulati et al., 2000). At present, the term "strategic alliance" is predominantly used within academic literature when discussing diverse forms of inter-firm partnerships (Gomes et al., 2016).

Given that the scholars usually mean the same, the question of nomenclature will not be gone into further and strategic alliance is defined below.

The word alliance originates from the French word 'allier' and refers to the 'act of allying' or state of 'being allied'. In the business world, a commonly cited definition of strategic alliance is that by Cravens and Piercy (2003; 413): "*A strategic alliance is an agreement for cooperation among two or more independent firms to work together toward common objectives*". Even though this definition touches a core element of the strategic alliance (achieve a common goal) and is recognised by leading scholars who have adopted it (e.g., Brookes, 2016; Business Dictionary, 2019) or changed it only slightly (i.e., several scholars such as Van der Heijden (2012), Todeva and Knoke (2005), and Ireland et al. (2002) emphasise that goal achievement is accomplished by 'sharing resources'), it is criticised as being too broad and simplistic because it neglects the 'strategic' component of the term. In this respect, alliances can be temporary or permanent, long-term or project-based (Todeva & Knoke, 2005). Although there are multiple different views on strategy and its essence, whether outside-in view[6] (Porter, 1979), insight-out view[7] (e.g., Barney, 1991; Wernerfelt, 1984), or a combination of both (Grant, 1991); deliberate[8] strategy (Porter, 1979) or emergent[9] strategy (Mintzberg et al., 1998), most scholars concord that strategy implies a long-term direction the organisation wants to go in respect to the alliance performance in order to achieve a competitive advantage (Johnson et al., 2011). Spekman et al. (1998; 748) provide a holistic definition that covers both major aspects, "strategic" and "alliance" viz.:

> "A strategic alliance is a close, long-term, mutually beneficial agreement between two or more partners in which resources, knowledge, and capabilities are shared with the objective of enhancing the competitive position of each partner".

---

[6]Proponents of the outside-in view (e.g. Davis, 2000; Keller, 1998) claim that the enactment of strategy concentrates predominantly on externally centred actions and is based on the idea that strategy relies on external influences such as customer preferences or competition.

[7]This perspective posits that the success of an organisation is mainly influenced by the capabilities and resources residing within the organisation (Abimbola & Kocak, 2007).

[8]A deliberate strategy is a result of the management and strategic planning process and focuses on developing a strategy before its implementation (Johnson et al., 2011).

[9]An emergent strategy results as a reaction to outside forces which allow a quicker adaption to the dynamic situation (Capon, 2008).

This definition illustrates that strategic alliance is a means of implementing corporate or business strategy (enhancing competitive position) (Ring, 2000). Beyond, it shows that alliance formation is grounded on reciprocity which means that it usually implicates sharing the risk, reward (financial and non-financial), and some kind of control among partners (DePamphilis, 2012; Oliver, 1990). This is substantiated by the French scholar Jolly (2002), who attached four conditions for a business partnership to be a 'real' strategic alliance and illustrates some practical implications of entering into a strategic alliance: beside resource sharing, each partner must be aware that both will lose some degree of autonomy in order to reach their mutual goal. Furthermore, the mutual engagement should yield results that would not emerge in the context of a single action. Ultimately, outside of the alliance, the majority of each partner's business remains independent.

In academic writings strategic alliance is often used interchangeably with the term "strategic partnership" (Vergauwen et al., 2010). Despite the wide-spread understanding that both terms can be equated, some try to draw a line by asserting that a strategic partnership refers more to equity-based relationships whereas strategic alliance focuses more on an exchange relationship without shared ownership (e.g., Glover & Wassermann, 2003). In contrast, scholars such as Barringer and Harrison (2000) and Ring and Van de Ven (1994) espouse that alliances are "*relationships with more specific characteristics, such as equity*" (Lowensberg, 2010; 1092).

Equity is a form of capital which is raised through the sale of organisational shares (giving up ownership) in exchange for cash. The buying organisation (investor) purchases interests in the partner organisation and thus becomes an associate (ownership) (Emery & Weed, 2006). Although the attribution of equity to one of the terms is ambiguous and remains open to discussion (Glover & Wassermann, 2003; Culpan, 2002; Barringer & Harrison, 2000; Ring & Van de Ven, 1994), scientists agree that the strategic alliance concept entails partnerships with equity (shared ownership) (Lowensberg, 2010; Sankaran et al., 2005; Inkpen, 1998). In this respect, equity partnerships generally comprise some form of direct investment in the partner and can broadly be classified in alliances with partial acquisition (unilateral alliances, in which one of the parties acquires equity in the partner) and cross-equity transactions (each organisation holds a stake in the partner) (Pekar & Margulis, 2003).

This paper acknowledges that there are different preferences in the usage of the term strategic alliance and strategic partnership. However, while the term strategic alliance is prevalent in the academic management literature (Gomes et al., 2016), strategic partnership predominates in the (German) football landscape

(Boor et al., 2016; Nagy, 2013; Oettgen, 2008). As the study concentrates on partnerships in the football business the term strategic partnership is primarily used throughout this study and is based essentially upon the following criteria found between the many perspectives considered above:

- long-term partnership between two parties (contractual agreement with or without shared ownership of up to 49%)
- exchange relationship, which is based on shared resources
- joint accomplishment of mutual strategic goals
- is linked to the strategic intent of both partners
- a major part of each partner's business remains independent

If a (contractual) strategic partnership is (additionally) based on equity it will be referred to as a strategic equity partnership.

However, this strategic partnership definition is preliminary. As the study's main goal lies in theory generation it is significant how the term is classified from the actors in the field (football clubs and corporate sponsors). Therefore, it makes sense not to compose a premature definition before empirical data is gathered and analysed. Consequently, the discussion about the definition of strategic partnership is reserved for the empirical part of the study. To simplify reading, "partnership" and "alliance" will be used as substitutes.

3.3.2 Different Forms of Strategic Partnership

The academic literature proposes that strategic partnership implies a diversity of organisational forms (Spekman et al., 1998). Since there is no clear-cut distinction between diverse forms, it appears expedient to scan the literature for the different types of partnerships to get a better understanding and help make a valid classification.

Spekman et al. (2000; 36) have a broad understanding and categorise alliances as "*everything on a continuum between the two extremes of arm's length transactions and mergers and acquisitions*[10]". In a similar vein, Todeva and

[10]'Merger and acquisition' (M&A) is a general term, which refers to the integration of corporations. Whereas a merger is a combination of two organisations to establish a new company, an acquisition is the purchase of one company by another in which no new corporations is established (Nicholas et al., 2002).

Knoke (2005) classify 13 different forms. Even though both classifications present an overview about various types of alliances it could be criticised, because these classifications neither differentiate the nature of the partnership (i.e., strategic or non-strategic) nor do these provide information about the partnership function around which an alliance is created. Hence, these categorisations appear fairly generic and vague to some extent. Giving this scope, Spekman et al. (2000) as well as Todeva and Knoke (2005) also encounter resistance as they include mergers and acquisitions in their understanding of strategic alliances.

However, here it seems worth differentiating that a merger implies an exchange of stocks between two partners whereas an acquisition is a kind of takeover in which one organisation gains control over the other by acquiring a majority stake (more than 50%, i.e., a controlling interest) (Dreher & Ernst, 2016; Cravens et al., 1993). Referring to Cravens et al. (ibid.), acquisitions should not be categorised as a strategic alliance. This is justified with a 'loss of corporate identity' of one of the partners and also conforms with Jolly's (2002) aforementioned condition of 'not losing independency' on each partner side. Further support of that view was provided by Dussauge and Garrette (1999) who emphasise that the strategic autonomy of both parties has to remain albeit the partnership affects the strategic direction of the cooperating partners.

Cobianchi (1994) provides a remedy of grouping different types of partnerships by mixing two dimensions, namely: the alliance function/area (e.g., sales, marketing) and the governance structure of the partnership (contractual vs. equity-based). The focus on structure and function seems to be valuable as other scholars build upon the same features. Kuglin (2002) distinguishes five types (sales alliance, solution-specific, geographic-specific, investment alliance, joint venture) and Lowensberg (2010) refers to structure too by presenting four modes (vertical and horizontal[11], equity, and non-equity alliances). Following the discussion about terminology, Das and Teng (2000) also agree that 'structure' is a distinguishing characteristic but this time it is argued from a resource-based point of view. They propose four distinct forms which are based on the type of resources (either property-based or knowledge-based) that are combined by two parties, i.e.,

[11]Whereas horizontal strategic partnerships are established between partners operating in the same business area, a vertical strategic alliance is a partnership between a company and its suppliers (Lowensberg, 2010).

joint ventures[12], minority equity, bilateral contract-based[13], and unilateral contract-based[14] alliances.

Kale and Singh (2009), building on a classification of Yoshino and Rangan (1995), present a clear overview of the various partnership forms in the alliance literature and provide a valuable distinction between pure contractual agreements and equity partnerships as shown below:

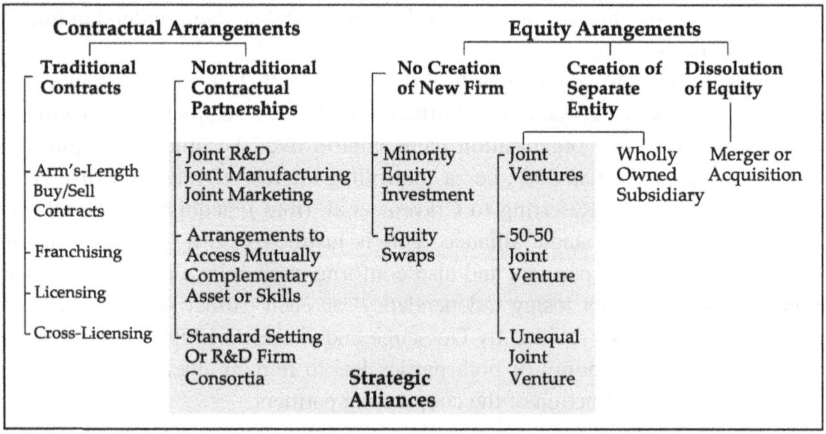

Figure 3.1 Forms of Business Partnerships. (Source: According to Kale & Singh, 2009; 47)

With respect to joint ventures it can be summarised that this partnership form has traditionally been perceived as a form of strategic alliance as Figure 3.1 shows. However, Cravens et al. (1993; 57) state, that

[12]A joint venture emerges when an independent company is created by at least two other firms (Hitt et al., 1996).

[13]"*Alliances are bilateral contract-based when the partners have sustained production of property rights. These alliances require partners to put in resources and work together on a continuing basis. For example, joint R&D, joint marketing and promotion, joint production, and enhanced supplier partnership*" (Das & Teng, 2000; 43).

[14]"*Alliances are unilateral contract-based when they embody a well-defined transfer of property rights, such as the 'technology for cash' exchange in licensing agreements. Licensing, distribution agreements, and R&D contracts are the main forms of unilateral contract-based alliances. The key feature here is that individual firms carry out their obligations independently of others. The level of integration is relatively low in unilateral contract-based alliances*" (Das & Teng, 2000; 43).

> "the key distinction between the strategic alliance and the joint venture is that the latter organisational form consists of the formation of a separate independent organisation by the venture partners. The joint venture creates a new organisation to perform one or more business functions".

Hence, Culpan (2002) proposes that joint ventures are rather a combination of an alliance and an in-house approach.

The discussion reveals a problem in many alliance-research studies: the lack of a clear working definition. The vast majority of research papers refer to the general term strategic alliance, without indicating exactly which particular kind of alliance they are investigating (e.g., equity or non-equity, joint venture, buyer/seller contracts, etc.). Even though the distinct forms share some basic characteristics of an alliance, several scholars build on different meaning. It is further assumed that each alliance form requires idiosyncratic treatment (Bell et al., 2006), in particular when equity or non-equity partnerships are the subject of research. Other studies state the particular form of alliance under investigation but generalise their findings to generic alliances. Therefore, these studies face the problem of contradictory findings and non-generalisability which can lead to confusion and misinterpretation of study results (conceptual blurring; Jiang et al., 2008). Bell and his allies (2006; 1611) describe this state as "chaotic" and infer an academic gap because

> "without considering the idiosyncratic nature of alliances [research] might also end up in spurious findings [...] and does not contribute much to the development of proper theory"

in the field.

3.3.3 Sponsorship As a Form of Strategic Partnership

While the form of a 'joint marketing partnership' has already been mentioned by Yoshino and Rangan in 1995, Dinkel (2002) was one of the first who denoted sponsorship as a strategic partnership between the sponsor and sponsee (Bühler, 2006).

The concept of sponsorship originates from the Greek word "*horigia*", derived from the words "*horos*" (dance) and "*ago*" (leads) (Quester & Thompson, 2001). Initially, sponsorship was loosely associated to a variety of inter-firm agreements, in which one company provides some kind of resource in the form of money, people, or equipment, and the partner organisation is the beneficiary of the resource (exchange for a direct association) (Kahuni et al., 2009). As marketing strategy has developed over the previous 30 years, probably no part has experienced more considerable changes than sponsorship (Meenaghan, 1998).

In the early 1970s, sponsorship was predominated by a philanthropic nature. This changed during the 1980s, as sponsorship developed towards a sales-oriented approach (Berrett & Slack, 1999). During the 1990s, the sponsorship agreement became primarily a B2B relationship (Farrelly & Quester, 2005b) and throughout this development, various definitions of sponsorship have been given. One of the most accepted definitions is that of Meenaghan (1993; 9):

> "Sponsorship is the provision of assistance either financial or in kind to an activity by a commercial organisation for the purpose of achieving commercial objectives".

Later on, Meenaghan and Shipley (1999; 328) advanced this definition by stating that sponsorship is a chance to construct "*a particular kind of brand imagery*". However, Olkkonen et al. (2000) view sponsorship as 'relationships and networks' and Amis et al. (1999; 259) classify it as a "*strategic investment that can be the basis of competitive advantage*". These definitions show the conformity with the former definition of strategic alliance and refer to the nature of achieving not only marketing goals but strategic goals. In respect to sport sponsorship, the classification of Pope (1998; 1) strengthens this view by stating that sport sponsorship can be expressed "*in terms of corporate, marketing or media objectives*".

Since football takes centre-stage in respect to sponsorships, some scholars attempt to deliver a football-specific definition. For example, Groscurth (2005) presents the following:

> "A strategic sponsorship partnership in the football business is a sponsoring cooperation between clubs/associations and corporations, which is oriented towards economic goals and characterised by systematic, long-term and joint marketing activities of both partners".

Similarly, and in accordance with the definition of 'strategic alliance', Bühler's definition of strategic football sponsorship (2006; 69) emphasises that this kind of business-related partnership is "*based on reciprocity*". By using the term partnership, Groscurth and Bühler captures the delineation of Dinkel (2002) and point to the obligation for both parties involved to aim for mutual goals. Both scholars further emphasise the commercial endeavour of sponsor and sponsee by referring to "*economic goals*" and "*various sponsorship objectives*" respectively which are "*all based on a commercial intention*".

Following the discussion about strategic alliances and strategic sponsorships it becomes obvious that various types grouped under the 'strategic partnership umbrella' are of a (slightly) different nature (Bell et al., 2006). Meanwhile, sponsorships and strategic football sponsorships are acknowledged as a form of strategic partnership (Prigge & Vöpel, 2014; Farrelly & Quester, 2005a).

It can be summarised that irrespective of partnership form each type of strategic partnership seems to encompass some salient characteristics, which are *"linked to the strategic mission of each partner firm"* (Inkpen, 1998; 224). However, strategic partnerships in this study rest upon the five characteristics listed in Section 3.3.1.

3.3.4 Strategic Equity Partner vs. Investor

As illustrated above strategic partnership entails contract-based partnerships, equity partnerships, or a combination of both. Still, if the partnership is purely contract-based, the contract entails all the rights and duties for both parties (e.g., joint marketing partnerships, sponsorships, or R&D alliances). If an organisation sells (additional) shares, the acquiring organisation has a share in the profits or debts of the partner and gets voting and controlling power in return (Prigge & Vöpel, 2014).

A strategic equity partnership (share deal) can also be seen in the light of a financial investment, in which one organisation acquires shares in the other (equity investment). For example, whenever a football club announces an equity partnership, the media commonly refers to the term investor (acquiring organisation), strategic partner, or sometimes "shareholder" (both terms are used interchangeably; Laskin, 2018) as the partner of the club (Ruf & Theweleit, 2018; Oediger, 2017b; Heun, 2016). Therefore, in order to avoid confusion and misconception it appears necessary to demarcate the term investor from the concept of strategic equity partnership.

As opposed to strategic partnership, which has its roots in the strategic management discipline, investor is a term coined from a financial perspective and is defined as *"a person, organisation, or country that puts money into something in order to make a profit or receive interest"* (Cambridge Dictionary, 2011; 458). This definition appears vague as it neither specifies what is meant by the pronoun 'something' nor does it point to one of the key characteristics of a strategic partner (e.g., an exchange relationship). This makes it difficult to notice the connection to a strategic equity partnership. Nevertheless, the definition still reflects the core of the investor's viewpoint, the focus on a financial return (Keythman, 2016; Poitras, 2016). VanDuzer et al. (2013; 538) concretise that an investor *"acquires assets (equity, dept securities, real estate, etc.)"* to achieve a financial return. Upon taking a closer look, different types of investors can be identified: private equity (PE) investors[15], institutional investors, and business angels[16], to name but a few. Irrespective of the type, people yet tend to utilise 'investor' as a collective term for various forms of investors (Laskin, 2018). The term investor in the present study refers to an investor (private person, organisation, or corporation) buying equity shares (capital in exchange for equity shares).

As per the definition and as the above discussion reveals investors have an explicit focus on generating cash or producing income (usually in the form of interest/dividends or an increase in share value) (Caselli 2010). Against this, the concept of strategic (equity) partnership is more holistic including an array of mutual strategic interests. Although a strategic equity partner comprises much more than purely financial objectives like an investor, both have in common the acquisition of equity stakes in which the investment organisation has a share in the business success of the partner and gets voting and controlling power in return (Prigge & Vöpel, 2014). To consolidate, a strategic equity partner is an investor but an investor is not automatically a strategic partner.

The voting and control power depend in large part on the amount of acquired shares. Usually, shares can broadly be classified into "minority" and "majority" shares. Whereas minority ownership is legally not defined (Gerke, 2002), it is commonly understood as less than 50% of the target organisation (Quimet, 2013). However, this paper relies on the categorisation of Burger et al. (2010) as this conforms with the classification prevalent in the German business landscape: a "minimal equity partnership" constitutes a stake of up to 4.9% in the partner. A "minority equity partnership" implies making a minority investment of 5% up to 24.9% in the partner. The minority partner generally has the option of increasing its stake. The magnitude of "blocking minority" differs depending on the country of origin between 25% and 33% (Lucks & Meckl, 2015).

[15]*"Private equity is about investments usually structured as equity or equity related instruments in unquoted (private) companies"* (Fraser-Sampson, 2011; 85).

[16]Business angels are defined as *"high net worth individuals who invest their own money, along with their time and expertise, directly in unquoted companies in which they have no family connection, in the hope of financial gain"* (Dana, 2011; 1).

In Germany, a shareholder has a blocking minority if he/she[17] owns a stock of shares between 25% and 50%. That means the equity holder or investor can block important decisions, for instance a change in constitution of a football club (Verein). Hence, 25% is a crucial barrier for the selling organisation if it wants to stay independent of any shareholder(s) (Lammert et al., 2009). A majority shareholder holds more than 50% (50+1) of a business (§16 AktG) and is referred to as "acquisition" or "takeover" (Dreher & Ernst, 2016). In addition, the rights and duties can differ on the specific governance structure of the selling organisation, which is regulated based on country-specific legislation (in Germany especially GmbHG viz. "Limited Liabilities Company Act", and AktG "Stock Corporation Act").

Depending on the perspective, equity deals relate to a differing amount of risk (Globermann & Nielsen, 2007). From the acquirer (investor) point of view, equity investments are associated with a high risk because if the 'selling organisation' goes bankrupt the purchasing organisation is not entitled to claim any repayments of its initial investment. Therefore, equity investors normally expect higher returns on investment (Prigge & Vöpel, 2014). For the selling organisation, equity money is an attractive financial option because in contrast to debt capital (e.g., credits), which requires paying back the money (normally in periodic interest payments) and in which creditors are able to force a business into bankruptcy if interests are not paid, equity money is not related to obligatory interest compensation. While selling shares means giving up control to the equity holder(s), dividend payments can be skipped which provides more spending flexibility (Keythman, 2016). Consequently, equity capital is an investment form which comes with a lower risk (from the perspective of the selling part) compared to other types of financing, in which interests are paid (Poitras, 2016).

3.4 Motives for Entering into Strategic Partnerships

3.4.1 Introduction

Analogue to the multitude of partnership forms there are just as many various motives presented in academic literature. For example, cost reduction, access to new markets, risk reduction, knowledge transfer, or economies of scale among

[17]The author is committed to the ethical principles of equality and impartiality; however, for clarity and brevity, reference is made only to the male form although both genders (he/she) are implied.

others are dominant in many studies (e.g., DePamphilis, 2012; Sluyts et al., 2011; Todeva & Knoke, 2005; Ireland et al., 2002). The approach of critically reviewing the motives for entering into strategic partnerships in this study differs from these theorists, whose efforts to itemise partnership motives has resulted in extensive lists of corporate motives without considering the larger benefits intended by business partners. This part is focused on comprehensive issues that might support groupings of motives associated with corporations' strategic effort in partnerships.

Eisenhardt and Schoonhoven (1996) have tried to classify the various motives into two key areas: strategic motives and social motives. Strategic motives are based on the idea that both partners anticipate an adequate payoff structure by entering into an alliance. This complies with Dyer and Singh's (1998) as well as Das and Teng's (2000) notion about gaining a competitive advantage. Social motives, in which the need to form a partnership emerges from social contacts and partnerships, are more prone to be entered into if the business people know each other. Though the latter motive appears to be irrational and fragile on first sight, Ring and Van de Ven (1994) suggest that creating personal relationships are essential to alliance success. Mitsuhashi (2003) and Uzzi (1997) confirm that "social embeddedness"[18], in particular trust and commitment, are crucial in the alliance formation process.

Das and Teng (2000; 37), arguing from an RBV, state two different core motives for why firms enter into strategic alliances: first, to *"obtain resources"* and second *"to retain resources"*. According to Das and Teng (ibid.), obtaining resources deals with gaining a competitive advantage whereas retaining resources concentrates on securing a competitive advantage. By so doing, Das and Teng (ibid.) correlate resources with the strategic view (gaining/retaining a competitive advantage) just like several authors did them (e.g., Tsang, 2000; Gulati, 1995; Oliver, 1990; Lorange & Ross, 1991, 1993).

Dyer and Singh (1998) corroborate that not only those resources which are owned by a single firm achieve a competitive advantage. Crucial resources can be extended beyond company boundaries by entering into strategic partnerships. This point of view is also supported by scholars in the sponsorship literature (e.g., Davies et al., 2008; Fahy et al., 2004; Meenaghan, 1991); this highlights the purpose of strategic partnerships (focus on competitive advantage), and engenders an interesting link between the RBV and brand positioning. Todeva and Knoke (2005) pick up on this strategic thought too and advocate the link to strategic

[18]Social embeddedness is *"the process by which social relations shape economic action"* (Uzzi 1996; 674).

positioning by stating that partnerships are formed for four major reasons, namely to 'address internal organisational problems', to 'consider economic benefits', to 'engage in strategic positioning' or for 'political' motives (e.g., overcoming legal barriers).

In order to present an integrative framework of why organisations enter into strategic (equity) partnerships, the review of alliance motives is guided by strategic motives. This is justified in the relevance of this approach in prior research that examines alliance formation as illustrated above (Lin & Darnall, 2014; Todeva & Knoke, 2005; Das & Teng, 2000; Eisenhardt & Schoonhoven, 1996).

3.4.2 Access to Distinct Resources—Knowledge Transfer and Learning

Many scholars (e.g., Cobbs, 2011; Kahuni et al., 2009; Urriolagoitia & Planellas, 2007; Cousens et al., 2006; Cliffe & Motion, 2005; Ireland et al., 2002; Das & Teng, 2000; Amis et al., 1999) regard a strategic partnership as a way to access (previously unavailable) distinct resources and to develop joint resources that can lead to a competitive advantage. Barney (1991; 101) classifies resources as

> "all assets, capabilities, organisational processes, firm attributes, information, knowledge, etc. controlled by a firm that enable the firm to conceive of and implement strategies that improve its efficiency and effectiveness".

The definition illustrates that resources belong to the strategic capabilities of an organisation and can be either tangible or intangible. Whereas tangible resources can be seen, touched, or quantified (e.g., facilities and money) and hence are relatively easy to imitate, intangible resources are invisible (e.g., knowledge, brand image) and therefore more difficult to imitate (Johnson et al., 2011; Vergauwen et al., 2010; Das & Teng, 2000). The relational and evolving nature of partnerships makes duplication increasingly difficult and the alliance as a resource more strategic (Cobbs, 2011). Hence, by combining resources in a unique way via alliances and by emphasising the strategic role of partnerships, several scholars (e.g., Kahuni et al., 2009; Urriolagoitia & Planellas, 2007; Fahy et al., 2004; Amis et al., 1997; Meenaghan, 1991) view a great opportunity to develop partnerships into a sustainable competitive advantage.

Knowledge is perceived as one of the most valuable, tacit, and strategic resources in an organisation (Meier, 2011; Lui et al., 2010; Farrelly et al., 2006; Ireland et al., 2002; Dyer & Singh, 1998; Grant, 1996). Referring to Birkinshaw

(2001), knowledge is even the most enduring source of competitive advantage. In their study on alliance management as a source of competitive advantage, Ireland et al. (2002) add weight to this view. This angle is based on the perspective that not resources per se, but rather processes, practices, and routines are subject to inimitability and causal ambiguity; and as they are context-related, they are the crucial differences that provide value solely to the organisation that makes use of them (Santala & Parvinen, 2007). This position comes to be known as Knowledge-Based View (Grant, 1996).

Knowledge acquisition refers to *"the extent to which the firm has learned from the alliance partner"* (Lui et al., 2010; 237). This definition represents a narrow view of knowledge acquisition, as it just encompasses learning 'from an alliance partner'. Other scholars have a more detailed view: whereas Beamish et al. (2016) distinguish between learning 'from' an alliance and learning 'in' an alliance, Inkpen (2002) differentiates three types of learning: 'learning about the partner', 'learning from the partner' and 'learning about managing business relationships', which is also referred to as 'alliance capability' (Sluyts et al., 2011). Partnerships deliver an exclusive opportunity to leverage the business capabilities with the support of the partner (Inkpen, 1998). For instance, learning may include gaining access to the marketing and management expertise of the partner (Spekman et al., 1998).

A fundamental precondition to make use of learning opportunities and knowledge exchange is that each partner is required to 'share his knowledge'[19] and is willing to transfer information (Dyer & Singh, 1998). That means, the partner must have the ability to recognise the value of knowledge and information, handle this, assimilate it into his own organisational context, and finally apply it in his specific business environment (Ireland et al., 2002). This ability is known as the 'absorptive capacity' of a firm (Barringer & Harrison, 2000) or is referred to as the 'dynamic capabilities'[20] of a company (Farrelly et al., 2006).

DePamphilis (2012), Farrelly et al. (2006), and Dyer and Singh (1998) specify that alliance governance structures facilitate the dissemination of information across partners and promote knowledge transfer. Wilson et al. (2008) agree by emphasising the ability to generate and maintain open communication as a key

---

[19]Dyer and Singh (1998; 665) classify knowledge-sharing activities as *"inter-firm interactions that permit the transfer, recombination, or creation of specialized knowledge"*.

[20]Dynamic capability is a firm's ability to integrate, build and configure internal and external competencies, suggesting that this should reflect its ability to achieve new and innovative forms of competitive advantage (Teece et al., 1997).

component in a partnership's learning process. Urriolagoitia and Planellas (2007) as well as Lui et al. (2010) stress that knowledge transfer depends on face to face interactions between partners. Referring to Lui et al. (2010), the amount of knowledge acquired by a company depends on three key components of relational capital: the amount of trust, the degree of transparency between partners, and the level of partner interaction. In this respect, Lei et al. (1997; 209) refer to an *"openness of organisational culture"* as a precondition for alliance learning. By establishing such a culture, partnership learning can contribute to a unique knowledge base. Spender (1996) notes that it should be taken into consideration that for the same reason that business rivals have difficulties imitating a company's knowledge, so the company may have difficulties to exploit it more effectively.

However, Birkinshaw (2001) remarks that alliance learning and knowledge transfer are a sensitive construct that may change the status of the partnership. Referring to Hamel (1991) there is a risk that the partner who first achieves its alliance learning goals is prone to leave the partnership. In this respect, he delineates alliances as a 'race to learn'. In contrast, Inkpen and Beamish (1997) put forward that an organisation which has learned and gained knowledge from its partner prefers to retain the partnership rather than to quit it.

Meier (2011) concurs with Gravier et al. (2008) that there is a lack of studies into the knowledge effects in alliances. There are some studies (Reid et al., 2001; Teece, 1998) which look into knowledge outcomes in the form of the accumulation of knowledge assets such as new technologies, new products, or patents. Others (Tsang et al., 2004; Hamel, 1991) focus on performance benefits. For example, Gravier et al. (2008), in their meta-analysis, provide evidence for a relationship between knowledge transfer and an increase in alliance performance. Unfortunately, the study fails to specify alliance performance. However, the scholars determine that empirical support for the knowledge-performance link in alliances remains limited. Meier (2011) provides an explanation for this shortcoming. On the basis of this, some academics such as Jiang and Li (2009) and Lane et al. (2001) differentiate between various knowledge outcomes, e.g., the work of Jiang and Li (2009) supposes that knowledge transfer and knowledge creation are disparate outcomes. However, even though Meier (2011; 16) agrees by expounding that knowledge creation refers to a management process, whereas knowledge outcome relates to the extent to which knowledge assets are accrued as an effect of knowledge creating activities, he also criticises that

> "these distinctions are only rarely reflected in the operationalization of variables and distinct outcomes tend instead to be merged, e.g., as one measure of organisational learning".

The characteristics and processes by which knowledge establishes a competitive advantage are complex and difficult to classify. It seems that further research is needed to arrive at robust measurements of knowledge effects in strategic alliances.

3.4.3 Brand Building—Awareness, Image, and Staff Motivation

Another encompassing resource to achieve a competitive advantage frequently finds expression in the partnerships' capability to develop the corporate brand[21], i.e., differentiation, positioning and image improvement, as well as potential for synergetic interplays (Van der Heijden, 2012; Nagy, 2011; Cobianchi, 1994).

Strategic partnerships are seen as an instrument in order to develop the corporate brand. This trend has intensified within the last decades as corporate branding has begun to move up the business agenda and is increasingly being acknowledged as a means which can generate differentiation and value creation (Knox & Bickerton, 2003; Balmer, 1999). In an age when many products and services seem to be equal and interchangeable, transparency generates an enormous strategic problem and forces organisations, irrespective of their size, to differentiate and position themselves by taking the needs of consumers into account. Since companies face difficulties obtaining an edge over their competitors, the focus of differentiation is shifting from products to organisations and corporate brands have become a central aim of marketing and strategy endeavours (Verma, 2009; Sarkar & Singh, 2005).

A corporate brand strives to establish the unique characteristics of an organisation (Rode & Vallaster, 2005) and allows companies to express things about themselves in a way that everyday language cannot convey (Ahonen, 2008). Referring to Kotler and Keller (2009), brand differentiation happens when the

[21]There are several definitions of corporate brand, which range from the more simplistic, e.g., as *"giving the organisation a clear stated sense of what it stands for"* (Inskip, 2004; 358) to the more complex, e.g., from Hatch and Schultz (2001; 7): *"A corporate-brand attracts and orients relevant audiences, stakeholders, and constituencies around the recognizable values and symbols that differentiate the organisation"*. CB extends product branding in such a way that the organisation and its name take centre stage and management tries to establish the organisation as a whole, which demonstrates its strategic importance and the resulting need to manage interactions with multiple stakeholders rather than customers only.

brand matches superior performance with an important customer benefit. This can help to establish a unique value proposition (UVP) and relationships with target customers, which work as a bond between customers and brands and are essential for competitive positioning (Mäläska et al., 2011; Keller, 2000). With reference to Marsden (2002; 307), positioning relates to the *"brand position in the mind of customers with respect to the values, which differentiate the brand's given or owned associations"*. According to Aaker (2004), positioning becomes the shaping of the brand's image so that customers recognise and understand what the organisation stands for. Jiang et al. (2008) and Das and Teng (2001) indicate that strategic partnerships support to promote a positive image and company reputation, and therefore the corporation enhances its trustworthiness in the eyes of stakeholders which, in turn, suggest fair dealings and good performances.

This trend is also identified in respect to sponsorship partnerships, in which sponsorships develop from a supporting marketing tool to the basis of brand strategies (Bühler, 2006; Cliffe & Motion, 2005). From a sponsor's standpoint, the shift from the classic view of sponsorship towards a strategic partnership perspective results from insights to incorporate sponsorships in corporate and brand strategies in order to maximise synergies. In this respect, some scholars consider sponsorship as a (mutual) 'value-creating resource' (Renard & Sitz, 2011; Fahy et al., 2004). Other academics such as Amis et al. (1999), Cliffe and Motion (2005), and Meenaghan (1991) view sponsorship as a 'distinctive strategic competence', which can act as an intangible asset, allowing corporations to boost their corporate brand, image and reputation, and therefore act as a means for sustained competitive advantage. Image is viewed as a strategic asset which tends to increase over the years and strategic partnerships are identified to foster up the company's brand image. In addition, sponsorships are perceived as a strong antecedent of brand loyalty and have the power to positively differentiate the sponsor from other companies.

Meenaghan (2001) emphasises sponsorship's ability to achieve favourable long-term image effects rather than short-term sales increases. He has further determined that consumers have a positive view of sponsorships and regard this kind of communication strategy, if well activated[22] (leveraged) (Sluyts et al., 2011), to be gentler, caring, and especially subtle compared to advertising. Many

[22] *"Activation refers to all marketing activities that a sponsor conducts to promote its sponsorship"* (IEG, 2010). It has to be considered that activation often includes investments which are above the amount of rights fee paid to the sponsored property (IEG, 2011).

scholars agree that sponsorship can effectively break through heavy promotional clutter and effectively differentiate a brand from its rivals (O'Reilly & Hornig, 2013; Westberg et al., 2011; Cornwell et al., 2001).

However, this form of differentiation often depends on consumers' perceived fit of specific values transferred via the sponsoring brand (Demir & Söderman, 2015). In this respect, the partnership typically reflects its unique culture, values and history, that are hard to imitate. One of the stated requirements to achieve this is to incorporate the sponsorship engagement into the strategic thinking of the corporation and to make a long-standing commitment to whatever is being sponsored (Demir & Söderman, 2015; Woisetschläger et al., 2015; Amis & Slack, 1999). This is substantiated by Cheng and Stotlar (1999) by underpinning the requirement for a long-term commitment to achieve mutual fulfilment.

Besides these positive effects, there are also studies report on the negative effects on the brand image of partner brands. Geylani et al. (2008) show that brand image can be impaired in alliances if the images of the partners are dissimilar. As a consequence, this may lead to 'uncertainty' in consumer perception. McQuerrey (2018) remarks that that there is no clear-cut distinction between the two partners in the customer's perception. Accordingly, the partner could be judged based on the actions of his ally.

A strategic partnership has not only the potential to lead to external brand strength[23] but also to internal brand strength (enhancement of brand identity) by improving employee morale and acting as a staff motivator (Olejniczak & Aicher, 2010; Cousens et al., 2006; Slack & Amis, 2001). According to Urde (2009; 616): *"A corporate brand cannot be stronger externally than it is internally"*. This is corroborated by Drucker (1998), who has emphasised that marketing in general has to bring the outside world inside the company and utilise that knowledge as a basis for strategic development. Many authors (Rode & Vallaster, 2007; Boyle, 2003; Urde, 2003; Harris & de Chernatony, 2001) substantiate that corporate branding requires a balanced organisation-wide approach and links an internal (identity) and external (image) aspect.

Varey (1995) was one of the first to reveal an employee-focused trend of corporations who target their partnership strategy to customers, but also considers how this could affect their employees. Two years later, Robins (1997) investigated how corporate decisions in general impact on staff. Coote and Cornwell (2004)

[23]Brand strength *"comprises the internal behavioural significance of a brand for internal stakeholder (e.g., employees) and external behavioural importance of a brand for its external stakeholders"* (Burmann et al., 2009; 391).

described the significance of sponsorship affecting employees' attitude and behaviour and Hickman et al. (2005) concur by presenting evidence that staff attitude and behaviour are positively influenced by sponsorships through the affinity with a sponsored organisation. It is further stated that sponsorship can act as an internal marketing tool which enhances employee loyalty and commitment (Hickman et al., 2005; Dolphin, 2003). Amis and Slack (1999) have already demonstrated that motivational talks with athletes or mutual product launches can help to generate pride and shape corporate culture.

Overall, strategic partnerships have the potential to be far more valuable than just an advertising message or an improvement in company image. When it is utilised in various ways across the organisation, a partnership can achieve external and internal effects.

3.4.4 Financial Motives for Strategic Equity Partnerships

The literature presents several possible reasons why organisations enter into strategic equity partnerships. Many scholars (e.g., Poitras, 2016; Caselli, 2010; Jones, 2008; Amis et al., 1997; Mintzberg, 1998; Carroll, 1996) espouse that by entering into an equity partnership, the corporations' managers must rationally expect a return on investment otherwise their own duties are being neglected (Dreher & Ernst, 2016). According to Andy Adcroft, senior lecturer in corporate strategy at the University of Surrey (Adcroft cited by Bolgar, 2010; Sect. 2):

> "If you're going on an acquisition spree as a company, you have to think about exactly what kind of opportunity you want to take. You have to justify this decision towards your stakeholders".

From the viewpoint of the acquiring partner, the financial goals are straightforward: dividend payments and/or an increase in share value are the most cited ones (Poitras, 2016; Keythman, 2016; Caselli, 2010). Krishnaswami et al. (2012) investigated equity motives from the perspective of the selling partner. They discovered that the selling partner in the dyad is mostly smaller compared to the buying partner. Although the authors fail to define what is meant by 'smaller' (smaller in respect to what?) it can be assumed that it refers to financial power (capacity).

Following their argumentation, the smaller partner favours a strategic equity partnership due to financial constraints. Hence, from the selling partner's stance, selling equity stakes is a vehicle for getting money. This is confirmed by former findings from Baker and Wurgler (2002) and Lerner et al. (2002) who even argue that companies subject to capital constraint rely on financing from their strategic partner(s). However, Krishnaswami et al. (2012) mitigate these outcomes somewhat. They add that if both partners are already in a contractual partnership (e.g., product market agreement) the smaller partner is likely to aim for an equity partnership instead of relying on it (if financial constraints exist). This is because a strategic equity partnership with an entrusted partner diminishes the *"adverse selection costs of external equity for these distressed firms"* (Krishnaswami et al., 2012; 8). This corresponds with research by Allen and Philipps (2000) who convey that minority equity partnerships are entered into to ease the financial constraints of the target firm. Likewise, Quimet (2013) as well as Liao (2014) discovered that equity provides direct financing.

However, while these scholars put financial motives in the spotlight of their investigations Todeva and Knoke (2005) as well as DePamphilis (2012) note that money alone rarely provides the basis for a successful long-term business alliance.

3.4.5 Strategic Motives for Strategic Equity Partnerships

A multitude of studies concentrate on the non-financial (strategic) aspects of strategic equity partnerships. Russo and Cesarini (2017) see equity as a type of partnership configuration (governance form) which is mainly used to reduce the risk of opportunistic behaviour. Accordingly, equity is chosen if the risk of opportunistic behaviour is high. Even though this finding is supported by Cravens et al. (1993), Fee et al. (2006) as well as Allen and Phillips (2000), who all state that minority acquisitions ease cooperation conditions (e.g., incomplete contracts) and/or promote collaborative behaviour, it ignores findings from a variety of studies which investigated strategic equity partnerships beyond being purely a form of governance.

Several scholars (e.g., Ashelm & Horeni, 2015; Prigge & Vöpel, 2014; Fahy et al., 2004) all agree that equity emphasises the long-term contribution and strategic role of the business partner. Similarly, Liao (2014) as well as Quimet (2013) see an equity purchase as an act of verifying a strategic partnership and Lin and Darnall (2014) remark that equity is a tool to enhancing the credibility of the relationship. Lowensberg (2010) and Das and Teng (2000) concur that strategic equity partnerships constitute a deeper relationship compared to pure contractual partnerships. Referring to Hertzel and Smith (1993), equity might also involve positive image effects as holding an equity stake seems likely to demonstrate the investment worthiness of the target organisation to other investors. Alike, Cousens et al. (2006) and

Dolphin (2003) in the sponsorship literature elucidate that, in contrast to non-strategic sponsorships, strategic partnerships provide chances for additional synergies, such as advanced image campaigns or the establishment of an emotional bond with customers. In line with the motto 'creating fans for brands' (Bolgar, 2010). However, these scholars do not explicitly refer to equity partnerships, they rather correlate their findings to the general term 'strategic partnership'. Therefore, it remains open whether they include strategic partnerships with shared ownership in their outcomes or not.

In a similar vein, many academics report about positive synergy effects in respect to equity acquisitions. While Quimet (2013) reports an improved information flow between partners, Kim and Inkpen (2005) discovered that equity promotes knowledge transfer because such a partnership is seen as stronger and more stable compared to non-equity partnerships. This is indirectly corroborated by Lui et al. (2010) who ascertain that a partnership built merely on contracts exacerbates effective knowledge transfer. These scientists base their findings on the increased level of trust that should exist in equity partnerships since equity increases the difficulty to exit from the partnership, thus intensifying the vulnerability of both parties to detrimental partner behaviour (Globerman & Nielsen, 2007). Although Das and Teng (2000) maintain that equity is an incentive for honest conduct and curbs opportunistic behaviour by referring to the "shadow of the future"[24] effect, this negative spillover is reinforced in equity partnerships due to the increased difficulty of exiting (Amis & Slack, 1999).

Other scholars spot exclusivity as another key reason to choose equity as a form of collaboration. For example, DePamphilis (2012) clearly states that equity reinforces exclusivity and power and Barringer and Harrison (2000) discovered an increase of market power via the erection of entry barriers for competitors as a major equity investment motive. Liao (2014) counters that a share deal is unlikely to affect market power, at least if it is related to minority acquisitions due to the limits for managing actions in the absence of control. Todeva and Knoke (2005) as well as Bleeke and Ernst (1991) offer additional insights and claim that the degree and depth of partnerships is much less affected by internalised costs and benefits than by the following:

- history of relationship
- present market positions of each corporation and
- their joint resource capabilities

[24]Companies that expect a relatively long-term partnership will be more careful about taking advantage of their partners (Todeva & Knoke, 2005).

Put another way, business partnerships are less driven by companies' retrospective financial logic than by their strategic (joint) purpose. Accordingly, Ring (2000) determines that the strategic intent for equity partnerships should be absolutely coherent with the organisation's overall strategic intent. Hence, corporations' decisions to partner cannot be verified in a rational way by the intention itself. On the other hand, these aspects merely support companies in defining post-facto justifications and rationalisations about their alliance decision. According to Todeva and Knoke (2005; 6):

> "A decision to cooperate is not a responsive action, but is fundamentally a strategic intent, which aims at improving the future circumstances for each individual firm and their partnership as a whole".

However, equity decisions are often discussed in respect to contracting issues in existing alliances (Liao, 2014; Quimet, 2013). Grossmann and Hart (1986), Hart and Moore (1990), as well as Hart (1995) spotlight an implication ('related cost to acquiring control') which equity purchases might have, if two organisations are already in a contractual partnership whose value depends on trades with its partner organisation. In such a situation, if the partner organisation necessitates a renegotiation of the contract, the investing organisation's bargaining power is restrained because the value of the partnership-specific assets depends on pursued trade. In this respect, Quimet (2013) refers to a 'holdup' problem. The other way around, the bargaining power of the target firm can also be limited if the value of the partnership depends on the continuation of the contractual partnership (continued trade). Moreover, Krishnaswami et al. (2012) found evidence that equity alleviates 'post-formation bargaining costs' that occur if the contrast in negotiating power is high.

3.5 Critical Success Factors and Effects

3.5.1 The Fit-Construct

When considering the "how" of entering into strategic partnerships each alliance is itself an individual matter with distinctive contextual characteristics based on the specific needs of the partnering organisations at the time of deal-making (Hecox, 2007). Thus, the success factors for entering into strategic partnerships, managing the complex interactions with stakeholders, and getting the desired effects are manifold. However, lessons gleaned from past research may shed light on some of the potential factors for partnership success.

With a vision in mind of searching for new efficiencies and competitive advantage, the initial critical step is to find and select the right partner (Todeva & Knoke, 2005). Elmuti and Kathawala (2001; 214) even say that finding the right partner *"is perhaps the most important step in creating a successful alliance"*. In the most general sense, there are two forms of partner selection, i.e., the passive approach (an organisation receives correspondence and interests) and the proactive approach, in which an organisation proactively acts to find a suitable partner (Mitsuhashi, 2002). Regardless who initiates the partnership, the majority of scholars agree that a 'fit' between the two parties is a key strategic requirement and one of the prime success factors for entering into and managing strategic partnerships (Russo & Cesarini, 2017; Santala & Parvinen, 2007; Cobianchi, 1994).

The concept of 'fit' generally implies the alignment of various organisational contingencies and can be traced back to the early work of Chandler (1962) and Ansoff (1965) who address a fit between corporate strategy and organisational structure. Over the years, the concept has developed into different ramifications, especially in the strategy literature.

For example, Porter (1985) tackles strategy and external conditions, Waterman (1982) amplifies that successfully implementing strategy requires a fit among elements in the McKinsey 7-S framework[25], and Mills and Snow (1994) demand a fit between strategy, structure, and processes. Contingency Theory (Lawrence & Lorsch, 1967) proposes that an organisation whose internal characteristics best match the external environmental demands will achieve greater performance.

Meanwhile, fit occupies an important place in respect to business partnerships too and emerges to shape the extent to which cooperating organisations achieve synergies that assist their success. Regarding this, 'fit' is chiefly related to the question whether there is a sufficient strategic basis for fruitful collaboration. While some refer to the term 'link' (Madrigal, 2001), 'congruence' (Woisetschläger & Michaelis, 2012; Meenaghan, 2001; Harrigan, 1988), 'alignment' (Douma et al., 2000), or 'complementarity' (Russo & Cesarini, 2017), the academic community concurs that fit is a dynamic construct which refers to different parts. For example, Ireland et al. (2002) emphasise a fit on three levels (strategic, relational, and operational), Russo and Cesarini (2017) accentuate strategic fit (alignment of complementary resources), partner congruence (fit in partners' goals and objectives), as well as cultural and organisational fit (compatibility). Das and Teng (2003) concur that fit refers to resources, too.

[25]The McKinsey 7-S framework consists of strategy, structure, systems, skills, staff, style, and shared values.

Complementary resources (strategic fit) imply a combination of resources whose mixture conduces to organisational success. Some academics (e.g., Murray & Kotabe, 2005) argue that an alliance partner should have similar but complementary resources in order to benefit from the resources implied in the partnership, because if the resources of both partners are the same, there will be no opportunity to take advantage. On the other hand, the same authors maintain that a certain degree of resource similarity (overlap) is required in order to effectively understand, incorporate, and make use of partner resources. If such an overlap is missing, an information gap could exist as to how to obtain and exploit the partner's resources. Harrison et al. (2001) reveal that complementary resources present opportunities for improved learning and the progress for new capabilities.

In contrast, Lin et al. (2009) suggest resource complementarity is negatively related to economic performance (i.e., return on assets). However, the level of complementary resources seems to be a vital aspect in setting a partnership's future outcome. Kim and Inkpen (2005) clarify the need for a balance between similar and diverse resources to establish a stable strategic alliance. Accordingly, having overly similar resources means that partners have little to learn from the associate which hampers the partnership from becoming deeper. Though, extreme resource diversity restricts an exchange and learning process and impedes managing the partnership effectively. In contrast, Dyer and Singh (1998) mitigate that a fit of resources is not a primary factor for alliance success. They rather see a fit in decision-making processes and operating systems as more important, whereby these components are also referred to as 'organisational fit' (Russo & Cesarini, 2017). Notwithstanding, referring to Nielsen and Gudergan (2012) competence similarity affects the extent to which alliance associates develop partnership-specific idiosyncrasies which may influence fit.

A number of academics have advanced the concept by adding that the corporate culture of both partners needs to be harmonious (cultural fit), otherwise the alliance is at risk of failure (Nielsen & Gudergan, 2012; Farrelly & Quester, 2005a; Das & Teng, 2003; Kaplan, 2002; Barringer & Harrison, 2000; Dyer & Singh, 1998). This was recently substantiated by Russo and Cesarini (2017) who refer to 'compatibility' as a cultural and organisational fit between associates. Related corporate cultures are cited to facilitate closer working relationships. If the people of both partners have similar mindsets, mutual goals become easier to attain and the risk of conflict is diminished. Moreover, understanding one another's culture might also positively influence inter-firm communication, knowledge transfer (Lyles & Salk, 1996; Cooper & Gardner, 1993), as well as the readiness to adapt to each other's management practices and working procedures (Russo & Cesarini, 2017). This corresponds to the aforementioned operational fit put forward by Ireland et al. (2002).

Findings by Cooper and Gardner (1993) suggest that contrasting corporate cultures is a main reason for alliance failure. Luo (1997), Das and Teng (2003), and DePamphilis (2012, 1987) coincide that cultural disparities are the 'culprit' for alliance failure. Jiang et al. (2008) further insert that cultural fit has to go beyond the top management level and requires that those responsible in managing the partnership on a day-to-day basis get in touch with their partner in order to check a fit and get detailed, first hand impressions about the partner organisation and its working procedures. In this respect, communication between potential partners is critical in order to encourage joint planning (Farrelly & Quester, 2005a).

Previous alliance research has also concentrated on partner characteristics and fit but mainly as an indicator for alliance results and long-term stability (DePamphilis, 2012; Lui et al., 2010; Saxton, 1997). Alliance stability is defined by Jiang et al. (2008; 178) as *"the degree to which an alliance can run and develop successfully based on an effective collaborative relationship shared by all partners"*. This definition implies that stability is not an outcome; it is rather a process-based, dynamic, and multi-dimensional construct. Jiang et al. (2008) further stress that stability is based on reciprocity, harmony, and fit. These components are said to be critical requirements for partners to accomplish anticipated synergies which can develop into a competitive advantage. Das and Teng (2000) add the perspective that stability means stable structures on the one hand, but also strategic flexibility on the other hand. Whereas structural rigidity provides a stable framework, which is crucial for active and harmonious processes to develop, Ernst and Bamford (2005), arguing from a change management view, state that flexibility is inevitable due to the ever-changing business environment and thus stable partnerships require timely and permanent modifications and fine-tuning as the alliance evolves. This is maintained in the sponsorship literature by Cousens et al. (2006) who corroborate that B2B relationships (should) change over time to adapt to the altering strategic direction of partnering companies.

However, there is overall agreement (e.g., Russo & Cesarini, 2017; DePamphilis, 2012; Nielsen & Gudergan, 2012; Douma et al., 2000) that the way in which various aspects of fit are unified, orchestrated, and incorporated within the partner's strategy is the prerequisite for successful partnerships. This dynamic concept is illustrated in Figure 3.2.

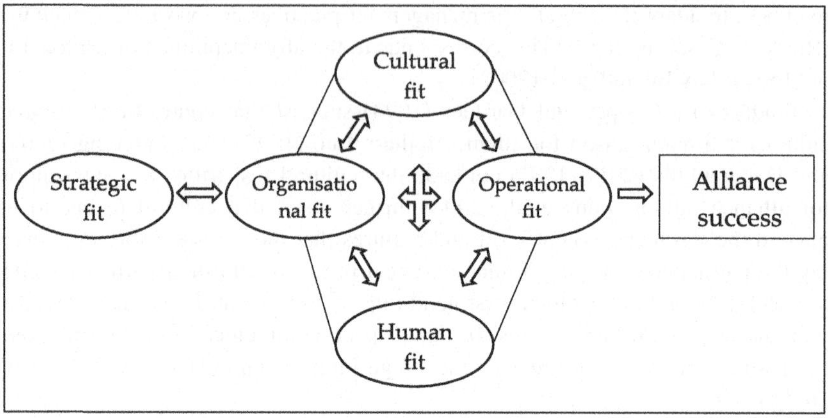

Figure 3.2 The Concept of Strategic Fit and Alliance Success. (Source: According to Douma et al., 2000; 582)

There is a discord in the academic discussion about the appropriate level of fit. Whereas Das and Teng (2003) as well as Draulans et al. (2003) are obscure in their formulation by talking about 'a certain degree' of fit and 'optimal fit', others such as Russo and Cesarini (2017) and Dyer and Singh (1998) are precise and demand a 'high level fit' among partners. In respect to cultural fit, Cooper and Gardner (1993) remark that even though a high fit is desirable, cultures do not need to become identical. Douma et al. (2000) distinguishes between 'good fit', 'mixed fit' and 'limited fit'. Although a good fit is favourable, alliances can also succeed if there is only a limited or mixed fit. Yet, the scholars clarify that the potential for conflict is high in that case. Hence, it is recommended to focus on strengthening the fit otherwise the strategic partnership is likely to fail (Douma et al., ibid.).

Related debates are also found in the sponsorship literature. In respect to sponsorships, fit can be classified as a strategic match between two business parties in terms of mission, goals, target audience, and values, and find expression in the perceived pertinence (between sponsor and sponsee) in the view of consumers (Mazodier & Quester, 2014; Woisetschläger et al., 2010; Cousens et al., 2006). Morgan et al. (2014) and Farrelly (2010) agree that a 'high fit' is a success factor that will generate positive results in the form of improved credibility, strong brand awareness, recall, and positive brand attitude (Simonin & Ruth, 1998).

In this respect, Meenaghan (2001) refers to the 'halo effect'[26] of sponsorship. However, there are also opposing studies (e.g., Olson & Thjomoe, 2009; Trendel & Warlop, 2007) which demonstrate a positive effect of 'low fit' sponsorships, as some people perceive a degree of incongruence appealing. Against this, Burmann and Nitschke (2005) advocate a 'moderate fit'. They argue that if the fit is too great, sponsorship has no (or little) image changing effect because consumers tend to be bored. Albeit there is generally consensus that fit is a determinant of sponsorship success, these conflicting results confirm that fit may change over time and should be regarded as a dynamic concept (Mazodier & Quester, 2014; Douma et al., 2000).

With reference to sport sponsorships, large-scale sponsorship partnerships can evolve into entire corporate and/or brand positioning strategies (Farrelly & Quester, 2005a) because sport has considerable non-verbal components entailing universal images of victory, hope, and pain, which has the potential to exceed cultural limits by achieving a fit. According to Farrelly and Quester (2005a) and Urriolagoitia and Planellas (2007), such sponsorship relationships can be the foundation for 'co-marketing alliances', in which the brand and corporate image of the partners are marketed together as a system. This is supported by a recent study of Woisetschläger (2015) about sponsorship relevance in the German 1st Bundesliga. Hence, many scholars (e.g., Demir & Söderman, 2015; Morgan et al., 2014; Cousens et al., 2006; Olkkonen et al., 2000) comply with the significance of evaluating a strategic fit on various levels (strategic, organisational, image/reputation, cultural, match of resource profile).

Overall, the fit construct arouses attention in the field of management and sponsorship and is perceived as a vital concept when it comes to entering into strategic partnerships. Fit does not only refer to a strategic match of partners in regard to values, objectives, and resources, it also implies a fit of operations and organisational culture. Manifestations of various kinds of fit indicate that organisations may seek to benefit from inter-partner fit in multiple ways simultaneously. However, fit should be viewed comprehensively. Referring to Nielsen and Gudergan (2012), treating individual components of inter-partner fit as independent and evaluating their outcome effects separately may lead to inconsistent results.

The controversial debate about the appropriate level of fit revealed a lack of concrete analytical schemes that propose suitable measures (Nielsen & Gudergan,

[26]'Halo effect' refers to the goodwill of sponsorship and occurs when the attributes of one factor are transmitted to another in such a way as it influences customer judgment (Egan, 2007).

ibid.). Nevertheless, while fit is perceived as a fundamental success factor for strategic partnerships, fit alone can barely be the sole basis for strategic partnership (success) due to the complex nature of partnership management (Hecox, 2007).

3.5.2 Trust and Commitment

Trust[27] has long been acknowledged as another critical success factor in the formation and management of partnerships (e.g., Parmigiani & Santos, 2011; Lui et al., 2010; Nufer & Bühler, 2011; Das & Teng, 2003; Hamel, 1991). Despite its centrality, many scholars have, to date, faced difficulty in coming to an overall definition of trust.

Das and Teng (2001; 255) see trust as *"a subjective state of positive expectations"*, others classify it as 'a reliance on the partner in a risky situation' (Hosmer, 1995; Moorman et al., 1992). While there is no universal definition, a more modern classification is adopted which is used in marketing and alliance literature and conforms to Cobbs (2011; 295) who defines trust as the *"confidence in a partner's reliability and integrity"*. Trust is further mainly established through open communication and perceived mutual understanding, which may result in shared decision making. Moreover, various experts categorise trust into multidimensional types. Ring (1996) distinguishes trust as 'fragile'[28] and 'resilient', McAllister (1995) states that trust is either 'cognition-based'[29] or 'affect-based'. Das and Teng (2001) based their research on Barber's (1983) classification of 'goodwill trust'[30] and 'competence trust'[31]. Even though many scholars utilise the terms 'benevolent trust'[32]

---

[27]In a partnership context trust can be classified as a psychological alignment including the intention to accept vulnerability based upon positive expectations of the intentions or behaviour of the other party in a partnership dyad (Farrelly & Quester, 2003).

[28]*"Whereas fragile trust is more calculative, resilient trust is said to be based on a perception of goodwill"* (Das & Teng, 2001; 255).

[29]Cognition is calculative and affect is about goodwill and responsibility (Das & Teng, 2001).

[30]According to Barber (1983; 14) goodwill trust is *"the expectation that some others in our social relationships have moral obligations and responsibility to demonstrate a special concern for other's interests above their own"* (Barber, 1983; 14).

[31]Competence trust refers to *"the expectation of technically competent role performance"* (Barber, 1983; 14).

[32]Benevolent trust is rooted in the belief that the business partner will behave with goodwill toward the partnership (Cullen et al., 2000).

(relational/emotional) and 'credibility trust'[33] (rational) (Beamish et al., 2016; Cobbs, 2011; Globermann & Nielsen, 2007; Farrelly & Quester, 2005b), the terms share the same meaning (as goodwill and competence trust). Since this differentiation is widely acknowledged in the research community and presents a clear distinction, it will be adopted in this study.

In addition, a multitude of writings (Russo & Cesarini, 2017; Farrelly & Quester, 2005b; Cooper & Gardener, 1993) examine trust in tandem with commitment[34], which is also seen as a key ingredient of long-term business relationships. Anderson and Weitz (1992; 19) present a valuable description by stating that commitment is the desire *"to develop a stable relationship"* and the *"confidence"* in the stability of the partnership. Especially in strategic partnerships many scientists (Farrelly & Quester, 2003; Kaplan, 2002; Meenaghan, 2001; Dyer & Singh, 1998) assume that both parties search for stable relationships, as the underlying motives of a strategic partnership require a long-term direction to attain a sustainable competitive advantage.

Spekman (1988; 79) has highlighted the crucial role of trust in respect to alliance negotiation, investment, collaboration, learning, knowledge transfer, and performance by denoting trust as the *"cornerstone of strategic partnerships"*. This was recently proven by Morgan et al. (2014) in a sponsorship context. Russo and Cesarini (2017) underpin the vital role of trust and commitment in respect to effective alliance daily operations. If the partners trust each other there is an increased information flow and high trust eases the exchange of sensitive information and knowledge.

Nielsen and Gudergan (2012) confirm an increased knowledge transfer and further add that trust lowers the cost of coordination. Furthermore, Gulati (1995) discovered that trust and commitment promote a sense of belonging among allies and reduce opportunistic behaviour. Though building trust is cited one of the most difficult tasks in managing partnerships (Cooper & Gardner, 1993) it becomes obvious that trust is a multidimensional phenomenon as it correlates to various aspects. For example, in a sponsorship context, partner image and reputation (e.g., in respect to management capability) are intertwined with trust as both can be a contributor to building trust and hence both influence the success of a partnership (Saxton, 1997). Beyond this, trust is frequently related to business people

---

[33]Credibility trust is the trust (confidence) that the alliance partner has the purpose and ability to meet their duties and adhere to their promised contributions (Cullen et al., 2000).

[34]Relational commitment has been classified as "*a willingness by the parties involved in the sponsorship dyad to make short-term investments with the expectation of realising long-term benefits from the relationship*" (Farrelly & Quester, 2003; 535).

and their traits and finds expression on a personal level. Some even argue that this can be the foundation for entering into a strategic partnership (social motives by Eisenhardt and Schoonhoven, 1996; social embeddedness, Uzzi, 1996). This can be demonstrated by the public statements in the context of the extension of the strategic partnership contract between FC Bayern München and sport equipment manufacturer Adidas. According to Karl-Heinz Rummenigge, chairman at FC Bayern München (Rummenigge cited in Sportspromedia, 2011; sect. 6):

> "We're delighted that the decades-long partnership between FC Bayern and Adidas, which has always been characterised by mutual trust and respect, will continue for a further period of at least eight years. Our 50 years of trust has grown into a partnership between friends".

This view on the partnership is shared by their corporate partner, according to Herbert Hainer, CEO (at that time) at Adidas (Hainer cited in Sportspromedia, 2011; sect. 4):

> "I'm delighted and proud. Adidas and FC Bayern Munich combine much more than a long-standing cooperation as sponsor and supplier. Our partnership is unique in football. It is founded on trust and mutual support".

On the one hand, the statements illustrate that a former sponsorship relationship seems to be beneficial for the development of a long-term strategic (equity) sponsorship. By the same token, the statements clearly show that trust is an evolving issue which accrues over time and is amplified if business people know each other (Das & Teng, 2001). (Goodwill) Trust has been cited by both Adidas and FCB as key factor in this process. This concurs with findings from Geh (2011) and Cobbs (2011) who have found theoretical and empirical evidence that trust is a key component in reducing the complexity of partnership operations.

However, it has to be considered that business partnerships which are heavily based on trust also come with certain risks. For instance, staff turnover can lead to a loss of trust because personal relationships break down. This could also have negative effects on shared corporate knowledge (Morgan et al., 2014).

Despite the general agreement that trust is an indispensable component in business partnerships, Das and Teng (2003) claim that 'key antecedents' i.e., trust of partnership success has not been sufficiently investigated yet. Nielsen and Gudergan (2012) concord by stating that research on trust is largely 'anecdotal' with little indication for economic benefits. For example, although Aulakh et al. (1996) elucidate the significance of trust building ex post and correlate trust with a positive information flow, they nevertheless did not find a significant relationship between trust and performance. Yet, extant literature gives the impression that trust has a positive, although sometimes indirect effect on alliance performance (Nielsen & Gudergan, 2012).

3.5.3 Prior Business Relationships

While trust is related to informal relationships between business people Gulati (1995) interrelates trust to prior business partnerships. By so doing, prior business partnerships affect trust positively. This is evidenced by scientists in the field. Referring to Parkhe (1993), a former relationship between partners accompanied with a history of trust plays an essential role in ex-ante alliance design choice (partnership continuation). Other scholars such as Doz (1996), Reuer et al. (2002), and Mitsuhashi (2002) sustain this view by emphasising that prior relationships facilitate the arrangement of future partnerships, offer valuable experience in managing partnership developments and support trust building. According to this view, it is the features of the relationship between partners as an ongoing pattern that should be the aspect for understanding partnership behaviour and performance.

As already discussed above, some academics (e.g., Lui et al., 2010; Kim & Inkpen, 2005) recommend equity as a form of alliance governance structure in order to improve partnership stability. This assumption contrasts to earlier findings from Gulati (1995) in which it is argued that a prior relationship between companies acts as a proxy for trust and makes companies less likely to opt for equity as a governance form. However, Gulati's work has only focused on R&D partnerships and cannot be referred one-to-one to other partnership forms. Nevertheless, Globermann and Nielsen (2007) provide indirect support for Gulati's finding.

The effects of prior relationships on alliance performance are ambiguous. Saxton (1997) depicts that prior ties lead to initial satisfaction, but have no impact on long-term advantage. Nielsen and Gudergan (2012) agree by elucidating that the collaboration becomes more effective because transactions are increasingly surrounded in social relations as the interactions continue. Frequently the business partner can become a vital source of creativity that improves the value of the firm and therefore supports a competitive advantage (Ireland et al., 2002; Dyer & Singh, 1998).

However, there are also opposing findings. Nielsen and Gudergan (op. cit.) explain that prior affiliation indicates a history of collaboration which can lead to inertia as partners stick to old patterns and may also neglect to pay attention to prospective alternatives. Beamish and Inkpen (1995) even argue that prior ties increase the likelihood of partnership instability due to enhanced resource similarity over time and the awareness of attained goals. This conforms indirectly with Lavie and Rosenkopf's (2006) notion that allying with new partners might widen the scope of the organisation and support access to new knowledge and business opportunities. In opposition to this, Ireland et al. (2002) and Barringer and Harrison (2000) maintain that accumulated learning may lead to knowledge-sharing routines and may enhance the absorptive capacity of a company. With regard to strategic equity partnerships, a prior relationship (e.g., in the form of a sponsorship) can facilitate the absorptive capacity through acquired knowledge throughout the (sponsorship) partnership as well as the trust that has matured between the organisations (Lund & Greyser, 2016). Hence, partnerships based on a history of collaboration can effectively transfer know-how across interfirm boundaries (Dyer & Singh, 1998).

Despite contradictory findings about short-term and long-term effects, the majority of academics perceive prior ties as beneficial for future partnerships and their stability in terms of accumulated experience, partner process familiarity, information about each other's culture, communication, and working preferences (Jiang et al., 2008; Saxton, 1997). Other scholars such as Doz (1996), Reuer et al. (2002), and Mitsuhashi (2002) perpetuate this view by emphasising that prior relationships facilitate the arrangement of future partnerships, offer valuable experiences in managing partnership developments and support trust building.

3.6 Summary of Strategic Partnership Literature

This section has analysed the general B2B literature concerning strategic partnerships. Diverse theoretical frameworks are taken into account and it is justified that this study uses a variety of frameworks in order to investigate and understand the subject comprehensively. Definitions of key terms are provided, and different forms of strategic partnerships are discussed.

The motives for entering into strategic partnerships are critically reviewed based on far-reaching issues that support groupings of motives associated with corporations' strategic efforts in terms of partnerships. The core motives refer to access to a variety of critical resources such as knowledge and competences. Also, boosting the corporate brand is a primary motive for corporations to enter into strategic partnerships. In addition, the financial and strategic considerations of strategic equity partnerships are acknowledged. The discussion has shown that equity is chosen to achieve financial returns for investors (investor/financial perspective). Moreover, equity is said to enhance cooperative conditions (e.g., information flow), is an indicator of the credibility of the partnership, and increases the partnership's exclusivity. However, there are contrasting views as to whether equity increases market power (Liao, 2014; DePamphilis, 2012). If the partnership is based on two levels (contractual and equity) this might have implications on the bargaining power of the partner, if the value of the partnership-specific assets depends on pursued trade (Quimet, 2013; Grossmann & Hart, 1986).

It is demonstrated that the concept of fit in its various facets, trust, and commitment are critical success factors for entering into and managing business partnerships. Moreover, prior relationships seem to be positively related to trust and also for continuation of the partnership. However, the latter outcome faces resistance as former relationships can also lead to inertia (Nielsen & Gudergan, 2012) and hamper a partner's progress because a company may neglect to pay attention to better prospective alternatives.

4 Strategic Equity Partnerships in the Football Business

4.1 Introduction

The preceding part delivered a review of the general partnership literature regarding the motives, critical success factors, and effects of strategic partnerships. Since this study is designed to study strategic partnerships between corporate sponsors and professional football clubs in Germany, the peculiarities of the football business are illustrated in this section. That means, beside academic sources (mainly from the area of sport management and marketing), information is reviewed and analysed from football media, in particular public statements, non-academic newspapers, club homepages, and general sport (football) websites.

Initially, the specific characteristics of the football game are outlined and it is elucidated that the business (and competition) of football is subject to different prerequisites compared to corporations in the economy. Next, it is clarified how the concept of strategic partnership is classified and applied in the German and international football business. Different types of equity partners are discussed against the concept of strategic partnership and the motives of four equity partner (investor) types are illuminated. Subsequently, the factors which attract corporations to enter into equity partnerships with German football clubs are investigated as well as the impact related with this partnership form is illuminated. This includes an examination about impediments, in particular the interactions between club and club members/fans.

T. Duffner, *Strategic Equity Partnerships in Professional Football*, Event- und Impaktforschung, https://doi.org/10.1007/978-3-658-31301-2_4

4.2 Background Information on the Business of Football

It has long been acknowledged that the football business is—similar to the general field of sport economics—characterised by three main peculiarities: the organisation of the sport, its production process, and the customer demand for the product football (Oettgen, 2008; Büch & Frick, 1999).

Football clubs are organised in a system of higher authorities (governing bodies), viz. FIFA[1] and UEFA[2] that issue licences and supervises the club's operations. Furthermore, each country has a national football authority, which directives are binding for clubs (Nagy, 2011). Within this organisational structure, football is a co-produced match by two competing teams within their national leagues or within the international (European) competition of UEFA Champions League or UEFA Euro League (team production, in which the consumer/fan in the stadium becomes a prosumer[3]; Alchian & Demsetz, 1972; Franck, 1995). Football clubs operate on an international labour market and, in particular since the Bosman ruling[4] (C-415/93) in 1993, highly talented players have become brand names and use the ruling to negotiate contracts according to their market value when their contracts expire. The change of bargaining power from clubs towards players resulted in an increased international competition to attract the best player's talent and raises the prices for player's salary (Fordyce, 2005).

The game is distinguished by the unpredictability of outcomes of matches due to a whole series of unexpected factors, such as player injuries, form of the day, luck, and eminently the quality and performance of the opponent (Nagy, 2012; Quitzau, 2003). Even though several scholars such as Capasso and Rossi

---

[1]FIFA is an acronym for Fédération Internationale de Football Association.

[2]UEFA is an acronym for Union of European Football Associations.

[3]The term prosumer is a combination of the term consumer and producer. In football, people who attend the match are on the one hand consumers and on the other hand they act as an external factor who essentially influence the atmosphere in the stadium (Schade, 2012; Teichmann, 2006).

[4]The Bosman ruling stated in its first case, that Bosman and all other EU football players have the right to a free transfer after contract end (it does not affect a transfer when a player is in contract) with the provision that they were transferring from a club within one EU Association to a club within another EU Association. Though the ruling does not touch internal transfers within the same association domestic transfer rules apply also to the case because clubs expected that if they do not apply to it at national transfers the EU will intervene (Parrsih, 2003).

(2012) as well as Michie and Oughton (2005) propose that a balanced contest between clubs is necessary to render match results uncertain and thus attract fans ('Louis-Schmeling Paradoxon'[5]; Neale, 1964), the organisation of clubs within the league system implies a competition for the best places in the table. Each tabular improvement of a team means a tabular decline of another team (destructive competition; Whitney, 1993).

While it is indisputable that winning (achieving and maintain the best possible sport performances) is the key objective for football clubs (Nagy, 2012; Frick, 2007; Sloane, 1971), there have been heated discussions in academic and non-academic contexts about the influence of money on sporting success (scores). Indeed, many authors find empirical evidence that sporting success correlates essentially with economic success. For example, Barajas et al. (2005), Szymanski and Kuypers (1999), as well as Hall et al. (2002) have revealed a statistical relationship between player salary spending and sports results as well as a link between sports results and revenues for professional sports organisations. In respect to football clubs, Hovemann and Wieschemann (2009) find evidence for a correlation between capital expenditure and an increased likelihood of wins. Recently, Wilkesmann (2014) proved a positive relation between player salary and club scores in the German 1st Bundesliga. These findings are in concert with previous results from Frick (2005) and are also confirmed by Gerrad (2008) in the context of the English Premier League. Carmichael et al. (2010) endorse that, in regard to the EPL, higher revenue is positively related to on-field success. In 2012, Kuypers and Szymanski supported this correlation based on an investigation of the Big Five. Accordingly, when a club attains great economical results (i.e., turnover, revenues), this is typically accompanied by improved sports results and vice versa.

In addition, Pinnuck and Potter (2006) ascertain that money is not only related to on-field success, but, as a consequence of winning, this also increases intangible results such as the image of the club. Overall, the interdependency and coor dination between sport and financial performance/goals is of utmost significance for the competitiveness of football clubs as illustrated in Table 4.1 on page 68.

[5]The Louis-Schmeling paradoxon is based on the principle that an athlete (or team) needs an (equal) partner to produce the sport performance. The competitiveness of the opponent is the key aspect for the attractiveness of the match (sport) and hence for earning revenues (Quitzau, 2003).

Table 4.1 Goal Alignment of Football Clubs to Raise Investor Interest. (Source: Own Illustration, referring to Keller, 2005)

Stable sport performance	Sustainable profitability
Requirement for exploitation of economic success Measures: - Meaningful player transfers - Promoting of young talents - Create sport and financial stimuli - Maintain good infrastructure	Basis for long-term economic success - Liquidity, turnover - Brand building - Solid economic management

Since the financial situation has an impact on sporting performance, Rohde and Breuer (2017) as well as Rudd (2012) constitute that TV revenues have increasingly become a key income source for clubs. In this context, Rehm (2018), Chemnitzer et al. (2015), and Schmitt (2015) state that German clubs face an essential drawback compared to other European leagues. Indeed, on average, TV broadcasting in foreign clubs (Spain, England, Italy, and France) makes up about 40–50% of overall revenue compared to German clubs, where broadcasting counts for 25–30% of overall income[6] (Chemnitzer et al., 2015). By looking at TV revenues from national TV rights it becomes evident that the EPL clubs enjoy an exceptional position as their current TV contract exceeds every other European top league by far as illustrated in Figure 4.1 (TV-right revenues in billion Euros per season, divided into countries) on the next page.

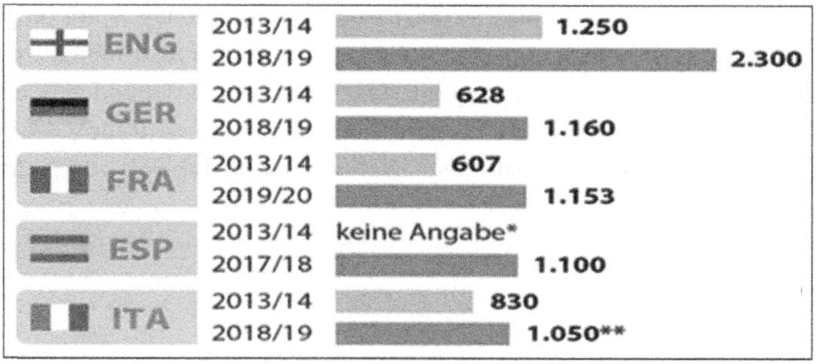

Figure 4.1 National TV Revenues in European Top Leagues. (Source: According to Hirsch, 2018, retrieved from Der Standard, 2018)

[6]In general, there are four main revenue sources of football clubs: revenues from media and broadcasting, sponsoring, ticketing, and merchandising (Schade, 2012).

Even though the DFL (Deutsche Fußball Liga, national football association in Germany) raised revenue from TV broadcasting[7] to approximately €1,16 billion per season (as of 12/2017), the difference vis-à-vis English clubs still remains considerable. Compared to Italy, France, and Spain the graphic illustrates that German clubs are competitive with respect to national TV revenues. However, Rosentritt (2016) adds for consideration that, on taking a closer look, German clubs have an idiosyncratic distribution of national TV revenues which is more solidary to the lower tier leagues compared to other European top leagues. For instance, German clubs allocate the biggest amount to clubs in the 2nd Bundesliga (around 15%). In the Big Five, the contribution to the lower tier leagues is around 5% (Wöckener & Tenbusch, 2016). While this strengthens a balanced contest nationally, it nevertheless results in lower TV revenues for the 1st Bundesliga clubs, who fight for international competition.

In addition, with respect to international TV revenues German clubs trail behind the European competition as demonstrated in Figure 4.2 (international TV revenues in European top leagues in the 2017/2018 season, in million Euros).

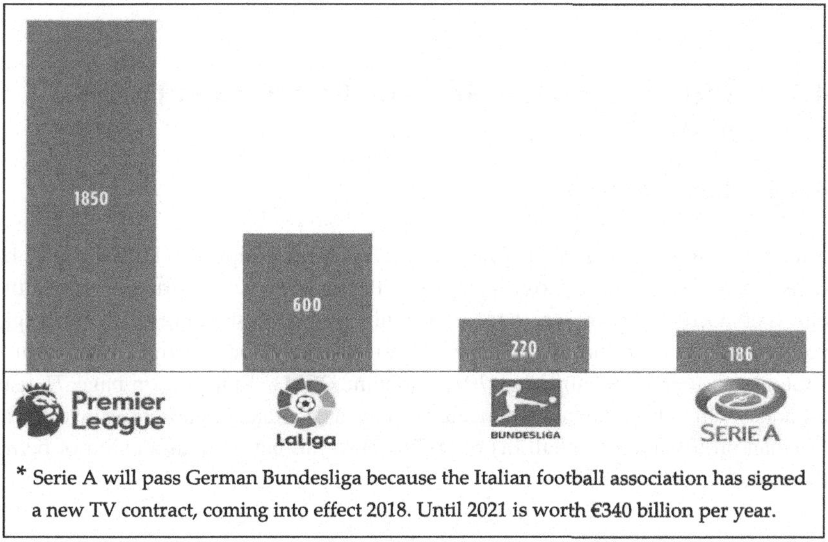

Figure 4.2 International TV Revenues in European Top Leagues in 2017/2018. (Source: Acccording to Rehm, 2018, retrieved from Manager Magazin, 2018)

[7]In the Big Five, TV revenues are central marketed by their national football associations.

Overall, based on the background that revenues are positively related to sporting success, the different TV revenue streams from the various football leagues have a considerable impact on club revenues and hence on the international competitiveness of football clubs.

Just like the TV revenues typically have a positive effect on the aggregated results, so, too the idiosyncratic governance structures of each football country affect on the competition of clubs. Adam and Hovemann (2018) as well as Lammert et al. (2009) assess that the 50+1 rule restricts German clubs to generate additional funds by selling majority shares. Even though the development towards investor ownership of clubs in international leagues also has negative effects such as the dependency of the owners and exorbitant player salaries (Lammert et al., 2009), Oediger (2017b) and Rohde and Breuer (2017) espouse that the cash injections from investors in foreign leagues put pressure on German clubs to exploit new income streams in order to fight for the best players and remain internationally competitive.

Taken as a whole, the need to generate additional financial and strategic options for German clubs in order to keep pace in international competition (i.e., to attract players) becomes obvious.

4.3 Different Types of Strategic Partners and Their Motives

4.3.1 Introduction

The increasing formation of strategic equity partnerships in Germany can be considered as a strategic move to enhance the club's revenue structure (from the club perspective). However, there is no universal understanding of the strategic partnership concept and diverse views exist in theory and practice about what a strategic partner is (Schürmann, 2015; Ashelm, 2011). Table 4.2 on page 71 lists alliances which have been announced by clubs as a strategic partner or investor in German professional football (as of 06/2019) so far, but without a claim of being exhausted.

Table 4.2 Overview of Equity Partners in German Football. (Source: Own Illustration)

Club	Shareholding	Equity partner/ announced	Investment in €/ features	Sponsorship/ since
1st Bundesliga				
FC Bayern München	FC Bayern München AG • FC Bayern München e.V. 75 % • Adidas 8.33 % • Audi 8.33 % • Allianz 8.33 %	• Adidas (2001) • Audi (2009) •Allianz (2014)	• 75 million • 90 million • 110 million Strategic Partners	• Equipment (1966) • Car sponsor (2002) • Stadium title (2000)
BVB Borussia Dortmund 09	Borussia Dortmund GmbH & Co. KGaA • Borussia 09 e.V. 5.53% • Evonik 14.78% • Bernd Geske 8.8% • SIGNAL IDUNA 5.43% • PUMA 5.0% • Streubesitz 60.46%	• Signal Iduna (2014) • Evonik (2014) • Puma (2014)	• 24 million • 61.5 million • 23.3 million Strategic partners	• Stadium name right sponsor (2005) • Lead sponsor (2007) • Equipment (2012)
Hertha BSC Berlin	Hertha BSC GmbH & Co. KG aA • Hertha BSC e.V. 90.3% • KKR 9.7%	• KKR (2014)	• 61.2 million Financial investor	• No sponsor (seat on supervisory board)
SG Eintracht Frankfurt	Eintracht Frankfurt AG • Eintracht Frankfurt e.V. 67.88 % • Freunde des Adlers GmbH 18.55 % • Freunde der Eintracht Frankfurt AG 10 % • BHF Bank 5 % • W. Steubing AG 3.57 %	• Freunde des Adlers (2018) • BHF Bank (2013) • W. Steubing AG (2010) • Freunde der Eintracht (2000)	• 15 million • 1.25 million • Not public • 4.5 million Strategic partners	• Seat on board • Seat on board

(continued)

Table 4.2 (continued)

Club	Shareholding	Equity partner/ announced	Investment in €/ features	Sponsorship/ since
RB Leipzig	RasenBallsport Leipzig GmbH • RB Leipzig e.V. 1% • Red Bull GmbH 99%	• Red Bull (2009)	• Unknown Investor/strategic partner/ owner	• Lead sponsor (2009) • Stadium name right (2010)
VfB Stuttgart	VfB Stuttgart 1893 AG • VfB Stuttgart e.V. 88.25% • Daimler AG 11.75%	• Daimler AG (2018)	• 41.5 million Strategic partner	• Stadium name (1949) • Lead Sponsor
FC Augsburg	FC Augsburg 1907 GmbH & Co. KG • FC Augsburg e.V. 1% • Klaus Hofmann & Investor group 99%	• Klaus Hofmann & investor group (2014)	• Unknown Maecenas WWK (strategic partner)	• Club president • Main sponsor & stadium name
Hannover 96	Hannover 96 GmbH & Co. KG • Hannover 96 Sales & Service GmbH & Co. KG (limited partner) 100% • Hannover 96 Management GmbH (100% subsidiary of Hannover 96 e.V.)	• Hannover 96 Sales & Service GmbH & Co. KG	• Unknown Maecenas	• Club president (Martin Kind)
TSG 1899 Hoffenheim*	TSG 1899 Hoffenheim Fußball Spielbetriebs GmbH • TSG Hoffenheim e.V. 4 % • Dietmar Hopp 96 %	• Dietmar Hopp (co-founder of SAP) (1995)	• Around 350 million Maecenas	• Maecenas (1995) • SAP lead sponsor

(continued)

Table 4.2 (continued)

Club	Shareholding	Equity partner/ announced	Investment in €/ features	Sponsorship/ since
VfL Wolfsburg*	VfL Wolfsburg GmbH • Volkswagen AG 100 %	• VW (2001)	• Around 100 million/ season • Owner	• Lead sponsor (1952) • Stadium name right
Bayer 04 Leverkusen*	Bayer 04 Leverkusen Fußball GmbH • Bayer AG 100%	• Bayer AG (1999)	• Around 25 million per season Owner	• Lead sponsor (1933) • Stadium name right
2nd Bundesliga				
SV Ingolstadt 04	FC Ingolstadt 04 GmbH • FC Ingolstadt 04 e.V. 80.1 % • Quattro GmbH 19.9 %	• Audi (2013)	• 25 million Strategic Partner	• Lead sponsor (2013)
Hamburger SV	HSV Fußball AG • Hamburger SV e.V. 76.19% • K.-M. Kühne 20.57% • Helmut Bohnhorst 1.22% • Familie Burmeister 1.35% • A. Margaritoff 0.67%	• Klaus • Michael Kühne	• Diverse support: credits, player transfers, etc.) Maecenas	• Fan & Maecenas • Stadium name right holder (2004)
DSC Arminia Bielefeld	DSC Arminia Bielefeld GmbH & Co. KGaA • Arminia e.V. 71.4% • B. Ostwestfalen 28.6%	• Bündnis Ostwestfalen (2017, association of 11 sponsors)	• Around 12 million Strategic Partner	• Sponsors • Lead sponsor & stadium name

(continued)

Table 4.2 (continued)

Club	Shareholding	Equity partner/ announced	Investment in €/ features	Sponsorship/ since
MSV Duisburg	MSV Duisburg GmbH & Co. KGaA • MSV Duisburg e.V. 89.9% • Capelli New York 10.1%	• Capelli New York (2015)	• Not specified (high sum of one-digit million) Strategic partner/investor	• Equipment (2018)
SSV Jan Regensburg	SSV Jahn Regensburg GmbH & Co. KGaA • SSV Jahn Regensburg e.V. 90% • Diverse investors 10%	• Various investors since 2010, i.a., Global Sports Invest AG	• Unknown Investor	• No sponsorship
3rd Liga				
TSV 1860 München	TSV München von 1860 GmbH & Co. KGaA • TSV München von 1860 e.V. 40% • HAM International 60%	• HAM International Ltd. (2011)	• Around 38.3 million Oligarch (Hassan Ismaik)	• No sponsor • Yahya Ismaik (brother of Hassan Ismaik): SC Chairman
KFC Uerdingen 05	KFC Uerdingen 05 Fußball GmbH • KFC Uerdingen e.V. 2.5% • KFC Uerdingen Entertainment GmbH 97.5%	• KFC Uerdingen Entertainment GmbH (2016/2017)	• Unknown Maecenas/ oligarch (Michail Ponomarew)	• Club president

(continued)

Table 4.2 (continued)

Club	Shareholding	Equity partner/ announced	Investment in €/ features	Sponsorship/ since
VfL Osnabrück	VfL Osnabrück GmbH & Co. KGaA • VfL Osnabrück e.V. 82.09% • Assmann Büromöbel GmbH & Co. KG 5% • Michael Koch 5% • Stadtwerke Osnabrück AG 4.91% • Nicole Welz 3%	• Assmann Büromöbel (approx. 2013) • Michael Koch (2013) • Stadtwerke Osnabrück (approx. 2013) • Nicole Welz (approx. 2013)	• Unknown Strategic partners & Maecenas	• Assmann (sponsor) • Stadtwerke (sponsor)
FC Würzburger Kickers	FC Würzburger Kickers AG • FC Würzburger Kickers e.V. 51% • Flyeralarm GmbH 49%	• Flyer Alarm Future Labs GmbH (2014)	Strategic partner	• Stadium name right (2013)
SC Fortuna Köln	Fortuna Köln Spielbetriebsgesellschaft mbH • Fortuna Köln e.V. 0.255% • DFC GmbH 99.745%	• DFC GmbH (2008) (Michael Schwetje holds 87%)	• Unknow Investor (Michael Schwetje)	• Business executive (Michael Schwetje)
FC Carl Zeiss Jena	FC Carl Zeiss Jena Fußball Spielbetriebs GmbH • SC Carl Zeiss Jena e.V. 5% • Staprix NV 95%	• Staprix NV (2013)	• 2 million (+diverse loans Investor (Roland Duchatelet)	• No sponsor

(continued)

Table 4.2 (continued)

Club	Shareholding	Equity partner/ announced	Investment in €/ features	Sponsorship/ since
SV Wehen Wiesbaden	SV Wehen 1926 Wiesbaden GmbH • SV Wehen 1926 Wiesbaden e.V. 10% • FI Fußball Invest GmbH & Co. KG 90%	• FI Fußball Invest GmbH & Co. KG (2008) (Parent company: Hanvest Holding/Brita)	• 2.25 million Strategic partner	• Brita: Stadium name (2007/2008) • Club president = CEO of Brita (Markus Hankammer)

*Exemption of the 50+1 rule

Due to diverse governance structures of the football clubs (i.e., their professional unit) and some special legal constructs some partners hold more than 50% of capital shares. However, this do not refer to the voting rights of the clubs (except for the clubs denoted with a *), as the club (Verein) has to hold the majority of voting rights (50+1) (Bauers & Hovemann, 2019b)

As illustrated above, German football is interwoven with a variety of commercial associations and different kinds of strategic partnerships, viz. contractual sponsorships (Oettgen, 2008; Süßmilch, 2004), equity partnerships with sponsors (Chemnitzer et al., 2015), Maecenasship[8] (Reich, 2007), oligarchs (Welling & Westhoff, 2018), and partnerships with financial investors (Keller, 2006).

Based on these versatile views from practitioners and theorists, the author explicates, delimits, and critically discusses various strategic partnership types in the football landscape together with their motives. This should ideally add to conceptual clarity to the concept of strategic partnership in German football.

4.3.2 Maecenas and Oligarchs

Maecenas, also known as a 'sugar daddy' (Will, 2015) or 'patron' (Nagy, 2011), have occupied an increasing role in financing European football clubs. Prigge and Vöpel (2014) as well as Chemnitzer et al. (2015) describe a Maecenas as an altruistic person who is highly passionate in football and who has an emotional attachment to the club. Besides, this kind of "goodwill investor" (Welling & Westhoff, 2018) is often in search of public recognition (Chemnitzer et al., 2015) and a club is perceived as a global trophy asset, boosting the Maecenas' business profile and providing access to vital connections (Boor et al., 2016).

Maecenasship has a long tradition in German football. One of the first prominent patrons was Hans (Jean) Löring who started to support (without holding shares) FC Fortuna Köln in 1967 and led the club into the 1st Bundesliga (Rosentritt, 2013). Nowadays, Dietmar Hopp[9] (who has invested around 350 million Euros equity money in TSG Hoffenheim since the 1990s and holds 96% of shares) and Klaus-Michael Kühne[10] (who supports Hamburger SV and holds a 20.57% share) are two of the most famous sugar daddies in German football.

---

[8]In contrast to sponsorship, which is an exchange relationship, a Maecenasship is a unilateral form of support (financial or non-cash benefit) and the Maecenas is as a private person, who is altruistic. As a rule, Maecenasship refers to a financial support (Will, 2015).

[9]Dietmar Hopp is the co-founder of software giant SAP. He has supported TSG Hoffenheim since the beginning of the 1990s, when Hoffenheim was just an ordinary amateur club. According to Forbes (2016b) Hopp and his family's net worth is US$9 billion.

[10]Klaus-Michael Kühne is majority owner of the logistic company Kühne + Nagel. According to Forbes (2016a), Kühne's net worth is US $ 10.9 billion.

Clubs benefit financially but are often dependent in monetary terms on their Maecenas and have to accept (hidden) managerial influence (Oediger, 2017b; Chemnitzer et al., 2015). Referring to Reich (2007), clubs are exposed to the arbitrariness of their patrons, who are free to withdraw their support at any time. Due to this dependency Reich (ibid.) has judged this business model as 'not sustainable' for German football clubs. Against this, based on the ever-increasing financial challenges for clubs, Chemnitzer et al. (2015) disagree by stating that Maecenasship is a suitable financing option for clubs. They lessen the argument put forward by Reich (2007) by emphasising the emotional bond of the patron to his or her club. Nevertheless, they also recommend clubs to invest the money provided by their sugar daddy into the infrastructure of the club or to establish the club brand in order to sustainably enhance the competitive position and work towards 'monetary emancipation' (independency of the patron). This is in line with the assessment of Breuer and Hovemann (2006) who indicate Maecenasship as a suitable financial option for investments in the clubs' infrastructure (sport facilities).

Welling and Westhoff (2018) distinguish a second form of sugar daddy in the form of oligarchs ("geopolitical motivated investors") who have slightly different investment motives. Referring to Oediger (2017), oligarchs are super rich people who often see football clubs as their personal hobby, as Roman Abramowitsch, investor of FC Chelsea, stated: "*I don't want to throw my money down the rathole, I just want to have fun*" (Abramowitsch cited by Oediger, 2017a; 2). In contrast to Maecenas, who are emotionally attached to their club, Welling and Westhoff (2018) argue that oligarchs (e.g., in Germany Hasan Ismaik at 1860 München) do not have an evidently emotional bond to their club. However, they provide their club with substantial sums of (private) money. In return, oligarchs are often interested in holding majority shares in order to have a controlling influence in the club (Nauright & Ramfjord, 2011).

Nowadays, many clubs in Europe enjoy the support of an oligarch. For instance, in the EPL this business model predominates the strategy of many clubs (e.g., Sheik Mansur bin Zayed Al Nahyan at Manchester City, Stan Kroenke at Arsenal London, Farhad Moshiri at FC Everton, Vichai Srivaddhanaprabha at Leicester City). Overall, English clubs attract more foreign investors than elsewhere. According to Barnard et al. (2019), at the end of the 2018/2019 season about 60% of clubs in the top two divisions in England had a foreign owner. In Germany, oligarchs occupy a minor role as a strategic partner because a controlling influence is prevented in Germany due to the 50+1 rule.

4.3.3 Financial Investors

Whereas patrons grant money from private persons, strategic equity partnerships are also entered into with financial (institutional) investors, such as private equity (PE) companies (e.g., KKR[11] and Hertha BSC Berlin). PE companies invest substantial sums of equity money in stakes of other businesses and try to reshape these organisations with the overall aim of selling their stakes for a profit (generating profit through the increase of share value) (Hufnagel, 2011).

In contrast to venture capital (a specific form of private equity), which is directed at 'early-stage' organisations with high growth potential, private equity firms concentrate their investment on a variety of companies, often mature organisations, which require access to capital either to stay competitive, enhance growth, or recover from economic trouble (Chemnitzer et al., 2015). Beside a shift of shareholder composition - from entering into a partnership - the private equity company usually provides knowledge, support, and management advice or even takes over the control of the partner business (Caselli, 2010).

There is general consensus among scholars (e.g., Poitras, 2016; Keythman, 2016; Caselli, 2010) that the PE firm is normally not interested in any synergy effects as their primary goal is focused on generating profits. Hence, Welling and Westhoff (2018) describe this type of club shareholder as a "classic investor". However, referring to von der Heijden (2012) as well as Pinnuck and Potter (2006), profits in the form of dividends cannot be expected from an equity partnership with a football club since their highest priority is to maximise sporting success. This is acknowledged by Oediger (2017b) who therefore assumes an increase of share value as a primary investment motive for financial investors in football clubs' shares. Scholars such as Prigge and Vöpel (2014) suppose an increase of share value (accretion) as a primary reason for investment, too.

There is a controversial debate in the academic sports literature of whether financial investors are suitable to act as a strategic partner for football clubs. According to Kern (2007), PE companies do not qualify for a strategic partnership due to their (exclusive) profit-oriented purpose. He favours partnerships with commercial partners who have the same or similar goals as the football club has, e.g., media companies, equipment suppliers, or sponsors. This view is supported by Prigge and Vöpel (2014) who remark on the difficulty of anticipating additional business interests of PE firms and suspect that those interests are in

[11]KKR stands for Kohlberg, Kravis Roberts & Co L.P. and is a private equity investment company located in New York.

accordance with club interests. Accordingly, Prigge and Vöpel (ibid.) do not consider such agreements as 'real' strategic partnership. Against this, Keller (2006) identifies private equity firms as an attractive financial opportunity in which the PE firm can act as a strategic partner. This understanding is seen in the practical example of Hertha BSC Berlin and KKR (holding of 9.7% of shares in the club, which can be extended to 33% via a call-option) as both talk about a strategic partnership (Herdtstück, 2018; Duff, 2014). However, Keller (op. cit.) concentrates on the financial aspects without going into details about further strategic synergies.

In a similar vein, Hovemann and Schubert (2006) address private equity in the form of venture capital as a viable financing opportunity. Just as Keller (2006), Hovemann and Schubert (op. cit.) as well as Seemann and Schollmeier (2008) also focus on the monetary features of PE partnerships in a subsequent discussion. Seemann and Schollmeier (ibid.) view German football clubs as appealing investment objects for PE firms, since such companies invest predominantly in growth markets and prefer alliances with strong brands. Both criteria seem to apply to German football clubs as shown by studies from Boor et al. (2016), Netzer et al. (2015), and Metrum (2004), among others. Moreover, the above-mentioned scholars explicitly indicate that those clubs beyond the 1st Bundesliga have immense growth potential, too.

4.3.4 Strategic (Equity) Sponsors

Süßmilch (2004) advocates the view that only those actors are in-line with the concept of strategic partnership who have further strategic interests (long-term synergies) beyond profits, such as sponsors. He refers to the conviction of academics who view the roots of strategic partnerships in the German football business in the marketing discipline, because many of those strategic equity partnerships have arisen out of long-term sponsorship collaborations (Chemnitzer et al., 2015; Prigge & Vöpel, 2014; Henseler et al., 2007). Oettgen (2008) concurs with Süßmilch (2004) that a sponsorship partnership is the basis for a "real" strategic partnership since sponsors, in contrast to financial investors, have various strategic interests. This is supported by Cousens et al. (2006) who insist on going beyond a narrow framework of interests that places the motivation for the partnership on monetary advantages at the expense of the value-added benefits of strategic relationships. This implies non-imitable advantages such as networks or competences.

Corporations invest in football sponsorships for a variety of reasons. Hermanns (1997) tried to organise the objectives in economic objectives (which have an impact on profits) and psychological objectives (image improve, increase in awareness). Gillies (1991) classifies corporate and marketing objectives. Pope (1998) follows the categorisation put forward by Sandler and Shani (1993) who add media objectives as another type. Bühler (2006) questions whether these differentiations make sense and stated that all objectives can basically be related to commercial intents. However, there is agreement among academics that increasing awareness and an image boost are the key objectives for football sponsoring (Bühler, 2006; Walliser, 2003; Hermanns, 1997).

In 2005, the Pilot group published a study about the objectives of German football sponsors. An increase in awareness (88%) and improved image (78%) were ranked highest. This result was recently confirmed by an investigation conducted by Nielsen Sports in 2018. This time, there is a slight shift towards image objectives (84%) which have passed awareness objectives (80%). The Nielsen Sports study discloses promoting customer loyalty (54%) and access to new target groups (48%) as additional sponsorship objectives, while Hermanns (1997) has already named staff motivation, too. Based on this, Walzel and Schubert (2018) and Plewa et al. (2016) extend the focus on staff motivation by incorporation the social responsibility as another goal for sponsorship endeavour. Football clubs appear to be extremely well suited to attain various sponsorship goals due to their loyal fan base, large media exposure (Adam et al., 2017), and the social role of the sport in general. This was already discovered by Seydel (2005) who showed that fans perceive sponsors of their club as more appealing compared to other corporations operating in the same market.

Although Bühler (2006) espouses football sponsorship as an effective strategy for positive image effects and synergies, he stresses the need to remember that image is a sensitive construct and there is an inherent risk associated with any kind of business partnership, in particular when football clubs are involved. For instance, in 1995 the lead (shirt) sponsor of Hamburger SV (1st Bundesliga club at that time), the Milchstrassenverlag, withdrew their logo of their brand "TV Spielfilm" from the team shirts due to a series of loses as the sponsor was concerned that their brand would be associated with the club's losing image (Pepels, 2001).

On the other hand, image correlations may affect the club, too. For example, there are numerous reports describing the negative impact of the lead sponsoring engagement of Wiesenhof[12] at the 1st Bundesliga club SV Werder Bremen in 2012, due to the sponsor's (negative) public image of mass breeding, unhygienic conditions, and animal abuse (Salzborn, 2017; Wallrodt, 2015; Kreiszeitung,

[12]Wiesenhof is a brand belonging to the PHW-group, a leading poultry company in Germany.

2014; Lange, 2011). The short- to medium-term consequences of this included the loss of club members, fan protests, outrage in social media, and a fan boycott of the shirt (Salzborn, 2017; Wallrodt, 2015). While both partners should be aware of the negative consequences of image spillover (Kahuni et al., 2009), Westberg et al. (2011) found evidence in their qualitative study that transparency, pro-activity, and media management appear to be fundamental aspects in lessening image damage and degenerative episodes.

Besides the "classic" sponsorship that may act as a strategic partnership, Oettgen (2008) further classified (strategic) sponsorships into two forms: sponsorships without a stake in the club and partnerships in which the sponsor holds shares (has a stake) in the club and therefore simultaneously becomes a shareholder/investor. The latter is the kind of partnership which was first denoted as a strategic partnership in German football when Adidas (sponsor) bought shares in FC Bayern München (Adam & Hovemann, 2018; Groscuth, 2005). This partnership form (specified in Chapter 3 of the dissertation as a strategic equity partnership) can be seen as a 'hybrid type', as the partnership consists of two levels: the (commercial) contractual agreement and the shareholding. A multitude of scholars such as Welling and Westhoff (2018), Chemnitzer et al. (2015), and Prigge and Vöpel (2014) agree that German clubs enter into strategic equity partnerships for the sake of generating income. From the strategic equity partner's point of view these scholars concur that the key motives are to generate further synergies or to intensify the existing sponsorship partnership.

The debate above has shown that various forms of strategic partnerships in the football business exist. These partnerships are mainly discussed from a financial viewpoint rather than a strategic stance. While majority equity partnerships (mostly in the form of patrons) are commonplace in other European football leagues, in German football the trend for strategic equity partnerships is discernible. The next section addresses the factors which makes German football clubs attractive in the eye of (potential) equity partners.

4.4 Critical Success Factors for Strategic Equity Partnerships

4.4.1 The Clubs' Growth Potential and Brand Building

There are different views in respect to what attracts corporations to buy club shares. According to Seemann and Schollmeier (2008) as well as Huth et al. (2018) German clubs can be seen as start-ups with enormous growth potential.

This is justified by the very good infrastructure, modernity of stadiums, as well as the highest attendance figures of all European football leagues (Adam & Hovemann, 2018; Breuer et al., 2018) as shown in Figure 4.3 (average game attendance in the most famous football leagues in the world between 2013 and 2018 in thousands).

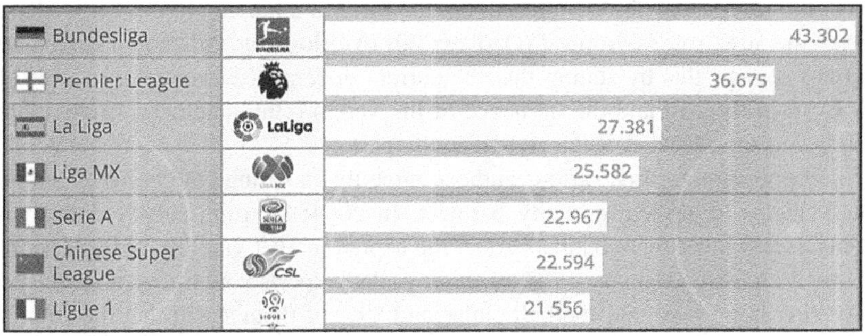

Figure 4.3 Attendance Figures in Big Five of European Football. (Source: According to Richter, 2019, retrieved from Statista, 2019)

By comparing the attendance figures among the Big Five, the German 1st Bundesliga is the only football league which exceeds 40,000 people on average per match regularly (43,879 in the 2017/2018 season; DFL, 2019). This results in high media attention that strategic partners can use to market their corporate brand (Adam & Hovemann, 2018).

The positive development of German football is also discernible in other areas: Netzer et al. (2015) published a McKinsey study with the title "growth engine Bundesliga", in which the authors report on the growth development of professional football in Germany. Between 2008 and 2014 all relevant revenue streams increased enormously, e.g., sponsoring (56%), merchandising (52%), media rights (47%), and ticket sales (40%). While Netzer et al. (ibid.) forecasts that this positive trend will continue in the years to come, this study conforms with the assessment from Prigge and Vöpel (2014) as well as Dworak (2010) about investor motivation and also complies with findings from Poitras (2016), Keythman (2016), and Caselli (2010) in the general alliance literature.

In addition, Pramschüfer (2016), Hofmann (2016), and Teevs (2014) contend that the persistent discussion about the 50+1 rule and its possible removal in the near future could be appealing for investors. This was supported by Klaus Filbry[13] in 2017 who, in an article by Oediger (2017b), argues that investors want to position themselves for the time after 50+1 by entering into minority equity partnerships. He uses the metaphor of 'unimproved land' to describe the possession of minority shares in a German football club. Referring to Filbry, the share value could rapidly rise if 50+1 is removed. The advantage to those partners who buy club shares now finds expression in the form of a pre-emption for new shares when the 50+1 rule is dropped (Oediger, 2017b). However, Adam and Hovemann (2018) counter this by stating that the current governance structures (i.e., 50+1) in German football and the influence of the Verein (club members) in the club's management reduce attractiveness to equity partners.

In opposition to this, various authors agree that a strong club brand is the primary factor in attracting equity partners. In 2004, Metrum, surveyed financial analysts and investment bankers about the capital market viability of professional football clubs in Germany. 67% of those polled experts could generally imagine investing in professional football clubs, and 89% of them stated that the strength of the corporate (club) brand is the primary investment criterion.

While Post and Druker (2018) as well as von Overloop (2015) specify that brand strength consists chiefly in a high brand awareness and a positive image, Bodet and Chanavat (2010) and Pons and Richelieu (2008) substantiate that clubs with a valuable brand are most attractive to strategic partners and investors. Indeed, Renard and Sitz (2011) support this view by stating that sport clubs need to build their own brand identity and values as an essential first step in order to permit the greatest leverage of sponsorship opportunities.

Based on this perspective, active branding becomes central to the club's strategy. This view is further intensified in light of the specific characteristic of the game (i.e., uncertainty and the unpredictability of outcome of matches). While these attributes can be a blessing by providing fans (and prosumers) with a high emotional service, Schade (2012) adds for consideration that these features impede club managers' work because they offer no stability and predictability for business planning. Consequently, Nagy (2012) and Quitzau (2003) infer that this makes football clubs a risky investment option.

However, Renard and Sitz (2011) emphasise that investors and sponsors expect business partners (clubs) who are stable and profitable. Also, Schade

[13]Klaus Filbry is a business executive at SV Werder Bremen and responsible for the business portfolios finance and marketing. He is also a chairman of the board of SVW.

(2012) remarks that the inherent risks associated with the nature of football means that parts of heterogeneous customer groups[14] of the match (viz. fans and spectators) are susceptible to frustration. This pushes club managers to find ways to lessen and manage these risks. Therefore, Schade (2012) reinforced the view of Rennard and Sitz (2011) by postulating that active management of the club brand becomes fundamental as this has a twofold benefit: Schade (op. cit.) purports that establishing the corporate brand offers the opportunity to detach the commercial performance (revenues) from the sporting success of clubs which is an opportunity to grow independently of (unpredictable) on-field results. As a consequence, sport clubs have the chance to enhance customer loyalty and to influence prosumers in terms of e.g., visiting future matches or consuming merchandising products, which can minimise the risk of losing disappointed prosumers (Murphy, 2018; Schade, 2012). This, in turn, supports the aforementioned required stability (Rennard & Sitz, 2011) of clubs in the eyes of a business partner and potential shareholder.

Nevertheless, Nagy (2011) counters the argument of Schade (2012). Nagy (op. cit.) invokes that, in practice, the maximising of intangible value in the form of brand building can usually only be attained at the cost of other result aspects. This could have implications on money spending for improving the team. Thus, he determines that image modification often has an indirect impact on club investments. Post and Druker (2018) as well as Breuer et al. (2018) endorse that the sporting success of the club is a vital component in establishing the club brand.

4.4.2 Internationalisation and Market Development

Meanwhile, many football clubs have recognised the need to establish their club brand (Murphy, 2018; Bodet & Chanavat, 2010; Pons & Richelieu, 2008). In light of the increasing commercialisation[15] of the football business, this trend expands to market the club brand internationally. Pons and Richelieu (2008) already constituted that the focus of internationalisation[16] is on market development in order

[14]Football clubs have several key but very heterogeneous target groups: direct/indirect audience (fans, day visitors, VIP guests, TV-audience), media, sponsors, licensees, and marketers (Schade, 2012).

[15]Commercialisation is "*the organisation of something in a way intended to make a profit*" (Cambridge Dictionary, 2019).

[16]In the management discipline internationalisation implies transborder creations and exploitations of commercial goods and services (Oesterle, 1999).

to generate new income streams for the club. In 2018, Adam and Hovemann investigated the activities to promote the internationalisation of clubs. With marketing tours, training camps, test matches, selling of commercial rights, and transferring foreign players (from the target markets) clubs try to open up new markets and bring the club brand to the attention of new target groups (Adam & Hovemann, op. cit.).

Internationalisation and the move to promote the brand abroad are not solely initiated by the club itself, Murphy (2018) highlights that clubs are often accompanied by their strategic partners, viz. sponsors and equity partners. Scholars such as Adam and Hovemann (2018) and Post and Druker (2018) concur that strategic partners can be a big support in marketing the club brand abroad. Post and Druker (ibid.) even argue that incorporating strategic partners in the international strategy of clubs is a fundamental success factor. According to that, the corporate partner can provide support in the form of know-how, access to their network, and organisational infrastructure (Adam & Hovemann, 2018).

On the other hand, strategic partners have recognised that football clubs have the capacity to reach beyond national boundaries, link with various markets and therefore benefit from the club's brand awareness (Murphy, 2018; Morgan et al., 2014). In this respect, Salz et al. (2015) refer to a win-win situation. However, just as brand building needs to be considered in light of sporting success (Nagy, 2011), Breuer et al. (2018) explain that internationalisation cannot be seen as detached from the sporting success of the club. This can be traced back to the slogan of "think local, act global" (Kapferer, 1998). Accordingly, brand success abroad rests upon success in the local market.

While German clubs achieve a high level of brand awareness nationally, a ranking of internationalisation (promoting the brand abroad) of clubs from Advant Planning (2015) shows that German clubs trail behind competitors from e.g., the English Premier League. This is supported by Schmitt (2017) who adduces that German clubs have neglected to take advantage of the "first-in effect"[17] (also "first mover effect"; Bodet & Chanavat, 2010) and fail to establish unique brand associations. While sponsorship partnerships have always tended to take a distinctly international flavour for English clubs, the tendency to focus on English clubs for international oriented sponsors has intensified in the last decade (Hess, 2015).

[17]First in (first mover) effect refers to a club which is the first one to enter a specific new area (e.g., a region in China). The people in that region keep on liking and supporting the first club (team) they have been familiar with (Bodet & Chanavat, 2010).

Figure 4.4 illustrates the relative frequency of international[18] shirt sponsors compared to national[19] shirt sponsors in the first leagues of England, Spain, Italy, and Germany in the 2017/2018 season.

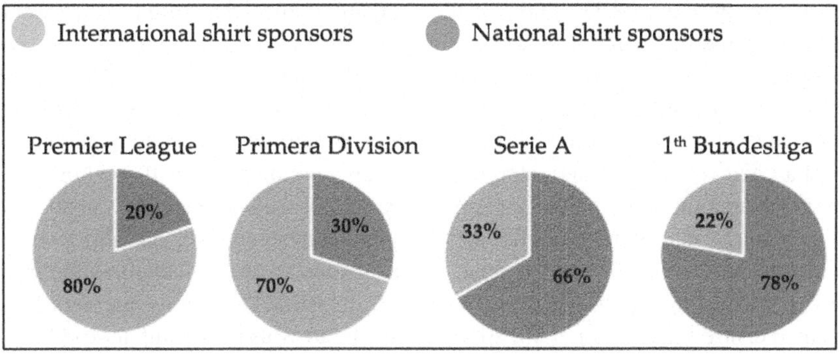

Figure 4.4 Sponsoring Structure of European Top Leagues. (Source: Own llustration)

The graphic clearly displays that the Serie A (66% of shirt sponsors) and the German Bundesliga (78% of shirt sponsors) have a predominantly national shirt sponsorship structure while 20% of the shirt sponsors at the EPL and 30% at the Primera Division are national ones.

Against the background that a shirt sponsorship's main purpose is to create brand awareness and reach (Schmitt, 2017), it mirrors the status that corporate sponsors see more potential to achieve that with clubs from other European top leagues, in particular in England and Spain instead of clubs from the 1st Bundesliga. Schmitt (ibid.) infers that German clubs have a 'backlog demand' to catch up in marketing their club brands internationally.

[18]In this context international refers to the respective country (football league) and delineates shirt sponsors whose headquarter is outside the own country (abroad).

[19]In this regard national means shirt sponsors (corporations) which are headquartered in the same country.

4.5 Effects on Club Members and Fans

4.5.1 Fan Rejection as Impediment

In Germany, commercialisation of the football business has often been associated with the outsourcing of the professional football unit to a corporation. For instance, in the 2018/2019 season only four clubs (out of 18) in the 1st Bundesliga were still operating in the governance form of the Verein. Since club interests have shifted from the former non-profit oriented club towards economic/commercial aspects (Quitzau, 2009), club management is no longer elected by club members but appointed by the supervisory committee of the commercial football unit. The financial contribution of club members via membership fees has also lost significance in German football as other financial sources, in particular income from TV broadcasting, sponsoring, and money from (strategic) equity partners have gained centre stage (Boor et al., 2016). Referring to Walsh and Giulianotti (2007), this leads to a shift of the clubs' management focus to the interests of other stakeholders (commercial partners, i.e., sponsors, marketing partners, shareholders) rather than club members and fans.

The trend towards the commercialisation of the football business has risen an intense discussion about the retention or repeal of the 50+1 rule. A repeal of the rule would provide clubs the opportunity to sell majority shares and therefore ensures equal opportunities in European football (Adam & Hovemann, 2018; Lammert et al., 2009). Hence, numerous football experts[20] (e.g., Lothar Matthäus, Oliver Kahn, Ralf Rangnick, among others) are in favour for a cessation of the rule and a multitude of sports law experts (e.g., Punte, 2012; Summerer, 2008; Weiler, 2006) expect the rule's abolition in the near future given its 'legal limbo'[21] (Hofmann, 2016, Teevs, 2014).

The 50+1 rule raised also attention at sport economists. Many scholars such as Lammert et al. (2009), Hovemann et al. (2010), Lammert (2014), Adam et al. (2017), and Bauers et al. (2015) address various ways to bypass the rule. Although they make valuable recommendations as to how to adapt the rule to prevent bypassing the rule has not happened an adaption yet. There are already

[20]In this context expert refer to people who are denoted as such by the media and public. Football expert are often ex-football players.

[21]Legally, a lawsuit in European Court of Justice against the 50+1 rule is expected to abandon the rule, e.g., due to a violation against European competition law (article 101 & 102 AEUV or article 63-66 AEUV) (Lopatta et al., 2014; Stopper, 2009).

some clubs excluded[22] from the 50+1 rule, which intensifies the discussion about the rule's effectiveness. For example, VFL Wolfsburg, which is fully owned by the automobile manufacturer VW AG (before 2007 VW held 90%), and Bayer 04 Leverkusen, which is fully owned by the pharmaceutical company Bayer AG. Recently, the case of RB Leipzig attracted attention when the drinks manufacturer Red Bull circumvented the rule and established RasenBallsport Verein Leipzig (RB Leipzig[23]) in 2009 (Red Bull owns 99% of the club).

While Adam and Hovemann (2018) as well as Oediger (2017b) agree that an abolition would increase the investment incentives for equity partners to buy club shares in German clubs and therefore introduce new financing opportunities, there are also contrasting views among clubs as to whether the rule should be repealed. Bauers et al. (2013), in a quantitative investigation, find evidence that 79% of the professional football clubs in Germany favoured retention for the 50+1 rule based on the main argument "exclusion of controlling influence by investors". This is supported by an assessment from Dierig (2014b), who stated that many of those responsible for the clubs fear a dependency from external investors and are worried about restricted decision-making. Already these days, in exchange for an (minority) equity investment, a strategic partner usually gets a seat on the board of directors at the club (e.g., FC Bayern München, Borussia Dortmund, VfL Wolfsburg, Bayer Leverkusen, Eintracht Frankfurt, TSG Hoffenheim, Hertha BSC Berlin, and Hamburger SV). This strategy, which is known as "interlocking directorates"[24] (Barringer & Harrison, 2000), creates a governance structure in which the partnering company can exert (residual) control[25] on the

---

[22]If a company or person has substantially supported a club with money for a continuous period of at least 20 years, the club is barred from the 50+1 rule and it is feasible for that company/person to hold a controlling stake in the club (Stopper, 2009).

[23]By adapting the license from SSV Markranstädt and renaming the club in RasenBallsport Leipzig e.V., the club was allowed to start in the 5th league. The abbreviation RB Leipzig reflects the company initials from Red Bull. The club is part of the marketing campaign of Red Bull and the long-term goal is to qualify for international competition. Therefore, Red Bull spends a lot of money to promote the club, which leads to controversial discussion within the football community because some perceive the major investments funded by of Red Bull as leading to competitive distortion.

[24]Interlocking directorates appear when a CEO or executive of one company sits on the board of another company (club) (Barringer & Harrison, 2000).

[25]Referring to Das and Teng (2001; 254), control is about "*influencing the behaviour of the partner*".

activities of the club (Globerman & Nielsen, 2007). In addition to the concern of controlling influence, a football club has still to accommodate their club members and fans, who are often termed the "heart of the club" (Herberger et al., 2013).

Research on the issue from the fan perspective (e.g., Bauers & Hovemann, 2019a; Bühler, 2017; Pilz, 2011) has shown that the vast majority of club members and fans are in favour for the retention of the rule (e.g., according to Bauers and Hovemann, 91.3% in 2011 and 90.1% in 2017). Beside this central finding Bauers and Hovemann (2019a), in their fan surveys from 2011 and 2017, developed arguments (hypothesises) for the retention and arguments for the repeal of the rule. The arguments of "exclusion of controlling influence by investors", "preservation of co-determination by club members/fans" (both arguments around 80% in 2011 and 2017), and "preservation of fan's identification" (77% in 2011, 69% in 2017) were discovered to be the crucial reasons for the retention of the rule. By way of contrast, the arguments "increase of international competitiveness" (24.8%), "exclusion of the benefit allowing clubs to use the exception rule" (13.4%), and "exclusion of the benefit allowing clubs to use the rule's bypasses" (12.2%) were main arguments of fans in favour of the repeal of the rule. The study makes a valuable contribution as this is the first quantitative study found to illuminate the background of fan opinions regarding the 50+1 rule and quantitatively verifies the findings from Pilz (2011) that 50+1 has a significant, symbolic meaning for fans in terms of protecting the social roots of football (fan's co-determination) and the fan's identification. Adam et al. (2018) and Bauers et al. (2015) determine that a cessation of 50+1 would reinforce the commercialisation of German football which, in turn, would intensify the conflict between commercial interests and the sociological and ideological interests of fans.

However, in contrast to the fan survey from Bühler (2017) who found that 85.4% of fans endorse preservation of the 50+1 rule, Bauers and Hovemann (2019a) focus on a differentiated classification of fans based on two criteria: they distinguished between club members and non-club members (also referred to as fan group). According to that, club members have a higher interest than fans (non-club members) due to their co-determining right as a member of the club. Against this, fans are characterised by a general interest in football.

Second, they took the number of stadium visits as an indicator of the level of fan interest (interest in football) and compared whether fans with a high number of stadium visits rate the arguments differently to those who visit the stadium just occasionally. The latter criterion was also the basis of a fan categorisation applied by Schade (2012).

Even though the scholars used the same criterion for classification, they correlated the interests of fans with the number of stadium visits differently. Schade (2012) designates "real fans" as those who visit the stadium three times per season or more. In contrast, Bauers and Hovemann (2019a) determine a number of 16 or more stadium visits. Bauers and Hovemann (ibid.) discovered that club members and fans with a high number of stadium visits rate the arguments for the retention of the 50+1 rule higher and the arguments for a repeal of the rule lower vis-à-vis their reference group. Nevertheless, the difference remains low. Bauers and Hovemann determine that all groups of football fans favour the retention of the rule and fans base their opinion on the same arguments (i.e., "exclusion of controlling influence by investors", "preservation of fan's identification", and "preservation of co-determination by club members/fans").

Nevertheless, while the majority of the authors refer to fans in general, Schade (2012) as well as Schwier and Fritz (2003) add that football fans should not be considered as a homogenous group. Königs (2002) classifies football fans into "organised" and "individualist". Setzen (1999) is more accurate and differentiates between five different groups: the fans/supporters (who try to actively influence the atmosphere in the stadium), the core audience (fans, but not supporters), the critical fans (who are interested in the event), the media audience (e.g., TV viewers), and the service customers (users of business seats and VIP lounges). The former two groups (which refers to König's "organised fans") have in common that they are characterised by a high number of stadium visits per season irrespective of sporting success, and are seen as the most significant group influencing the atmosphere in the stadium (Setzen, 1999). The supporters, in addition, often show their attachment to the club by following their team to away games. Gabler (2009) agrees with Setzen (1999) but refers to "football-centred" fans.

Although the "football-centred" fans are said to have the most impact, it has to be taken into consideration that service customers are becoming increasingly significance (in respect to the club's revenues), as these largely consist of business people (e.g., sponsors, Maecenas, and corporations) (Dörnemann, 2002). Irrespective of the fan group, Beech (2010) states that fans (in their role as prosumers) are essential for the (public) attractivity of the sport and its entertainment value.

Fans' dislike of investors and the debate about the repeal of the 50+1 rule can also be regarded in the light of the concept from Hirschman (1970). In his book "Exit, Voice, and Loyalty" he examined the correlation between organisations and their stakeholders (i.e., customers) in terms of opportunities of action for customers (either "exit" or "voice") if the organisation changes the quality of its products or services. With the exit option, customers just change to a competitor.

These customers are often characterised as not loyal. In contrast, customers can also make use of their "voice" in order to signalise their dissatisfaction with the performance of the company or the quality of products and services respectively. This option is chosen if customers are loyal, meaning they have a high emotional bond to the company. Based on this, economic experts speak for opening up the German football market for external investors (repeal of 50+1) as the free market will adjust, as otherwise customary. Quitzau (2014) contradicts and captures the logic of Hirschman (1970) and Erberich (2017a). In contrast to "normal" customers who can choose between exit and voice, football fans and club members have no opportunity for exit. Although they have the opportunity of "protest" (Erberich, 2017b), the option of "exit" to the effect that they switch to a different club if the quality of the service is bad (no sporting success), does not exist due to their emotional bond to their club (Roose & Schäfer, 2017; Quitzau, op. cit.). Indeed, while Adam et al. (2017) convey an emotional bond of football fans too, Johnston (2014; sect. 1) goes one step further by stating that football fans are the "*most loyal customers in the world*". In order to protect their right, within their scope of exerting influence on club management (e.g., through membership, inclusion of fan organisations, or public protests in the stadium), fans try to put pressure on the club board.

Based on the example of RB Leipzig, it is evident that nearly all fans from the so-called 'traditional clubs'[26] protest against the (perceived unlimited) investment of Red Bull which is perceived as a kind of "financial doping" (Bauers et al., 2013) that ruins the "romance of football" (Dierig, 2014b).

4.5.2 Possible Attributes of Raising Fan Acceptance

Some scholars (e.g., Schade, 2012; Alexa, 2009) focus their research interest on how the brand personality of a club affects the attachment and behaviour of fans. Alexa (2009) developed the PEBT model (measurement model for brand personality) which is an acronym for four brand personality components (professionalism, emotionality, down-to-earthiness[27], and tradition). In his empirical study,

[26]'Traditional club' is not a clearly defined term. However, referring to Klein (2008) a traditional club is characterised by the following attributes: 1) established and grown independent of a corporation 2) has a history which developed over decades 3) which is associated with famous players or results 4) which possesses a deep fan base.

[27]This is a translation of the German word "Bodenständigkeit".

he ascertains that the latter three components positively affect the commitment of football fans to their club. Professionalism has no significant impact on fan attachment. Overall, Alexa (2009) comes to the result that a strong brand personality has a positive impact on the attachment and commitment of the club's fans.

Similarly, Schade (2012) examined whether the club's brand personality influences the behaviour of internal (e.g., employees) and external (e.g., fans and sponsors) target groups in a sport-related context (handball, football, basketball). By exploring different aspects of brand personality (and brand image) he inferred that "regional affinity" has a positive impact on identification with the club. Identification is a crucial factor for generating the commitment and loyalty of target groups and therefore seems to be a suitable aspect to consider for brand differentiation and positioning (Schade, ibid.).

Both findings, those of Schade (2012) and Alexa (2009), can be related to the study of strategic equity partnerships. For example, the regional affinity of a club's (potential) equity partner could have positive implications on the acceptance of the club members and fans. However, this remains unexplored yet.

In a similar vein, Tsiotsou et al. (2014) stated that a fit of brand personality in sport sponsorships has positive effects on brand involvement and self-expression. Hence, they recommend that sport managers should enter sponsorship relationships with corporations whose brand personality fits with the personality of the club. Although this study is not related to fan acceptance regarding equity partners of clubs, it indicates that the brand personality of an investor might have an effect on the acceptance of club members and fans.

4.6 Summary of Strategic Equity Partnerships in the Football Business

This section considered the concept of strategic partnership in detail as it is understood and applied in the German football business. Different forms of strategic partnerships are identified, viz. sponsorships, strategic equity partnerships, Maecenasship, partnerships with oligarchs and financial investors. These types are critically discussed in respect to the concept of strategic partnership and with regard to the investment motives of the equity partners. While there is accordance that selling shares is an attractive option for German clubs to strengthen their financial basis, each type of equity partner/shareholder focuses on idiosyncratic motives.

Maecenas and oligarchs see football clubs as a personal hobby and an opportunity for business networking. While Maecenas have predominantly social motives and have a high emotional bond to "their" club, oligarchs are mainly emotionally unattached, they rather see clubs as their personal hobby and aim to boost their business profile (Welling & Westhoff, 2018). There are controversial views as to whether financial investors are qualified for a strategic partnership since many scientists face difficulties in anticipating the underlying motives of a financial investor. Therefore, they see this form of partnership simply as a financing option for clubs. Lead sponsorships are perceived as strategic partners because these sponsors have various strategic motives such as increasing brand awareness, image improvement, and the development of new markets. The reasons why sponsors buy additional clubs shares (choose equity) are said to be based on "advantages in other form", "mutual reputation and image effects" (Prigge & Vöpel, 2014), "safeguarding" (Welling & Westhoff, 2018; Oediger, 2017b), or an "intensification" of the sponsorship partnership (Welling & Westhoff, op. cit.).

This Chapter also illustrates the key attracting factors for entering into a strategic partnership with a football club. In particular, the enduring public interest, the positive development of German football over the last years, the growth potential of clubs, and the club brand are main factors. Additionally, the opportunity for market development and the support of internationalisation are attracting factors for club shareholders. This part further illuminates the effects of equity partnerships on German football clubs. It is shown that equity partnerships increase the commercialisation of football.

In the centre of discussion is the repeal or retention of the 50+1 rule. There are contrasting views among club authorities and football experts about the 50+1 rule. On the one hand, a cessation would lead to equal opportunities among clubs in Europe. On the other hand, those clubs which support the rule fear a flood of investors in case of abolition and concomitant a dependency from an external shareholders and restricted decision making.

Research on the fan perspective regarding investor presence in Germany is mainly connected with the debate about 50+1 (e.g., Bauers et al., 2018). It is revealed that club members and fans in Germany have traditionally been part of the ownership structure of the club (co-determination), are highly emotionally involved in their club and occupy a critical role in the management of German football clubs. Consequently, selling club shares to investors is a sensitive issue in the eye of club members and fans. Several studies (i.e., Bauers & Hovemann, 2019a; Bühler, 2017) confirm that the majority of fans are in favour of the retention of the 50+1 rule and against investor presence. This opinion is mainly based on the arguments of "exclusion of controlling influence by investors", "preservation of co-determination by club members/fans", and "preservation of fan's identification" (Bauers & Hovemann 2019a). It is shown that fan resistance (e.g., protests in the stadium) is one way to demonstrate the fans' opinion.

The last part introduced three studies (Tsiotsou et al., 2014; Schade, 2012; Alexa, 2009) that examined how the brand personality of a sport organisation may affect fan behaviour. According to this, regional affinity and a positive image of a sponsor has a positive effect on fan identification with the club.

5 Research Design

5.1 Introduction

With regard to the research question and sub-questions, general motives for entering into strategic (equity) partnerships (RQ), the critical success factors (SQ 1) and the effects of strategic partnerships (SQ 7) were addressed as presented in the literature. Moreover, impediments (SQ 2) have also been touched. However, the lack of empirical research on the topic in the football business has clearly been outlined. This part takes this research one step further by depicting an overall research design that is appropriate to respond to the research question and sub-questions adequately.

In line with the study's objectives, collecting and analysing empirical data within the specific field of football club partnerships in Germany ought to contribute to a richer theoretical and practical understanding on the issue by looking at the underlying motives, critical success factors, processes, and impediments for entering into strategic equity partnerships in the German football business. It should further allow investigations as to how an additional shareholding affects the strategic intent of clubs and sponsors and how an equity stake adds value to the partnership.

This Chapter provides details about the entire research process by describing the research design[1]. It discusses the underlying research philosophy and proceeds

[1]According to Creswell (2009; 5) the research design implies "*the intersection of philosophy, strategies of inquiry and specific methods*".

Electronic Supplementary Material The online version of this chapter (https://doi.org/10.1007/978-3-658-31301-2_5) contains supplementary material, which is available to authorized users.

T. Duffner, *Strategic Equity Partnerships in Professional Football*, Event- und Impaktforschung, https://doi.org/10.1007/978-3-658-31301-2_5

with explicating and justifying the research strategy (grounded theory) adopted to address the phenomenon under study. Research methods utilised for data collection, site, and sampling are justified and processes for analysis and theory development are elucidated and clarified with examples. It is illustrated how all of the main parts of the study work in concert to address the research question and problem with the aim of maximising the validity and credibility of the findings (Greene, 2006). Research ethics are taken into consideration and potential limitations associated with the chosen research design are acknowledged and further discussed at the end of the study (Section 7.4) as part of an overall evaluation of the research study.

5.2 Philosophical Position—The Researcher's Paradigm

5.2.1 Introduction

All research rests on underlying philosophical assumptions about what represents valid research (Birks & Mills, 2015; Fischer, 2010; Vidal, 2008). Humans have different views about the world and reality (ontology[2]) and the process by which knowledge is developed and changed into meanings (epistemology[3]) (Christ, 2013). In interaction with techniques utilised to examine a specific problem (methodology) and the role of researchers' values (axiology[4]), these aspects create a holistic view and are expressed in a researcher's "paradigm", which is "*the set of common beliefs and agreements shared between scientists about how problems should be understood and addressed*" (Kuhn, 1962; 45). However, there is no general consensus among scholars about the term "paradigm" since others refer to this as "research philosophies" (Esterby-Smith et al., 2015; Saunders et al., 2009), "worldviews" (Creswell, 2009), and "research methodologies" (White, 2000).

[2]Ontology refers to "*assumptions that we make about the nature of reality*" (Esterby-Smith et al., 2006; 31).

[3]Epistemology concerns "*the study of the nature of knowledge*" (Fischer, 2010; 15).

[4]Axiology is "*a branch of philosophy that studies judgments about values*" (Saunders et al., 2009; 110).

Within social sciences a wide range of philosophical stances are identified which differ amongst academics. These paradigms are generally based on two major, traditionally opposing views: positivism and social constructivism (interpretive research). Whereas positivists essentially base their research on quantitative data, thorough observation and measurements of the objective reality (ontology) that exists (Saunders et al., 2009), social constructionists concentrate predominantly on qualitative methods. In this respect, the focus lies on the subjective meanings of people's experiences in order to identify the complexity of aspects (Robson, 2002).

There is an ongoing debate between the relative value of quantitative (positivism) versus qualitative (constructivism) research, which led to the "*paradigm war(s)*" (Pratt, 2016; 2) of the 1990s. Consequently, a diversity of alternative paradigms is promoted, which embraces insights from both positivism and constructivism to challenge this dichotomous way of thinking. Two famous ones are denoted as lying between these extremes: pragmatism and critical realism (Christ, 2013; Johnson et al., 2007; Luck et al., 2006). However, appointing a paradigm involves more than merely mentioning a tradition or school for research. It is about scrutinising the phenomenon under study and challenging and developing a personal worldview. Both aspects contribute to paradigm selection. Even though some researchers and scholars (e.g., Glaser & Strauss, 1967; Glaser, 2005) do not comment on the underlying ontology of their research, many academics such as Pratt (2016), Cresswell (2006), and Esterby-Smith et al. (2015) concur with McPhail and Rexroat (1979; 457) who maintain "*all recipes for generating knowledge rest upon assumptions about reality*".

5.2.2 Critical Realism

This research study is based ontologically on critical realism (CR). CR is a philosophical approach which has its roots in the work of Roy Bhaskar. The key to a critical realist position is the acknowledgement of unobservable objects: things which cannot be measured via our senses, yet still exist. Critical realists argue that what we experience are sensations, the impressions of the incidents in the real world, not the incidents directly (Saunders et al., 2009). The real world is more than people commonly perceive. CR supposes a stratified ontology across three domains.

The "real domain" adopts the assumption that the physical world is independent from human thoughts. However, knowledge and thoughts affect human perception. Hence, people may create a subjective reality, which is known as the "empirical domain". The actual incidents ("actual domain", the linking part between the "real" and "empirical" domain) have real causes, but that empirical insights of the "real domain" are only possible through examination and observation of actual incidents. Experiences are generated from real causes and effects in concert with subjective perceptions (Weed, 2009). Therefore, descriptions in study results are understood to be different from factual ("real") reality (Johnson et al., 2007).

The critical realist approach serves to maintain the significant macro-level research quality characteristic of being able to make a generic formal contribution to knowledge across substantive subjects (Levers, 2013; Weed, 2009). Moreover, critical realists also pay attention to 'why' phenomena occur (Bhaskar, 2010). Understanding the 'why' in the research design is a core element in CR ontology in order to explain and comprehend the phenomenon, which mirrors a key purpose of the present study.

5.2.3 Symbolic Interactionism

Epistemologically, this research is informed by a subjective, interpretive stance in the form of symbolic interactionism (SI). Critical realism accepts an interpretive epistemology and sustains that meaning has to be understood rather than to be measured (Sayer, 2000). Subjectivism is based on the conviction that knowledge is *"always filtered through the lenses of language, gender, social class, race, and ethnicity"* (Denzin & Lincoln, 2005; 21). While it is not rejected that an external ("real") reality exists (Levers, 2013), a subjective epistemology appreciates knowledge as value-laden (axiology). Data collection and observations are influenced by the researcher (observer) and the researcher is affected by the participants (observed) (Birks & Mills, 2015; Levers, op. cit.). Subjectivism has a clear affiliation to SI, especially as both perspectives concur that the researcher is part of what is viewed, rather than separate from it (Charmaz, 2006).

Symbolic interactionism is a sociological, theoretical perspective, which has its roots in American pragmatism[5] (Charmaz, 2006; Glaser, 2005). The philosophical ideas of pragmatism are mainly informed and translated into a workable social science by George H. Mead. His work has been the cornerstone for the develop-

[5]Pragmatists argue that reality "may be out there", but people can only comprehend its existence through sensations. People perceive the same reality differently. In accordance with subjectivism, knowledge is value-laden (pragmatic, epistemic values) and rather a process (Creswell, 2009). From a pragmatist perspective, the goal of science is to enhance the world (problem solving), and not to study for the sake of knowledge (Creswell, 2009; Charmaz, 2006).

ment of SI, even though Mead never used this term. Herbert Blumer (1969), one of Mead's pupils, has refined Mead's ideas and has coined the term symbolic interactionism. He formulated three premises on which SI is established (Locke, 2003).

First, people act toward things based on the meaning they allocate to those things, that is, meaning guides action. Second, the meanings people attribute to things arise from social interaction (communication between humans). Third, the meanings are processed and modified through interpretation in specific situations. Meaning is a process rather than fixed (Aldiabat, 2011; Locke, 2003).

One of the key premises of SI is that a researcher must enter the particular, social world of the people they study to comprehend the situation and environment from the subject's perspective as well as to discover new, first-hand insights (Saunders et al., 2009; Goulding, 2002). Since business and management research situations are not only complex, but also unique (especially in the football context), the SI perspective is deemed highly appropriate to investigate strategic equity partnerships.

The underlying philosophical approach of a critical realist ontology related to an interpretivist epistemology in the form of symbolic interactionism allows for an appreciation that the researcher is not able to measure a phenomenon directly and, therefore, interpretation of the meaning constructed through the interaction of the researcher and the research participants is implied. There is an awareness of a possible reality "out there", although a reality about which data and knowledge will be partial and biased and hence the nature of such reality will continually be a matter of revision (Weed, 2009).

The research paradigm is considered to fit to the research question, which requires an in-depth understanding of a real-life phenomenon (problem) and to enter the world of the research subjects to comprehend their world from their perspectives. This will improve the researcher's capacity to elaborate a practical, rich, deep, and explanatory theory (Chamberlain-Sataun et al., 2013).

5.3 Emphasis of Study Design and Research Strategy

5.3.1 Qualitative Focus of the Study

The research strategy provides a general guide to the research and contains the specific processes with which the research is conducted (Bryman, 2006). Although different terms are used for this concept e.g., "research methodologies"

(Mertens, 1998), this study prefers the classification put forward by Creswell (2009) and Bryman (2006), who refer to "research strategies".

Research strategies are guided by the research question and are linked to the specific research design. Traditionally, one distinguishes between "quantitative" and "qualitative" designs, which Robson (2002) refers to as "fixed" and "flexible" designs respectively. The majority of scholars acknowledge a third key design as a mix between quantitative and qualitative, which some scholars term the "multi-method" (Bryman, 2006) or "mixed-methodologies" (Teddlie & Tashakkori, 2006).

Quantitative research is based on deductively[6] testing theories and examines relationships among variables (Bryman, 2006). However, this thesis is not about testing existing theories, rather it aims to develop a (new) theory in a field, which has rarely been studied to date. The complexity of theory development and density of the research topic demand an in-depth understanding of strategic equity partnership processes and mechanisms and thus a (predominant) qualitative research strategy is required.

A qualitative strategy aims to explore phenomena concerning social or human problems and allows investigation of complexities and distinctions of a study. Data are typically analysed inductively[7] and gathered in the participant's setting (Saunders et al., (2009). Several qualitative strategies are identified, with reference to Kolb (2012) and Biggam (2011), "ethnographies", "action research", "grounded theory", "case studies", and "phenomenology research" are proven to have academic credibility.

Ethnography is not appropriate because it focuses on investigating behaviour in a broader field of culture. Action research concentrates on integrating change into the research process itself by joint collaboration between the researcher and participants applying an action research spiral[8] (Robson, 2002). Whilst the author appreciates the benefits of an action approach and learning from experience, this is not feasible for this research project.

Case study research enables the investigation of *"contemporary phenomenon in its real-life context"* (Yin2014; 16) with close observation of how a specific

---

[6]Deduction tries to explain causal relationships between variables and is defined by Fisher (2010; 313) *"as the process of inferring particulars from a general statement"*.

[7]Inductive research is an approach to conducting research which focuses on building a theory emerging from data (Saunders et al., 2009).

[8]Action research is characterised by an iterative process, called "action research spiral", consisting of diagnosing, planning, taking action, and evaluating (Saunders et al., 2009).

population behaves (Yin, ibid.). Case studies overlap, largely, with all other naturalistically oriented qualitative research strategies (Locke, 2003). Since a case study has not only been regarded as a strategy, but also as a method (Biggam, 2011), which allows for paradigmatic flexibility and methodological openness (Luck et al., 2006), Wolcott (1992; 36) has annotated that case studies appear *"to fit everywhere in general and yet nowhere in particular"*. This is in line with comments of Stake (1994; 236), who regards case studies rather as a *"choice of object to be studied"*. Consequently, the author perceives cases more as empirical units (inputs to or outcomes from the research process) than a legitimate research strategy.

Since strategic equity partnerships with sponsors in the corporate football context have not yet undergone empirical investigation, the study necessitates a strategy that calls for an in-depth examination, allows for flexibility in data collection and also embraces a systematic and rigorous approach to data analysis and theory generation (Loonam, 2014).

5.3.2 Grounded Theory Essentials

Grounded theory (GT) is a research methodology, which has been placed among the most influential and widely used forms of qualitative research (Esterby-Smith et al., 2015). The key purpose of GT research is to generate inductively a theory which is flexible enough to make a wide range of situations comprehensible and sufficiently general to be *"applicable to the whole picture"* (Glaser & Strauss, 1967; 242). GT also utilises a deductive component to allow theoretical sampling[9] to take place which is exclusive to grounded theory research (Kanealy, 2008). Especially in fields where complex social interaction is rarely studied and understood, and no theory exists yet, GT is recommended as the primary and most effective methodology for application (Chamerblain Salaun et al., 2013; Fendt & Sachs, 2008; Calman, 2006).

Initially employed in health science, GT is becoming increasingly popular in business and management research as it develops context-based explanations of

[9]Theoretical sampling is a distinctive characteristic of GT. It is *"the process of data collection for generating theory whereby the analyst jointly collects, codes, and analyses his data and decides what data to collect next and where to find them"* (Glaser & Strauss, 1967; 45). Strauss and Corbin (1990; 176) described it as *"sampling on the basis of concepts that have proven theoretical relevance to the evolving theory"*.

phenomena (Maital et al., 2008; Fendt & Sachs, 2008). Scholars such as Weed (2009) and Sotiriadou and Shilbury (2008) call for the use of GT in the field of sport management to investigate sport-related phenomena and their embedded processes due to GT's emphasis on theory development. GT is also characterised as a style of analysis that does not rely on specific disciplinary views (Strauss, 1987) and thus fits to (sport) management research, which can be considered as a hybrid discipline (Kanealy, 2008).

Originally developed by Glaser and Strauss in 1967, the methodology has diverged into three distinct versions: classic or "Glaserian" Grounded Theory (Glaser, 1978, 1998, 2001, 2003, 2005); evolved Grounded Theory ("Straussian") linked to Strauss (1987), Strauss and Corbin (1998), Corbin and Strauss (2008, 2015) and constructivist Grounded Theory, which arises from the work by Kathy Charmaz (2006, 2009, 2016). These differences mainly occur due to varying philosophical perspectives. Whilst there are different schools of the methodology, essential grounded theory tenets (methods) remain the same as illustrated in Table 5.1.

Table 5.1 Essential Grounded Theory Methods. (Source: Own Illustration, referring to Calman, 2006)

Common core features		Glaser	Strauss & Corbin	Charmaz
1.	Simultaneous data collection & analysis	✓	✓	✓
2.	Coding: codes and categories developed from data and not from literature (theoretical sensitivity)	✓	✓	✓
3.	Discovery of social processes in the data	✓	✓	✓
4.	Inductive construction of abstract categories	✓	✓	✓
5.	Theoretical sampling	✓	✓	✓
6.	Writing analytical memos	✓	✓	✓
7.	Constant Comparative Method (CCM)	✓	✓	✓
8.	Integration of categories into a theoretical framework	✓	✓	✓

Even though some scholars (e.g., Fendt & Sachs, 2008; Kanealy, 2008) recommend making a clear distinction as to which school of GT to follow, this study adopts the perspective put forward by Birks and Mills (2015) and tries to utilise a balanced view of GT (methods) without embracing a dichotomous position, because it is believed that things are rarely black or white, in particular in respect to interpretive research. Nevertheless, due to diverging use of terms (e.g., with regard to analysis) in the various GT schools, this paper adopts the terminology put forward by Strauss and Corbin (1990, 1998) in order to provide clarity in terminology and to avoid misconceptions.

At the forefront, the GT process, consisting of data collection and analysis, is iterative and evolving. The context in which the research takes place (e.g., organisations, the actors, and their interrelations) is of great significance, and is supposed to relay a conceptual understanding of subjects that compose the naturalistic world. In other words, it permits theoretical generalisation[10] (Fendt & Sachs, 2008). As the phenomenon cannot be understood fully in advance, it is not feasible at the beginning of the study to see exactly where one will be led by the data and analytical progress (Corbin & Strauss, 2015; Weed, 2009). Grounded theory allows a flexible approach to data collection (Glaser & Strauss, 1967). According to the motto 'all is data', any type of quantitative (e.g., questionnaires, surveys) and/or qualitative data such as reports, images, observations, interviews, and focus groups can be used (Calman, 2006). Data collection is guided according to the concept of theoretical sampling and theoretical sensitivity. In search of information, the researcher will initially go to the most obvious site and collect data from a group of people who have experienced the phenomenon under study (Charmaz, 2006). As data are gathered, they are simultaneously analysed using three coding strategies (open, axial, and selective coding) with the overall goal of developing a conceptual theory. Data analysis is therefore related with progressively increasing the conceptual level from raw data to abstract, interrelated ideas as illustrated in Figure 5.1 on page 106.

[10]Theoretical generalisation refers to the development of theoretical concepts or propositions which are supposed to be of wider application. Conclusions or constructs are generated in a local setting or single study, which are then used in developing wider theory, which is relevant to other settings (Ritchie et al., 2013).

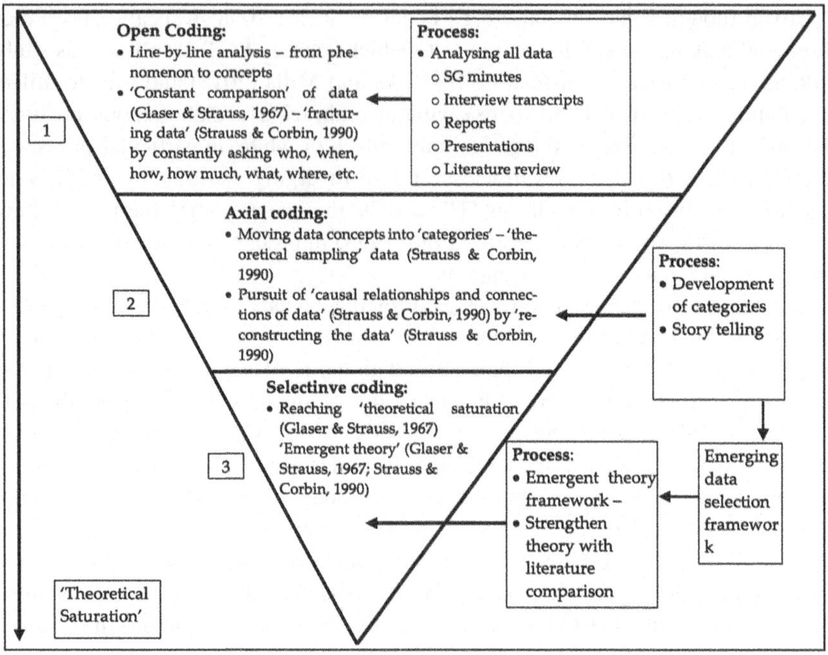

Figure 5.1 Grounded Theory Coding Process. (Source: According to Loonam, 2014; 62)

It has to be taken into account that GT coding is not a straight-line process. Rather, coding is flexible and transitions between the three coding stages are fluid; if required, one can return to the data and make a 'fresh' coding which also allows weighing of significance of codes, concepts, and categories (Birks & Mills, 2015; Charmaz, 2006).

The analysis begins with open coding[11] (line-by-line, code everything for everything), a procedure in which unknown facets or aspects can be discovered via the two central tools of asking (theory generating) questions about the data

[11]Coding means that labels are attached to segments of data that represent what each segment is about. Coding is a tool to distil data, sort them, and provides a sense for comparing diverse segments of data (Charmaz, 2006).

and constant comparison (via Constant Comparing Method[12]). Principal questions to be posed to the text are in particular those listed in Table 5.2:

Table 5.2 Principle Questions of Coding Procedure. (Source: Own Illustration, referring to Birks & Mills, 2015)

What	What is it about? Which phenomenon is being tackled?
Who	Who are the actors? Which roles do they have? How do they interact?
How	Which aspects of the phenomenon are addressed and which are not addressed?
Where, when, how long?	Time, process and location.
Why	What are the reasons for their acting? What is the attention? What is the purpose?
With what	What are the strategies? What are the tactics in order to attain the goals?

Specifically, data (in this study expert interviews) are analysed for incidents and experiences which results in denoting codes that stand for conceptual recurrences and similarities in the pattern in the data (Birks & Mills, 2015). By continuously comparing incidents with incidents within an interview, initial concepts[13] (codes) are generated.

Concepts (codes) can be either substantive or in-vivo codes. In-vivo ('within the living') codes take participants words as representative of a wider concept in the data (Strauss & Corbin, 1998). While some argue that in-vivo codes are very subjective, these have the benefit of reflecting a particular view of respondents which reinforces the authenticity of data interpretation. Therefore, in-vivo codes can be a source of vital analytical insights about the world of interviewees (Urquhart, 2013). Against this, substantive codes are taken from extant theory or

[12]The constant comparative method (CCM) *"combines systematic data collection, coding, and analysis with theoretical sampling in order to generate theory that is integrated, close to the data, and expressed in a form clear enough for further testing"* (Kolb, 2012; 83). CCM encapsulates four steps: *"(1) comparing incidents, applicable to each category, (2) integrating categories and their properties, (3) delimiting the theory, and (4) writing the theory"* (Glaser & Strauss, 1967; 105).

[13]*"A concept is a descriptive or explanatory idea, its meaning embedded in a word, label or symbol"* (Holloway, 2008; 43).

a researcher's experiences. For those kinds of codes, although not a must-have, Charmaz (2014) and Saldana (2013) each argue in favour of the use of gerunds when denoting concepts (codes) to stand for data as a way to classify process in the data. This approach is also recommended by Birks and Mills (2015) and will be applied in this work.

In order to pre-empt confusion in respect of GT analysis terminology, the difference between code, concept, and category will briefly be clarified. In essence, the three terms all refer to similar things, but are not used consistently among GT scholars and even vary within writings of the same scholars (Loonam, 2014; Glaser 2005; Strauss & Corbin, 1990, 1998). The words differ in terms of their level of abstraction and sophistication. The earliest outcome of the first analysed (open coded) interview is a list of codes. All codes in this interview are then compared with each other. Codes which refer to the same incident but which have a different label (name) are subsequently merged into a label called concept. This allows redundancies to be discarded and reduces the number of codes to a smaller number of concepts (Chamberlain-Sataun et al., 2013). These concepts are again compared against each other and against codes from incoming (new) interviews, which eases and corroborates the negotiation and renegotiation of views to develop the emerging grounded theory. Eisenhardt (1989) and Sotiriadou and Shilbury (2008) underscore the importance of constant comparison because it provides new insights from the data which supports the creation of an empirically valid theory. If various concepts refer to a similar phenomenon, these concepts are collapsed into higher lever conceptual 'categories' with which future codes and concepts are compared. Categories are then compared with categories. Thereby, it is not unusual that the name allocated to a concept is elevated to become the label of a category (Birks & Mills, 2015).

Beside data collection and analysis (coding), memos are written throughout the whole GT process. Memos are analytic notes about concepts, comparisons, hypotheses about categories and their relationships, and any other impressions and thoughts about the data (Sotiriadou & Shilbury, 2008; Charmaz, 2006). Memos help to map the research, extract meaning from data, act as building blocks, and document the development of the theory (raise data to a conceptual level). Memos further facilitate reorientation vis-à-vis the research when the analysis becomes complex (Goulding, 1999). Hence, memos are described as the *"cornerstone of quality"* (Birks & Mills, 2015; 40) and contribute to the enhanced credibility of the study.

Through the process of studying data, comparing them, and writing memos, the research is able to define categories that best match and interpret the data.

This necessitates axial coding[14] (second stage of analysis), which is more sophisticated than open coding and implies the process of abstraction onto a theoretical level by connecting (building relationships of) various concepts (and categories) to categories (the axes) and identifying patterns in the data (Glaser & Strauss, 1967). Building relationships between concepts (how categories and concepts relate to each other) is an inevitable step to move the analysis from rich descriptions towards theory building.

Corbin and Strauss (1990) recommend using "the paradigm" as a supportive tool in revealing relationships between categories. With the aid of the paradigm, a phenomenon (a category, that keeps the bits together) can be connected in respect to its context, casual conditions, intervening conditions, strategies, and consequences (all referred to as sub-categories). A sub-category examines the phenomenon by asking when, where, who, how, and with what consequences. This approach provides categories with greater explanatory power, hence corresponding with the concept of advancing theoretical abstraction from the data (Strauss & Corbin, 1990). However, according to Charmaz (2006; 61), *"the frame may extend or limit your vision, depending on your own subject matter and ability to tolerate ambiguity"*.

As it is not intended to force the data into a preconceived framework, this paper adopts the advice put forward by Urquhart (2013) for the need to be flexible about how categories relate. This also conforms with Corbin and Strauss' (2015; 90) comment that the paradigm is *"only a tool and not a set of directives"*. Böhm (2000) even recommends, although a proponent of the Straussian version of GT, to use the coding families commended by Glaser. Glaser (2005) added eleven more coding families to his original six coding families in order to connect categories and even says that analysts can develop their own connection patterns. This is supported by many GT scholars in the field (e.g., Mey & Mruck, 2007; Böhm, 2000; among others) who encourage people to create their own coding paradigms which best fit their research context (circumstances) and aid theory generation. This appears as an enrichment for axial coding and therefore this advice will be followed in this study.

Within axial coding, properties of categories and sub-categories are required to be identified in the data in order to saturate those and provide depth to the evolving theory. According to Strauss and Corbin (1998; 101), properties are

[14]Axial coding is the appreciation of concepts in terms of their dynamic interrelationships (Goulding, 1999).

"the characteristic of a category, the delineation of which defines [a category] and gives it meaning". Properties can be dimensionalised on a continuum (and the dimensions can be connected to conditions), therefore bring in variation into categories which is an indication of the depth and reach of the theory (Strauss & Corbin, ibid.).

The sampling strategy at this stage is concentrated on sampling for variation and contrasting cases in order to promote the depth of the evolving theory (Truschkat et al., 2005). Moreover, classifying properties and their dimensions while taking the conditions under which they operate into account will disclose insufficiencies in the data, which can be addressed by the use of theoretical sampling. Theoretical sampling (what data come next?) is proceeded based on concepts and categories that have demonstrated *"theoretical relevance to the evolving theory"* (Strauss & Corbin, 1990; 176). Theoretical sampling aims at theory development and not representativeness of a population (Fendt & Sachs, 2008). That means, sampling is not predictable before embarking on the primary research. In search of the emerging theory the researcher is free to continue data collection with cases, or other qualitative and quantitative methods, in order to refine the categories and advance the theory (Kanealy, 2009; Charmaz, 2006). This is consistent with the *"encompassing principle"*, which focuses on the recognition that the research objects *"are complex, multi-dimensional outcomes that require interpretation from multiple perspectives"* (Chalip, 2006; 7). Additionally, theoretical sampling allows "micro analysis", which is composed of comparative (case) study analysis to provide suitable guidance *"grounded in a proper appreciation of contextual specificity"* (Chalip, 2006; 8).

Data are again constantly compared and eventually grouped into one (or more) core category[15] (categories) (Goulding, 1999), which keeps all the bits together (relates meaningful with other categories; Glaser & Holton, 2004). While Glaser (1978, 2005), Strauss and Corbin (1990, 1998), and Birks and Mills (2015) state that identifying a core category is a key factor for the integration of a grounded theory, other scholars such as Charmaz (2006) and Urquhart (2013) are more flexible and admit to have two or even three core categories respectively. However, the scientists agree that generating a core category should be the focus of theory generation.

[15]According to Glaser (1978; 95) a core category must meet the following criteria: *"(1) It must be central and account for a large proportion of behaviour; (2) it must be based on recurring themes drawn from the data; (3) it must relate meaningfully to other categories; (4) analysis should be based on the core category; (5) it should be modifiable"*.

Once the core category is identified, selective coding (third stage, coding just for the core categories) starts for the purpose of theoretical integration[16] and to elaborate the core category (Truschkat et al., 2005). This process continues until theoretical saturation[17] is reached, where no new insights for theory building can be found in the data. By using the storyline[18] technique theoretical integration should be eased, which enhances the explanatory power of the theory. As such, the storyline has a twofold purpose: it not only supports the production of the final theory, it is also a vehicle by which the final theory can be presented to the reader. The salient point is that the storyline is both profound in terms of analysis and comprehensible for the audience (Birks & Mills, 2015; Charmaz, 2006). This is maintained by Dey (2007) who supports to the presentation of the grounded theory within a narrative in order to improve cohesion and 'digestibility'.

In terms of style, the focus of grounded theory writing should be on conceptuality (theoretical statements about relationships) instead of description (Strauss & Corbin, 1990). Glaser (1978) further recommend to use indicators marginally and only for support purpose. Simultaneously, indicators clearly should illustrate that the theory is grounded in the data, which contribute to Steinke's (2000) quality criteria of "empirical anchoring". Nevertheless, 'thick' description should be avoided in grounded theories (Mills & Huberman, 1994).

The result of continually reviewing the data, refining questions, and re-evaluating these changes is a theory which is "grounded in the data", is relevant to a specific situation (substantive), and can subsequently be developed into a formal theory (theory of middle-range) (Strauss & Corbin, 1998). The theory is only positioned in the context of the literature and extant theory following analysis and construction of the GT. This complies with the spirit of GT of not forcing analysis in preconceived theories (Charmaz, 2014; Glaser & Strauss, 1967).

---

[16]Theoretical integration is the process of "*pulling together of the abstract theoretical scheme into a final grounded theory*" (Birks & Mills, 2015; 181).

[17]Theoretical saturation refers to the point, until no new insights from the data (primary research) are obtained (Kanealy, 2009).

[18]According to Birks and Mills (2015; 180), storyline is a "*strategy for facilitating integration, construction, formulation and presentation of research findings through the production of a coherent grounded theory*".

5.3.3 Choice and Justification for Grounded Theory

As evidenced from discussions on management research, it appears that academics put greater emphasis on theory verification than on theory generation (Levers, 2013; Weed, 2009; Maital et al., 2008). However, with an overlapping and diverse topic such as sport management in general, and strategic equity partnerships in a corporate-sport context in particular,

> "academics need to be willing to cast away from the safe harbours of verification and firmly set their sights on the open seas of exploration. If our academy [management] limits its exploration of phenomena, then as scholars we limit the field of management inquiry" (Loonam, 2014; 5).

Qualitative research provides some renowned benefits. Data obtained in qualitative studies concentrate on naturally occurring events on what 'real life' is and are gathered in close proximity to a specific setting, that allows powerful new concepts or adjustments of present ones to be produced (Guercini, 2014). As Maital et al. (2008; 3) indicate: *"God is in the details, and the details are in the stories"*. The recent influx of various qualitative studies in sport management studies, for example Cooper et al. (2017), Stride et al. (2017), Hemme et al. (2017), and Weed (2009) is an indicator for the increased acceptance of qualitative studies in the field. Recently, Davis et al. (2012; 71) commented that GT is a valuable approach to theory building and *"is consistent with the normal scope of a doctoral dissertation"*.

Costa (2005) notes, if the discipline of sport management it to make a difference, sport management research cannot be based on knowledge and studies that have exclusively been conducted in non-sport settings because they neglect the unique features of the sport context. This is reinforced by Chalip (2006) and Sotiriadou and Shilbury (2008) who argue that GT in sport management studies supports a shift in research boundaries. They suggest departing from merely testing existing mainstream management theories and fitting them in predetermined variables in the sport management context. Instead, Chalip (op. cit.) accentuates the requirement of researchers to clarify to what extent mainstream theories and insights from social science are effectively applicable in the sport management context. Hence, researchers need to spot the utility and limitations for sport management of concepts that are extracted from other (mainstream) disciplines ("Derivative Model"). Moreover, researchers are encouraged to take into consideration exploring subjects in their sport-related context as they emerge. That means one has to identify and examine sport specific components ("Sport-focused Model") as illustrated in Figure 5.2.

	Derivative model	Sport-focused model
Inspiration:	Mainstream management marketing, economic, ..., theory	Search for theory that is grounded in sport phenomena
	↓	↓
Objectives:	Affirm existing theory OR Locate sport as a (possible) boundary condition	Create new theory OR find relevance of existing (mainstream) theory
	↓	↓
Outcome:	Apply known theory OR Discover lack of relevant theory	Build sport management practice on a demonstrably pertinent conceptual base

Figure 5.2 Complement Models of Sport Management Research. (Source: According to Chalip, 2006; 3)

In accordance with Costa (2005), Sotiriadou and Shilbury (2008), and Weed (2009), to name but a few, researchers need to delve into sports specific phenomena and build theory that is grounded in the management of sports. It is therefore essential that the phenomenon of strategic equity partnerships in the corporate football context is researched in its natural setting to comprehend its social constructions in order to supply a meaningful guide to action (Strauss & Corbin, 1998).

By using GT, the chosen research strategy is distinguished by the potential to justify both, the "Sport-focused Model" (theory emerges from the specific field of research) and the "Derivative Model" (checking congruence with existing management theory after theory development). This is justified with the idiosyncratic nature of German football, the co-determination of club members and especially the existence and uniqueness of the 50+1 rule. In particular, these aspects have implications on how clubs are managed and therefore justifies a concentration on German clubs. In addition, the phenomenon of strategic equity partnerships with corporate sponsors appear in Germany merely.

This study is interested in the business motives of corporate sponsors and clubs especially based on the background of divergent ambitions between clubs (sporting success) and corporate sponsors (profit). Due to the focus on corporate business motives, equity partnerships with other types of equity partners such as Maecenas and oligarchs are excluded from investigation, because they tend to have rather social and/or personal motives as illustrated in section 4.3.

This study uses sport management as a context for primary research to conclude that grounded theory is a viable and recommended methodology for the main purpose of theory generation for several reasons: first and foremost, the nature of the research question indicates the research goal (a question that explores motives and processes rather than testing a hypothesis). The literature review has clearly demonstrated the inadequacy of existing research and a theoretical vacuum to explain and answer the research question(s). Hence, the topic under investigation is directed towards an exploratory rather than a verification study. GT is well suited to advance an understanding in the corporate-sports partnership field because the power of GT lies in its ability to explain rather than to describe what is actually occurring in practice (Birks & Mills, 2015; Weed, 2009).

Academics concur that GT generates more than narratives (Levers, 2013; Weed, 2009; Lincoln & Guba, 2005; Glaser & Strauss, 1967). In fact, GT creates credible propositions of relationships among concepts (categories) and clusters of concepts that are rooted in the data (Strauss & Corbin, 1998). According to Fendt and Sachs (2008; 5): *"Listen to the situation and let the data speak"*. Hence, GT helps to create views and to learn why and how corporations and clubs enter into and manage strategic equity partnership in the corporate football context.

GT is also selected because it is consistent with the researcher's epistemology and ontology. The goal is to discover knowledge about "*actual production of meanings and concepts used by social actors in real settings*" (Gephart, 2004; 457) and not to explore an objective, external reality. The underlying assumption of using GT in this sport management-related research study is that sports and management are socially constructed. The premise is to let interpretations arise from research participants in the field (whereby knowledge is "co-created" or biased by the researcher in his role as interviewer) and finally to compare the results with available concepts on the issue. Grounded theory not only allows interpretation of participants' subjective perspectives, but also provides a means of abstraction of such experiences into theoretical concepts via GT's exclusive characteristics of its three coding procedures, constant comparative method, and theoretical sampling (Breuer et al., 2018; Sachs & Fendt, 2008). These key features offer access to the naturalistic world under study, come close to the lived experience of the participants, and provide the opportunity to make sense of them. Moreover, the flexible approach to data gathering and the structured approach to data analysis are expected to be useful in dealing with a mass of qualitative data and encourage valuable, interesting insights from interactions among research participants in their real business world (Maital et al., 2008; Sachs & Fendt, 2008).

However, the symbolic interactionists' dedication to apprehending social reality 'in situ' rather than 'in toto' accord to the maxim of *"local determinism"* on the one hand (Shalin, 1991; 245), and immediately prompts questions about the generalisability of research on the other hand. Either way, academics (especially in business and management) are permanently told of the ever-changing business environment (Abimbola & Vallaster, 2007). This view by itself lessens the argument of generalisability. Additionally, if people accept that organisations are unique then this reinforces the above statement (Chamberlain-Salaun et al., 2013). Besides, the methodology is conceptually dense. It implies provisional conceptual relationships submitted in discursive form, and it delineates patterns of action and interaction between and among social actors, *"developed from complex and constant iterative interplay among the data and between data, memos, and the literature"* (Fendt & Sachs, 2008; 448).

Overall, the chosen research design composed of a critical realist ontology, a symbolic interactionists epistemology, a mainly qualitative research strategy, and the grounded theory methodology is deemed consistent and to be highly appropriate to conduct this research study. Figure 5.3 on page 116 summarises the overall research approach.

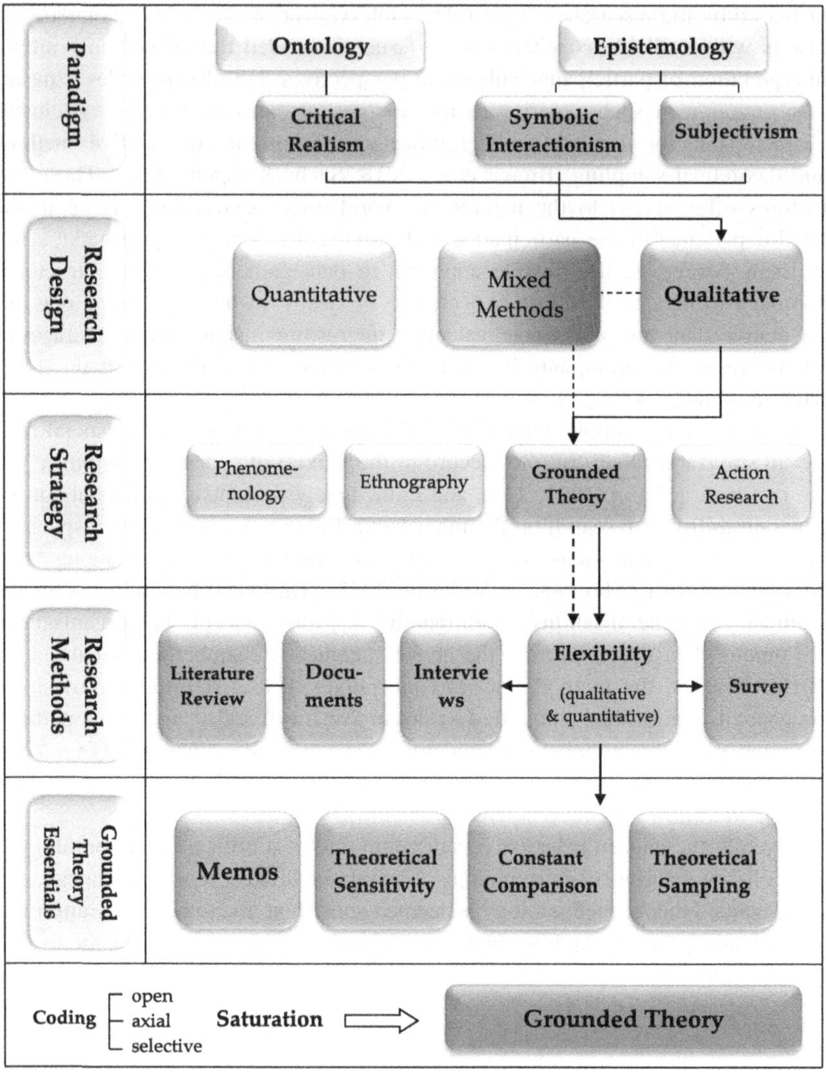

Figure 5.3 Overall Research Approach. (Source: Own Illustration)

5.4 Implementation of the Study Design

5.4.1 Theoretical Sensitivity and the Role of Literature

While the founding fathers of GT recommend preventing any preconceptions and to entering the research field with no prior review of the literature (no theory before data), the timing of the literature review in a GT study has been the subject of controversial debate over the last decades. Today there are various different views that try to integrate existing theory with the concept of theoretical sensitivity. As Dey (1999) has noted, the goal is to enter research with 'an open mind but not an empty head'.

The researcher acknowledges that literature may bias data collection and analysis. However, the key to ensuring theoretical sensitivity is not to be directed by theory (literature) but rather to be informed by it (Loonam, 2014). In concert with the principle of constant comparison and continuous memo writing, theoretical sensitivity can be further maintained. Existing literature is seen as another data source, which may well enhance the study (Locke, 2015; Giles et al., 2013; Calman, 2006). Moreover, a preliminary literature review is required by university authorities to demonstrate that the research field is worthy of study and that the research problem really exists. To satisfy both university demands and the principles of GT, the present status of research into strategic (equity) partnerships in the sports field is placed at the beginning of the thesis (Chapter 2, as an elaboration of the research gaps). The general alliance literature follows in Chapter 3. Chapter 4 addresses the football specific partnership literature.

The author has complied with the advice of Loonam (2014) and Sotiriadou and Shilbury (2008) and has covered a wide range of literature in order to facilitate a conceptual approach and to provide enough background knowledge. That means strategic partnership beyond the sports business have critically been reviewed including a variety of other B2B industries. This also serves as a foundation to elaborate practical solutions, as Mahony and Pitts (1998; 263) stated:

> "Sport management researchers will be more helpful to practitioners if they base their suggestions on a well-developed, theoretically based body of research, some of which may not have immediate implications for sport managers".

While some scholars (e.g., Bell et al., 2008) contend that the theoretical diversity of a topic might lead to study distortion, rendering the comparison of study results more difficult, and also impede theoretical progress, many others (e.g., Urriolagoitia & Planellas, 2007; Hecox, 2007; Cousens et al., 2006; Farrelly et al., 2006; Daellenbach et al., 2006; Bell et al., 2006; Olkkonen et al., 2000) argue that theoretical diversity might be beneficial to theoretical development of an academic area, because multiple perspectives allow insights into partnerships at different layers of 'visibility and interpretability' to be developed (Daellenbach et al., 2006). In a similar vein, Davies and his allies (2008) endorse the investigation of sports sponsorships from a strategic alliance perspective, as related literature (i.e., alliance and investor literature) could provide valuable insights for developing alternative frameworks and perspectives on managing strategic sponsorships.

Accordingly, due to the interdisciplinary field of study the author has included a broad realm of theoretical perspectives rooted in two broad areas of literature which shaped his current state of knowledge: sport (football) sponsorships and strategic alliance/partnership literature respectively inter-organisational relationships (the latter two pooled under the generic term "partnership literature"). In practice, recognised academic sports sponsorship journals, partnership specific journals as well as academic books were researched and these gave crucial academic insights into the field of B2B partnerships. As sponsorship is integrated in the marketing field, general marketing topics are touched on. The partnership literature not only embraces contractual cooperative agreements, it also contains equity partnerships and therefore the investor perspective (including a financial/M&A view).

Furthermore, the study takes the advice put forward by Breuer et al. (2018) to include non-academic publication into a grounded theory study in order to provide particularly context specific information. In this regard, it is explicitly referred to journalistic texts. Since football is of high public interest and many information are available via non-academic articles in the form of general sports (newspapers, professional journals, public announcements) and specific football media (sports magazines, press releases from clubs, and sport websites) these sources are utilised to add to profound insights into the topic, its current developments, and actual events.

Overall, only the literature written in English or German has been taken into account in order to lessen the risk of inappropriate results due to mistranslation. In order to ensure theoretical sensitivity and become aware of (and acknowledge) the own pre-conceptions, reflection has been used before embarking on the primary data collection phase.

5.4.2 Reflection of Preconceptions

Many GT scholars (Birks & Mills, 2015; Breuer et al., 2015; Strauss & Corbin, 1990) concur that facing one's own theoretical preconceptions is essential to stay theoretically sensitive and to avoid forcing the data into preconceptual frameworks, because human beings use, consciously or unconsciously, comparisons with things they know or which they are familiar with in order to perceive their social reality (Truschkat et al., 2005). By implication, this has an influence on how research data is analysed and interpreted. Especially in the German scientific GT community, reflexivity has become a crucial part in the GT process (Breuer et al., 2018). Self-reflection[19] is seen as an appropriate method to make one's own preconceptions transparent. Furthermore, regular self-assessment of thoughts to identify gaps in knowledge, explore feelings, and find methods for improvements in a process of learning helps one to become more organised and goal-orientated (Sugarman et al., 2000). Therefore, the research process is reflected with respect to the researchers' preconceptions which are mainly rooted in his academic and professional background. Since reflection aims to explore the researcher's subjective perspective, the following statements in this section pertain to the author's viewpoint. Accordingly, evidence for statements is not provided and the first-person perspective is avoided in the interest of the stylistic consistency of the dissertation.

The interest in this research topic is rooted in the personal background of the author as a professional football player. The job as a footballer provides insights into the business of football and the specific values which predominate around many actors in the football industry. Growing up in the field leads to an awareness that money is a core element in a football club. However, money is invested in order to boost the team to sporting success. It has often been observed that clubs spare neither trouble nor expense to drive their first team forward. Sometimes it appears that club authorities do not hesitate to spend the club's money for short-term sporting success, irrespective of financial prudence and with devastating effects in the absence of sporting success. As a consequence, it seems that many of those responsible for a club fail to see the bigger picture in the long run.

By the same token, the personal worldview of the researcher is influenced by his educational background at university level. As a management student,

[19]Reflection is defined in many different ways, e.g., Boud et al. (1985; 19, cited by Sugerman et al., 2000) explained it is *"a cognitive activity where people recapture their experience, think about it, mull it over and evaluate it"*.

academic knowledge is shaped by theories in the area of business and management. Making a profit as an overall goal of a corporation was one of the key principles taught. Expressions such as 'cash is king' and 'generating shareholder value' have accompanied the entire academic career. Generating cash vs. winning football matches—these were two key preconceptions before embarking on this research project.

In addition to that, it was presumed that marketing goals of corporations can effectively be achieved with a (pure) sponsorship partnership without spending substantial sums of money to hold a stake in a football club. The first strategic equity partnership between FC Bayern München and Adidas gave rise to the question how shareholding fits in the strategy of a corporation, in particular based on the background of the differing objectives between football clubs and corporate sponsors and also due to the need for corporations to justify their investments to the own stakeholders. Initially, it was assumed that FC Bayern München represented an exception because the club has long been one of the most successful clubs in Germany as well as in the world—with respect to financial and sporting results. However, as the trend for strategic equity partnerships has evolved and other clubs entered into minority equity partnerships with sponsors too, the question of why corporations choose this strategy occurred again. While for clubs a financial benefit appeared obvious due to the one-off payment, the added value for the sponsor remained concealed to the author. Consequently, the third preconception prior to this research study was that marketing goals can also be achieved with a (pure) sponsorship partnership without spending substantial sums of money to hold a stake in a football club.

5.4.3 The Case Study Approach

With respect to the research question(s) the author has selected a case study method for data collection. Case research allows for the holistic study of a phenomenon with close observation of how a specific population behaves in a particular context (Yin, 2014). The aim is to *"probe deeply and to analyse intensively multi-various phenomenon"* (Cohen & Manion, 2007; 258). Case research has been perceived as a major source of grounded theory and theory building (Eisenhardt, 1989; Glaser & Strauss, 1967) because it is in line with the GT's principle of investigating a phenomenon in context in which research and theory are in their formative stages (Wahyuni, 2012; Brown, 2008), as is the case of strategic equity partnerships in the corporate-football environment in Germany.

This view is reinforced by Strauss and Corbin (1998) and Guercini (2014) who espouse that grounded theory is designed to be conducted flexibly and creatively rather than pursued dogmatically. Moreover, Jiang et al. (2008) demand the use of case studies in alliance research in order to support the development of different theoretical concepts and to get more detailed information. Just as GT, within the framework of case study research various qualitative and quantitative methods can be utilised and connected (Creswell, 2008). While qualitative expert interviews predominate in this study, a quantitative online survey among football club members and fans is also applied.

5.4.4 Theoretical Sampling

Identifying which case to research first is a difficult choice (Goulding, 1999). The decisive criterion for qualitative sampling is its relevance in respect to the research problem. As recommended by Kanealy (2009), the researcher is allowed to choose a case that is deemed (at the planning stage) to make a useful contribution to the research question (initial purposive sampling). Likewise, Danermark (2002) suggests examining extreme cases in which the phenomena can be considered in pure or extreme form. Therefore, the present study is initially based on the case of FC Bayern München and its corporate partners (Adidas, Allianz, Audi, and Telekom) for the following reasons:

first and foremost, FCB is the first club in Germany to have established enduring equity partnerships with three big sponsors (Adidas, Allianz, and Audi). Therefore, FCB is the club with the most experience in the management of strategic equity partnerships. Second, the equity partnerships can be viewed as a success story, as FCB has developed into one of the three richest clubs worldwide, increasing its turnover from € 162.7 million in the 2002/2003 season (in which the first strategic equity partnership was initiated) to € 657.4 million in the 2017/2018 season (FCB website, 2018). Third, Adidas (equipment), Allianz (insurance), and Audi (car manufacturer) are three big players in their respective industries and can provide diverse, valuable experience due to their myriad business backgrounds. Finally, Telekom (lead sponsor), as a non-equity partner, may deliver precious insights into why they have not chosen equity as a partnership form.

Furthermore, the case of SG Eintracht Frankfurt (Eintracht) would also appear to be of relevance for enhancing this study. The Eintracht case is the first and only one (up to now) in which a strategic equity partner cut off from the club.

In 2001/2002, Octagon (US sports marketing agency) bought 49% shares of the club. Just one year later, Eintracht experienced dissolution and Octagon sold its shares back to Eintracht. This case offers the opportunity to investigate reasons why Octagon cut off the partnership, what the underlying reasons and processes were, as well as how the club handled this difficult situation.

After analysing (open coding) the first interviews (first coding block) the author included the case of BVB Borussia Dortmund 09 (BVB) as this added the perspective of a B2B business to the study. BVB partnered in 2006 with its current lead sponsor Evonik, which bought shares (15.43%) in 2014. Additionally, BVB is the only club in Germany which is a publicly listed company (GmbH & Co.KG aA) and therefore could introduce new insights about background information and peculiar features, too.

In the course of theoretical sampling, a different view was gained from the case of SV Werder Bremen (SVW). According to numerous public announcements, the club is in search of a strategic equity partner but has failed to find a proper partner to date. This provides information about the difficulties experienced by clubs finding a strategic equity partner. In addition, the interview with the club authority has yielded precious information in regard to theoretical sampling. The club was in negotiations with a sponsor about a strategic equity partnership and had already agreed a shareholding on the board level. In the final analysis the supervisory committee of the sponsor was divided over the shareholding and thus the deal failed. In the case of SVW, it came to light that the club is supported by a consultancy company in order to find the right partner. To understand this interaction and to get an objective perspective, an interview was conducted with a managing partner of that consultancy company.

During the time of collecting and analysing data VfB Stuttgart (VfB) announced the shareholding of its long-term sponsor Daimler AG. This was deemed as an opportune occasion to include a very current perspective which allows existing categories to be further deepened. Also, the decision-making process between Daimler AG as the parent company and its subsidiary company Mercedes Benz Bank (lead sponsor of VfB) could be investigated. The interview with the lead sponsor of VfB revealed that Daimler AG involved its M&A department in the decision-making process. The procedure that the M&A department was mainly involved in decision-making was new. Therefore, this perspective enriched the primary research with another point of view.

Based on these interviews, the corporate and club perspective has come to a point of saturation. Overall, the following organisations (7 clubs and 15 corporations) are represented within this study as shown in Table 5.3 on page 123.

Table 5.3 Partaking Research Organisations. (Source: Own Illustration)

Football Clubs	Corporations	Industry
FC Bayern München	Adidas	Manufacturer of sport articles
BVB Borussia Dortmund 09	Evonik	Special chemicals (B2B)
SG Eintracht Frankfurt	Allianz	Insurance
SV Werder Bremen	Puma	Manufacturer of sport articles
VfB Stuttgart	Signal Iduna	Insurance
FC Ingolstadt	Daimler AG	Automotive
VfL Wolfsburg	Mercedes Benz Bank	Financing
	Audi AG + VW	Automotive
	Wiesenhof	Foodstuff/poultry
	Network Corporate Finance	Management Consultation
	[Anonym] sponsor	Anonym
	Octagon	Sports right marketer
	Telekom	Telecommunication/media

One central issue which came to light during the qualitative investigation was how clubs and corporations deal with the interests of club members and fans. Their view and their needs were considered in the (equity) decision-making process by both the club and corporate partner. Consequently, and in line with the principle of theoretical sampling, this perspective is added to the study by using an online survey as the final data collection stage. The details of the survey will be outlined in Section 5.4.6.

5.4.5 Qualitative Data Collection via Expert Interviews

Qualitative data is collected in personal interviews. Interviews are fundamental sources of grounded theory and case study information and are deemed to offer the advantage of allowing closer access to participant's views (Fisher, 2010). As the focus of the study is on theory building it is imperative—referring to several scholars such as Pryziborski and Wohlrab-Sahr (2014)—to interview experts in the field. In terms of the characteristics that define an expert, the literature presents diverse opinions (Bogner et al., 2009). For example, based on the definition of Meuser and Nagel (1991), Bähring et al. (2008; 93) classify an expert as a person that *"possesses a considerable amount of specialised knowledge of their subject on the basis of many years of professional experiences"*. Gläser and Grit (2004) opposes that specialised knowledge does not have to be based on professional experience but can also originate from studies, research, or autodidactic acquisition. Irrespective of the origin of knowledge, the crucial aspect is the existence of specialised knowledge.

Bogner et al. (2009) add that specialised knowledge refers to specific interpretive knowledge ("know-why") and procedural knowledge ("know-how"). This conforms with the understanding from Pryziborski and Wohlrab-Sahr (2014) who state that an expert of an organisation is a person who either takes strategic decisions, justifies them, or is involved in strategic management and decision-making processes. As the buying/selling of organisational shares is a wide-ranging (financial and strategic) decision, it can be categorised as a top management decision. Thus, the researcher tried to win those top managers for interviews who actually take the final decision or who are mainly incorporated in decision-making. Interviewing these top-managers seems to be highly appropriate as they can provide the information, insights, and knowledge (know-why and know-how) which is required to answer the research question (why and how are equity partnerships established and managed).

Experts are approached based on the principle of snowball[20] sampling. This strategy is especially suitable for the recruitment of a group of people who are difficult to access, such as experts and top managers (Pryziborski & Wohlrab-Sahr, 2014). The initial access to the field (first expert interview) was attained with the help of the researcher's employer SV Werder Bremen. Truschkat et al. (2005) note that the closer the contact to the research field the easier it is to get support for the research project. As the professional background of the researcher is in the football business (as an active football player at the time of doing the research), this turned out to be true in respect to this research study.

Whilst gaining access to experts (business and club leaders) is said to be difficult (Truschkat et al., 2005) without first providing such individuals with some background information, basic information (i.e., motivation, personal situation, topic, purpose of research, overriding issues) was included upon approaching the

[20]Snowball sampling is an approritate sampling method when characteristics to be possessed by samples are rare and difficult to locate. This method includes primary data sources nominating another relevant primary data source to be utilised in the research (Dudovski, 2018; Pryziborski & Wohlrab-Sahr, 2014).

experts (via e-mail) in order to increase the likelihood of participation. As experts have very restricted time schedules, the requests also demanded flexibility and spontaneity on the part of the researcher in order to adapt and react to the experts' schedules.

All requested experts agreed to be interviewed except for one, who denied a personal meeting for an interview. This participant nevertheless referred to a colleague and offered additional support via telephone if necessary. Overall, 24 interview partners were recruited, 23 males and one female. Out of the 24 participants, 16 experts were top managers on the C-level[21] or member of the supervisory committee. Some of these even had a double position combined with a seat on the supervisory committee at the sponsored club. Eight experts were in the position of head of their department (e.g., sponsoring, marketing, M&A). The detailed sequence of interviews is presented in Table 5.4 on page 126.

Expert interviews require good communication skills, openness, and flexibility on the part of the interviewer. In accordance with the principle of theoretical sensitivity, the researcher opts for a non-directive interview[22] (Gray, 2009). In contrast to structured interviews, which are based on standardised questions, the unstructured form of the non-directive interview provides the interviewees with the opportunity to express their stories and thus allows the researcher to get in-depth insights into complex situations (Foddy, 1995). Further, this form of interview takes the expert status of the interviewees into account and the expert can refer to key themes he deems significant for the topic. Furthermore, the researcher is able to remain as open and adaptable as possible which minimises the influence of pre-conceptions. Thus, there is no pre-set of questions but a guideline with fundamental topics (the interview is based on the research questions viz. motives and processes of equity partnerships) that the researcher intends to investigate. This guideline is an instrument to pre-structure the interview, but is used flexibly. That means, all interviewees are faced with the same opening question (which eases the comparison of interviews) in which the participants were encouraged to set any focus areas they deem to be relevant (Jamshed, 2014).

---

[21]C-level is a collective term for a number of chief officers, i.e., CEO (chief executive officer), CFO (chief financial officer), CMO (chief marketing officer) and CHRO (chief human resource officer) (Von Loh, 2018).

[22]The non-directive interview is a form of an unstructured interview. It seeks to gather in-depth information and usually does not have pre-planned set of questions (Jamshed, 2014).

Table 5.4 Overview on Interview Participants. (Source: Own Illustration)

Date	Job Position	Form of Interview
First stage of inquiry		
01 March 2017	C-level	Interview via Skype
02 March 2017	C-level	Interview on site
20 March 2017	C-level	Interview on site
22 March 2017	• C-level • Member of the supervisory board/later on C-level	Focus group on site
23 March 2017	Head of Department	Interview via Skype
27 March 2017	C-level	Interview on site
27 March 2017	C-level	Interview on site
27 March 2017	C-level	Interview on site
30 March 2017	Head of Department	Interview on site
Second stage of inquiry		
27 April 2017	C-level & supervisory board	Interview on experts' place
10 May 2017	C-level	Interview on site
Third stage of inquiry		
11 June 2017	C-level & supervisory board	Interview via Skype
17 June 2017	Head of Department	Interview on site
19 June 2017	C-level & supervisory board	Interview on site
24 June 2017	Head of Department	Interview via Skype
25 June 2017	C-level	Interview on site
30 June 2017	Head of Department	Interview on site
25 September 2017	Head of Department	Interview via Skype
27 September 2017	• C-level & supervisory board • Head of Department	Focus group via Skype
05 October 2017	C-level & supervisory board	Interview on site
27 November 2017	• C-level & supervisory board • Head of Department	Focus group on site

In line with the proposal put forward by Corbin and Strauss (2015), the interview form (and guideline) evolves during the primary research process towards a more structured form. It encompasses more concrete question about emerging concepts in order to confirm or discard those concepts. This entails that replies to questions create new (other) questions which fine-tune the process in order to gain required information and fully elaborate categories. However, openness (and the opening question) remains the same for the aforementioned reasons. All research participants offered additional support following on from the interview should further information be required or information be vague. In addition, many experts helped to secure access to other experts in the field for further interviewing (snowball sampling).

The interviews took place between March and November 2017, with early interviews informing latter ones. Three interviews were conducted in the form of a focus group as three of the experts recommended including those responsible who were mainly involved in the preparation of the equity deal-making. This proposal was gratefully received.

All interviews were conducted personally and face-to-face. The majority were performed on the site of the organisation which is distinctive for expert interviews (Pryziborski & Wohlrab-Sahr, 2014). One interview was performed at the experts' private residence and six interviews were led via video-telephony (Skype) at the insistence of two participants or because of travel and time constraints on the part of the researcher. However, due to the features of video-telephony the characteristics of the face-to-face situation remained the same. The interviews were held in German except of one interview which was performed in English (native language of the expert). All interviews were recorded and lasted between 47-120 minutes and resulted in 439 pages of transcription which constituted the bulk of the data to be analysed (all transcriptions are accessible on the attached storage medium). A summary memo (postscript interview memo) was written immediately after each interview in order to note first impressions and to capture immediate interpretation thoughts of respondents' views and experiences. Additionally, the researcher noted the circumstances under which interviews took place, made notes of emerging data, and referenced the relevant sources employed to arrive at concrete findings in order to maintain a chain of evidence[23].

All interview situations proceeded in a similar way. Initially, the researcher introduced himself and tried to start a phase of 'small talk' in order to establish a faithful, relaxed atmosphere and degree of intimacy. Subsequently, the research topic and purpose were explained. The interviewees had the opportunity to ask questions and have any concerns addressed. In order to enhance the trustwor-

[23]A chain of evidence "*allows an external observer to follow the derivation of any evidence from initial research question to ultimate case-study conclusions so that the observer should be able to trace the steps in either direction*" (Yin, 2014; 127).

thiness of the research process, each interview participant received an informed consent form[24] (Appendix I) in advance of the interview and declaring their agreement to be involved in the study. The informed consent form was signed, one consent form for the researcher and one consent form for the interviewee. Participants were informed of their right to cancel the interview or their participation in the project at any time without having to name reasons. All interviewees accepted the recording of the interview. The anonymity of participants' personal information was assured. In order to increase the likelihood of accessing sensitive information, the research participants were explicitly informed of their right to prevent the researcher from publishing sensitive information. Sensitive sections were blackened in the transcripts. Even though some sensitive sections are not allowed to be published, this still enables the researcher to evaluate the information and achieve a better understanding of the whole phenomenon and context.

After the opening question, the researcher drew on relevant topics put forward by the interviewees with the aid of immanent questions[25]. Therefore, field notes were created during an interview in order to ensure follow-up questions of significant areas without interrupting the interviewee's thought process. If all immanent questions were saturated, the researcher asked about topics he considered of relevance with regard to the research questions. In that situation, the interview guideline secured that all (supposed) vital aspects were touched on and proved to be significant or not from the perspective of the expert. Moreover, the guideline ensured some kind of comparability (Pryziborski & Wohlrab-Sahr, 2014). The interview continued until the point of saturation (until participants had exhausted their whole story).

Since the researcher has a professional background in the football business and an academic background in management studies, precious time was saved by the need not to deduce responses so as to elucidate basic principles. Likewise, research participants and the researcher share the same passion, that of football, and most interviewees valued the fact that an active footballer was writing a doctoral dissertation. As a result, interviews were relaxed and mostly genial. It is assumed that such an atmosphere increased the flow of replies as well as

[24]The informed consent form explains each participant the rationale and nature of the study, potential risks, why they are candidates, and informs about participant rights. The informed consent form is signed by the participant and the researcher.

[25]Immanent questions refer to the immediate responses (topics) of interviewees (Pryziborski & Wohlrab-Sahr, 2014).

the depth of answers and led to responses that would not normally have been achieved (Boyce & Neale, 2006).

All interviews were transcribed referring to Dresing and Pehl's (2015) 'simplified system of transcription' (Appendix II). That means, small talk issues are not transcribed which is consistent with Strauss and Corbin's (1987) stance of recording and transcribing interviews.

Interviews are combined with document analysis (Yin, 2014) to present background information and to detail broader organisational and partnership structures. Official documents such as press releases, website articles, financial statements, reports, presentations, and strategy documents are reviewed. The analysis of documentary secondary data provides a valid way in which to address the research purpose, especially given the fact that the public interest of football leads to the publication of valuable data. As documents generally offer consistent and precise information, they are deemed appropriate in adding to the robustness of outcomes (Lund & Greyser, 2016; Morgan et al., 2014). To further amplify the credibility of the study a concept library is utilised (a detailed electronical database including a code book and a memo book), in which all data and information are stored that allow the researcher to order, maintain, and organise data systematically (Loonam, 2014; Yin, 2014; Brown, 2008).

5.4.6 Quantitative Data Collection via Online Survey

An online survey was chosen in order to incorporate the perspective (opinion) of football fans and club members in Germany. Survey research is deemed appropriate because this allows for a collection of information from a larger population, therefore ensuring an accurate sample (Saunders et al., 2015). As the research phenomenon concerns the German football business the questionnaire was designed in German.

Online-based data collection has several benefits. An online survey provides the chance to increase the reach of the survey because of a viral marketing effect (i.e., the link could be shared with other social network users). Moreover, participants are largely excluded from bias due to the survey situation and anonymity could be guaranteed. Respondents also had the chance to pause the questionnaire and to continue at a later time, providing flexibility to participants. In addition, this allows participants to take enough time for completion which increases the chance to get profound replies (Selm & Jankowski, 2006). Possible distortion in the form of multiple participation could be avoided by the inclusion of cookies[26].

The population is derived from all German-speaking football fans in Germany. Football fans are not a homogeneous group (Schade, 2012; Schwier & Fritz, 2003). There are a variety of different groups of fans who differ in terms of their level of interest, involvement, and consumption behaviour (Gabler, 2009; Hill, 2002; Setzen, 1999). While the number of football club members is recorded by the DFB (7,090,107 million in 2018), Bühler (2017) assesses that it is not possible to make a precise statement about the constitution of the "football fan" population. This is exacerbated by the difficulty to come to an overall definition of what a fan is (Hills, 2002). Therefore, with reference to Hills (2002) and Rohr (2006) the survey is directed at those individuals (fans) who have an enduring interest (involvement) in football (Rohr, 2006; Hills, 2002). This aspect is guided by the amount of football consumption per season. In this study, those individuals are considered as fans who consume football at least 10 times per season or more, irrespective of the form of consumption (e.g., via TV, stadium visits, or the internet). The chosen distribution channels (all sport and football related) will largely ensure that the target group is reached.

The survey is based on a questionnaire (Appendix III), which was programmed with the survey tool 'questback' (EFS Survey), and includes 10 content questions, which are posed in a logical sequence. The content questions are designed to explore the views of fans and club members regarding the four types of shareholders (equity partners) identified in the expert interviews (strategic partner (sponsor), financial investor, Maecenas, oligarch). The aim here is to close the research gap of previous studies which concentrate on the term investor only.

First and foremost, the overall acceptance of the four shareholder types is inquired (multiple answers possible). Relevant issues were extracted from the expert interviews, in particular the "importance of a positive image of a shareholder", the relevance of the "regional affinity" of a shareholder, the "size of shares acceptable to fans", the "distribution of shares to a number of different shareholders of a club", and the "importance of a club's priority right to repurchase the shares". Based on this and in line with the principle of theoretical sampling, the literature was additionally reviewed in order to contribute to an elaborated questionnaire. In particular, the quantitative work by Bauers and Hovemann (2019a), but also the qualitative study from Pilz (2011) enriched the questionnaire content by considering "arguments in favour of a shareholder" and

[26]A cookie is a small text file that provide a way for a website to identify a user and keep track of the user's preferences (Pcmag, 2018).

"arguments against the admission of a shareholder". This allowed a holistic investigation of the fan perspective on the phenomenon.

The content questions are complemented by four socio-demographic questions at the end of the questionnaire. This order is used in order to increase the readiness to provide information, because the focus and concentration of participants is primarily directed towards answering content questions of a complex subject. The socio-demographic part requested whether participants are club members or non-club members. This offers the opportunity to divide the population into a "non-club member" ("fan group") and "club member group". A segmentation of the two groups enables the findings to be related to the respected work of Bauers and Hovemann (2019a). Furthermore, fan behaviour in respect to football consumption and stadium visits is requested too, allowing conclusions to be drawn as to whether the target group was reached and providing information about the type of participants (e.g., the aforementioned discussed types/group of fans) and their level of interest/involvement in football.

The very last question referred to whether participants are interested in being informed about the results after data analysis and publication. In that case, participants had to enter their e-mail address (voluntary). This neither affects the replies given (as the question is posed at the end) nor does it restrict anonymity due to the voluntary nature of the information. Since the questions build on from each other answering was compulsory. Yet, it was possible to not give an answer by using the option "not specified", "I have no opinion on the subject", or "none of the above". In order to guarantee a consistent logical sequence, filters are used throughout the questionnaire.

While the content questions aimed to cover all relevant aspects, efforts were also made not to overtax participants in order to minimise the drop-out rate. Thus, the content questions are composed of a mix of single-item scales and multi-item scales. Single-item scales have practical advantages such as ease of administration and parsimony (Diamantopoulos et al., 2012). Furthermore, single items are less time consuming and therefore may lead to better survey effectiveness (Bergkvist & Rossiter, 2007). Against this, a multi-item scale is appropriate in order to illustrate the various facets of an issue. A combination of both types is said to lessen the drop-out rate (Bergkvist & Rossiter, ibid.) but also allows the complexity of the issue to be accommodated.

There are contrasting views in the literature regarding the required indicators of multi-item scales. While Churchill (1979) demands 10 items, Bollen (1989) contradicts and requires three to four items. Weiber and Mühlhaus (2010) state that the majority of studies utilise between three and six items. This advice was followed in this study.

The majority of answer options were based on a 5-point Likert Scale (totally agree—totally disagree; very important - unimportant). A Likert scale is deemed to be an effective and reliable way to investigate a participant's attitudes and preferences in greater detail (Joshi et al., 2015). The use of an uneven scale prevented distortions as participants were not forced to opt for 'one side', which may have appeared if even scales had been used. Although an uneven scale has the drawback that participants might tend to choose the middle option ('golden mean'), empirical findings are indicative of uneven scales (Franzen, 2014; Weiber & Mühlhaus, 2010). In addition, the answer choices were labelled. Franzen (2014; 707) concurs with findings from Krosnick (1999) and Tourangeau et al. (2007) that *"if designation [...] is possible, this should be chosen",* since this increases reliability. In order to ensure a high response rate, the questionnaire was designed based on the general advice put forward by Pötschke (2009), Schnell et al. (2008), and Theobald (2007) for online questionnaires as listed below:

- the answer option "not specified"
- the opportunity to interrupt the questionnaire and continue later on
- avoid scrolling
- ensure the anonymity of participants and provide that information at the beginning of the survey.
- a progress bar
- an attractive, professional survey design

In addition, the author ascribed importance to the questions' wording which is based on the following principles recommended by May (2001): use of simple language to convey the meaning, prevention of ambiguities and leading questions, removal of vague terms in order to avoid vague replies, and ensuring that participants have the required knowledge to answer the questions.

To guarantee the latter aspect, the questionnaire includes an introductory part to the topic in which participants are informed about the basic terms (i.e., definitions of the four types of shareholders). Even though it is supposed that club members and fans have touchpoints (e.g., via media or fan discussions) with the general topic of strategic partnerships and shareholders in football, this pre-information was regarded as essential in order that all participants answer the questionnaire based on the same basic understanding. Moreover, technical terms in interrogation are explained on the respective question sheet (desktop).

A pre-test was conducted in order to assure the comprehensibility of questions, the structure of the questionnaire, and to determine the average duration time. Furthermore, the pre-test enabled (via an open answer field) arguments that club members and fans deemed crucial but which had been previously neglected, to be integrated. With the aim of getting feedback from a diverse audience, the pre-test was conducted with people ranging from academics of different disciplines (sport economics, marketing), football fans, and club members.

In order to generate a representative sample, several distribution channels were utilised. First, all fan representatives and fan projects by clubs from the 1st Bundesliga, 2nd Bundesliga, 3rd Liga, and the 4th League (Regionalliga) were contacted via e-mail and asked to forward the invitation containing the online survey link to their fans. Those representatives who did not answer got a follow-up e-mail after seven days and another reminder e-mail after 17 days. In addition, the survey was promoted via a website article and Twitter post (via a retweet[27] to the website article) of SV Werder Bremen. In order to address a broad audience, the survey link was published by "Kicker Sportmagazin" in their social network (Facebook) three times in the interval of two weeks. Moreover, the distribution was promoted by the website and smartphone app of a daily newspaper, the "VDV" (Vereinigung der Vertragsfußballer; football union) and "DieFußballecke.de" in form the of a press release.

The distribution was carried out in stages in order to minimise divergence loss due to information overload especially via social media platforms. The poll was online from 26th April until 17th June 2018. The starting time was deemed favourable as the topic was under discussion at that time in the media due to the proposal from the club president of Hannover 96 (1st Bundesliga club) to take over the majority of voting shares of the club (Kicker, 2018). However, the survey ended with the start of the World Championship 2018, as the focus of media and football fans shifted towards this event.

Overall, a total of 12,923 people accessed the survey link. 1,610 (completion rate of 12.5%) finished the questionnaire completely, representing 996 (62%) club members and 587 (36%) non-club members (2% of respondents not specified). The sample is adjusted to exclude those participants who apparently have no enduring interest in football. These are those participants who answered the question "how many times do you consume football per season overall" with "not at all" (3 participants) and less than 10 times per season (18 participants). Consequently, 21 participants (due to interactions) are eliminated from the sample, resulting in an adjusted sample of 1,589 participants. The detailed description of the survey sample is illustrated in Table 5.5 on page 134.

[27]A retweet is a post of a previously posted (public) message (Adividera, 2018).

Table 5.5 Survey Sample Characteristic. (Source: Own Illustration)

Sample characteristics	Absolute frequencies	Relative frequencies
Overall sample (net)	n = 1,610	100%
Club members	996	61.9%
Non-club members	587	36.5%
Not specified	27	1.7%
Overall consumption of football/season	n = 1,610	
not at all	3	~ 0.1%
1-3 times per season	8	~ 0.3%
4-6 times per season	6	~ 0.3%
7-9 times per season	4	~ 0.2%
10-12 times per season	22	~1.4%
13-15 times per season	32	~1.5%
16-18 times per season	58	2.5%
>18 times per season	1477	93.4%
Stadium visits per season	n = 1,589	
not at all	74	4.7%
1-3 times per season	370	23.3%
4-6 times per season	248	15.6%
7-9 times per season	143	9%
10-12 times per season	126	7.9%
13-15 times per season	97	6.1%
16-18 times per season	147	9.3%
>18 times per season	384	24.2%
Favourite Club	n = 1,589	
Yes	1572	98.9%
No	17	1.1.%
Favourite club of participant	n = 1,589	
1st Bundesliga	1130	71.1%
2nd Bundesliga	140	8.8%
3rd Liga	235	14,8%
Regionalliga	41	2.6%

(continued)

Table 5.5 (continued)

Sample characteristics	Absolute frequencies	Relative frequencies
Other	19	1.2%
Not specified	24	1.5%
Age of participants	n = 1,586	
Younger than 18	40	2.5%
18-30	724	45.6%
31-40	470	29.6%
41-50	206	13%
51-60	108	6.8%
61-70	32	2%
Older than 71	5	~0.3%
Not specified	3	~0.2%

In order to make a profound statement about the quality and representative status of the sample, it is essential to know the size of the population and its constitution (Schnell et al., 2008). Since precise information on the underlying population (i.e., football fans in Germany) is not given (Bühler, 2017), a statement based on scientific standards about the representative status of the present sample cannot be made. Even though this is not possible it can be assumed, based on the number of participants (1,589), that the sample provides a fairly realistic image of the fan opinion as per classification in this study.

In order to identify relevant limitations of empirical findings, the sample is considered differentially (Schnell et al., 2008). Upon taking a more detailed look, two groups are overrepresented in the sample: younger fans (between the age of 18-30) and middle aged (between the age of 31-40) fans (Institut für Demoskopie Allensbach, 2017a, 2017b, 2017c). The differential analysis of the groups show that these do not rate the issues of the content questions differently compared to their reference group.

The open answer fields in the questions regarding the "arguments in favour of a shareholder", "arguments against a shareholder" and "justification of share allocation" were excluded from consideration because these are only infrequently completed by 2.7% (in favour), 2.5% (against), and 1.8% (allocation of shares) and yield no significant insights.

5.4.7 Data Analysis

The interview data is analysed based on the key principles of grounded theory described previously. In order to improve the comprehension and get a sense of how coding was practically applied, each of the three coding stages is demonstrated by an example. This chronological presented process is rather a circular procedure in the actual research process.

In the open coding stage, data is fractured via microanalysis (line-by-line coding) in which central ideas are identified. The grey marked text passages are open coded as seen in the next two tables (interview excerpt, IP 1, 2; 44) (Tables 5.6 und 5.7).

Table 5.6 Interview Excerpt for Open Coding. (Source: Own Illustration)

The critical factor in an equity partnership is, all of the equity holders have their interests aligned in the same place. I think the fundamental issue with [club] was the membership of the Verein probably thought here was the sugar daddy from America that was going to spent us lots of money, bringing lots of players. You know, [Club A] would be fantastic. Listen, I am a fan of a football club, I am a [club B] season ticket holder, and I am very passionate about my team. And [club A] is fantastic, has a huge fan base, very passionate, which is terrific. But you know that fans only care about winning on the pitch. On the other hand, you have a very large American corporation whose ultimately aim is to make money. Those two things, which are not necessarily incompatible but fans are not interested in their team making money. In fact, they want their football team to spend any penny and more on players. And even here in [name of football league]. You know there is a huge amount of money now, but fans want better players. They are not interested in making money.

Table 5.7 Example of Open Coding. (Source: Own Illustration)

Text passage (grey marked)	(code number) Code
Critical factor	1. Property of "having aligned interests"
All the equity holders have their interest aligned in the same place	2. Having aligned interests (condition)
the membership of the Verein probably thought here was the sugar daddy from America that was	3. Differing role expectations

(continued)

Table 5.7 (continued)

Text passage (grey marked)	(code number) Code
going to spend us lots of money, bringing lots of players.	4. Increasing revenue stream
I am very passionate about my team	5. CEO passion for football 6. Dimension of passion: very
And [club a] is fantastic,	7. Enthusiasm
has a huge	8. Dimension of fan base: huge
fan base,	9. Huge fan base (property)
very passionate, which is tereffic	10. Property: passion of fans; dimension of passionate: very
fans	11. Fans as personification of the club
only care about winning on the pitch	12. Focussing on sport success
very large American corporation whose ultimately aim is to make money	13. Making money (in vivo)
fans are not interested in their team making money.	14. Differing ambitions
In fact, they want their football team to spend any	15. Fans having power on club
penny and more on players. but fans want better players. They are not interested	16. "their" = claim of ownership (fans as personification)
in making money.	17. Differing ambitions

Following this procedure, during the first step of open coding, each interview revealed a number between 85 and 187 of initial codes. Using the constant comparison method, the number of different codes could be reduced between 85 and 100 effectively, depending on the interview. Table 5.8 on page 138 exemplifies the process of constant comparison of codes which refers to the same incident but that have been coded with a different label initially.

Table 5.8 Outcome of Constant Comparison Method. (Source: Own Illustration)

Constant Comparison Method	
Interview codes with the same meaning	Codes
Aligning mutual strategic goals, requiring compatibility of goals, requiring same interests	Having aligned interests
Prior access to club, prior relationship, insight into management, prior insight to shareholder personal	Having prior insight
Creating synergies, adding business value, supporting own business progress, pursuing business concept, supporting corporate goals, mutual benefitting, supporting own business progress	Creating win-win
Sound economic club management, achieving sound finances, requiring club management with interest in earning money, sound economic management, expecting not to lose money, not losing money	Operating in the black
Equity is the basis for sponsorship, shareholding as a strategy to back up sponsoring, substantiating sponsorship with equity, backing up sponsorship, securing long-term collaboration	Securing long-term sponsoring
Creating customer touchpoints, getting media presence, increasing awareness	Increasing awareness

The initial number of interview codes could subsequently be merged and increased by the level of abstraction (again via constant comparative method) to an initial number of 32 higher ordered concepts. Table 5.9 illustrates the outcome of the concepts and respective codes of an open coded (line-by-line) interview, thereby presenting a chain of evidence (Urquhart, 2013). The number behind the codes is the frequency of occurrence of that code within the sample interview.

Table 5.9 Example of Concept Development. (Source: Own Illustration)

Concepts	Codes (number of occurrence)
1. Case-specific context	Initiation by club (2), building new stadium (3), incorporating further investors, capital increase
2. Industry context	Differing ambitions: profits vs. trophies (3), football attracting society, being under public eye, having pressure from club members if no image fit, increasing importance of money
3. Macro context	Increasing fight for symbols (5), differing business values (2), not relying on contractual bond, not accepting limits (2)

(continued)

Table 5.9 (continued)

Concepts	Codes (number of occurrence)
4. Enhancing revenue structure	Enhancing revenue potential (6)
5. Substantiating self-conception	Securing self-conception as a top club (2)
6. Shareholding	Shareholding to raise money (2), shareholding as unique move (2)
7. Managing the dyad	Connecting shareholding and sponsoring (3), handling sponsorship and equity separately (2), contract length demonstrating emphasis, sport success strengthening sponsoring goals (2)
8. Reasonableness of shareholding	Evaluating economic reasonableness (3), accretion of club shares, expecting not to lose money (2), equity features: accretion, dividends, availability (4)
9. Securing	Securing long-term bonding (6), equity being preventative measure (2)
10. Retention	Retention factor (2), implementing an obstacle (3), equity making sense if strategic though is existing, Seat of CEO in supervisory committee
11. Having a say	Having no big influence, dimension: low
12. Screening	Considering to add money to sponsorship, forecasting club growth, comparing different equity models, scenario planning (2)
13. Pre-conditions of club	Sport success at club (4), favourable site conditions (3), club history, operating in the black (2), using money sustainably (3)
14. Negotiating	Negotiating shareholding, approaching to fee based on partner service, expedition service, appreciating personal and corporate support, window of opportunity
15. Sponsoring goals	Creating awareness, getting media attention (4), transporting positive image (2)
16. Inflowing CEO passion	Inflowing CEO passion (3)
17. Amplifying emotional attachment	Subtle conviction for continuation (3), emotional attachment (6)

(continued)

Table 5.9 (continued)

Concepts	Codes (number of occurrence)
18. Partnership management	No gifts for shareholding (3), living the partnership (2), requiring steady mutual effort/input, playing both sides against each other would mean more money, exchanging information
19. Having aligned interest	Planning security at club (2), jointly yielding the best for both (2), having mutual interests (3)
20. Promoting aspects for partnership	Proximity to partner, having personal relationships
21. Corporate mission	Not being financial investor, sport being core business (3), being a global brand, sponsoring controversial of non-core, depth of partnership depending on core business
22. History of partnership	History of partnership (3), measuring sponsoring success/goal attainment
23. Yielding opportunity	Yielding opportunity (3)
24. Sounding board (in vivo)	Having competent supervisory committee, sounding board (in vivo), having economic experience, sense of unity, good interaction between partners, interaction not directly related to shareholding, introducing corporate interests, sitting at supervisory committee before shareholding, sitting at supervisory committee must-have, strong connection at committee
25. Deepening involvement	Closer relationship (2), deepening (4)
26. Understanding of one's roles	Understanding of one's roles (3), knowing one's own competence
27. Quality people	Quality people at club (3), people factor (2)
28. Supporting internationalisation	Supporting internationalisation (2)
29. Networking	Benefitting from corporate network, networking (3)
30. Equity reinforcing domain of interest	Equity reinforcing domain of interest (3), equity supports problem solving (2)
31. Threatening factor	Changing CEO (2), player transfers as risk
32. Signalising commitment	Equity as sign of support (2)

These codes and concepts are extracted from the early stage of analysis (one interview). They were regarded provisionally and are not elaborated. Also, the allocation of codes to concepts is provisional at this stage. Codes and concepts may be re-sorted and re-named if a better fit is identified during the process of analysis (Birks & Mills, 2015; Charmaz, 2006). Hence, the number of concepts were extended in the subsequent interviews (during the course of theoretical sampling), in which new relevant concepts could be classified. Furthermore, existing concepts were enriched with incoming codes. Against this, other concepts appeared not to be relevant over the analysis process. This process is depicted in two provisional theoretical models of different stages of theory development in Appendix VI. The following list (an excerpt; a full index of initial codes and provisional concepts is found in Appendix IV) exemplifies how codes and concepts were merged into initial categories (Table 5.10).

Table 5.10 Example of Increasing Level of Abstraction. (Source: Own Illustration)

Early list of codes	Early list of concepts	Higher level categories
Fit with business values Fit of image Having same management culture Having aligned interests	Compatibility	
Having football expertise Having economic expertise Integrity Having know-how	"Quality people" (in vivo)	Connecting with a symbol
Fan base high Having high media presence Having sport success Being a communication platform Being a symbol	Charisma of the club	
Raising brand awareness Improving image Emotionalising Connecting with the target group	Strengthening the corporate brand	
Exchanging information Updating partner Mutual source of inspiration Being honest	Requiring open communication	

(continued)

Table 5.10 (continued)

Early list of codes	Early list of concepts	Higher level categories
Dealing fairly Requiring mutual effort Transparency, Integrity Shareholding as additional bonding	Conduction business	Partnership management
Supervisory committee leading to closeness Amplifying emotional attachment Intensifying long-term partnership Personnel stability leading to closeness Deepening trust	Deepening involvement	Deepening involvement
Success of sponsorships Prior insight Having prior insights	History of partnership	History of partnership

The concepts could finally be clustered (via axial and selective coding) into five major categories: *connecting with a symbol, becoming a brand symbiosis, shareholding, fear of loss*, and *securing* (the core category). In order to comprehend the 'delimiting' (Glaser, 1978) as well as to retrace the initial codes, concepts, and categories, a 'codebook' (an inventory of all numbered codes related to text passages and the allocation to concepts) was created and electronically stored. Similarly, a 'memo book' (Appendix V) was generated that keeps all the memos of the study (numbered, including date, heading, and a reference to codes/concepts/categories).

Within the scope of axial coding the concepts and categories are preliminary scaled and ordered with the help of the study's specific heuristic framework (the paradigm) which allows possible networks of relationships between concepts and sub-categories to be identified (Strauss & Corbin, 1990). This paradigm is based on that from Strauss and Corbin (1990) but is adjusted to the specific context of the study to include "basic requirements" instead of intervening conditions, and "attracting factors". That better fits the nature of the study and expresses that the research phenomenon focuses on the motives of the decision-making process of why strategic equity partnerships are entered into and what attracts the parties (SQ 1) to enter into an equity partnership. Causes (casual conditions) refer to the reasons why something happens or why something is done (RQ and SQ 3). The study's specific paradigm is illustrated in Figure 5.4.

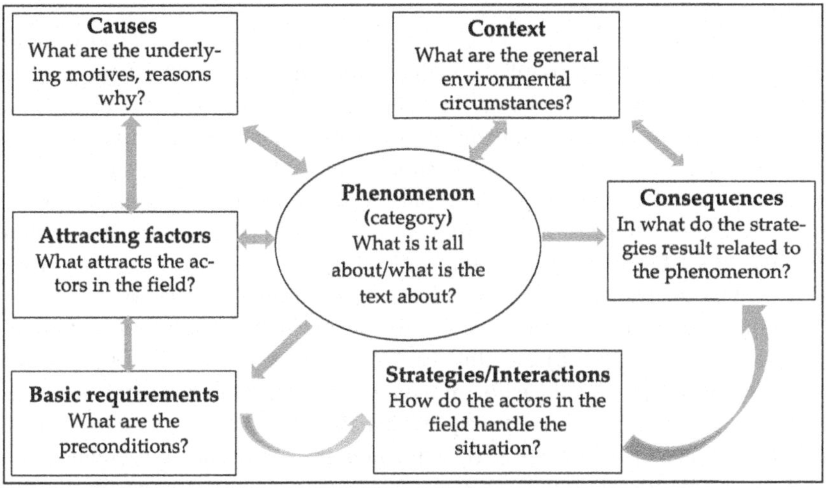

Figure 5.4 The Study's Coding Paradigm. (Source: Own Illustration, referring to Strauss & Corbin, 1990)

It should be noted that there is no intention to force the data into a preconceived framework. The paradigm rather acts as a supporting tool which is applied flexibly in order to best match the data (various categories). Therefore, not each category consists of all parts of the paradigm. For example, for some categories the paradigm consisted of three parts only, which refers to Corbin and Strauss' (2008) 'adjusted' paradigm, i.e., conditions (circumstances that lead to a particular response), actions/interactions (actions made by individuals or organisations to situations, or problems) and consequences (outcomes of inter-/action to events). This approach complies with the recommendation by Strauss and Corbin (1998) and Corbin and Strauss (2015) to not force the data into the paradigm or any other theoretical framework. Therefore, the theoretical framework of categories is flexible and is adjusted in a way to fit the data best.

However, codes within the theoretical category may have classified (answered questions) in multiple paradigmatic areas. In addition, the paradigm not only supports the data analysis but also to present the categories and concepts to the reader (form of representation). This allows the visualisation of relationships between sub-categories and concepts and illustrates the elaboration and diversity of the theory.

The following conventions have been agreed to assist the reader in identifying and integrating aspects of theoretical importance within the figures which represent the categories. Codes are hallmarked by utilising the bullet point (-). In contrast, properties and their dimensions (dimensions explain the variation within each property) are highlighted by the bullet point (). In-vivo codes are market by double quotes (e.g., "yielding opportunity"). Relationships between the various parts are illustrated using arrows. Bidirectional arrows point to interrelationships whereas monodirectional arrows imply "lead to" or "is related to". This procedure enables the reader to delve into the details of the evolving theory.

In order to present a clear structure for understanding and to prevent confusion, the theory (Chapter 6) is outlined as follows: first, in order to 'set the scene', the write-up starts with a depiction of the research context in which the actors see themselves operating. This context is divided into three areas, i.e., a case-specific, an industry, and a macro context. By explaining the context at the beginning, vital background information and environmental coherences of the specific field of inquiry are given. Next, the author explains the emergence of the theory on the basis of the major categories which are used as headings to provide some structure. The development of categories is based on empirical data and supported by the use of document analysis where appropriate.

The illustration of a category starts by describing and explaining the keynote of the category (introductory subsection of the category). In addition to that, definitional information is given to elucidate the essence of a given category. This complies with the advice put forward by Birks and Mills (2015) as well as Birks et al. (2009). While the conceptual relationships are explained the terms highlighted in italics are empirical concepts (categories, concepts codes, properties, or dimensions) that emerged from the data. Afterwards, the integration of codes, concepts, and sub-categories (of a category) is graphically illustrated by the use of the paradigm. This is to assist the reader to follow the interconnectedness of conceptual components and supports to present the findings in a consistent and coherent way. Each term of the diagrams is grounded in the data and represent either a code, property, dimension, concept, or a category.

Furthermore, references to the findings (specific text passages of the interviews) are made by incorporating quotations which reflect codes and concepts that supported the development of a category *"taking advantage of the superb chain of evidence afforded by grounded theory"* (Urquhart, 2013; 162). However, with reference to Glaser (1978), the credibility of the theory is mainly achieved by its integration and the delineation of concepts and categories. It is further recommended that quotations and descriptive statements about the data rather serve as *"illustration and imagery"* (Glaser, 1978; 134). This conforms with Strauss' (1987) advice that grounded theories should be written conceptually and longer illustrations should be minimised. Therefore, following the advice of Strauss and Corbin (1998; 283) quotations are often *"woven in with the analysis within the same or closely related sentences"*. Yet, extended quotes are appropriate for case illustrations (Strauss & Corbin, ibid.).

Each interview transcript is denoted with a "IP" (interview participant) and a number (including numbered pages and line numbers which refer to the storage medium). This procedure is pursued in order to ensure the participants' anonymity but also allows to reference back to the respective interview passage.

Since the interviews are conducted in German (except for one, which was led in English) but the dissertation is written in English, all interview quotations are translated (a translation by the author) into the English language to ensure consistency within the study. Nevertheless, in order to enable the reader to have direct access to the original text passage, this is presented in the footnote on the respective page. This complies with the advice put forward by zu Knyphausen-Aufseß (2009).

The vital role of memos as a fundamental part of analysis has already been highlighted previously. While memos are incorporated in the depiction of the emergent theory, some parts of original memos will be included where suitable to assist the reader in understanding and making sense of the grounded theory. Throughout the storyline, relevant (original) memos will be referenced since they provide insight into an integral part of the (in-depth) analysis process (Birks & Mills, 2015).

Overall, all categories are interrelated with the core category. In those categories in which some concepts and sub-categories refer to the club or corporate view only, these concepts will be highlighted by referencing to the respective view. This procedure allows idiosyncratic aspects related to a specific perspective to be sketched.

By means of triangulation[28], the survey data, which mirror the view of the club members and football fans, are statistically analysed (descriptive statistics) using SPSS[29]. Descriptive statistics provide information about the distribution of replies and allow the data to be described systematically (e.g., in the form of distribution frequency) in order to convey the substance of the data (Löffler, 2009). Moreover, by the use of contingency tables, the correlation of two variables can be displayed. Via miscellaneous forms of tables and diagrams the presentation of results should be facilitated. In regard to diagrams, distribution frequency is predominantly depicted using relative frequency (rf) as this provides a better overview compared to absolute frequency (Glück, 2018). The survey results are integrated in other categories wherever (thematically) appropriate and necessary in order to enrich the evolving theory. In accordance with the principle of consistency the survey results were translated into the English language too.

There is overall consensus in the scientific community that referencing to existing literature (theoretical integration) is an inevitable step. Corbin and Strauss (2015) advocate the integration of theoretical description, interpretation, and discussion of data to offer the reader a comprehensive understanding. By cross-referencing to the work of others it is possible to support and validate existing theories and by this means emphasise and strengthen the value of the own contribution (Birks & Mills, 2015). In order to prevent reiterations in the write-up cross-referencing to existing literature (comparing and contrasting) is made within the scope of categories in a separate section labelled 'theoretical integration' at the end of the respective category. A segregation of external theory and own empirical findings is recommended by leading grounded theorists (Glaser & Strauss, 1967) and buttressed by Glaser (2013), Charmaz (2014), and Birks and Mills (2015) in more recent years since this allows the reader exactly to see the outcomes from theory development. Via tables connections to existing literature are illustrated allowing to see accordances, contradictions, and extensions of the empirical findings at a glance. How the grounded theory answers the research question and sub-questions is finally summarised in Chapter 8.

---

[28]Data triangulation is *"a means of seeking convergence across qualitative and quantitative methods"* (Creswell, 2009; 14). Triangulation is included in the logic of grounded theory (Assmann, 2012) and allows data consistency to be cross-checked (Wahyuni, 2012), and thereby contributes to improved internal validity (Darke et al., 1998).

[29]SPSS (Statistical Package for the Social Sciences) is a software tool for statistical analysis.

5.5 Evaluation of Research Quality and Trustworthiness

The evaluation of research, ascertaining of trustworthiness[30], and taking research limitations into account are crucial components in accurately manifesting the integrity of a study (Kolb, 2012). Whether of a methodological nature, researcher's bias, a lack of transparency, or translation errors, it is crucial that the researcher acknowledges and discusses limitations as these affect research results (Yin, 2014; Creswell, 2009). Albeit it is complex to demonstrate the absolute accuracy of research, various criteria have been identified to evaluate the quality of this research project, ranging from the concept of validity[31] and reliability[32] (commonly used in quantitative studies), to criteria, which focus on the assessment of qualitative studies (e.g., credibility and transferability). Table 5.11 on page 148 summarises different sets of criteria.

Lincoln and Guba's (1985) four criteria of qualitative research focus on whether the research is conducted in a way, in which the issue under study is accurately identified and explained. The author put much effort into the literature review and investigated a broad field as suggested by Loonam (2014) and Sotiriadou and Shilbury (2008).

The paper clearly demonstrates that the topic of strategic equity partnership in the corporate football business has not yet been empirically investigated and is thus an area worthy of study.

---

[30]Trustworthiness has been classified as the conceptual soundness from which the value of qualitative research may be assessed (Bowen, 2009).

[31]Validity can be divided into three main aspects: whereas construct validity refers to whether the research instruments are accurate operational measures for the concepts being studied, internal validity seeks *"to establish a causal relationship, whereby certain conditions believed to lead to other conditions, as distinguished from spurious relationships"* (Yin, 2014; 46). External validity implies defining the domains to which the results can be generalised (Esterby-Smith et al., 2006).

[32]Reliability refers to the extent to which the operations of the study (data collection and analysis) yield consistent findings and can be repeated with the same results (Saunders et al., 2009).

Table 5.11 Evaluation Criteria. (Source: Own Illustration)

Universal/quantitative criteria	Qualitative criteria	Grounded Theory criteria	Grounded Theory criteria
• Validity • Relevance (Hammersley, 1992) • Reliability • Validity • Objectivity (Lincoln & Guba, 1985)	• Credibility • Dependability • Transferability • Conformability (Lincoln & Guba, 1985) • Intersubjective traceability • Indication of research process • Empirical anchoring • Admit limitations • Reflective subjectivity • Coherence • Relevance (Steinke, 2000, 2010; Breuer et al., 2018)	• Fit • Workability • Relevance • Modifiability • Parsimony • Scope (Glaser, 1992) • Credibility • Originality • Resonance • Usefulness (Charmaz, 2014)	• Data quality • Theory quality • Research process • Empirical grounding (Strauss & Corbin, 1998)

Glaser's quality factor of "relevance" is tackled in the introductory part of the study. Relevance is also related to fit (another term for validity) and workability (also referred to as "authenticity"; Golden-Biddle & Locke, 1993). If the theory fits the data and has explanatory and predictive power (workability), then it is relevant (Birks & Mills, 2015). Since the theory is grounded in the data, this provides empirical justification for relationships between concepts. In particular, the study can be perceived as relevant in respect to its theoretical contribution as it is the first empirical study about the topic in the field that develops theory from the specific area of sport management by using GT. Moreover, since experts in the field are interviewed and recommendations are derived from the theory the study contributes to practical relevance.

A common malaise of qualitative research is the lack of neutrality and impartiality (Chamberlain-Sataun et al., 2013; Glaser, 1978), in particular regarding the use of expert interviews as the primary data collection source. The interviews were conducted personally which could mean that the interviewees felt uncomfortable by virtue of the face-to-face situation. This may lead to distorted answers. Also, other biases may occur due to a lack of experience on the part of the researcher as regards conducting interviews (Saunders et al., 2015).

While it is acknowledged that a researcher is not likely to convey and reproduce the interview in all of its facets, this disadvantage could be lessened by recording each interview, noting the circumstances under which the interview took place as well as writing a post-interview memo directly afterwards. However, experiences in conducting interviews cannot be acquired without practice, they have to be personally made. While the researcher entered the empirical field with some experiences in leading interviews it is acknowledged that this ability was enhanced during the course of primary research.

Glaser's (1998) check about "fit and workability" also refers to whether concepts appropriately articulate the pattern in the data which it contends to conceptualise, and how the main concerns of participants are resolved respectively. In order to illustrate to readers how data interpretation and analysis was practically applied and actually implemented ("intersubjective traceability", Steinke, 2010) each coding stage is exemplified. Corbin and Strauss (1990; 18) put much emphasis on the generation (via the coding-categorising activity) of a set of concepts grounded in the data. A grounded theory monograph

> "should permit a quick, if crude, assessment of concepts merely by a check of the index to determine whether the listed concepts seem to be technical or common-sense ones, and whether there are many of them".

By the use of diagrams as a form of representing categories (and their codes and concepts) this should be ensured. In addition, to meet this requirement, a concept library is applied including a code book (Appendix IV) and a memo file (Appendix V) in order to ensure and document a rigorous research process. This should also facilitate understanding of how different codes were merged into concepts and various concepts merged into categories. The author not only tried to explain conceptual linkages between categories, but also to chart their relationships (with arrows) which supports Steinke's (2010) criterion of "coherence". Interpretations in form of concept/category development and concept linkages are further supported based on concrete examples of empirical data ("empirical grounding", Strauss & Corbin, 1990; "empirical anchoring", Steinke, 2010).

The criterion of "modifiability" (Glaser, 1998) refers to how the emerging theory is modified by new data. Referring to Glaser (ibid.), there are no right or wrong theories, but the researcher must have the ability to alter and adapt the theory to incorporate new data. By depicting diagrams from different stages of the study (theory) (Appendix VI), adaption should be illustrated.

Strauss and Corbin (1996) also maintain that doing grounded theory requires creativity from the researcher, in particular in terms of analysis. However, creativity does not refer to 'artistic freedom', rather it is the inevitable subjective personal contribution in the targeted, controlled research process. People with a deductive-nomological research logic criticise the subjective personal contribution as this involves the risk of 'idiosyncratic aberrance' (Strübing, 2018). With the goal of scrutinising his own interpretation (and analysis process), using synergies, and thinking 'out of the box', the author made use of six 'peer research support groups' (as recommended by Mey & Mruck, 2007) within the frame of grounded theory methodology workshops, which increases the fit, workability, and credibility (Lincoln & Guba, 1985). The members of the support groups reviewed excerpts of interview transcripts, provided coding thoughts, coded excerpts of interview transcripts from their point of view, discussed ideas, gave feedback about the research study (process), and presented a forum for debating the researcher's concepts and impressions. While this caused a reconsideration of former coding outcomes and led to conducting fresh coding in some places, referring to Birks and Mills (2015) this is a common procedure in GT studies and can also be regarded in the light of the "double-loop learning concept" by Argyris and Schön (1978). Overall, Savage (2005) infers that this tool improves the value of qualitative studies.

Finally, one of the inherent methods of grounded theory, constant comparison, is acknowledged as a proper tool to enhance the trustworthiness of the study. Birks and Mills (2015) have published three factors that influence the quality of grounded theory research: researcher's expertise, methodological congruence, and procedural precision. Based on these factors, Birks and Mills (ibid.) present practical explanations (questions) to each of these factors, which assist the researcher in dealing with both the applicability of grounded theory and the processes by which the theory is derived. As this framework can also act as a self-check for the researcher, application is deemed useful. While some criteria can be assessed before embarking on the primary research process (pre-check), others can only be judged at the end of the research journey (post-check). However, the framework provides beneficial insights on which aspects to concentrate on during the whole research project, and thus it will act as a guideline for the researcher. The checklist is illustrated in Appendix VII.

With regard to the online survey, much emphasis was put on ensuring the objectivity and increasing the validity (construct, internal, and external) and reliability of the study. The author focused on an elaborated questionnaire and concentrated on lucidity in interrogation and the avoidance of repetitions (accuracy of pre-information, wording, order of questions, and structure of answers), therefore serving to ensure validity. A bias due to the negatively connotated term investor was intended to be prevented by way of avoiding investor as an overall term for all types of (strategic) equity partners. Instead, the term shareholder was used and the four types of shareholders were explained at the beginning of the questionnaire. Against this, misunderstandings of the fundamental content could not entirely be ruled out due to the complexity of the topic. However, they could be minimised via explanations and definitions in the introductory part of the survey as well as further explanations of technical terms related to specific questions. Yet, by virtue of the online survey situation participants had no chance for queries. Thus, possible insecurities could not be completely avoided.

The survey was designed with an appealing and professional visual layout including a university and a survey logo and the questionnaire was extensively tested in regard to its functionality on various mobile devices and different operating systems in order to guarantee a smooth participation process. Internal consistency should be attained via the use of a pre-test. The pre-test revealed an average duration of around 10 minutes. In practice, it became apparent that the average duration was 13:45 minutes (calculated by the survey programme). Based on this, it can be assumed that participants completed the questionnaire conscientiously and seriously. Referring to Saunders et al. (2009), the completion rate of the survey of 12.5% can be regarded as above average since the average completion rate of online surveys is 11% or lower.

The online survey situation allowed respondents to pause the questionnaire and to continue at a later time, providing flexibility to participants which increases the objectivity of implementation. In addition, online questionnaires provide better control as most participants answer from their own personal computer or mobile device (Saunders et al., 2009). Since users were not attracted with an incentive, it can be assumed that they participated because they had a real interest in the topic.

Last but not least, the study could be limited in respect to linguistical and grammatical aspects on two levels. First, linguistical errors might occur due to the fact that English is not the native language of the author. To remedy this, the dissertation is being proofread by a native English speaker who works as a translator. Nevertheless, linguistic flaws can never be completely eliminated. Furthermore, the translations of the interview passages into the English language is an interpretation as such. Although much focus and care were placed on the translation of interview passages into the English language, this still remains a (corresponding) translation by the author. In order to minimise this limitation, the original interview passage was placed in the footnote to allow the reader to trace back.

To sum up, this research project does not claim to be a stringent grounded theory as presented in textbooks because the research reality did not allow to implement all GT methods dogmatically, namely the rigorous use of theoretical sampling and the assurance of a pervasive, circular process between data collection and analysis. In particular, due to their stressful jobs and time constraints, access to top managers was restricted in terms of time and required spontaneity, as such interviews had to be arranged at short notice and scheduling was not predictable. The author did, however, engage in open and axial coding in three big blocks before new interviews were conducted. Still, adaption of the research process to the actual research setting is sometimes inevitable (Birks & Mills, 2015).

The founding fathers of grounded theory state that GT methods should be applied flexibly. This is confirmed by Truschkat et al. (2005) who noted that it is even often required to adjust the methodology to satisfy the actual research circumstances. They nevertheless advice that this should only be done if the GT essentials are appropriately taken into account. For that reason, the study arrogates to be in line with the basic GT principles because these are appropriately adjusted and (flexibly) applied throughout the project. Also, the use of quantitative survey data to enrich the categories is in line with GT principles ('all is data').

5.6 Ethical Considerations

Research ethics[33] have been of great interest throughout the dissertation. Formal approval was already obtained prior to starting the research project. The author put much attention to core ethical principles such as transparency, voluntary input, no harm, data confidentiality, and anonymity of participants. Therefore, the study is conducted with special care and sensitivity, places great attention on honesty, treating people fairly, and protecting participants' rights, interests, and privacy.

Throughout the theoretical sampling process any discrimination due to age, nationality, or any other is prevented. Therefore, sampling and case study selection is guided by clear criteria towards theory generation and data saturation. Additionally, the sampling process and concrete measures within the study are

[33] *"Research ethics refer to the application of a moral code of conduct when human participants are the focus of empirical research"* (Biggam, 2011; 249).

made transparent to all participants and case companies in personal conversations and/or via e-mail.

To ensure participants were properly informed before participating in the interview/study an informed consent form was presented and signed by the researcher and all participants before starting interviews. This includes the right of participants to withdraw from the study at any point without stating any reasons. To avoid deception and falsification, interviews were recorded and the parts for publication were subject to participant checking. Overall, these ethical considerations may enhance a positive research atmosphere throughout the process of data collection and analysis.

5.7 Summary of Research Design

This Chapter explains and justifies the research design by discussing and presenting the study's philosophical position related to ontology, epistemology, and methodology. Due to the exploratory nature of the research question a mainly qualitative research approach is deemed appropriate which still allows a variety of methods (qualitative and quantitative) to be utilised. By implication, this Chapter thoroughly justifies the use of grounded theory as the study's underlying research methodology.

Grounded theory enables consideration of various perspectives of strategic equity partnerships between sponsors and football clubs to be integrated into the study via the flexible use of qualitative and quantitative data. It further provides in-depth insights into the phenomenon and fosters theory development on the specific field under study.

Qualitative and quantitative data collection methods have been described and the circular process of theory generation (data collection and analysis) has been explained and illustrated step-by-step. Essential grounded theory methods were introduced and how they are applied in this study. A reflective commentary provides insights into theoretical preconditions. Finally, ethical considerations were addressed and limitations acknowledged.

their consent to all participants and case companies in personal conversations [illegible]

To ensure participants were properly informed before participating in the survey, a standardized consent form was presented and signed by the interviewer and all participants before starting interviews. This includes the right of participants to withdraw from the study at any point without stating any reason. [illegible] interviews were recorded and the participants [illegible]

5.7 Summary of Research Design

[illegible]

6 Empirical Findings and Discussion

6.1 Introduction

This Chapter presents the empirical findings of the study by use of the storyline technique and discusses the results against the existing body of knowledge from the literature review as outlined in Chapter 2, 3 and 4. Initially, the broader contextual relationships of the research field are described in order to deliver a framework for orientation. Based on this, the theory is illustrated and explained through the categories, sub-categories, and concepts. The main categories can be found in the different sections of this Chapter and the corresponding sub-categories and concepts are embedded within each subsection. Each section/category is completed by a 'theoretical integration' part in which the empirical concepts are compared and contrasted in relation to the literature.

As has been announced in Chapter 3, at the end (Sect. 6.9) it will be drawn on the definition of strategic partnership and strategic equity partnership to present a valid definition in this specific research context. Finally, a summary of the empirical findings is presented.

Electronic Supplementary Material The online version of this chapter (https://doi.org/10.1007/978-3-658-31301-2_6) contains supplementary material, which is available to authorized users.

T. Duffner, *Strategic Equity Partnerships in Professional Football*, Event- und Impaktforschung, https://doi.org/10.1007/978-3-658-31301-2_6

6.2 Overview of the Research Context

6.2.1 Introduction

The overall research context is classified into three different context layers (i.e., *macro context, industry context*, and *case-specific context*) in which the research phenomenon is embedded. This consists of the conditions and circumstances under which the agents in the field (clubs, football fans, and sponsors) operate and in which strategic equity partnerships in the corporate football business in Germany are entered and managed. This part will 'set the scene' by introducing the terms of the context to the reader. How the context is related to the main categories of the study will be explained during the course of theory development (context as a component of the paradigm).

6.2.2 Macro, Industry, and Case-Specific Context

The *macro context* describes the overall trends in the broader business world and refers to societal, economical, and international trends which have wider implications on the phenomenon. The concept of *differing ambitions* refers to the contrasting nature between the two key agents in the research field, professional football clubs in Germany and their corporate sponsors.

Football clubs operate in a system which is characterised by an intensive link to club members and fans (fans as the third key agent) who are very *emotional* and who are perceived as the *personification of the club*. Football clubs and their fans' main interest is to win football matches, according to IP 1 (4; 2):

> "In fact, they [the fans] want their football team to spend every single penny and more on players. [...] You know there is a huge amount of money now, but fans want better players. They are not interested in making money".

Whereas football clubs are managed to achieve the best sporting results, the corporate sponsor's ultimate goal is to make money. IP 1 (4; 21) emphasises that, at the end of the day, a corporation *"needed to make money and they needed to win football matches. They are not entirely incompatible, but they are not entirely compatible either"*. These *differing ambitions* imply that both clubs and corporations are run with a different *management focus*. IP 5 (77; 12) explains the concept of *differing ambitions* and its link to the concept of *fans as personification of the club* in the following way:

> "If I make a profit of 10 million in a corporation the press will celebrate. If a make a profit of 10 million as a sport club and I am at the bottom of the table they string me up. In turn, if I claim a 10 million loss but I am under the first four in the table I am the greatest. Completely different to the economy. You need success and if you have success there is quiet on the interest-rate front".[1]

While this statement indicates the differing *management focus* the military diction used by IP 5 illustrates the power of fans and reveals the focus of the corporate's and club's management efforts. It also demonstrates the *differing ambitions* and it becomes evident that for clubs *"[...] the highest priority is the maximisation of sporting success while avoiding insolvency"*[2] (IP 9, 140; 22).

Nowadays, football is a source of permanent attention in society *(football attracting society) independent from the trade cycle.* This feature of being *"top of the pops"* (IP 22, 391; 8) is a main reason for the *growing football business* and underlines football's social emphasis. The high attractiveness of football has various implications. Due to increased media attention in which the agents in the field are permanently *under permanent public eye,* football clubs are seen as an effective *"communication platform"* to convey advertising and communication messages.

The media appear as another main agent in the area as clubs generate major income streams via e.g., TV-broadcasting rights. Moreover, the media act as a national and international distributor for club sponsors (and their communication messages). IP 9 (135; 24) even says that football clubs have become *"media companies"* which *"successfully merchandise a specific content, and this content is football"*.[3] While this can be blessing for clubs and their commercial partners in

---

[1] *„Wenn ich in einem Wirtschaftsunternehmen 10 Millionen gewinn mache, feiert mich die ganze Presse. Wenn ich in einem Sportverein 10 Millionen Gewinn mache und bin auf dem letzten Tabellenplatz, dann hängen sie mich auf. Das heißt, wenn ich 10 Millionen Verlust mache und bin unter den ersten 4, bin ich der Große. Völlig anders als es in der Wirtschaft draußen ist. Also sie brauchen auch Erfolg. Und wenn sie Erfolg haben auf die Dauer, ist auch Ruhe an der Front"* (IP 5, 77; 12).

[2] *„[...] höchstes Ziel ist eben letztendlich die Maximierung des sportlichen Erfolges unter Vermeidung der Insolvenz"* (IP 9, 140; 22).

[3] *„[...] sie letztendlich heutzutage ein Medienunternehmen geworden sind. Das ist/ sie vermarkten erfolgreich einen bestimmten Content und dieser Content ist Fußball"* (IP 9, 135; 24).

times of success, being *under permanent public eye* implies that the (business) actions of clubs and corporations are transparent. This can have diverse negative effects on the management of clubs and their business partnerships too *(intensifying consequences)*, because *"there are just issues in which you become a plaything for the media. Either way, we are always in the focus"*[4] (IP 24, 436; 10). Upon analysing the diction used by IP 3 (57; 2) it becomes obvious that the relationships with the media are conflict-laden: *"This starts by entering a deal with the devil, the media"*.[5]

In modern times, the business environment has become highly competitive for clubs and corporations. This results in a *change of business values* in which money occupies a major role *(increased focus on money)* on both sides. This is accentuated by IP 8 (122; 23) who stated that *"nowadays relatively large amount of emphasis is placed on money and of course partly beyond a pecuniary engagement"*.[6] With respect to the football business, the focus on money becomes obvious due to the *correlation between revenues and sport success*. IP 8 (130; 36) mentioned: *"There is a correlation between revenues and success in football"*.[7]

For clubs, money gains centre stage as it serves as a tool for winning football matches and securing the club's competitiveness. This is amplified given the *unique nature of football* in the various football leagues across Europe. This implies different preconditions of clubs in generating (additional) money, e.g., in terms of *diverse governance structures* (i.e., the opportunity to sell majority club shares, the 50+1 rule in Germany). IP 9 (156; 22) states that *"[...] in England these [equity partnerships] are all majority participations"*.[8] However, this not

---

[4] *„[...] es gibt einfach Themen, da wird man so zum Spielball von Medien. Wir sind ja sowieso immer im Fokus"* (IP 24, 436; 10).

[5] *„Das fängt ja schon an eben damit, dass du einen Pakt mit dem Teufel, den Medien eingegangen bist"* (IP 3, 57; 2).

[6] *„Es geht da heutzutage schon relativ viel ums Geld und es geht natürlich teilweise noch ein bisschen ein Engagement über die reine finanzielle Geschichte hinaus"* (IP 8, 122; 23).

[7] *„Es gibt eine Korrelation zwischen Einnahmen und Erfolg im Fußball"* (IP 8, 130; 36).

[8] *„Du siehst ja, in England sind das alles Mehrheitsbeteiligungen"* (IP 9, 156; 22).

only applies for the EPL but for all other leagues across Europe. As a result of this, German football clubs are faced with *increased revenues from international competition.* This is exacerbated by higher TV revenues especially in England which demands that German clubs find ways to address this in order to remain internationally competitive. With reference to IP 12 (210; 12):

> "That is why growth is required because we see that we [club name], in the international context of the Champions League, are faced with competitors who are able to reckon with different revenue streams. Take a look at England which is confronted, or rather blessed with a huge increase in TV money. [...] In the Bundesliga, the competition is just differently structured".[9]

The 50+1 rule leads to heated discussions not only among German clubs in connection with competitiveness, but also among football fans as IP 12 (230; 21) outlined:

> "And you will see, if you repeal the 50+1 you will start a race among investors or those who see themselves as such but who, in fact, are not. If Russian oligarchs or Arabs come on board with massive cash injections then they will totally dismantle sporting competitiveness".[10]

The central relevance of fans in the management of a club emerged as a crucial topic in the research field for clubs and corporate partners which leads to the category *fear of loss* (which will be referred to posterior) and which has implications

[9] *„Wachstum ist deswegen notwendig, weil wir eben sehen, dass wir heute, wir als [Clubname], im internationalen Konzert der Champions League insbesondere Wettbewerber haben, die mit ganz anderen Revenue-Streams rechnen können. Schauen sie nach England, die mit explosionsartig Steigerungen im TV Geld konfrontiert sind, oder beglückt sind. [...] In der Bundesliga haben wir den Wettbewerb etwas anders strukturiert"* (IP 12, 210; 12).

[10] *„Und da werden sie sehen, wenn sie die 50+1 Regel kippen, dann haben sie ja das Rennen der Investoren, oder Derjenigen, die sich als solches bezeichnen, aber keine sind. Wenn die russischen Oligarchen oder Araber plötzlich an Board bekommen, die mit massiver Cash Injektion in die Clubs unterwegs sind, dann werden die die sportliche Wettbewerbsfähigkeit total auseinandernehmen"* (IP 12, 230; 21).

on the management of the corporate club partnership. IP 15 (278; 23) provided background information:

> "Mutual activities for the benefit of the club and also for the benefit of the fans. Naturally, one must not lose sight of the fact that there is a fan culture which is extremely sensitive and it is not our interest to do anything negatively on fan culture".[11]

The *case-specific context* involves the individual situations and circumstances of clubs and sponsors in a concrete case, which affects the formation of a strategic equity partnership. In all individual cases, entering into a strategic equity partnership follows a trigger. The underlying motives will be explained during this Chapter within the scope of the core category *securing*. Depending on the individual case, one partner initiates the shareholding to the other. The recipient of the shareholding inquiry is faced with a *"yielding opportunity"* in which fundamental parameters are evaluated (i.e., *need*, the *availability of shares, compatibility,* etc.). If these criteria are assessed positively, in-depth *"screening"* is started. The critical point is that entering into a strategic equity partnership is complex and requires many aspects to be considered for both partners.

The research is embedded in three layers of context that provide crucial background information in order to understand the issue under investigation. Figure 6.1 on page 161 presents an overview of that context and illustrates the relationships between its concepts.

[11] *„Gemeinsame Aktivitäten im Wohle des Vereins und auch im Wohle der Fans. Und natürlich immer im Auge: Vorsicht, es gibt eine Fankultur, die sind extrem sensibel und wir haben auch kein Interesse und wollen auch nichts tun, was diese Fankultur negativ tangiert oder stört"* (IP 15, 278; 23).

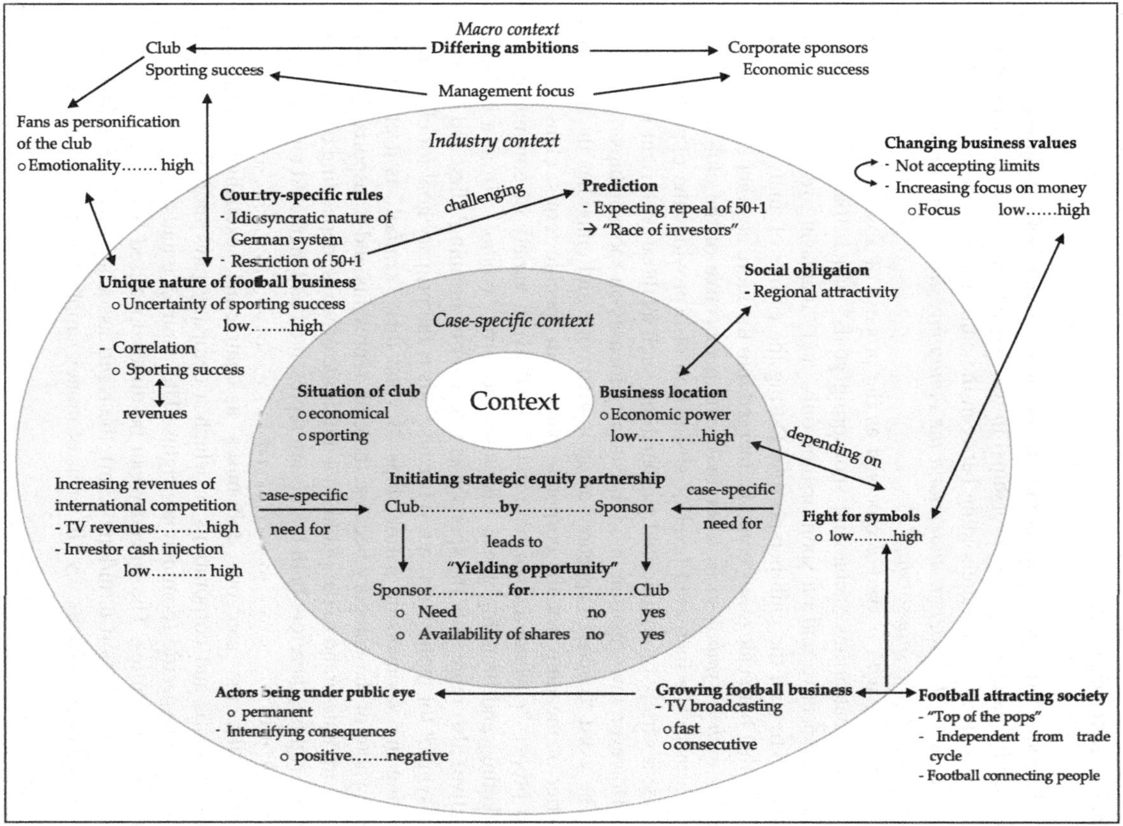

Figure 6.1 Empirical Research Context. (Source: Own Illustration)

6.3 Connecting with a Symbol

6.3.1 Introduction

This category looks at why corporations and professional football clubs enter into commercial partnerships (sponsorships) in the first place. This is fundamental in order to understand a shareholding between the club and sponsor, as IP 15 (269; 8) explained: *"In order to understand the equity investment one has to supply a background to the sponsorship".*[12]

Connecting with a symbol emerged as the process of abstraction of the two provisional categories "achieving sponsoring goals" which focused on the corporate perspective and on sponsorships only, and "increasing revenue streams" which centres on the club perspective. During the course of analysis, it became evident that both categories could be merged into the more abstract category *connecting with a symbol* so as to embrace the perspective of the club and corporate partner. The increased level of abstraction also provides the opportunity to include a variety of commercial partnerships, such as those with right marketers, too. However, investigation into this category focuses on sponsorships.

The word *"symbol"* appeared as an in vivo code and embodies the club as a 'carrier of meaning' for the corporate partner. In specific terms, clubs are seen as a proper *"communication platform"* to achieve a variety of communication, marketing, and branding goals. Likewise, the term *"symbol"* (from a club perspective) also represents the sponsor as a 'carrier of meaning', first and foremost as a symbol for money (revenues) because this is the primary goal for clubs upon entering into sponsorship partnerships. Beyond this, *"symbol"* is deemed to fit the keynote of the category because the club represents and transports the sponsor's corporate brand to the public in a multitude of ways (depending on the sponsorship rights), therefore both brands are represented and marketed together to the outside world.

Basically, the category epitomises a contractual, exchange partnership between clubs and corporations in which a company pays money to a club in exchange of specific (commercial) rights. The contract entails all the rights and duties of the parties. The category can be dimensionalised based on its properties of *duration* (short-term/long-term), the *rights* associated with the partnership (dispersed/exclusive), its *size* (in terms of money supplied to the club in exchange

[12]*„Man muss, um das Aktieninvestment verstehen zu können, muss man ein bisschen ausholen in Richtung Sponsoring"* (IP 15, 269; 8).

of rights), and the *scope* of the partnership (national/international), which depends on the business reach of the parties involved. *Connecting with a symbol* subsumes diverse concepts that can be classified into the sub-categories of *attracting factors, causes, basic requirements, partnership facilitating, strategy,* and *context.* How these sub-categories and concepts work in concert are explained in the following.

6.3.2 Attracting Factors, Causes, and Strategy

While the high attractivity of football has already been illustrated as a contextual element, the sub-category *attracting factors* comprises those aspects that make a specific club appealing for a corporate partner. The central attracting property of a club is the capacity to elicit surgency which is reflected in the concept *"charisma of a club"*. The *"charisma of a club"* finds expression in a *huge fan base, media presence, (media) reach*, and *high brand awareness*. This concept strongly correlates to the *sporting success* and the *brand image* of the club. For example, a huge fan base affects the club's (social) media reach (e.g., in terms of followers at Twitter). Similarly, the greater the sporting success, the higher the (media) interest and public attention which, in turn, raises the reach and brand awareness of the club as well as positively affecting the *"charisma of the club"*, according to IP 12 (221; 1):

> "The better our sporting performance the better our charisma, both nationally and internationally, and the easier it is to attract new/not necessarily strategic partners but sponsoring partners who attribute a higher value to the sponsoring rights".[13]

While this quotation refers to the club's charisma, the appealing role of charisma is a mutual concept and refers to the sponsor too, as can be extracted by the following statement from IP 24 (411; 14): *"It is the goal that one benefits from the mutual charisma"*.[14] Consequently, on the one hand, the club's charisma is a

[13]*„Ja, desto mehr unsere sportliche Leistungsfähigkeit, desto mehr unsere Strahlkraft ist, national wie auch international, desto einfacher ist es natürlich möglich, neu / jetzt nicht unbedingt strategische Partner, aber Sponsoring Partner zu gewinnen, die auch den Wert, den Sponsoringrechten einen höheren Wert beimessen"* (IP 12, 221; 1).

[14]*„Das ist schon das Ziel, dass man einfach davon profitiert der gegenseitigen Strahlkraft"* (IP 24, 411; 14).

central attracting factor for companies to partner with a football club. On the other hand, the corporate charisma is a supportive aspect in attracting further sponsors for a club. A pool of accepted sponsors indicates the opportunity to connect with other organisations (sponsors) for the sake of *networking* and *generating business*.

The objectives of why clubs and corporations enter into sponsorships are subsumed in the sub-category *causes*. By entering into a sponsorship relationship, football clubs and corporations both have the objective of *increasing revenues*. However, the difference between the two parties is that for clubs *increasing revenues* is a *direct* objective (and outcome) as well as primary goal due to the *correlation between sporting success and revenues* (industry context). For sponsors, *increasing revenues* is rather an *indirect* goal because the sponsor chiefly uses the partnership for *strengthening the CB* (the primary corporate goal) which, in turn, aims to generate revenues. IP 12 (212; 10) presents the "logic" of the corporate football sponsorship:

> "And the more successful a brand or a club such as [club name] is in respect to sports, the stronger the emotionalisation and positive values related with success are reflected in the sponsoring partnership. And ultimately, this is depicted economically via money".[15]

Corporations try to find ways to connect with their target group (*meeting target group* as a basic requirement) and attract attention in society as a whole and also among (potential) customers. Due to the aforementioned significance and attractiveness of football in society *(football attracting society, football connecting people),* football clubs are seen as a "*platform*"for *strengthening their CB*. According to IP 14 (251; 23): *"That means football as a platform to promote the own brand is extremely interesting".*[16] The concept *strengthening*

---

[15] *„Und desto sportlich erfolgreich eine Marke ist oder ein Club wie [Clubname], desto mehr Emotionalisierung, positive Werte, verbunden mit Erfolg und so weiter liegt auch in so einer Sponsorenpartnerschaft. Und das wird am Ende ja ökonomisch abgebildet durch Geld"* (IP 12, 221; 10).

[16] *„Das heißt, Fußball ist als Plattform, um mit seiner Marke zu werben, schon natürlich hoch interessant"* (IP 14, 251; 23).

the CB contains a variety of concepts which represents a sponsor's goals, such as *emotionalisation, creating awareness, image transfer, and employer branding.*

The image and awareness objective have in common that their emphasis (and effects) can differ over the years of a sponsorship. For example, *creating awareness,* in concert with *improving image,* one of the traditional sponsorship goals, is of great relevance at the beginning of a sponsorship relationship due to a *"novelty effect".* Over time, *creating awareness* loses its initial impact as *"the marginal return of our engagement [lead sponsoring] at [club name] is lessened on the one hand, because the novelty effect is not present"*[17] (IP 14, 258; 18). By *improving image,* the sponsor tries to transfer specific image factors of the club to its own brand in order to change the attitude and perception of consumers. Awareness and image objectives are normally achieved within a timeframe of three to five years, with reference to IP 17 (308; 3):

> "In the past, one engaged in sponsoring for a limited time of approximately 3-5 years only and then one decided to quit because the awareness goals and also the image goals have largely been achieved anyway".[18]

However, a longer-term sponsorship which goes beyond that timeframe provides the opportunity to transfer other partnership-related image effects, for example continuity and reliability: "A *long-term partnership has a positive impact in terms of images aspects such as reliability and continuity and this again helps"*[19] (IP 14, 258; 25).

Emotionalisation emerged as another dominant concept in the empirical data. *Emotionalisation* builds upon the *high emotionality* of football and football fans and refers to the intent to create sympathy among a target group and infusing one's own brand with the positive emotions of football. The priority of pursuing this goal via a sponsorship can be related to the corporate mission.

[17]*„[...] der Grenzertrag unseres Engagements [Hauptsponsoring] wie [Clubname], der wird auf der einen Seite geringer, weil eben der Neuigkeitsaspekt eben nicht da"* (IP 14, 258; 18).

[18]*„Früher hat man ja oft Sponsorships für eine bestimmte Zeit nur betrieben, man musste so Mindestlaufzeiten von 3-5 Jahren machen, hat dann aber irgendwann entschieden, wir gehen da wieder raus, weil ich meine Bekanntheitsziele dann sowieso erreicht habe und die Imageziele auch im Großen und Ganzen [...]"* (IP 17, 308; 3).

[19]*„Also, eine lange Partnerschaft zahlt natürlich auch ein in Imagewerte wie Verlässlichkeit, Kontinuität und da hilft es dann wieder"* (IP 14, 258; 25).

Frequently, those corporations whose *core business* is based on intangible goods, products and services, characterised by only few touchpoints with clients, or whose core business is detached from sport in general (e.g., insurance companies) use sponsorships with football clubs predominantly to *emotionalise* their own brand. With reference to IP 10 (164; 16):

> "Where we come from. We have always said we primarily want to use sponsoring in order to emotionalise the brand. We are in an industry in which intangible goods exist".[20]

Corporations further enter into sponsorships to be perceived as an attractive employer (*employer branding*) who cares for its employees (*internal focus*) and, in addition to this, make the company attractive for potential jobholders (*external focus*). This concept primarily operates in a context in which the club and sponsor are located in the same region. *Employer branding* interrelates to the concept of *"social obligation"*. Companies deem to feel responsible for their native region. Due to the positive *impact of football on society* (context), corporations seem to perceive a sponsorship with a football club in the same region (due to a regional affinity) as an appropriate strategy to demonstrate social responsibility and show good *"corporate citizenship"*. This is mirrored in the following statement from IP 22 (397; 6):

> "This is expected by the fans, the employees but also the region, that you become involved as an attractive employer. Logically, it is still obvious that this is a region-specific sport engagement. It is rather a social obligation instead of a corporate-strategic obligation".[21]

Strengthening the CB is interdependent with the concept of *"door opener"*. *"Door opener"* is a higher ordered concept that embraces the concepts *establishing new business contacts* (personal), *penetrating markets*, and *positioning the brand* in the target markets. It refers to the club and corporate perspective equally. Table 6.1 on page 167 provides evidence for the concept and reflects the process of abstraction.

[20] *„Wo wir herkommen. Wir haben immer gesagt, wir wollen vor allem das Thema Sponsoring einsetzten, um die Marke emotionalisieren. Wir sind in einer Industrie, wo nichtgreifbare Güter existieren"* (IP 10, 164; 16).

[21] *„[...], das erwarten dann zum einen die Fans, die Mitarbeiter, auch die Region, dass man sich da als attraktiver Arbeitgeber auch engagiert. Aber logischerweise war immer klar, es ist ein regionalspezifisches Sportengagement, es ist eher eine gesellschaftliche Verpflichtung, aber jetzt nicht die unternehmensstrategische Verpflichtung"* (IP 22, 397; 6).

Table 6.1 The "Door Opener" Concept. (Source: Own Illustration)

Higher ordered concept	Concepts	Empirical proof
"Door opener"	Establishing new business contacts	*"And it helps to open the doors. It does not support the generation of business, but it does help to open doors. I'd say contacts to other big companies and also to other markets. Gaining access* via *VIP contacts here and there was really very, very positive. Very, very positive"*[a] (IP 22, 405; 21). *"Someone who, in addition to this, opens the door for the club, establishing new business contacts"*[b] (IP 4, 60; 30).
	Penetrating new markets	*"They recognised that they have a door opener with the partnership with [club]. In fact, nationally and internationally because they are known"*[c] (IP 12; 208, 35). *"The idea with [club] was this market penetration"*[d] (IP 6, 89; 1).
	Positioning the brand	*"Of course, the idea is that the partners are all top brands [...] and with their brand strength they are easily able to position and transport us in the various countries"*[e] (IP 2, 15; 11).

[a]*„Und es hilft schon, die Türen zu öffnen. Es hilft dir nicht das Geschäft zu machen. Aber zu mindestens tust du dich leichter, mal eine Tür aufzumachen. Ich sage mal die Kontakte zu anderen großen Unternehmen, auch zu anderen Märkten. Oder da mal über VIP Kontakten hier und da mal reinzukommen war wirklich sehr, sehr positiv. Sehr, sehr positiv"* (IP 22, 405; 21)

[b]*„[...] jemand der eben darüber hinaus dem Verein Türen aufmacht, neue Geschäftskontakte damit eröffnet"*(IP 4, 60; 30)

[c]*„Sie haben dann gemerkt, dass sie mit der Partnerschaft Borussia Dortmund Door Opener haben. Und zwar national als auch international, weil man sie kennt"*(IP 12, 208; 35)

[d]*„Die Idee war mit [Club], diese Market Penetration"*(IP 6, 89; 1)

[e]*„Die Idee dabei ist natürlich die, dass die Partner alle Top-Brands sind, [...] und mit ihrer Markenstärke uns natürlich wesentlich leichter positionieren und transportieren können in den unterschiedlichen Ländern"* (IP 2, 15; 11)

The emphasis on *penetrating markets* and *positioning the brand* can be aligned based on the dimension *focus* (regional/international). This principally depends on whether the sponsored club aims to qualify for international competition. In this case, the sponsorship is internationally focused. On condition of partnering with a club with national sport ambitions the sponsorship is rather nationally focused. However, this is just a principal focus which is open to change or alignment.

The presented sponsorship goals bear on the type of sponsorship *strategy* (sub-category) between the club and corporation. The four major types of sponsorships identified in the research area, which have major implications on the research phenomenon, are the lead (jersey) sponsoring, stadium name right sponsoring, kit (equipment) sponsoring, and car sponsoring. These types of sponsorships do not only constitute the biggest sponsoring sums, but are also the sponsorships with which clubs prefer to enter into strategic equity partnerships in German football. According to IP 12 (207; 14):

> "Of course, our first contacts are the core sponsors, namely the lead sponsor, kit sponsor, and naming right partner for the stadium, because these also depict the biggest sponsoring volumes".[22]

Even though the various sponsorship goals apply for all types of sponsorships, there are still some focus areas associated with the specific sponsorship form. Table 6.2 on page 169 builds upon Memo 196 (from 21 November 2018) that provides an impression of the emphasis of goals with respect to the four sponsorship types.

[22] *„Und da sind natürlich die Kernsponsoren für uns die ersten Ansprechpartner, sprich Hauptsponsor, Ausrüster oder Namensrechtsgeber für ein Stadion, weil die auch die größten Sponsoringvolumen abbilden"* (IP 12, 207; 14).

Table 6.2 Memo 196—Goals of Different Sponsorship Types. (Source: Own Illustration)

196_Memo_Emphasis of sponsorship types_21 November 2018

Emphasis

low high

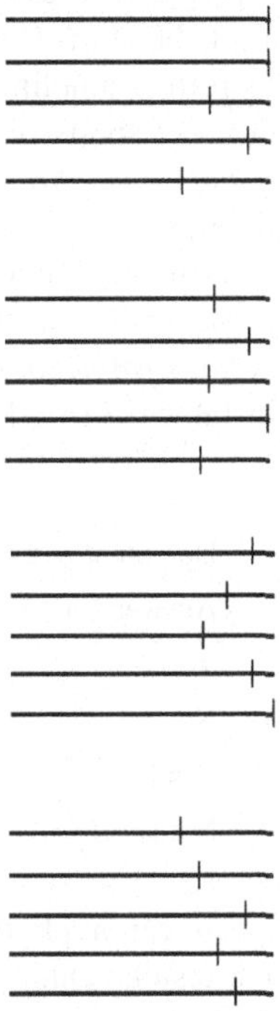

Lead sponsoring
- Awareness/media attention
- "door opener"
- image effect
- emotionalisation
- employer branding

Stadium name right sponsoring
- awareness/media attention
- "door opener"
- image effect
- emotionalisation
- employer branding

Kit sponsoring
- awareness/media attention
- "door opener"
- image effects
- emotionalisation
- employer branding

Car sponsoring
- awareness/media attention
- "door opener"
- image effect
- emotionalisation
- employer branding

The dimensions presented in the table are not fixed but rather flexibly adjusted depending on a case-specific context and also differ according to specific business situations and circumstances. Therefore, this illustration acts as a rough orientation on the *emphasis of goals related to the four types of sponsorships*.

A lead sponsorship attracts the most media attention and awareness since the brand logo of the sponsors is visible on every jersey from the club. Wherever the club appears in the media the club represents its lead sponsor, too. Therefore, one of the main goals associated with lead sponsoring is *creating awareness*. Although this refers to the kit sponsor too, the kit sponsor usually only has a small logo on the attire compared to the lead sponsor whose advertising space is spread across the front of the shirt. Both sponsorship types have in common that an awareness effect is further amplified by jersey sales. Another key goal of the kit sponsor (as a producer of sportswear) is to enhance the credibility of their company *(authenticity of the sports brand)*. However, *creating awareness* and *improving image* also rank high.

Improving image appears to be a main goal of the lead sponsor too, even though there are controversial views on this issue. This is mainly based on the *majority of fans having a favourite team* (industry context) which is verified by the fan survey as shown in Table 6.3 (n = 1,589).

Table 6.3 Fans Have a Favourite Team. (Source: Own Illustration)

Do you have a favourite club?		
Answer options	**Frequency**	**Percent**
Yes	1572	98,9
No	13	0,8
Total	1585	99,7
Not specified	4	0,3

Being thrilled about a team can imply that fans are against the opposing team, at least in respect to match results. Due to the fact that a lead sponsor is on the front of the team shirt, a lead sponsor also plays against another lead sponsor. The perception of *"being against"* might be conveyed to the sponsor and therefore could have a negative impact, according to IP 22 (397; 16):

> "That was a conscious decision because we are neither the main sponsor at [club name] nor are we main sponsor here. I do not want that [company A] plays against [company B] or [company C] against [company D] in [location]. This is not our intention".[23]

[23]„*Das war auch eine bewusste Entscheidung. Denn wir sind weder beim [Club] auf der Brust, noch sind wir hier auf der Brust. Ich möchte auch nicht [Unternehmen A] gegen [Unternehmen B] spielen, oder [Unternehmen C] gegen [Unternehmen D] in [Ort]. Das ist nicht unsere Intention*" (IP 22, 397; 16).

In contrast to a lead sponsor, a stadium name right sponsor focuses its sponsorship on *emotionalisation* and *improving image* by aligning their strategy to the football match event. With reference to IP 15 (275; 11):

> "That is why we have said that tricot sponsoring is not an issue for us because one is always against someone else. One plays in the [stadium name] in which a good match takes place but one always playing against someone else. [...] What we want to avoid is that someone plays against [corporate name]".[24]

Moreover, since a stadium name right sponsorship is fixed to the location of the stadium it has (mainly) a regional focus. This type of sponsorship seems to require a very long-term view in order to get the desired effects in particular in relation to 'traditional clubs'. Many club fans have a positive association to the original stadium (name) of their club because often the name has existed (except in the case of a new construction) as long as the club itself. Fans, therefore, link the stadium name with previous victories and the history of their club. According to IP 15 (270; 22):

> "All those who know the tradition of the club, a club which embraces its past like hardly any other, they are naturally connected with stadium [stadium name A] and later [stadium name B] from its history, so one has to carefully consider renaming the stadium into [new stadium name]. This is of course/clear and all those involved were well aware that it would encounter massive resistance from the fan base".[25]

This statement illustrates that a stadium name right sponsoring can arouse conflicting reactions in particular on the part of the club's fans. Whereas the other types of sponsorships are widely established and accepted, a stadium name right sponsorship is still a sensitive issue. A look at the sponsorships of Bundesliga clubs is evidence of this. All clubs engage in main (jersey), kit, and car sponsoring. However, 14 out of 18 club in the Bundesliga market their stadium name rights in the 2018/2019 season (document analysis, Stadionwelt, 2018). Selling the stadium name appears as another step towards commercialisation and

[24] „*Und deswegen haben wir auch gesagt, die Trikotwerbung ist für uns deshalb kein Thema gewesen, weil man ja immer gegen spielt. Man spielt im [Stadoinname], da findet ein gutes Spiel statt, aber man spielt immer gegen. Wenn jetzt auf dem Trikot steht gegen [Unternehmen], wir wollen gar nicht, dass irgendjemand gegen [Unternehmen] spielt*" (IP 15, 275; 11).

[25] „*Wer die Tradition dieses Vereins kennt, der ja nun auch die Tradition wie kaum ein anderer Verein lebt und natürlich auch mit dem Stadion [Stadionname A] aus der Historie heraus, später [Stadionname B] in einer Art verbunden ist, das man sich schon gut überlegen musste, so ein Stadion umzubenennen in [neuer Stadionname], das ist natürlich schon / das war allen Beteiligten klar, das wird auch auf massiven Widerstand in der Fangemeinde stoßen*" (IP 15, 270; 22).

is often perceived as a "loss of tradition" (Wolf, 2012). This fan concern becomes a central phenomenon in the theory and will be meticulously explained within the frame of the category *fear of loss*.

6.3.3 Basic Requirements and Facilitating Partnership

The mutual preconditions (basic requirements) for a sponsorship are largely manifested in the concept of *compatibility*. Especially in industries linked to high emotionality such as football, compatibility between partners is significant, according to IP 3 (40; 25):

> "Ultimately, this is the same as with other mergers. Strategic compatibility has to be verified. And in a context which is linked to emotions, such as football, this is extremely important".[26]

Compatibility essentially refers to whether there is a sufficient strategic basis between the club and sponsor for effective and successful collaboration. For both partners it is fundamental to have e.g., the same *goals*, *business values*, *image*, and similar (compatible) *management cultures*. The latter concept refers to the way of thinking and the basic beliefs and affects how the business people interact as it implicates the *norms*, (*business* and *ethical*) *values*, *management style*, and *mindsets* the associates bring to the partnership.

In terms of *compatibility* of *image*, two opposing approaches are classified. On the one hand, the *image* can be *similar* which allows the image to be positively strengthened mutually. On the other hand, the *image* can also be *opposing* which allows one party (normally the sponsor) to benefit from the club's image. Although corporations try to improve their image by *connecting with a symbol,* the *compatibility* of image is, from a club's view, linked to the sponsor's branch. Irrespective of the specific company, the branch in which a firm operates is a criterion for clubs when to entering into a sponsorship. This refers to branches of a controversial nature. IP 20 (378; 16) specified: *"If they fit into the canon of values. Like I said, something like the arms industry or human rights abuses are issues which [club name] pays very close attention to"*.[27]

[26] *„Das ist im Endeffekt das gleich wie bei anderen Fusionen, dass die strategische Kompatibilität halt vorher überprüft werden soll. Und da, wo es halt noch mit Emotionen verbunden ist, wie im Fußball, ist es halt besonders wichtig"* (IP 3, 40; 25).

[27] *„Ja, gerade also ob Sie da in den Wertekanon hineinpassen. Wie gesagt, so etwas wie Rüstungsindustrie oder Menschenrechtsverletzung das sind Themen, wo der [Club] sehr, sehr intensiv darauf achtet"* (IP 20, 378; 16).

Compatibility is furthermore linked to the *organisational colours*. Whilst the compatibility of organisational colours is a desired state, it does not appear to be a disqualifier for a partnership. Sponsorships can be based on different company colours; however, this depends on the idiosyncratic viewpoint of the sponsor (variation in the data):

> "This is aggravated by the fact that our company colours completely differ to [club A colours]. In contrast, our colours are those of [club B colours]. […] To cut a long story short, we have found solutions for everything"[28] (IP 15, 270; 29).

Nevertheless, if the sponsor and club have the same colours *compatibility* is invigorated.

Beyond the concept of *compatibility*, *trust* acts as a pivotal requirement. *Trust* is merely associated to the people who represent the club and the sponsor and refers to those individuals involved in the decision-making process. While there is accordance that a moderate amount of *trust* is a basic requirement in order to enter into a sponsorship, *trust* intensifies over time (process character) if the partnership develops positively. Hence, *trust* is found at grassroots level as a basic requirement and has also a dynamic component. Moreover, *trust* is closely linked to the concept of *"quality people"* as it refers to the people's expertise *(their professional qualities)* and *integrity* (personal qualities). These two elements serve as a foundation for *trust* to be intensified.

The 'people factor' has further implications when entering a sponsorship relationship as it works as a factor for *facilitating partnership*. Personal relationships between those responsible for the partnering organisation ease the way to come together and may act as a *"door opener"* for a partnership, as IP 22 (387; 15) disclosed:

> "Good relationships, including personal relationships already existed between our business with [company A] and we already knew people such as [person A] and [person B], also [person C] and [person D]. And I think, this was the initial origin".[29]

[28] *„Erschwerend kommt hinzu, dass wir Unternehmensfarben haben, die nun mit [Vereinsfarben] gar nichts zu tun haben, sondern die [andere Farben] sind. […] Und lange Rede kurzer Sinn, wir haben für alles Lösungen gefunden […]"* (IP 15, 270; 29).

[29] *„Gute Beziehungen, auch persönliche Beziehungen von unserem [Geschäft] zum Beispiel mit [Unternehmen A] vorhanden waren und man einfach so Persönlichkeiten wie den [Person A] und [Person B], auch den [Person C] und den [Person D] kannte. Und ich glaube, das war eigentlich so dieser erste Ursprung"* (IP 22, 387; 15).

The concept of *having personal relationships* occupies a predominant position within the whole research area. The statement from IP 15 (270; 15) puts it straight and also highlights the connectedness between *trust* and *having personal relationships:*

> "And additionally, one knows each other and there was a sort of trust from the long-term contact. And that was a vital requirement. Trust as a vital requirement for getting into a conversation".[30]

Having personal relationships promotes a partnership (if the key basic requirements are met) because the people already have personal access to each other.

Another concept as part of *facilitating partnership* is *propinquity* (emotional and spatial). The spatial component of *propinquity* refers back to the concept of *employer branding* and *social obligation* in a way that local (spatial) proximity could be a facilitating factor to sponsor a club, given the sense of social responsibility. The emotional component is linked to the personal level and is expressed via the concept *CEO passion (emotional attachment)* for football. An *emotional attachment* to a club is rather a subtle concept which affects the accomplishment of a corporate-club partnership. IP 20 (380; 7) confirmed in honesty:

> I: "How important is such an emotionality to the club. You have mentioned that you are a fan of [club name]. Does it matter in respect to the sponsoring, the equity story?"
>
> B: "Well, I ought to say no but then I would lie to you. I think this is very important in this region".[31]

As stated in the quote, *emotional attachment* is a crucial ingredient in the decision-making process for a sponsorship (and a shareholding). Overall, business decisions are based on rational criteria but personal relationships and an emotional attachment to the club also affect partnership formation positively. This concept will be reconsidered and deepened in the category *shareholding essentials* as it provides insights into the specificity of football and the football business. Figure 6.2 on page 175 presents a detailed summary of the category and its sub-categories.

---

[30] *„Und dazu kannte man sich und da war auch ein gewisses Vertrauen da, aus dem langjährigen Kennen. Und das war eine wichtige Voraussetzung. Also Vertrauen als wichtige Voraussetzung, dass man überhaupt ins Gespräch kommt"* (IP 15, 270; 15).

[31] *„Wie wichtig ist so eine Emotionalität auch zum Club. Sie haben ja schon angesprochen, dass Sie persönlich Fan vom [Club] sind. Spielt so etwas eine Rolle, beim Sponsoring, bei der Equity Geschichte? R.: Also ich sage jetzt mal, ich müsste eigentlich nein sagen, aber dann würde ich Sie anlügen. Ich glaube, das spielt hier in der Region eine sehr große Rolle"* (IP 20, 380; 7).

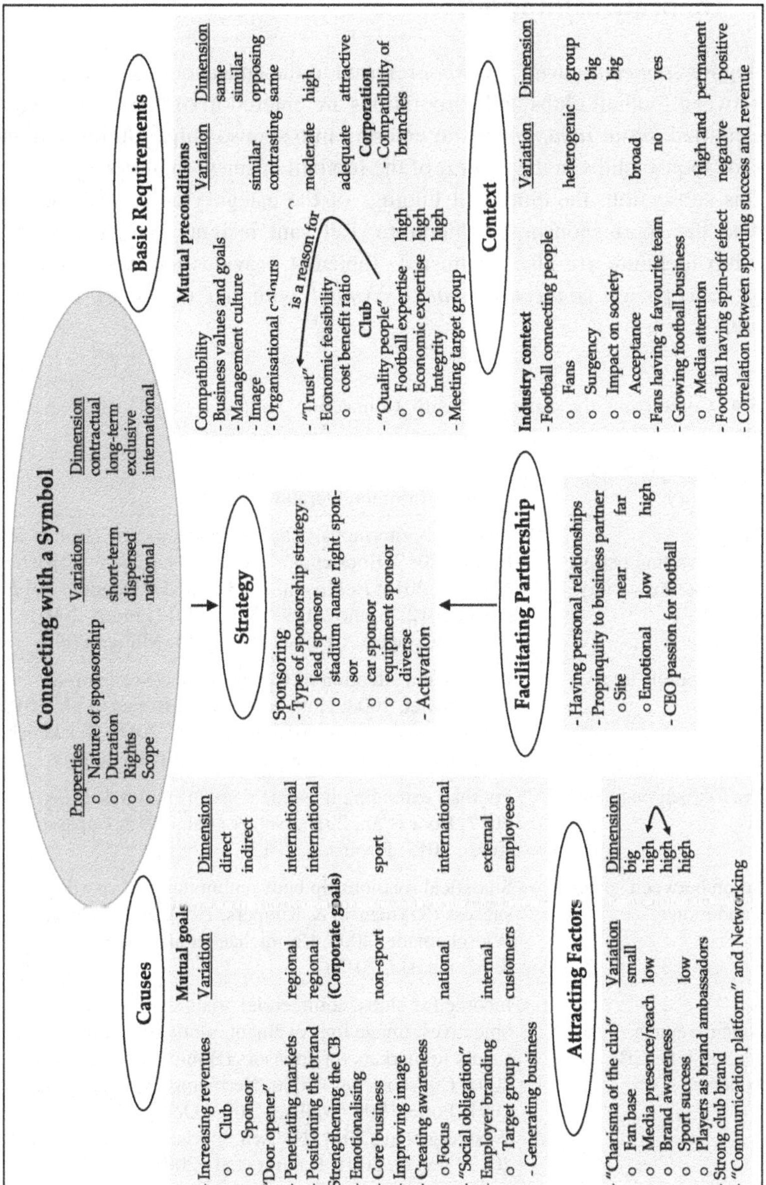

Figure 6.2 Connecting. (Source: Own Illustration)

6.3.4 Theoretical Integration

The category *connecting with a symbol* referred to the endeavour of why sponsorships between football clubs and corporations are entered into. *Attracting factors* were identified, *basic requirements* to entering into sponsorships illuminated and *causes* for sponsorships in the *context* of the football business explored.

In this subsection, the empirical findings of the category are discussed with respect to the sport sponsorship literature. Relevant insights from the general partnership literature are also contrasted. Table 6.4 provides an overview about relating concepts of *connecting with a symbol* with the outcomes from the literature.

Table 6.4 Contrasting the Literature with Connecting with a Symbol. (Source: Own Illustration)

Empirical concepts from grounded theory	Findings from the literature review
Context Football connecting people Football attracting society	Football is enormously fascinating to society (Rohde & Breuer, 2017; Boor et al., 2016; Statista, 2016; Capasso & Rossi, 2013; Robinson, 2013; Van der Heijden, 2012; Rudd, 2012; Grundy, 1998; Nagy, 2011; Frick, 2007; Prigge & Vöpel, 2014; Schmitt, 2015; Müller, 2008)
Being under public eye	High media attention of football clubs (Seemann & Schollmeier, 2008; Huth et al., 2018; Breuer et al., 2018; Adam & Hovemann, 2018; Rosentritt, 2016; Wöckener & Tenbusch, 2016; Schade, 2012; Quitzau, 2009)
Growing football business	Football extending its value domain (Sarter & Mies, 2017; Boor et al., 2016; Netzer et al., 2015; Capasso & Rossi, 2013; Robinson, 2013)
Correlation between sporting results and money	Statistical relationship between money and sporting success (Szymanski & Kuypers, 1999; Hovemann & Wieschemann, 2009; Carmichael et al., 2010; Kuypers & Szymanski, 2012)
Causes Increasing revenues Strengthening the CB "Door opener"	Income for clubs, commercial goals such as awareness objectives, image improvement, motivating employees, access to markets for sponsors (Bühler, 2006; Süßmilch, 2004; Cousens et al., 2006; Hermanns, 1997; Gillies, 1991; Pope, 1998; Walliser, 2003; Oediger, 2017b; Westberg et al., 2011; Nielsen Sports, 2018; Adam et al., 2017; Seydel, 2005; Kahuni et al., 2009)

(continued)

Table 6.4 (continued)

Empirical concepts from grounded theory	Findings from the literature review
Employer branding	Corporate social responsibility (Walzel & Schubert, 2018; Plewa et al., 2016)
Contribution Emphasis of goals related to type of sponsorships "being against"	-
Basic requirements Compatibility	The concept of fit, congruence, and alignment (Alexander, 2009; Madrigal, 2001; Woisetschläger & Michaelis, 2012; Woisetschläger et al., 2010; Meenaghan, 2001; Harrigan, 1988; Douma et al., 2000; Kahuni et al., 2009; Motion et al., 2003)
Trust	Trust is emphasised as a vital requirement (Das & Teng, 2001; Cobbs, 2011; Beamish et al., 2016; Globermann & Nielsen, 2007; Farrelly & Quester, 2005b; Spekman, 1988; Morgan et al., 2014; Russo & Cesarini, 2017; Nielsen & Gudergan, 2012; Gulati, 1995; Saxton, 1997)
"Quality people"	Trust is related to a personal level (Saxton, 1997; Eisenhardt & Schoonhoven, 1996)
Personal relationship	Informal relationships facilitate transactions (Saxton, 1997; Gulati, 1995)
	Contrasting view (insignificance of personal relationships at the beginning of a partnership; Urriolagoitia and Planellas, 2007)
Attracting factors "Charisma of the club"	Attractivity of football (Boor et al., 2016; Schuster & Unterhitzenberger, 2014; Chemnitzer et al., 2015); appeal of football clubs (Prigge & Vöpel, 2014; Netzer et al., 2015; Capasso & Rossi, 2013; Robinson, 2013; Rudd, 2012; Nufer & Bühler, 2011; Szymanski, 2001)
Communication platform	Sponsorship as business building activity (Fahy et al., 2004; Dolphin, 2003; Chemnitzer et al., 2015; Henseler et al., 2007; Süßmilch, 2004).
Propinquit	Regional affinity (Schade, 2012, Alexa, 2009)
Extension	
CEO passion for football Emotional attachment	There is no source which explicitly mentions a direct impact between the establishment of a sponsorship and CEO passion respectively the impact on emotional attachment on business decision making.

It is widely accepted that football arouses great interest and attention in society and attracts people all over the world (Van der Heijden, 2012; Nagy, 2011; Frick, 2007). While Capasso and Rossi (2013) as well as Rudd (2012) substantiate the great appeal of football to people (as a sport) and to corporations (as a business), Boor et al. (2016), Statista (2016), Netzer et al. (2015), and Schuster & Unterhitzenberger (2014) give some very useful insights (facts and figures) into the growing football business.

The *correlation between money and sporting results,* which is manifested in the *unique nature of football* and acts as a main principle in a football club's management, is common knowledge and has previously been investigated and confirmed by several scholars (e.g., Hovemann & Wieschemann, 2009; Schilhaneck, 2008; Frick, 2006; Hall et al., 2002; Szymanski & Kuypers, 1999). With regard to football's attractivity, the empirical concepts *(football connecting people, football attracting society, growing football business)* conform with existing knowledge.

Adam et al. (2017) and Seydel (2005) underpinned that football clubs are ideal for image transfer and increasing awareness due to their loyal fan base and large media exposure. This is supported by scholars such as Murphy (2018), Post and Druker (2018), Schade (2012), and Bodet and Chanavat (2010) who examined that the club brand is the central aspect which makes clubs appealing to potential sponsors. Von Overloop (2015) specifies that brand strength consists chiefly of high brand awareness and a positive image. Renard and Sitz (2011) demand that sport clubs need to build their own brand identity and values as an essential first step in order to permit the greatest leverage of sponsorship opportunities. The significance of building upon own brand strength for clubs was further underpinned by Kuper (2009) who specified that the club brand is one fundamental strategy for clubs to remain competitive. These insights are also reflected in this grounded theory within the sub-category *attracting factors*. In particular, attractivity is manifested in the *charisma of a club* which constitutes the club's inherent aspects (e.g., fan base, media reach, brand awareness, etc.). Additionally, the various sponsorship opportunities to use a club as a *communication platform* in various forms become appealing for corporate partners which is consistent with findings from Chemnitzer et al. (2015), Henseler et al. (2007), Süßmilch (2004), Fahy et al. (2004), and Dolphin (2003).

The literature further reports about a variety of reasons why companies sponsor football clubs. For example, Bühler (2006), Walliser (2003), Oediger (2017b), and Westberg et al. (2011) all agree that image improvement and brand awareness are the primary goals for football sponsorships. Nielsen Sports (2018) and Hermanns (1997) add staff motivation and market penetration as further vital ambitions. These goals overlap with the empirical findings (sub-category *causes*) and are mainly expressed in the concept *strengthening the CB*.

While the various forms of football sponsorship are widely discussed, this study endeavours to dimensionalise the focus of different sponsorship types (lead, kit, car, and stadium name rights sponsoring) which allows the idiosyncratic focus of the four main sponsorship types in the football business to be reviewed. Beyond this, the empirical findings add to the discussion about sponsorship disadvantages by detecting that a lead (tricot) sponsor always *plays against* someone else (the other lead sponsor of the rival club). This might have negative effect on the image which is an impediment for some companies to enter into this type of sponsorship.

In terms of the *basic requirements* of sponsorships, scholars from diverse disciplines agree that the fit construct, in its various designations such as congruence and alignment, is a key aspect in the management of business partnerships. Fit largely corresponds with the higher-ordered empirical concept *compatibility*. The term compatibility has already been used by Russo and Cesarini (2017) to describe a cultural and organisational fit between associates. While cultural fit has gained prominence through many scholars within the last decades (e.g., Nielsen & Gudergan, 2012; Farrelly & Quester, 2005b; Das & Teng, 2003; Kaplan, 2002; Barringer & Harrison, 2000; Dyer & Singh, 1998), in this GT cultural and organisational fit are included too via the related concept of *management culture*. However, *compatibility* in this study is far-reaching as it encompasses a fit of image and values (business and ethical values), thereby matching with the findings from sport sponsorship scholars such as Woisetschläger (2015), Demir and Söderman (2015), Morgan et al. (2014), and Cousens et al. (2006). Even though Olson and Thjomoe (2009) and Trendel and Warlop (2007) showed a positive impact of 'low fit' the empirical data is consistent that high *compatibility* is the basis for an effective working relationship in a corporate football partnership.

There is agreement among scholars that trust is essential in any business partnership (Russo & Cesarini, 2017; Morgan et al., 2014; Spekman, 1988). Eisenhardt and Schoonhoven (1996) as well as Gulati (1995) and Saxton (1997) indicate trust as a social motive for partnering and relate trust to a personal level respectively. The empirical data clearly reflect the crucial role of *trust*. Trust, in this study, appears as a dynamic concept which intensifies during a partnership, therefore substantiating findings from Saxton (1997).

Within the emergent theory the concept of *trust* is not only related to personal traits but essentially relates to trust in the expertise and competence of the people involved *(quality of people)*. Beyond this, this study emphasises the key role of trust between the business parties before deal making, hence presenting *trust* as a precondition for entering into a partnership.

Moreover, the interconnectedness of trust and personal relationships between individuals of the collaborative organisations emerged as a relevant aspect. In this research context, personal ties are important in all phases of the corporate club partnership and even before a sponsorship is started because personal relationships often act as a first *"door opener"* to enter into a sponsorship partnership *(facilitating partnership)*. This finding contrasts to those of Urriolagoitia and Planellas (2007) who allege that informal relationships do not play a vital role at the beginning of a partnership. However, the facilitating aspect of personal relationships is indirectly verified by Gulati (1995) and Saxton (1997) who refer to trust on a personal level as a facilitating component in exchange transactions.

This study also supports findings from Morgan et al. (2014) that informal processes facilitate partnership deal making. In particular, personal relationships lead to informal interactions between business people and support the entering into business partnerships. However, this grounded theory extends the insights from the literature by adding the concept of *CEO passion for football*. In essence, the theory finds clear evidence that a corporate CEO's passion *(emotional attachment)* can be a main facilitating factor to engage in football sponsorships. This challenge the commonly accepted view of rational decision-making in business management (e.g., Poitras, 2016; Caselli, 2010; Jones, 2008; Mintzberg, 1998) and provides evidence that an emotional component has an impact on specific business decisions.

While *connecting with a symbol* has explained the reasons and processes for entering into a sponsorship between a club and corporation the next section provides insights into the process of how a sponsorship develops into a strategic partnership *("brand symbiosis")*.

6.4 Becoming a Brand Symbiosis

6.4.1 Introduction

This category label has its origin in the in vivo code *"brand symbiosis"*. The term "symbiosis" implies an association of two partners of a different origin who collaborate for the sake of mutual benefits (Duden, 2016; 1730). On the one hand, there is a corporate sponsor (focused on profits) who partners, on the other hand, with a football club (originating from a non-profit nature). *"Brand symbiosis"* is combined with the gerund "becoming" in order to reveal the process character of the category.

Becoming a brand symbiosis can be seen as an advancement of *connecting with a symbol* (the corporate club sponsorship). The category describes and explains the progress from an initial sponsorship which acts as a formal marketing communication platform towards a strategic sponsorship partnership *("brand symbiosis")* in which each partner benefits in various ways. During the *history of partnership*, based on several positive actions and *interactions* due to the partners' contributions and *mutual effort*, the sponsorship develops into an effective ongoing partnership related to the attainment of pre-set sponsorship goals *("track record", consequences)* over time. This circular, symbiotic process of alignment leads to a *deepening involvement* between the club and sponsor accompanied by an increasing level of *trust*.

"Brand symbiosis" is characterised by the properties *strategic direction, high importance,* and *high effort* (e.g., managerial time, personnel). *Becoming a brand symbiosis* entails the sub-categories *connecting with a symbol* (which acts as a basic requirement), *interactions, deepening involvement, "sounding board",* and *consequences* which interconnect during the process of *history of partnership*. Although the sub-categories (and their concepts) are partly addressed separately they are rather mutually dependent and interrelate due to their process characteristic. For example, as a process of permanent interactions *(partnership management)*, experiencing the collaboration positively, and the achievements of partnership goals (consequences), a *deepening involvement* occurs during the *history of partnership*.

However, it has to be considered that *becoming a brand symbiosis* is not inevitable for all corporate club sponsorship relationships. There are still many sponsorship (commercial) partnerships in the football business which do not develop into a *"brand symbiosis"* for a variety of reasons. Nevertheless, the focus of this study is about strategic equity partnerships in German football. *Becoming a brand symbiosis* is a crucial step in the development of a sponsorship partnership towards a strategic equity partnership. Therefore, the category embodies the development of a corporate-club sponsorship towards a strategic equity partnership.

6.4.2 History of Partnership, Interactions, and Deepening Involvement

Becoming a brand symbiosis builds upon the category *connecting with a symbol* (precondition). Within the sponsorship, each partner contributes based on its own *management culture* and with its partnership goals in mind. The *management cultures* need to be *compatible* (basic requirement of *connecting with a symbol*) in order to facilitate coordinated actions and effective *partnership management*. Although *compatibility* is to be assessed prior to entering a formal sponsorship (in the frame of *connecting with a symbol*), the *compatibility* of *managements cultures* is a matter of assessing the partnership a posteriori. *Partnership management* constitutes the main concept of the sub-category *interactions* between the club and sponsor. How people behave towards each other is ideally characterised by *mutual respect, open communication, dealing fairly* (*honesty* and *transparency*), and *mutually inspiring business ideas* and acts as a building block for a compatible and collaborative environment. *History of partnership* reflects this process character.

As interactions succeed the partnership adds more value to both the sponsor and club in terms of growing *partnership experience* and *partnership results*. This progress is embodied by achieving a "*track record*" which refers to the attainment of pre-set goals (ascertained via *measuring sponsorship goals* such as awareness and image objectives, etc.) as well as to interpersonal components *(being on good terms with partner)*. IP 12 (214; 32) explained the process as follows:

> "To have a partnership strategy is about a medium till long-term issue. You have to experience a track record in order to see whether one fits together. Thus, in respect to the brands, personnel, the beliefs, how to shape the future".[32]

As a consequence of positive interactions and by attaining a "*track record*", the club and sponsor become more deeply involved with each other *(deepening involvement)*. This is confirmed by IP 10 (166; 31):

> "We have seen a good deal of maturing. We have also seen minor successes over time and have realised that the partnership holds greater potential. So we thought, let us take the next step, id est from a small a bigger step and from this step to the [next step; anonymised word] and this ultimately evolved into a gigantic partnership".[33]

---

[32] *„Eine Partnerstrategie haben, hat was mit Mittel- bis Langfristigkeit zu tun, und dann muss man ja erst mal ein Track Record miteinander spielen, dass man sieht, passt man denn zusammen. Also von den Marken, von den Personen, von der Vorstellungen, wie man gemeinsam in die Zukunft gehen will"* (IP 12, 241; 32).

[33] *„Und da ist einiges gereift und wir haben über die Zeit auch kleine Zwischenerfolge gesehen und gemerkt, das birgt eigentlich für mehr, lass uns die nächste Stufe eingehen. Sprich, von der kleinen auf die nächste gegangen. Von der Stufe auf die [Unternehmen] [anonymisiertes Wort] gegangen und noch mal eine riesen Partnerschaft gegangen"* (IP 10, 166; 31).

This statement indicates a step-by-step approach of *deepening involvement.* As the sponsorship matures it prospers and is attributed to an increased *formal* (more rights and money) and *emotional attachment.* An increased emotional attachment results from the frequent interactions and becomes manifested in the way the partnership is experienced. IP 10 (175; 10) depicts that *"[...] it feels like collaborating with a colleague from a different department",*[34] which indicates a sense of unity. Accordingly, the interrelationship of *partnership management* and *outcomes* is a circular process of *deepening involvement.* For instance, the closer the club and sponsor collaborate the better the *insights into partner management* and the better attuned their business interactions. Additionally, ongoing and *frequent interactions* promote interpersonal *trust.* In essence, the club and sponsor start to orchestrate complementary resources and the club incorporates the sponsor into its strategic planning, as IP 2 (15; 7) disclosed: *"Since all big partners with whom we collaborate are those we integrate in our strategy".*[35] Consequently, the sponsorship extends in terms of associated rights *(content)* and *sponsorship fees* and evolves into a strategic partnership. With reference to IP 2 (19; 10), this strategic partnership is characterised as follows:

> "I would say that these are usually bigger compared to a normal sponsorship and therefore the effort and the amount of people guiding them is far greater. Of course, they have more rights. More rights mean that they preoccupy a multitude of issues. It is not only about doing things operationally or communicatively. In terms of content these are, in part, fundamentally different issues".[36]

The statement reflects an additional effort associated with a strategic partnership in terms of personnel, rights, and collaborative content. An abstract of Memo on page 184 provides an insight into the in-depth analysis of the term "big partner" regarding partnerships and thus allowing the properties of a strategic partner in this research field to be identified.

---

[34] *„[...] ich würde fast sagen es fühlt sich so an, als würde ich mit irgendwelchen Kollegen einer anderen internen Abteilung zusammenarbeiten"* (IP 10, 175; 10).

[35] *„Denn alle großen Partner, mit denen wir zusammenarbeiten, sind die, die wir in unsere Strategie einbinden"* (IP 2, 15; 7).

[36] *„Ja ich meine, die [strategischen Partner] sind meistens größer als ein ganz normales Sponsorship und dadurch ist natürlich der Aufwand und auch die Anzahl Derjenigen, mit denen man das Ganze betreut, viel größer. Die haben natürlich auch mehr Rechte. Mehr Rechte bedeutet, dass oftmals auch eine Vielzahl von Themen besetzt werden. Da geht es also nicht rein darum, etwas betrieblich zu machen oder nur Kommunikation zu machen. Das sind halt teilweise auch inhaltlich ganz andere Themen da"* (IP 2, 19; 10).

Table 6.5 Memo 44 - The Term Big Partner. (Source: Own Illustration)

Memo 44_ analysis of word_„big" partner_ 23 April 2017

This memo refers to the word "big partner". What exactly is meant by big partner? By use of a farfetched comparison the word "big" is set into the context of a big football match. This is commonly characterised by: high (public) attention, mindfulness and excitement, high concentration, high effort (organising, detailed preparation, etc.), and a high relevance. By considering these properties within the data, the following properties of big partners can be confirmed:

Properties	Dimension	
- effort (time, money)	low	*high*
- personnel	few	*lots*
- attention (and care)	low	*high*
- relevance	low	*high*
- rights	few	*widespread*
- issues	limited	*diversified*
- direction	tactic	*strategic*
	short-term	*long-term*

It becomes evident that "big partner" is used synonumously with strategic partner.

Inherent with the denotation of being a strategic partner *("brand symbiosis")* is the existence as a top sponsor of the club (supreme level of a sponsorship pyramid[37]). Since strategic issues have gained centre stage in a *"brand symbiosis"*, instead of concentrating on the communication objectives solely the partnership becomes more business oriented *(shifting partnership goals)*, as IP 17 (307; 36) highlighted:

[37]In a 'sponsoring pyramid' (a hierarchy) clubs list their sponsorships according to their relevance and impact (in terms of money, rights, and scope) for the club. The main partnerships are at the top, but differ in their designation from club to club. For example, some clubs refer to "top sponsors", "premium sponsors", or "champion sponsors", others to "platinum sponsors". However, they have in common that the partners at the top represent the most eminent sponsorships (document analysis).

"So, we have intensive opportunities to cooperate with [club name] in the business area. This is a good deal more compared to the past. There has been a real shift away from awareness and image in the beginning towards image and business".[38]

The business aspect finds expression in *having a mutual business concept*, which is an outcome of ongoing interactions and *deepening involvement. Having a mutual business concept* is a key characteristic in a *"brand symbiosis"* in which the affiliates start to see the synergies of the collaboration and begin to develop mutual business activities beyond the contractually defined sponsorship that create value for both partners, because the associates have realised that *"[...] we have two brands, [club] and [own company], they do something for each other which they could not achieve on their own"*[39] (IP 18, 324; 25).

For example, regarding the activity of penetrating international markets, the corporate partner supports the club in terms of its internationalisation strategy by providing its infrastructure to the club in the countries abroad and supporting touchpoints to vital political and economic networks. The club agrees to additional promotional activities in return, such as a factory visit in the country. In consequence, both partners benefit in the form of a *"door opener"*. In return, the sponsor benefits from an international brand awareness of the club. In this case, the club acts as a *"door opener"* for *generating business* and *penetrating markets.*

A mutual business concept can also be directed to merchandising activities e.g., in the form of establishing a *store* abroad or to build up *football clinics* and *junior football camps* around the world. In these activities the sponsor is perceived as an *"enabler"*, therefore contributing to a positive image and creating sympathy. The club can use these mutual activities as a scouting tool for young potential players. Furthermore, in the era of digitalisation there are several other opportunities for a mutual business concept, such building up a club TV channel, developing a mobile app for exclusive news and information about the club, and supporting the stadium experience via mobile devices.

[38]*„Also haben intensive Möglichkeiten, mit dem [Club] auch im Businessbereich zusammenzuarbeiten. Das ist deutlich mehr, als wir früher gemacht haben. Es hat sich absolut verzogen von Bekanntheit, Image am Anfang, jetzt deutlich zu Image und Business"* (IP 17, 307; 36).

[39]*„[...] wir haben zwei Marken, [Club] und [eigenes Unternehmen], die tun etwas füreinander, was sie aus sich heraus selbst nicht tun könnten"* (IP 18, 324; 25).

Evidently, in a *"brand symbiosis"* value is also added to the partnership in the form of the exchange of know-how *(exchanging know-how).* Even though knowledge exchange is nascent during the history of partnership (*"This [knowledge transfer] can occur everywhere"*,[40] IP 2, 20; 21) it is intensified in a *"brand symbiosis"* due to closer collaborations. Knowledge exchange can cover diverse areas, such as marketing, legal, or strategic issues and is reflected in *unilateral* and *bilateral* dimensions. The statement of IP 10 (175; 16) provides evidence of a mutual knowledge exchange: *"I think, we learn a lot from each other. Well, really mutually"*. This is confirmed by IP 22 (394; 11), who additionally explains in which area the sponsor can benefit from the club:

> "I think both sides benefit. On the one hand, football operations work differently, but one has to be open-minded. Let me put it this way, we learn about the player's world. How are the asset and liability structure evaluated? And this is not about the stadium it is about the players. How is the players' potential assessed, how it is evaluated".[41]

This statement gives rise to a precondition for the sponsor to benefit from a knowledge transfer, to be open-minded in order to assimilate the knowledge into its own company context. However, there is variation in the data (negative case) that *benefitting from knowledge exchange* pertains to the club's side only (*unilateral* dimension). IP 15 (282; 26) addressed the issue of whether the sponsor also benefits from a know-how transfer by answering: *"No, this is not the case"*.[42]

6.4.3 Sounding Board

The status of being a top sponsor of a club is often accompanied with having a representative of the sponsor on the club's *supervisory committee* although this is not compulsory and can differ according to partnership-specific circumstances (variation in the empirical data).

---

[40] *„Den [Wissenstransfer] kann es überall geben"* (IP 2, 20; 21).

[41] *„Ich glaub da profitieren beide Seiten daran. Auf der einen Seite klar, der Spielbetrieb tickt anders als ein Unternehmen. Da muss man sich auch auf das eine oder andere einlassen. […] Insofern sag ich mal ja, wir nehmen da auch schon mit, was die Spielerwelt bewegt. Wie dort die Vermögensstruktur beurteilt wird. Und Vermögensstruktur heißt ja nicht die Arena, sondern Vermögensstruktur heißt die Spieler. Das Spielerpotential, wie wird das eingeschätzt, wie wird das bewertet, wie wird das beurteilt"* (IP 22, 394; 11).

[42] I: *„Ist das eine gegenseitige Consultingrolle, also profitiert auch [Unternehmen] vom Know-How von [Club] oder ist das // B: Nein, das nicht"* (IP 15, 282; 26).

In this study, the term *"sounding board"* is interchangeably applied to also mean supervisory committee. However, *"sounding board"* became the label of the sub-category because the term emerged as an in vivo code in the data and therefore mirrors the specific meaning of the research field. Moreover, *"sounding board"* reflects the key features related with a club's governance body or *supervisory committee*, id est to act as a consulting and supervising body and to act as a supportive tool in terms of the club's strategic decision making.

While the number of members in a club's *"sounding board"* depends on the idiosyncratic club constitution, the *"sounding board"* has generally a key and multidimensional role in a corporate club partnership. First and foremost, the *"sounding board"* is a vital part of the club's strategic (non-executive) management body. For instance, one of the supervisory committee's tasks is to appoint and release the board (club management). In addition, a member of the *"sounding board"* has a voting right on specific issues, e.g., club spending in excess of certain thresholds needs to be approved by the *"sounding board"*. Second, within the scope of a share deal, being part of the club's *"sounding board"* becomes *binding* (tool for justification, will be explained in Sect. 6.5.2).

Even though a seat on the club's *"sounding board"* is optional in a *"brand symbiosis"* it is frequently a pre-stage in the process towards a strategic equity partnership since being part of the club's *"sounding board"* is another step in the *deepening involvement* between the parties, because *"[...] you are part of strategies, missions and action plans, as well as budgets"*[43] (IP 13, 239; 10). As a member of the *"sounding board"* a corporate partner has the opportunity to support the strategic direction as well as intervene in case of economical failure by *"having a say"* (e.g., via the voting right) on the club.

A fundamental issue concerning the *"sounding board"* is an aligned understanding of how to effectively collaborate in respect to the club's sporting affairs and overall strategy. This is expressed in the concept *"understanding of one's role"* which becomes especially pivotal for clubs as a requirement for a strategic partner. *"Understanding of one's role"* is linked to a clear split of responsibilities between commercial issues and sporting decisions. Clubs certainly expect no interventions from corporate partners into sport-related decisions. Therefore, an *"understanding of one's role"* is inevitably linked to *trust* among the partners and the people who are part of the supervisory committee, according to IP 7 (106; 8):

---

[43] *„[...] dann bist du ja Teil von Strategien und Missionen und Handlungsplänen und auch Budgets. Das heißt, du bist ja dann involviert in [unv. 13:20]"* (IP 13, 239; 10).

> "Well, you repeatedly come to the issue of an understanding of one's role, common values and finally how one wants to actively participate or the opposite".[44]

Regarding the personnel composition of the *"sounding board"* it is examined that one of the strategic partner's board members (most often the CEO) is usually part of the club's *"sounding board"* for several reasons: as previously explained, a strategic partnership at a football club is commonly associated with an emotional attachment to the club which often refers to the CEO, too. Accordingly, as an individual interested in football personal interests are common. Sitting at the club's supervisory board appears to be a question of prestige for those concerned which underpins a certain social status.

A CEO of a large enterprise commonly brings with him impressive expertise and economic experience. This equally refers to an external perception as well as to an internal self-perception connected with the position at hand, as expressed in the statement by IP 15 (283; 4): *"Well, there is clearly an exceptionally high level of expertise in the supervisory committee and one would like to contribute"*.[45] By way of analysing the diction employed by participants, the inherent social status becomes obvious. For example, IP 15 (282; 31) used military vocabulary:

> "That there has been the will from the club that each CEO is part of the supervisory committee. Of course, this has something to do with public image that the sponsors acknowledge that the top level of the company is on the board and that this is not a minor topic. Instead, it is the supreme army command on board".[46]

This statement highlights the reciprocal desire to have the strategic partner's CEO as a member of the club's *"sounding board"*. The statement also illustrates the

[44] *„Also, du kommst immer wieder an das Thema Rollenverständnis, gemeinsam Werte, und wie letzten Endes wie man sich einbringen will, oder eben auch nicht einbringen"* (IP 7, 106; 8).

[45] *„Also da ist schon eine brutal hohe Kompetenz im Aufsichtsrat und die will man natürlich auch gerne mit einbringen"* (IP 15, 283; 4).

[46] *„Und da war schon der Wille des Vereins, dass der Vorstandsvorsitzende jeweils dort im Aufsichtsrat sitzt, das hat natürlich auch was mit Außenwirkung zu tun. Das dann die Sponsoren zu bekennen geben, da sitzt die oberste Unternehmensspitze im Aufsichtsrat und das ist nicht Thema irgendwelcher nachgelagerter Themen, sondern da ist die oberste Heeresführung mit im Boot"* (IP 15, 282; 31).

relevance of the partnership for both parties and indicates a *signifying effect* of a highly qualified sounding board to the public. A *"sounding board"* made up of economic experts (CEOs) of *"[...] powerful organisations symbolises a corresponding strength within the clu*b"[47] (IP 22, 399; 15). This is not only beneficial in terms of transferring know-how (consulting) but also has a positive impact for attracting further sponsors.

IP 11 (195; 12) indicates another benefit for the club arising out of a competent supervisory committee: *"But what we do as a supervisory committee, we are of course a good sounding board because we have a lot of economic experience"*.[48] *Exchanging know-how* is once again fortified with a corporate seat in the club's *"sounding board"*.

6.4.4 Consequences

Although the consequences are dynamic and arise during the interplay of activities in the *history of partnership*, the sponsorship has developed towards a status which is characterised by specific features. That means the sponsor and club have obtained an effective way to coordinate their strengths and started to see an added value which emanates from a strategic partnership *("brand symbiosis")*. This added value refers to a variety of "brand-links" in which the parties *"[...] mutually develop a specific area in my company"*[49] (IP 9, 142; 6).

Overall, *becoming a brand symbiosis* evolves dynamically during the history of partnership, considerably influencing the developmental process of a sponsorship relationship towards a strategic partnership. The sub-categories are dependent on one another. During the *history of partnership* positive interactions incrementally lead to the achievement of intermediate outcomes which, in turn, affect further positive *partnership management*.

---

[47] *„[...] schlagkräftige Unternehmen symbolisieren auch eine entsprechende Kraft im Verein"* (IP 22, 399; 15).

[48] *„Aber was wir als Aufsichtsrat machen, wir sind natürlich ein guter Sounding Board, weil wir eine Menge Erfahrung haben aus dem Wirtschaftsleben"* (IP 11, 195; 12).

[49] *„Und das wichtigste ist letztendlich, dass du sagst, ich kann mit ihm gemeinschaftlich einen bestimmten Bereich in meinem Unternehmen entwickeln. Also hat er eine bestimmte Kompetenz, die ich nicht habe, die meine ergänzt"* (IP 9, 142; 6).

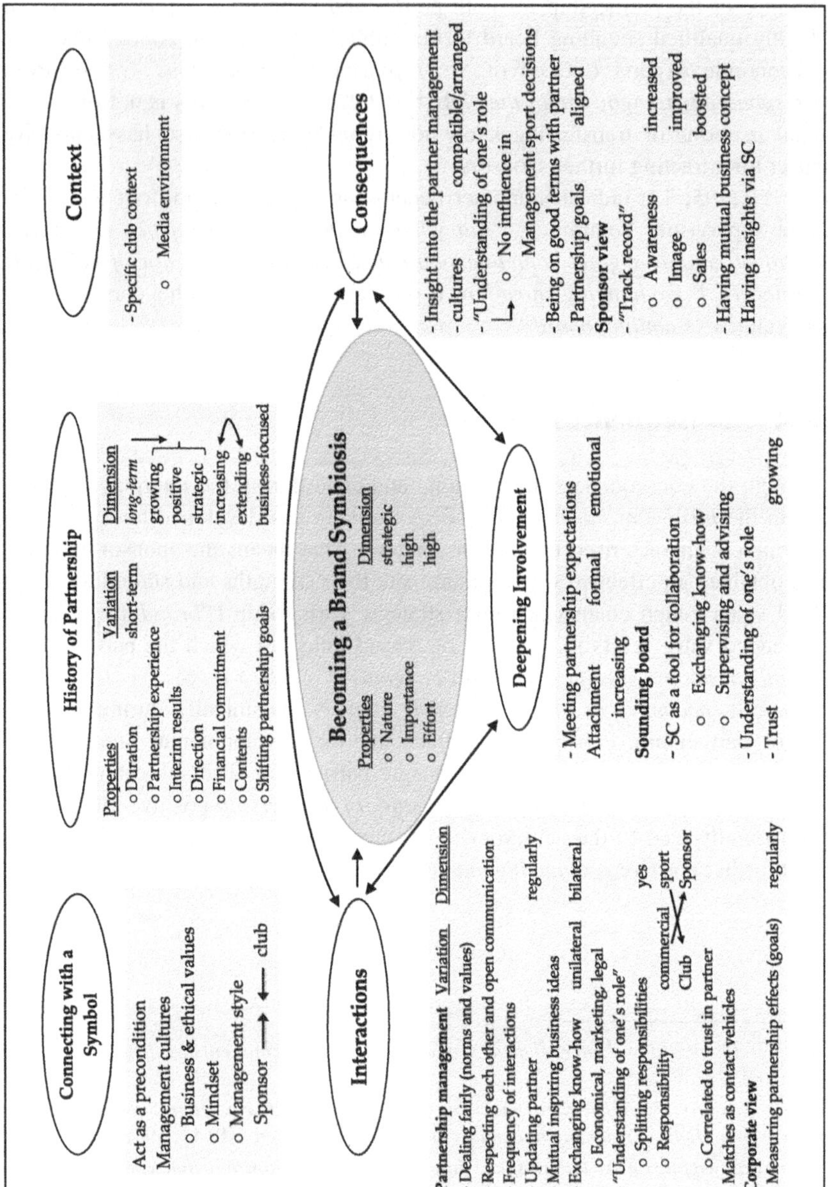

Figure 6.3 Becoming a Brand Symbiosis. (Own Illustration)

How people interact becomes a precondition for a long-lasting business relationship. Within this circular process of interactions and consequences a *deepening involvement* occurs which expresses an increased *formal* and *emotional attachment* between the club and sponsor and fosters a growing level of *trust. Deepening involvement* is an open-ended sub-category which is equally contingent on interactions and consequences. By *having a mutual business concept,* the club and sponsor invest jointly in order to attain mutual strategic goals. This business concept can be varied in nature. The key is that the club and sponsor make an effort to engage in ongoing relational investments (e.g., *mutually inspiring business ideas*), supporting interactions (e.g., in terms of international market penetration), open communication, inter-organisational knowledge exchange, and learning. Figure 6.3 on page 190 presents the results of the category.

6.4.5 Theoretical Integration

Becoming a brand symbiosis explained the process of partnership development from a sponsorship towards a strategic partnership. Table 6.6 presents a synopsis as to how the empirical concepts of the category *becoming a brand symbiosis* relate to pre-existing insights in the literature. It includes sport-related partnership as well as the general literature on strategic alliances.

Table 6.6 Contrasting Literature with Becoming a Brand Symbiosis. (Source: Own Illustration)

Empirical concepts from grounded theory	Finding from the literature review
Preconditions (connecting with a symbol), especially compatibility	Fit, alignment and compatibility on various levels (e.g., Farrelly & Quester, 2005b; Kahuni et al., 2009; Alexander, 2009; Madrigal, 2001; Woisetschläger & Michaelis, 2012; Woisetschläger et al., 2010; Meenaghan, 2001)
Exchanging know-how Mutual consulting	Retaining resources (i.a., Das & Teng, 2000; Dyer & Singh, 1998; Davies et al., 2008; Fahy et al., 2004; Meenaghan, 1991), knowledge transfer (Meier, 2011; Lui et al. 2010; Farrelly et al. 2006; Ireland et al. 2002; Birkinshaw, 2001; Dyer & Singh, 1998; Grant, 1996)
Shifting goals, generating business, having mutual business concept	Further synergies (Dworak, 2010; Chemnitzer et al., 2015; Prigge & Vöpel, 2014; Nagy, 2012; Süßmilch, 2004; Alexander, 2009; Kahuni et al., 2009; Morgan et al., 2014)

(continued)

Table 6.6 (continued)

Empirical concepts from grounded theory	Finding from the literature review
Penetrating markets, positioning the brand	Strategic positioning (e.g., Todeva & Knoke, 2005; Farrelly & Quester, 2005a)
Partnership management Open communication and dealing fairly	Open dialogue and transparency (Westberg et al., 2011; Motion et al., 2003; Hecox, 2007; Morgan et al., 2014; Doz, 1996; Reuer et al., 2002; Mitsuhashi, 2002)
Understanding of one's role	Role expectations (Urriolagoitia & Planellas, 2007; Hecox, 2007; Morgan et al., 2014)
Frequency of interactions	Investment of time, money and effort (Reuer et al., 2002; Mitsuhashi, 2002); intense interactions (Morgan et al., 2014; Hecox, 2007; Urriolagoitia and Planellas, 2007); ongoing interactions (Doz, 1996; Reuer et al., 2002; Mitsuhashi, 2002)
"Track record"	Partnership experience affects partnership outcomes (Motion et al., 2003)
History of partnership (process character)	Process character of the partnership (Urriolagoitia & Planellas, 2007; Motion et al., 2003), partnership develops over time (Hecox, 2007; Morgan et al., 2014)
Deepening involvement	Partnership intensifies (Alexander, 2009; Kahuni et al., 2009; Hecox, 2007; Morgan et al., 2014), Commitment (i.a., Russo & Cesarini, 2017; Farrelly & Quester, 2005b; Cooper & Gardener, 1993; Weitz, 1992)
Meeting expectations	How the partnership is experienced (Motion et al., 2003)
Increasing trust Emotional attachment	Trust as critical attribute to act as a strategic partner (Hecox, 2007; Morgan et al., 2014; Das & Teng, 2001; Cobbs, 2011; Beamish et al., 2016; Globermann & Nielsen, 2007; Farrelly & Quester, 2005b; Spekman, 1988; Russo & Cesarini, 2017; Nielsen & Gudergan, 2012; Gulati, 1995; Saxton, 1997; Eisenhardt & Schoonhoven, 1996)
Extension Sounding board	Emotional attachment (Tsiotsou et al., 2014; Urriolagoitia & Planellas, 2007).
Consequences Compatibility tested and confirmed	Interlocking directorates (Barringer & Harrison, 2000; Globermann & Nielsen, 2007; Lowensberg, 2010)
	Aligned goals and compatible environment established (Farrelly, 2006; Rennard & Sitz, 2011; Hecox, 2007; Urriolagoitia & Planellas, 2007), valuable synergies achieved (e.g., Urriolagoitia & Planellas, 2007; Morgan et al., 2014; Lui et al., 2010; Kim & Inkpen, 2005; Jiang et al., 2008; Saxton, 1997)

The academic community coincides that fit on various levels is a precondition to develop a business partnership into a strategic partnership (e.g., Woisetschläger & Michaelis, 2012; Alexander, 2009; Madrigal, 2001). Farrelly and Quester (2005a) ascertain that strategic compatibility, goal convergence, trust, and commitment are critical attributes that allow a sponsorship to act as a strategic alliance. In the same sense, Kahuni et al. (2009) found that the basis for developing a commercial partnership into a co-branding partnership is a fit in brand values and attitudes between the partners. While the preconditions to enter into a football club partnership have previously been highlighted in the concepts of *compatibility, quality of people,* and *trust* this study emphasises the process character of a corporate club partnership *(history of partnership)* in which the *compatibility* of the partners is tested within the *partnership management* on a day-to-day basis. It is during the *history of partnership* that both partners get a (deep) insight into the partner management and are able to evaluate compatibility in terms of e.g., management cultures, mindsets, aligned goals and values.

The way people behave with each other *(partnership management)* becomes essential in this grounded theory and a basic requirement for partnership progress. The characteristics of the daily collaboration such as *dealing fairly, open communication,* and *being honest* have been highlighted by Urriolagoitia and Planellas (2007) as well as Westberg et al. (2011) previously. Several scholars such as Morgan et al. (2014), Hecox (2007), Urriolagoitia and Planellas (2007), and Doz (1997) concur that ongoing interactions and the duration of collaborating together creates a closer relationship and supports the partnership in becoming more strategic. Motion et al. (2003) also relate the way in which the partnership is experienced as key to sponsorship outcomes which is in line with the empirical concepts of *"track record"* and *partnership management.* Furthermore, frequent and honest interactions support the building of *trust* and lead to a *deepening involvement.* The sub-category *deepening involvement* also entails an incremental rise in *emotional attachment* during the *history of partnership* which substantiates outcomes from Tsiotsou et al. (2014). Similarly, Alexander (2009) stated the need for co-branding partnerships to intensify in order to produce value beyond stipulated content.

However, *deepening involvement* is interrelated to the sub-category *"sounding board"* which, in turn, interrelates to the concept of *"understanding of one's role"*. Although Barringer and Harrison (2000), Globermann and Nielsen (2007), and Lowensberg (2010) address the issue of interlocking directorates as a common strategy in business to exert power (residual control) on the activities of the partner, the issue of the supervisory committee as a strategic instrument in football clubs is underrepresented in the football literature.

This study presents valuable insights into a club's supervisory committee as a crucial aspect in partnership management and progress within the scope of the sub-category *"sounding board"*. Being part of the club's supervisory board is another step towards deepening involvement which promotes further and closer collaborations and often acts as a pre-step to strategic equity partnerships. Moreover, the club's supervisory board is also a tool for informal partnership management which supports the partnership in becoming closer. Overall, detailed empirical information is given on the issue of a club's supervisory committee, therefore adding information on how corporations use the supervisory committee as a strategic tool in football clubs as well as how clubs benefit from board members' network and expertise.

The critical meaning of role expectations for building a compatible partnership environment is set out by Urriolagoitia and Planellas (2007), Hecox (2007), and Morgan et al. (2014). While role expectation in previous studies concentrated predominantly on daily operations, *"understanding of one's role"* extends this by explicitly linking behaviour roles to the supervisory committee. A brand symbiosis between the club and sponsor is characterised by clear responsibilities, namely that the sponsor does not intervene in the sporting decisions of the club. Thereby, the grounded theory connects the concepts *"understanding of one's role"* to *trust* among the partners and illustrate both concepts as fundamental features which need to be developed over time to become a strategic partner(ship).

Although a limited number of scholars investigated the development of sport sponsorships towards strategic partnerships only, there is overall agreement that a strategic partnership can achieve further synergies for both partners' businesses compared to purely commercial collaborations. Yet, some authors (e.g., Dworak, 2010; Süßmilch, 2004) neglect to classify what is meant with further synergies. In the marketing literature, Cousens et al. (2006) and Dolphin (2003) report on advanced image campaigns or the establishment of an emotional bond with customers. Against this, findings from the general alliance literature describe an improved information flow (Quimet, 2013), knowledge transfer (e.g., Lui et al., 2010; Dyer & Singh, 1998), strategic positioning, or entering new markets (e.g., DePamphilis, 2012; Sluyts et al., 2011; Todeva & Knoke, 2005).

The empirical findings indicate that a brand symbiosis is associated with *shifting goals* from purely communication goals (e.g., image transfer and awareness) towards strategic, business building goals which exceed contractually defined issues. Since both partners recognise the value of a deepening partnership, the added value of a brand symbiosis finds expression in the concepts of *mutual consulting, exchanging know-how, supporting internationalisation,* and *having a mutual business concept.* The latter concept is based on the idea of coordinating strategies and activities in order to generate business together. This is similar to the finding from Motion et al. (2003) that a co-branding partnership offers the chance to pursue new strategies assisted by an experienced associate. The expectation of partners to invest in the partnership and produce value beyond stipulated content has also been emphasised by Farrelly et al. (2006).

While becoming a brand symbiosis explicated the developmental process of a sponsorship towards a strategic partnership the next category sheds light on the variety of backgrounds in the processes to enter into an additional share deal with a club.

6.5 Shareholding

6.5.1 Introduction

Shareholding builds upon the category *"becoming a brand symbiosis"* and represents another step of *deepening involvement* (progress). *Shareholding* is a phenomenon which is formally related to a *share deal* (equity investment) between the club and sponsor. The club gets *money* in exchange for selling *shares* (an equity stake) to the sponsor who simultaneously becomes a shareholder of the club. Consequently, the partnership exists on a contractual sponsorship *("brand symbiosis")* and a *shareholding*, thereby morphing the partnership into a *strategic equity partnership* (consequence). How these two categories (partnership forms) are interrelated is explained in the sub-category *managing the dyad.* The basic requirements for *shareholding,* which are based on relational and financial criteria, are explicated in the sub-category *shareholding essentials.* While *shareholding essentials* are *screened* before deal making, the sub-category "*screening*" also entails various strategic considerations as preconditions to entering into a strategic equity partnership. The consequences of a *shareholding* are displayed in the sub-categories *"having a say"* and *signifying.*

An equity investment is commonly characterised by the financial parameters' (properties) *dividend payments, availability of invested money*, and *share value.* A share deal at a football club, however, needs to be seen in the light of the *unique nature of the football business* and *differing ambitions* between the sponsor and club. This specific *context* inheres that a football club is not intended to pay dividends to shareholders, as explained by IP 4 (40; 37):

> "If they want to have a return then it does not fit because it is incomprehensible that a football club should pay dividend to their shareholders if things are going well. Rather you could invest the money in even better players in order to further boost success".[50]

Based on the unique characteristics, a shareholding at a football club (from the investor's viewpoint) is associated with *low dividend payments* and *restricted availability* of the invested money as the following statement clarifies:

> "The capital is more or less bound but not flexible. Indeed, it increases in value but it is not easy to realise because [club name] will not be sold to anyone overnight, who takes over the shares. [...]. Therefore, at least for us, it is not suitable as a financial investment"[51] (IP 11, 193; 33).

The quote indicates that, from a financial point of view, an equity investment in a football club stake appears not to be a lucrative deal. Instead, a shareholding is based rather on a *strategic intent* (property), which is explicated in the core-category *"securing"*.

The related amount of money associated with a share deal is dependent on the club's *share value*. Valuation of a football club is a complex issue. Although different valuation mechanisms exist and are mentioned in the interviews (e.g., discounted cash flow method and Stuttgarter procedure) these do not apply for football clubs due to their unique feature of not having *"[...] free liquidity, as we invest all in players"*[52] (IP 9, 140; 38). Football club valuation is predominantly based on the brand equity which is determined by myriad aspects such as social media reach, fan base, occupancy rate of the stadium, or property of club terrain, to name but a few. With reference to IP 7 and IP 9 (140; 14), a common

---

[50] *„Wenn die eine Rendite haben wollen, dann passt es nicht. Weil es zum einen keinem vermittelbar ist, dass ein Fußballclub an die Aktionäre eine Dividende ausschüttet, wenn es gut geht. Und dann könnte man das Geld ja noch besser in Spieler investieren, damit es noch besser gut geht"* (IP 4, 40; 37).

[51] *„Das Kapital ist mehr oder weniger gebunden, aber nicht flexibel. Das erlebt zwar eine Wertsteigerung, aber die kannst du nicht so einfach versilbern, weil [Club] wird nicht von* heute auf morgen *an irgendjemanden verkauft, der dann alle Anteile übernimmt.* [...]. *Insofern ist zumindest für uns, als Finanzinvestment das nicht geeignet [.]"* (IP 11, 193; 33).

[52] *„Wir haben keine freie Liquidität, weil wir alle investieren in Spieler"* (IP 9, 140; 39).

and simplified procedure for a club valuation is *"[...] to multiply the club's turnover by a factor of between 2.5 and 3.5"*.[53] However, this is rather considered as an orientation.

Table 6.7 displays an excerpt of an overview of the share prices of the 1st Bundesliga clubs which have entered into an equity partnership up to the present day (document analysis). Based on turnover and total price of share deal, the club valuation and the factor of turnover (at time of deal making) can be calculated. The analysis refers to the last accounting year before deal making.

Table 6.7 Club Valuation. (Source: Own Illustration)

Club	Size of share	Price in Euros	Turnover of club in Euros/accounting year	Club Valuation	Factor
FC Bayern München*					
• Adidas	10%	75 million	176 million (2002/2003)	750 million	4.26
• Audi	9.1%	90 million	303 million (2008/2009)	989 million	2.8
• Allianz	8.33%	110 million	528 million (2013/2014)	1.320 million	2.5
Borussia Dortmund					
• Evonik**	14.78%	61.5 million	260 million (2013/2014)	470 million	1.8
• Puma	5%	23.5 million	260 million (2013/2014)	470 million	1.8
• Signal Iduna	5.43%	25.5 million	260 million (2013/2014)	470 million	1.8
VfB Stuttgart					
• Daimler AG	11.75%	41.5 million	112 million (2017)	353.2 million	3.1
Hertha BSC					
• KKR***	9.7%	21.3 million	104 million (2013/2014)	220 million	2.1

* Due to equity dilution each strategic equity partner now holds 8.33% stake in the club
** Evonik bought two stakes in 2014, the first one of 9.06% (€4.37 per share) and a second one of 5.72% (€4.7 per share)
*** This data is included to have a comparative case of a club valuation in an equity deal with a financial investor (KKR)

It should be considered that turnover and share price are approximated figures and rely on public information. Therefore, they might be prone to differ slightly to actual numbers. The table, nevertheless, provides a sense of the club valuation which varies according to the specific deal. However, it becomes obvious that

[53] *„[...] Umsatzmultiplikatoren, die liegen bei 2,5 bis 3,5 Mal Umsatz"* (IP 9, 140; 14).

a share deal with a 1st Bundesliga club is characterised by an *amount of money into the million* (property). IP 20 (377; 35) applied a metaphor by speaking about *"[...] not a slug from a small bottle, but a large gulp. You have to be ready to afford it"*.[54] This requires *financial feasibility* (basic requirement) on the part of the sponsor (equity partner) who can, accordingly, be categorised as a large enterprise. The quote from IP 23 (410; 6) complements the aforementioned statement: *"For medium-sized companies this is out of their league"*.[55]

An equity investment is not only related to high costs (for the sponsor) but also with a change in the property situation of the club. A club *"[...] has 100% equity and if you dispense something then it is gone. You do not get it back"*[56] (IP 9, 137; 38), which indicates a *fundamental decision* (property). Hence, a share deal is a vital business transaction related to high expenditures and far-reaching implications which requires a strategic managerial decision. This decision-making rests upon various relational and financial preconditions *(shareholding essentials).*

6.5.2 Shareholding Essentials

The sub-category *shareholding essentials* contains the mutual basic requirements for entering into a strategic equity partnership. There is agreement among research participants that relationship progress has its necessary criteria without the partnership cannot move to the next stage. Since a corporate club partnership is a process of *deepening involvement, shareholding* builds upon the existing sponsorship relationship. While it is possible to enter into a shareholding without a prior business partnership, on analysing the enduring (longer than 5 years) strategic equity partnerships in the 1st Bundesliga to date it is evident that a former sponsorship unfailingly proceeds a share deal. That means, all concepts implied in the categories *connecting with a symbol* and *becoming a brand symbiosis* apply to the phenomenon (category) *shareholding* in the form of a precondition.

---

[54] *„Sie haben ja unsere Zahl genannt, [anonymisierte Zahl] Millionen Euro, das ist ja nicht ein Schluck aus der kleinen Flasche, sondern das ist ja ein größerer Schluck. Da musst du auch bereit sein, dass leisten zu können"* (IP 20, 377; 35).

[55] *„Die mittelständischen Unternehmen, für die ist das alle eine Nummer zu groß"* (IP 23, 410; 6).

[56] *„Du hast 100% Eigenkapital und du gibst etwas davon ab und dann ist es weg. Du kriegst es nicht zurück"* (IP 9, 137; 38).

Accordingly, having a *history of partnership* seems to be a fundamental necessity for entering into a share deal. IP 2 (15; 29) addresses (from a club perspective) that a sponsor *"[...] should be a partner of us for a considerable time in order to be in line for a shareholding"*.[57]

The background to this precondition is to have *prior insights* into how the partner operates and how the partner organisation is managed. A *history of partnership* ensures that *compatibility* in terms of *management culture, values, mindsets, goals*, and *understanding of one's* role is proven. Without a prior relationship *"this is just extremely difficult to predict"*[58] (IP 7, 103; 35).

IP 1 (3; 28) emphasises the significance of *having aligned interests* between the club and (potential) shareholder(s) by stating that *"the critical factor in an equity partnership is that all of the equity holders have their interests aligned in the same place". Having aligned interests* refers to a mutual vision about the club future and the partnership as a whole. These interests need to be directed at a long-term and sustainable partnership, according to IP 7 (108; 30): *"There is a strategic interest for both sides. One focuses on a mutual, long-term positive development of the club"*.[59] The fact that the corporation has been a (long-term) sponsor at the club designates the partner's *strategic intent*, because it is the sponsorship *(connecting with a symbol)* which has been the reason why the company entered into a partnership with the club in the first place. IP 18 (349; 18) disclosed (from a corporate point of view) that *"there are strong brand-strategic considerations and less an investment in the sense that you can say: to the last penny I work out why they do it"*.[60] An inherent *strategic intent* of the corporate partner is equally significant for clubs because *"most notably, we do not want that this partner says in a week: I am going to resell my stakes to someone. It is important for us that it is sustainable"*[61] (IP 12, 212; 19). This is fortified by IP 23 (426; 4) who stated:

---

[57] *„[...] längere Zeit schon Partner von uns sein sollten, damit es überhaupt in Frage kommt, dass sie, dass sie ein Anteilseigner werden"* (IP 2, 15; 29).

[58] *„Und das, ist einfach extrem schwierig immer vorherzusagen"* (IP 7, 103; 35).

[59] *„Da ist ein für beiden Seiten ein strategisches Interesse. Man hat eine gemeinsame, langfristige, positive Entwicklung des Vereins im Blick"* (IP 7, 108; 30).

[60] *„[...], dass es sehr stark markenstrategische Überlegungen sind und jetzt nicht so sehr ein Investment in dem Sinne wo man sagen kann: Heller und Pfenning, ich rechne Ihnen das genau aus, warum die das gemacht haben"* (IP 18, 349; 18).

[61] *„Und vor allem wollen wir ja nicht, dass dieser Partner nächste Woche sagt: ich verkaufe meine Beteiligung an irgendjemanden. Das ist ja auch für uns wichtig, dass es nachhaltig ist"* (IP 12, 212; 19).

> "Again, the criterion has to be that an investor which comes to us wants to develop our business system as [club name]. Just providing money as a means of entry and showing up every so often is not a sufficient criterion".[62]

This statement indicates a corresponding concept of *having aligned interests*, id est to have a *subtle consensus of money use* which is generated out of a share deal. Since for clubs the most important success is sport related, there is a tendency to invest all available money into the squad in order to achieve the best sporting results *(correlation between revenues and money, differing ambitions)*. However, IP 9 (138; 10) states *"this is precisely not the concept of a strategic partner"*.[63] Just spending the money generated via a share deal into the squad is rather perceived as a kind of *"Maecenas, this is stupid money or money which is spent stupidly"*[64] (IP 9, 138; 11). Even though a club's sporting success is important for the strategic equity partner too in order to benefit from the club's charisma, a strategic equity partner has still a differential view on the club's issues due to its profit-driven nature, according to IP 22 (393; 31): *"We pose different questions to the economic reasonableness for one reason or another"*.[65] Especially, due to football's *unique characteristic* of *uncertainty* (context), strategic partners coincide that a predominant usage to strengthen the squad is not acceptable, as IP 11 (200; 9) underpinned:

> "And I am convinced that we would not have done it if we had a club ranked 8 or 9 that wanted to improve to rank 5 and therefore needed some money in order to buy players. Because you know players are being bought and sometimes it works out and sometimes it doesn't. But a new stadium, an infrastructure there you know that you have the precondition that the club can improve".[66]

---

[62] *„Aber noch mal, das Kriterium muss sein, ist dieser Investor, der zu uns stößt jemand, der uns, unser Geschäftssystem als [Club] weiterentwickeln kann. Geldabliefern und Eingangstür und ab und zu vorbeikommen ist kein hinreichendes Kriterium"* (IP 23, 426; 4).

[63] *„Das ist natürlich genau nicht das Konzept eines strategischen Partners"* (IP 9, 138; 10).

[64] *„Da ist ein Mäzenatentum, das ist ein dummes Geld oder Geld, was dumm ausgegeben wird"* (IP 9, 138; 11).

[65] *„Wir stellen andere Fragen zur wirtschaftlichen Sinnhaftigkeit von den einen oder anderen Dingen"* (IP 22, 393; 31).

[66] *„Wir hätten das, bin ich überzeugt davon, nicht gemacht, wenn wir, ich sage ich jetzt mal jetzt einen Verein, der auf Platz 8 oder 9 ist und sagt, ich will mich aber auf Platz 5 verbessern und jetzt brauche ich ein bisschen Geld, damit ich ein paar Spieler einkaufen kann. Weil, Sie wissen es selber, Spieler werden eingekauft und die funktionieren oder funktionieren nicht. […]. Aber ein neues Stadion, eine Infrastruktur, das weißt du, du hast Voraussetzungen, damit der Club dann besser werden kann"* (IP 11, 200; 9).

A *history of partnership* ensures that the club and strategic partner have *aligned interests* and a mutual *consensus of money use* in order to enhance the club's competitiveness in the long-run. Furthermore, a history of collaboration ascertains a relationship of *trust*. Trust in the *quality of people* (i.e., their *expertise* and *integrity*) is a pivotal, universal concept which affects the whole corporate club partnership. When it comes to a share deal, a *high amount* of *trust* is even more important. With reference to a sponsor's point of view, IP 15 (278; 29) reported:

> "Originating from the sponsoring right up to the shareholding today which would not have been possible without the sponsoring and without the trust of the people which has been established over years".[67]

The fundamental role of trust cannot be overestimated. This applies for clubs alike because *"if I dispense a part of my own then only to someone I trust. I think this is a good way of putting it"*[68] (IP 2, 28; 6). A lack of *trust* in the capabilities of those responsible can be a reason for a sponsor's restraint, as IP 23 (432; 31) propounds: *"We would never have done the outsourcing*[69] *based on poor personal requirements"*.[70] The *quality of people* becomes key as this is the foundation for sporting and economic success and therefore sustainable club development.

Beside these relational preconditions of *shareholding* an equity investment must be based on rational financial arguments *(economic reasonableness)* which essentially correlates to the *need for justifying*. This becomes evident due to the high *investment into the million* associated with a *shareholding* at a major league club and the profit-driven nature of a sponsor. IP 24 (411; 19) highlights the relevance of this:

---

[67]*„Entstanden vom Sponsoring bis hin heute zu der Beteiligung, die aber ohne das Sponsoring und über das Vertrauen, was über viele Jahre zu den handelnden Personen aufgebaut worden ist, wahrscheinlich auch nicht stattgefunden hätte"* (IP 15, 278; 29).

[68]*„Wenn ich einen Teil von mir selbst abgebe, dann nur an jemanden, zu dem ich auch Vertrauen habe. So kann man es glaube ich ganz klar sagen"* (IP 2, 28; 6).

[69]Outsourcing, in this context, refers to the legal requirement of a club to outsource their professional football unit into the legal form of a corporation in order to sell club shares.

[70]*„Wir hätten die Ausgliederung nie gemacht unter falscher personeller Voraussetzung"* (IP 23, 432; 31).

> "I have monitored the process in terms of M&A including the valuation too. Being able to justify it economically is a very important aspect for us. What we not do is to simply waste money, this is a no-go".[71]

Specifically, the financial properties (e.g., *share price, share value*) related with a shareholding and *forecasting future club growth* are two fundamental components for sponsors since these determine the *economic reasonableness* of an equity investment.

First of all, club shares act as pecuniary counter value for the investment. On that front, *value retention* of club shares is the most crucial aspect and the minimum requirement for a sponsor to justify an equity investment. IP 11 (187; 5) honestly admitted that *"at least we have expected that we do not lose the money"*.[72] Au contraire, an increase of share value is desirable and put forward as a main argument of justification, according to IP 8 (121; 15):

> "By having a look at the valuation, the crucial aspect is that the acquired share is worth far more nowadays. Independent of whether one can sell it at the free market. If you have a look on the balance sheet, the value, as assets, is absolutely ok".[73]

The importance of club valuation mirrors the economic-driven nature of the sponsor which can be dimensionalised on the continuum *not losing money/making money*. While *value retention* (not losing money) is the basic requirement and pivotal for justification, the following statement reflects the *making money* dimension, according to IP 13 (235; 28):

> "And that the price and the club valuation was characterised by an undervaluation and one could see how added value could be attained on the financial side too".[74]

---

[71] *„Ich habe das ja auch M&A haltig auch begleitet mit Bewertung auch so, dass man es wirtschaftlich rechtfertigen kann, das ist ein ganz wichtiger Punkt für uns. Wir machen hier nicht, wo wir einfach Geld nur verschenken, das geht natürlich nicht"* (IP 24, 411; 19).

[72] *„Zumindest sind wir davon ausgegangen, dass wir das Geld nicht verlieren"* (IP 11, 187; 5).

[73] *„Der wesentlichere Punkt, dass die, wenn du die Bewertung des Vereins anguckst, dann ist natürlich was wir damals erworben haben heutzutage deutlich mehr Wert. Unabhängig jetzt davon, ob wir es am freien Markt verkaufen könnten. Wenn du rein bilanztechnisch raufguckst, dann ist das natürlich als Wert, als Aktiva absolut ok"* (IP 8, 121; 15).

[74] *„Und, dass der Preis und die Bewertung des Vereins dann auch eine Unterbewertung hatte und man sehen konnte, dass man Mehrwert schaffen konnte, auch auf der finanziellen Seite"* (IP 13, 235; 28).

A positive share forecast or performance rests on a combination of *operating in the black*, which in turn is cross-connected to the *quality of people* (sustainable club management), the *clubs favourable site conditions* and the *growing football business*. Table 6.8 details the interrelationships between these concepts and displays cross-connections to other concepts.

Table 6.8 Concept of Economic Reasonableness. (Source: Own Illustration)

Concept	Codes	Properties and Dimensions			Correlating concepts
Economic reasonableness	- Getting dividends	- Amount - Emphasis	**low** **low**	high high	
	- Operating in the black	- Profitability - Relevance	**break-even** low	high **high**	- Quality of people
	- Increase in share value	- Scope - Relevance	value retention preferable	increase minimum	- Growing football industry - Need for justifying
Forecasting future club growth (positive)	- Favourable site conditions	- Stadium - Infrastructure - Site access - Commercial power of city	outdated stunted inconvenient low	modern advanced convenient high	
	- Sporting success	- Kind	in patches	steady	- Quality of people
	- Growing football market	- Kind	slow volatile	fast steady	- Football attracting society - Media interest

Although financial and growth issues are basics that need to be given for corporations as minimum preconditions, IP 23 (421; 32) clearly states that *"[...] it will not work to decide in favour for a Bundesliga club based on facts [..]"*.[75] This statement indicates the existence of non-factual aspects that seem to be required when entering into a shareholding with a football club. Indeed, there is overall agreement among sponsors that an *emotional attachment* to a club is included into the decision-making process, as IP 4 (54; 2) stresses: *"You do not*

[75] *„[...] auf Faktenbasis sich für einen Bundesligaverein zu entscheiden, [..] das wird nicht funktionieren"* (IP 23, 421; 32).

cause somebody to do that without some emotional component. Well, some kind of affinity for football is definitely required".[76]

The relational and financial components of *shareholding* are strongly correlated to the sub-category *"sounding board"*. While a seat on the club's *"sounding board"* is often a desirable status for the sponsor in a *"brand symbiosis"* (strategic sponsorship) being part of the club's *"sounding board"* is a *binding* component of a *shareholding*, as the insights of IP 22 (404; 37) illustrate:

> "Basically, this has been prepared by the club. The shareholding is associated with a seat which is pretty logical".
>
> "I: If you take a share you want to be part of it [smile]".
>
> "B: That is correct. How shall I justify if there is a loss. Well, then I say I have no insight. Tell me, are you silly? You took a share".[77]

The statement sheds light on the club's *"sounding board"* as a tool for justification (for the sponsor) in order to ensure a *"protection of own capital"* (IP 18, 343; 12). A seat on the club's *"sounding board"* guarantees that the strategic equity partner is continuously updated *(exchanging information)* about the business situation of the investment object (club) and ascertains to have deep insights into the club's management procedures (*having insights* via the *"sounding board"*).

Legally, the idiosyncratic club constitution determines as of which share size a shareholder is entitled to a seat on the supervisory committee. Irrespective of that, the vast majority of interview participants agree that *sitting on the supervisory committee* is inevitably linked (as a contractual fixed item) to a shareholding. However, there are also two negative cases in which a seat at the club's *"sounding board"* is contractually not fixed. Yet, in these circumstances being part of the

---

[76]*„Sie kriegen eigentlich kaum einen, ohne dass irgendeine emotionale Komponente dabei ist. Dann, sag ich mal eine Affinität zum Fußball muss er denke ich auf jeden Fall haben"* (IP 4, 54; 2).

[77]*B: „Das hat der Verein im Kern eigentlich vorbereitet, mit den Shares gibt es einen Sitz, was auch eigentlich fast sachlogisch".*

I: „Wenn man sich schon beteiligt will man auch dabei sein [lächeln]".

B: „So ist es. Weil wie soll ich rechtfertigen, wenn mal ein Verlustsituation ist. Ja da sag ich, ich habe da keinen Einblick. Sag mal, bist du doof? Du hast dich doch beteiligt" (IP 22, 404; 37).

"sounding board" is informally agreed based on a mutual understanding of how to run a strategic equity partnership (same *mindset*, high level of *trust,* and *understanding of one's role*). IP 4 (62; 14) expounds this mutual understanding from a club's viewpoint as follows:

> "In the supervisory committee you need someone who invested money into the company. And they have the right to be informed, to ask questions and to decide on the board. These are rights an investor must have".[78]

By analysing the existing strategic equity partnerships in the 1st Bundesliga (document analysis), it is confirmed that a seat on the supervisory committee is unfailingly associated with a shareholding of the club, *"well, basically to strengthen the voice of economical reasonableness and keeping in mind in which strategic direction the [club name] develops"*[79] (IP 18, 345; 21). Beside these shareholding essentials there are various *strategic considerations* involved in the decision-making process that are elucidated as part of the sub-category *"screening"*.

6.5.3 Screening

"Screening" is a fundamental part of the shareholding decision-making process and is closely interwoven with the sub-category *shareholding essentials.* A *shareholding* rests upon a meticulous *"screening"* process that is performed before the club and sponsor enter into a strategic equity partnership.

"Screening" is a collective term for various strategies applied in order to evaluate a business situation holistically. It equally refers to aspects of the own organisation (*internal screening*, e.g., need, fit to own strategy) and acts as a background check on the partner (*partner screening*, e.g., due diligence). Moreover, the *macro* and *industry environment* are evaluated allowing a prediction about the club's *growth potential* for the future (*shareholding essential*) as well

---

[78] *„Im Aufsichtsrat brauchen sie natürlich jemanden von denjenigen, die Geld ins Unternehmen investiert haben. Und die haben auch ein Recht, dass sie informiert werden, dass sie Fragen stellen können, dass sie auch über den Vorstand befinden können. Das sind Rechte, die ein Investor dann haben muss"* (IP 4, 62; 14).

[79] *„Also, im Grunde die Stimme der wirtschaftlichen Vernunft verstärken und eben mitdenkt, in welche Richtung entwickelt sich [Club] eben strategisch richtig"* (IP 18, 345; 21).

as about future circumstances which might have an impact on the partnership, to be made. This correlates to possible *"spin-off effects"* of the sports (due to its *unique nature*) and the *difficulty to resell the shares*. IP 15 (281; 6) explained it as follows:

> "However, because it is a new segment, at the end of the day the board has to decide on the special influences which football can have, in particular the spin-off effects positively as well as negatively, and it is its responsibility. To get rid-off the value short-termed is difficult here".[80]

Therefore, *"screening"* serves as a basis for a sound decision-making process.

Partner screening is closely linked to the financial preconditions and growth potential of the club. It predominantly focuses on the current economic situation of the partner which is assessed via *"due diligence"*. With respect to the sponsor, this relates to the aforementioned *financial feasibility*. Since a shareholding is linked to high expenses for the shares, the club wants to ensure that it partners with a financially reliable associate who operates on a solid financial basis in order to reduce the risk for failure due to financial constraints, according to IP 9 (141; 33): *"He needs to have deep pockets in order to afford it and to be a reliable partner in the long run. Therefore, he needs to be economically sound"*.[81]

While the sponsor already has an insight into the club management due to the *history of partnership*, a shareholding still requires an in-depth check of the club's financial situation. Moreover, the club's structural preconditions in terms of the *site conditions* are evaluated. In this respect, the *stadium, infrastructure,* and *business location* (economic power of the city) are assessed as these are one of the determining factors that promote a club's future growth. With reference to IP 11 (187; 1), this becomes evident:

[80] *„Aber da das dann ein neues Segment ist, muss der Vorstand entscheiden, ob er am Ende des Tages die besondere Einflussnahme, die eben Fußball haben kann, insbesondere die Abstrahleffekte, im positiven wie im negativen, das muss natürlich der Vorstand entscheiden und liegt in seiner Verantwortung. Den Wert kurzfristig los zu werden, das geht hier nicht gut"* (IP 15, 281; 6).

[81] *„Er muss tiefe Taschen haben, damit er sowas bezahlen kann, dass er nachher auch ein solider Partner ist auf die Dauer, also er muss wirtschaftlich grundsolide sein"* (IP 9, 141; 33).

> "Well, [club name], this is one of the top clubs, they have steadily grown over the last 25 years and they will further grow due to the infrastructure, victories, history, and the whole economic area".[82]

An assessment about the club's growth potential is further ascertained based on a "*screening*" of the *industry* and *macro context.* The football industry has experienced a permanent surge over the last years and is perceived as a growing market (*growing football business*). IP 16 (288; 17) even declared that "*football, professional football is, from our viewpoint, the growth market number one*".[83] IP 22 (392; 5) coins the in vivo code "*top of the pops*" by highlighting football's "*[...] premium capacity and the social interconnectedness*".[84]

As part of an industry and macro "*screening*" additional effort is put into *scenario planning*. IP 15 (286; 25) provides insights into this process:

> "What is the prospect, what is the planning like, what kind of club strategy, what is their vision, from which area could a share progress arise, how is the club positioned, how strong does the sporting success impacts and, and, and".[85]

This statement sheds light on the various aspects which might have an impact on the future club state and share value of the club. Via *scenario planning* the sponsor tries to predict different scenarios and include these into the decision-making process.

Internal screening refers to a partner's own key *strategic considerations* whether *shareholding* supports the inherent partnership goals and whether it

[82] „*Mensch, [Club], das ist einer der Top-clubs, die sind die letzten 25 Jahren nur gewachsen, und die werden auch weiter wachsen aufgrund der Infrastruktur, der Erfolge, der Historie, des ganzen Hinterlandes*" (IP 11, 187; 1).

[83] „*Fußball, Profifußball ist aus unserer Sicht der Wachstumsmarkt Nummer 1*" (IP 16, 288; 17).

[84] „*Und wenn man wirklich mal sieht, wie der Fußball sich in den letzten 10 Jahre entwickelt hat, auch was die Premiumfähigkeit anbelangt, auch was die gesellschaftliche Vernetzung anbelangte. Dann ist das schon top of the pops*" (IP 22, 392; 5).

[85] „*Wie ist die Perspektive, wie ist die Planung, wie ist die Strategie dieses Vereins, wo will der hin, wo können Kursentwicklungen heraus resultieren, wie ist er positioniert, wie stark sind die sportlichen Erfolge relevant und, und, und*" (IP 15, 286; 25).

fits to the own strategy. Legally, a stake of up to 49% is feasible in Germany to participate in a football club due to the 50+1 rule (*idiosyncratic nature of the German football system*). Within this range, part of the *strategic considerations* of a club is a choice about the *amount of shares* to be issued to equity partners in general. Since selling shares is a shift in the ownership structure of the club and means giving up voting rights a shareholding is a sensitive (conflict-laden) issue for the parties involved (especially for club members and fans), which is grounded in the origin of German football clubs (*idiosyncratic nature of German football, fans as personification of the club* and their *high emotionality*). Regarding this, clubs and sponsors agree that a share deal at a football club requires consideration of the unique club environment, i.e., the club fans occupy a vital position in the club's setting (context) and become a crucial feature in the decision-making process. With reference to the club perspective, IP 7 (112; 21) stated: "*Well, you cannot handle such an issue without the support of the members and fans*".[86] The following statement illustrates the corresponding corporate perspective: "*[…] We have no interest and do not want to do something which negatively affects the fans*"[87] (IP 15, 278; 25).

Consequently, it is essential to get a holistic overview of fan opinion with regards to the *amount of shares*. Therefore, the current fan perception towards the strategic options of clubs regarding the overall *amount of shares* to be issued to shareholders is taken into consideration as illustrated in Figure 6.4 (n = 1,589) on page 209.

[86] „*Also du kannst so ein Thema nicht ohne die Begleitung durch Mitglieder und Fans machen*" (IP 7, 112; 21).

[87] „*[…] wir haben auch kein Interesse und wollen auch nichts tun, was diese Fankultur negativ tangiert oder stört*" (IP 15, 278; 25).

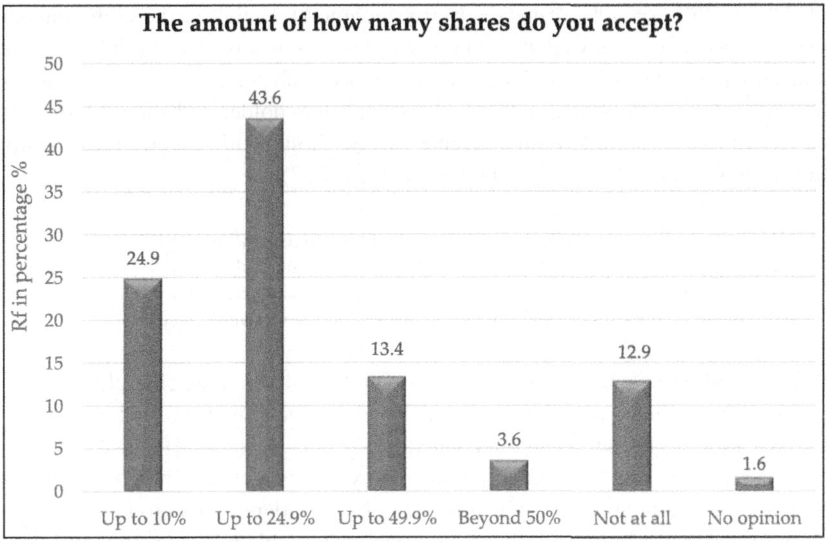

Figure 6.4 Fan Opinion on Amount of Shares. (Source: Own Illustration)

First and foremost, the bar chart shows that the majority of fans agree on minority equity partnerships of up to 10% (accumulated 81.9%). However, the *amount of shares* to be dispensed to external shareholders varies. Compared to the option "up to 10%" (24.9%) and "up to 49.9%" (13.4%), the blocking minority (up to 24.9%) is highly rated (43.6%). This is an indication that more than half of the club members and fans who agree on minority equity partnerships wish to preserve the club's exclusive decision-making power. The answer option "beyond 50%" was selected by 3.6% which implicates that 94.8% (100% minus 3.6% and 1.6% with no opinion) reject a majority shareholding. By implication, this provides (indirect) evidence for the exclusion of a controlling interest and the retention of the 50+1 rule.

The bar chart provides a general overview of fan opinion with regards to the *amount of shares* to be issued. Yet, since the majority of participants are fans from the 1st Bundesliga clubs (see survey characteristic, Table 7) this might be different in other club contexts, in particular at clubs from the 2nd Bundesliga and the 3rd Liga.

Some clubs such as VfB Stuttgart, Hamburger SV, and FC Bayern München already pursue the strategy of restricting the disposal of shares to a maximum of 24.9%, 25%, or 30% respectively (by incorporating this in the club constitution) instead of the allowed 49% in order to take the needs of their club members and fans into consideration. This should reduce club member and fan concerns towards a *fear of dependency* from an external shareholder and should lessen the danger of *fan resistance* (both concepts will be explained in greater detail within the category *fear of loss*), as explained by IP 2 (16; 7):

> "We have, I do not want to say due to compliance reasons, but we have stipulated that in our case it is not 50+1 instead the e.V. with the club members will always hold 70% of the corporation. [...]. In this way it is always clear that the majority is held by the club members and this is a system which works very, very well".[88]

Even though this is an effective strategy which works in a specific club context, it does not guarantee that this applies to all clubs because every club has its own idiosyncratic background and fan context (IP 7, 111; IP 9, 148; IP 12; 225).

In addition to the decision about how many shares a club wants to sell in general, another strategic aspect which needs to be considered refers to the *amount of shares* one partner holds. As illustrated previously (Table 6.7), the strategic equity partnerships in German football are based on minority shareholdings which differ from 5% at the minimum to around 15% (per partner, with regard to strategic equity partners).

First and foremost, an equity stake serves as a counter value for the sponsor's investment (one-off payment). Consequently, the exact size of shares for one partner is, inter alia, a matter of costs a sponsor is ready (or able) to expend and a question of how many shares a club is willing to dispense to one partner. From a strategic standpoint, there are fundamentally two criteria which have to be satisfied for both partners with respect to the stake size: the *amount of shares* needs to be high enough to show a sustainable strategic interest in the club but should concurrently avoid evoking the impression of taking influence or dominating the club (which indicates the connection to the category *fear of loss* and the concept *considering fan resistance*) as IP 15 (277; 35) unveiled:

[88] *„Wir haben uns selbst, ich will jetzt nicht gleich sagen aus Compliance-Gründen, sondern wir haben uns selbst eine Auflage erteilt, dass wir gesagt haben, bei uns ist es nicht 50 + 1, sondern der e.V. mit seinen Mitgliedern wird immer 70 Prozent behalten an der AG. [...]. Weil eben immer klar ist, die Majorität ist bei den Clubmitgliedern und das ist ein System, mit dem wir sehr, sehr gut fahren"* (IP 2, 16; 5).

> "Not just a few shares, which can be resold tomorrow. Instead, which is also important for the club, he has sponsors and these are so closely attached to the club that they are ready, first and foremost, to economically connect with the club and to engage in a way which shows we do not want to dominate the club. This is also vital for the fans".[89]

The statement shows that a strategic equity partner has no interest in taking influence into the clubs' issues which is confirmed by IP 2 (29; 18): "*I can honestly say it is certainly no hostile takeover [smile]. Instead one knows each partner a very long-term and this was just the next step*".[90] The expression "*very long-term*" relates to the concept *history of partnership* and "*just the next step*" indicates the process character *(deepening involvement)* of the partnership.

It is commonly agreed in this research context that a 5% stake is a considerable (minimum) size for one partner to demonstrate a strategic interest. Beyond this, related to expressing a strategic interest, the exact share size is not decisive, because "*[…] as long as there is no/let's say a distribution it does not matter if we are involved with 5% or 25%*"[91] (IP 16, 294; 18). While in some contexts the priority of a strategic equity partner is to hold a stake of around 5% (to express a strategic interest only), other corporations put more emphasis on the share size due to external image and positioning impact. This, in particular, refers to circumstances in which the club decides to incorporate more than one strategic equity partner. Generally, a club has three strategic options to allocate equity stakes:

- a certain stake to one partner
- the shares are equally issued between several strategic equity partners
- the shares are unequally issued between several strategic equity partners

[89] „*Nicht so ein paar Aktien, die man morgen wiederverkaufen kann, sondern schon, auch für den Verein wichtig, er hat Sponsoren, und die Sponsoren sind so mit dem Verein verbunden, dass sie auch bereit sind, erstens sich wirtschaftlich an diesen Verein zu binden und zu engagieren aber in einer Form, wo deutlich wird, sie wollen den Verein nicht domminieren. Das ist auch für die Fans wichtig*" (IP 15, 277; 35).

[90] „*[…] glaube ich, dass man klar sagen kann, es sind sicher keine feindlichen Übernahmen [lächeln], sondern, dass man hier [.] sich schon sehr, sehr lange gekannt hat und das einfach ein nächster Schritt war*" (IP 2, 29; 18).

[91] „*[…] so lange es ja auch keine / sagen wir eine gewisse Ausschüttung gibt, ist uns ja egal, ob wir jetzt irgendwie mit 5% oder 25% drin sind, weil nutzt ja nicht viel*" (IP 16, 294; 18).

The latter two options are affected by the strategy of the strategic equity partner, too. From a corporate perspective, on condition of numerous corporate club shareholders, the *amount of shares* has implications for the corporate status within the compound of several strategic equity partners. A shareholding can be built upon the strategy of *being* (and *signifying*) the *number one partner* of a club by holding a larger stake compared to co-shareholders. This strategy is mirrored in the following statement:

> "I have already mentioned it, for us it is very important that we are perceived in the one-to-one relationship with the fans and the sympathisers the [club name] has worldwide. That we are perceived as the number one partner and the undisputed number one partner"[92] (IP 18, 327; 33).

While expressing the status as *being the number one* partner of the club is a vital endeavour for some strategic equity partners to hold a superior stake, other shareholders put less significance into the *amount of shares* and even argue that the share deal as a whole is not of long-lasting interest in the public perception, as put forward by IP 20 (376; 3):

> "Well, this fizzles out at some point. Then, nobody cares about it. In two years, nobody under the sun knows anymore that [corporation] is part of it".[93]

Although there are contrasting views among corporate responsibles whether the *amount of shares* has a long-lasting effect on image and the public perception, the fan survey yielded interesting information about fan opinion regarding strategic options of how to allocate shares among one or several shareholders. First and foremost, fans appear not to have a uniform opinion as illustrated in Table 6.9 (n = 1,330[94]) on page 213:

[92] *„Und ich hatte es eben schon gesagt, für uns ist das eben sehr wichtig, dass wir eins-zu-eins in der Beziehung in der Wahrnehmung der Fans und der ganzen Sympathisanten, die [Club] weltweit hat. Das wir der Nummer Eins Partner und der unangefochtene Nummer Eins Partner wahrgenommen werden"* (IP 18, 327; 33).

[93] *„Aber das verpufft ja dann auch irgendwann mal wieder, dann interessiert das keinen. In zwei Jahren weiß kein Mensch mehr, dass [Unternehmen] jetzt mit dabei ist"* (IP 20, 376; 3).

[94] Participants had the opportunity to chose the answer choice "not specified" (n = 259).

Table 6.9 Allocation of Shares among Shareholders. (Source: Own Illustration)

How should the shares be allocated among shareholders?	
Answer options	Rf in percent %
1 Shareholder who holds all shares	14.4
Several shareholders holding different amounts of shares	42.6
Several shareholders holding an equal stak	32.9
I have no opinion	10.1

With regard to the allocation of shares, the majority of fans seem to prefer that the shares are allocated among several shareholders (overall 75.5%) instead of one shareholder who holds all the shares (14.4%). There is also the tendency for a preference for an unequal allocation of shares among several shareholders (42.6%) compared to an equal allocation (32.9%). The fans' opinion is inter alia based on the arguments presented in Table 6.10 (answers relate to the question in Table 6.9).

Table 6.10 Arguments of Share Allocation. (Source: Own Illustration)

Please reason your answer from the above question*		
n = 1,330[1] * multiple answers possible	Quoted Rf in %	Not quoted Rf in %
The influence of one shareholder who holds all the shares could be too big	61.7	38.3
In the case of several shareholders the club benefits from various competences of the shareholders	50.3	49.7
In case of several shareholders it is not possible to distinguish who is the main partner of the club	9.8	90.2
In case of several shareholders there is a risk of disturbance due to contrasting views between shareholders	22.6	77.4

[a]Participants had the opportunity to chose the answer choice "not specified" (n= 259).

The majority of fans (61.7%) did quote that the influence of only one shareholder who has all shares is too big. This indicates a *fear of dependency* of one big partner into the management of the club and also conforms with previous insights that the majority fans accept minority shareholdings of up to 24.9% which is a crucial barrier for investors (blocking minority). The admission of several shareholders to benefit from various competences yielded a split result.

Furthermore, 77.4% of fans do not see a risk of disturbance for the club in the case of several shareholders. The negated argument *"in case of several shareholders it is not possible to distinguish who is the main partner of the club"* is not quoted by 90.2% of fans. This means that fans can distinguish who the main partner of the club is in case of several shareholders.

While this is a general argument and not related the amount of shares an equity partner holds, by use of a cross table and a correlation determination (chi-square test) a statistical correlation between the two variables *"in case of several shareholders it is not possible to distinguish who is the main partner of the club"* and *"several shareholders holding a different amount of share"* could be identified, as depicted in Table 6.11 (n = 1,330[95]).

Table 6.11 Contingency Table - Amount of Shares and Several Shareholders. (Source: Own Illustration)

Several shareholders holding different amounts of shares * In case of several shareholders it is not possible to distinguish who is the main partner of the club					
			In case of several shareholders it is not possible to distinguish who is the main partner of the club		
			not quoted	quoted	total
Several shareholders holding different amount of shares	not quoted	Amount	666	**98**	764
		% of several shareholders holding different amounts of shares	87.2%	**12.8%**	100.0%
	quoted	Amount	**533**	33	566
		% of several shareholders holding different amounts of shares	**94.2%**	5.8%	100.0%
Total		Amount	1199	131	1330
		% of several shareholders holding different amounts of shares	90.2%	9.8%	100.0%

[95] Participants had the opportunity to chose the answer choice "not specified" (n = 259).

The two squares highlighted in gray illustrate the key information in the table. While *being perceived as the number one partner* is a strategic goal for some strategic equity partners and the reason to hold a majority stake compared to co-shareholders (IP 18, 327), this correlation can statistically be confirmed (P value 0.000) from the fan view as shown in Table 6.12:

Table 6.12 Chi-Square Test. (Source: Own Illustration)

Chi-square test					
	Value	df	Asymptotic Significance (2-sided)	Exact Sig. (2-sided)	Exact Sig. (1-sided)
Pearson Chi-Square	**17.926**[a]	**1**	**.000**		
Continuity Correction[b]	17.146	1	.000		
Likelihood Ratio	18.923	1	.000		
Fisher's Exact Test				.000	.000
Linear-by-Linear Association	17.912	1	.000		
n of Valid Cases	**1330**				

a. 0 cells (0,0%) have expected count less than 5. The minimum expected count is 55,75
b. Computed only for a 2x2 table

It can be stated that fans can distinguish who is the main partner of the club based on the *amount of shares*. Therefore, *being the number one partner* by holding a superior stake is one strategic option, may be justified in a specific context, and can be reflected in fan opinion.

The decision about the *amount of shares* can also be established on the strat egy of *being on eye level* with co-shareholders, thereby expressing an equally vital status by holding the same size of stake, as revealed by IP 22 (399; 23): *"This has always been the strategy of [name of the person]. Limited partners but all operating as equals"*.[96] Both strategic approaches interrelate to the corporate identity of the strategic equity partner. For instance, if a company's competitive

[96]*„Das war auch immer die Politik von Herrn [Name]. Begrenzte Partner, aber alle gleichrangig auf Augenhöhe"* (IP 22, 399; 23).

strategy is based on a differentiation strategy this strategic direction needs to be compatible with the share size. In this given context, a minority stake compared to other shareholders would not fit to the image of the partner as the following example elucidates:

> "With respect to the shareholding we would be the little partner vis-à-vis [company A], [company B], and [company C]. [Company D, own company] has a latent problem with this [smile]. As market leader and [type of sponsorship] then not to be the little partner. This is also the reason, either we are equal partners or not at all"[97] (IP 17, 311; 20).

It becomes evident that the *positioning* within a context of numerous strategic equity partners matters according to the own company's strategic direction and corporate identity (self-conception). The survey results confirm that the *amount of shares* an equity partner holds has a *signifying* effect with respect to status (who is the main partner of the club) from the perspective of fans. Furthermore, it can be extracted from the last-mentioned statement that the size of disposable shares might be a limiting factor for the club to incorporate further strategic equity partners if there is just "a rest amount of shares" available which is lower compared to the shares of already existing shareholders.

Another vital aspect as part of the strategic considerations of a sponsor is an assessment about the acceptance of a share deal with respect to the own stakeholders. IP 15 (277; 7) refers to a *"[...] political aspect. Shall we invest, is it right to invest in a football club"*.[98] While a justification of the investment to own shareholders is done via the aforementioned financial preconditions and a seat in the club's *"sounding board"*, the political deliberation can contain other

---

[97] *„Wir wären dann bei der Beteiligung der kleine Partner gegenüber [Unternehmen A], [Unternehmen B] und [Unternehmen C]. Da hat [Unternehmen D, eigenes Unternehmen] immer latent ein Problem mit [lachen]. Als Marktführer und [Sponsoringform] dann nicht der kleine Partner zu sein. Das ist dann auch ein Grund, entweder sind wir dann gleichwertiger Partner oder nicht"* (IP 17, 311; 20).

[98] *„So und dann kommt die politische Seite, wollen wir das aus politischen Gründen, ist es richtig, in einen Fußballverein zu investieren, wie ist die Reaktion der [Kunden], hat man da mit irgendwelchen Querbewegungen zu rechnen [..]"* (IP 15, 277; 7).

stakeholder groups (e.g., employees, customers, and public) whose consideration depend on the mission of the company and are dimensionalised on its relevance *(not at all important/very important).*

For example, for a company with a non-sport related core business or an enterprise with no regional affinity to the club an investment into a football club stake could meet with resistance among staff, based on the argument *"[...] you put money in this but you do not want to pay better salaries for your employees"*[99] (IP 5, 65; 17). In contrast, in a different corporate context (e.g., sport-related core business or a company in the same region of the club) a shareholding might rather be positively perceived by employees as the employer (company) demonstrates a form of social responsibility by supporting "their" (the employee's) club (IP 22, 386; IP 20; 380; IP 23, 409; IP 24, 410). Consequently, the internal impact of a football club investment needs to be balanced in a corporate-specific context.

To summarise, a share deal requires a multitude of *shareholding essentials* and is based on various *"screening"* processes and strategic considerations which need to be positively evaluated in order to realise a shareholding between the club and corporate sponsor. Figure 6.5 on page 218 provides a summary about the most vital components of the sub-category.

[99] *„Und dann bei der Betriebsversammlung aufgetischt wird, da gibt ihr Geld hin und dem Mitarbeiter wollte ihr keine höheren Löhne zahlen"* (IP 5, 65; 17).

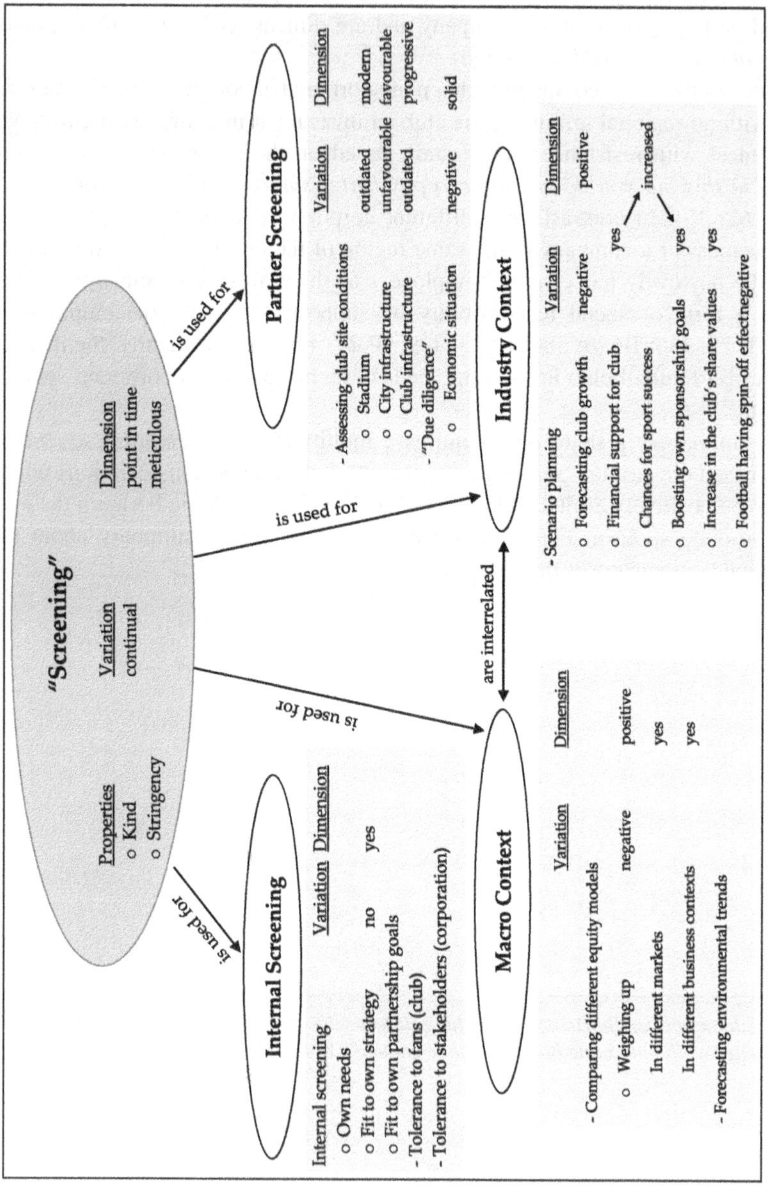

Figure 6.5 Screening. (Source: Own Illustration)

It is further shown that, by entering into an additional share deal, the corporate club partnership consists of a dyad of sponsorship and shareholding. How this dyad is managed is explained in the following sub-category *managing the dyad.*

6.5.4 Managing the Dyad

Managing the dyad is a connecting category that links the two categories *becoming a brand symbiosis* (the strategic sponsorship partnership) and *shareholding.* The term dyad is utilised in order to indicate that a strategic equity partnership is based on a two-level partnership: a contractual sponsorship and a partnership at the ownership level of the club. The term dyad means "two units treated as one (a pair)" and implies an equivocalness. Although the shareholding and sponsorship are legally and formally separated, the partnership as such is managed as one.

Basically, the shareholding and sponsorship are fixed in two different contracts, "*[...] which* per se *have nothing to do with each other*"[100] (IP 20, 369; 26). Whereas a sponsorship contract entails all the commercial rights and duties between the affiliates a shareholding is not related to commercial rights. It is rather an exchange relationship between an equity stake (shares) and money which is associated with specific rights that depend on the *amount of shares* and the club constitution, according to IP 4 (50; 37):

> "However, this is partly important to elucidate to the potential equity holders that there is no seat, neither a standing nor a business seat, no kind of advertising is associated/nor is there any entitlement".[101]

Yet, a shareholding contract may entail individual rights for the corporate partner, such as a contractual agreement to have a binding seat on the club's supervisory committee (*binding/not binding*). Still, a sponsorship can formally and legally exist without a shareholding at the club and vice versa.

---

[100] „*Das sind auch zwei unterschiedliche Verträge, die haben eigentlich* per se *nichts miteinander zu tun*" (IP 20, 369; 26).

[101] „*Aber es ist teilweise auch wichtig auch den potentiellen Eigenkapitalgeber klar machen, dass sie mit der Beteiligung keinen Sitz, weder einen Stehplatz, Business Seat, irgendwelche Werbung damit nicht / kein Anrecht darauf haben*" (IP 4, 50; 37).

However, the words used in the aforementioned statement from IP 20 (i.e., per se) indicate a restriction. The quotation of IP 17 (309; 9) also suggests a restraint by using the subjunctive (should): *"That we say these two things should be separated from each other"*.[102] Both statements hint to a subtle connection between a sponsorship and a shareholding. Indeed, within the course of in-depth analysis it becomes evident that, based on strategic considerations, a shareholding and sponsorship are connected substantially. Holding club shares without being a club sponsor would not be compatible with the communication and marketing strategy of the sponsor. The key reason behind this is that a credible relationship is difficult to convey to the public if a company is a top sponsor at a club and simultaneously a direct competitor is shareholder of the same club. Therefore, it is unlikely that a corporation will sponsor a club while a direct competitor is shareholder of the same club. IP 17 (311; 7) summed this up aptly: *"[...] This is a situation nobody wants to have. It does not make any sense for you to hold an equity stake and then [company B] is on the shirt [...]"*.[103] Furthermore, an exit from one of the partnership forms has implications on the other because it affects the interpersonal relationship and trust between the partners (among people), as explicated by IP 15 (283; 34):

> „If you separate from the overall investment according to the motto: We quit the sponsorship, we abandon [the sponsorship rights], then one has to ask the question whether it still makes sense since one questions the issue as a whole. And this refers to both sides because the two things are mutually dependent. And if it is said there is trust and on the one level it is gone one has to think about whether it affects the other. Consequently, there are correlations".[104]

[102] *„Das wir sagen, eigentlich sollten die beiden Dinge ein Stück weit getrennt voneinander sein"* (IP 17, 309; 9).

[103] *„[...] diese Situation will natürlich keiner. Weil es keinen Sinn macht, dass man Equity hat und dann ist [Unternehmen B] auf dem Trikot [...]"* (IP 17, 311; 7).

[104] *„Wobei es natürlich schon so ist, wenn man sich jetzt von dem Gesamtinvestment trennen würde nach dem Motto: Wir machen kein Sponsoring mehr, wir geben die [Sponsoringrechte] ab, dann muss man sich eigentlich die Frage stellen, was auf der anderen Seite dann die Kapitalbeteiligung noch Sinn macht. Aber dann stellt man das Thema ja insgesamt in Frage. Und dann muss man es auch auf beiden Seiten tun, weil das eine natürlich das andere in gewisser Weise befördert. Und wenn man sagt, man hat Vertrauen und wenn man das an der einen Ecke nicht mehr hat muss man überlegen, hat das nicht auch Auswirkung auf das andere. Also insofern gibt es da schon Wirkungszusammenhänge"* (IP 15, 283; 34).

While shareholding and sponsorship are substantially connected the dyad can also be contractually connected via a *"retention factor"*. A *"retention factor"* is a contractual item regarding the equity stake which regulates the shareholding in case of a possible exit from the strategic equity partnership as a sponsor (pre-defined exit strategy). IP 22 (390; 10) explains that with an end of the sponsorship strategy *"[...] we would refund the share to equivalent values. And this is properly contractually agreed"*.[105] That means, in case of a sponsorship termination the club or a different company/partner has to buy back the shares from the leaving strategic equity partner based on the current share value of the club. The *"retention factor"* is based on strategic considerations and gets the sponsor into a favourable position. Since the share price is an *amount into the million* the *"retention factor"* serves as an obstacle (cross reference to the sub-core category *deterring competitors*) for other companies who aim to supersede the actual sponsorship, with reference to IP 11 (186; 7):

> "Therefore, we have tried confidentially, I'd say, to connect these shares with a specific retention factor. That means, if today someone would participate at [club name], then we have the right to sell the shares".[106]

Even though the bonding (via the shareholding) is not inextricable an additional equity investment still serves as an obstacle. The statement of IP 11 (202; 25) clarifies: *"It is all solvable but is it definitely more difficult for us to enter [club name] if [company B; current sponsor] has an equity as you have to buy it"*.[107] However, the *"retention factor"* is an optional contractual clause in the shareholder contract and not included in every corporate club partnership (variation in the data). Irrespective of an existing contractual *"retention factor"*, the equity stake still serves as an obstacle due to the aforementioned strategic considerations to achieve consistency in the communication strategy.

---

[105] *„Dann würde auch mit einem Ende einer Sponsoringstrategie auch verbunden sein auch die Anteile, ich sag mal, schon wieder zu gleichen Werten zurückgibt. Und das haben wir im Vertrag sauber hinterlegt*" (IP 22, 390; 10).

[106] *„Darum haben wir auch dann im Vertrauten versucht, eben diese / diese Anteile, ich sag einmal [.], mit einem gewissen Retention Faktor zu verbinden. Das heißt, wenn heute jemand anders einsteigen würde bei [Club], dann haben wir das Recht, die Anteile auch zu verkaufen*" (IP 11, 186; 7).

[107] *„Es ist alles lösbar, so ist es nicht. Aber es ist definitiv schwieriger für uns bei [Club] jetzt rein zu gehen, wenn [Unternehmen] ein Equity hat, weil das musst du erst raus kaufen*" (IP 11, 202; 25).

An additional shareholding also signifies a closer and stronger tie and acts as a stabilising factor *(demonstrating stability)* for the whole partnership, as an exit of a strategic equity partnership is rendered difficult due to the share deal, according to IP 22 (404; 12): *"Yes, this is a more stable anchor and one simply can't say I resign"*.[108] This stability is intensified even further due to the binding seat in the club's *"sounding board"*. As a member of the club's *"sounding board"* the strategic equity partner is involved in the fundamental decisions of the club, i.e., this allows inclusion in the strategic decision-making process about future club shareholders (change in the club's ownership structure of the club) and enables co-determination on this issue.

While there is a strategic connection within the dyad of sponsorship and shareholding, in practice the daily partnership management is not different due to an additional share deal, as IP 10 (175; 4) clarified:

> "If I had to separate the investment versus strategic partnership, since we have both, I think I could not do it. This would be stupid. We are a partner. To get to the point, this is very intensive".[109]

Although the daily operations are not altered by a shareholding, an equity investment has an impact on the strategic management of the partnership since, for example, a seat on the club's *"sounding board"* becomes compulsory.

Sitting on the club's supervisory committee can be a conflict-laden situation within the club's *"sounding board"* because of the dual role of being a commercial partner (sponsor) and shareholder at the club. IP 15 (276; 12) outlines as follows:

> "As a shareholder I say: yes, get still more money from the sponsors as this is good for the share price. If I am on both sides this is maybe not so funny. In this case I say: wait a minute, slowly, slowly, slowly, this is an economic issue".[110]

---

[108] „*Ja, das ist ein stabilerer Anker, wo man nicht einfach sagt jetzt kündige ich mal kurz*" (IP 22, 404; 12).

[109] „*Wenn ich jetzt trennen müsste, Investment versus strategische Partnerschaft, da wir ja beides haben, ich glaub das könnte ich gar nicht. Wäre auch blöd. Wir sind halt ein Partner. Das ist schon eigentlich sehr intensiv, das trifft es erst mal*" (IP 10, 175; 4).

[110] „*Als Anteilseigner sage ich: Jawohl, holt von den Sponsoren nur noch mehr Geld rein, weil das dem Aktienkurs guttut. Wenn ich auf beiden Seiten bin, finde ich das vielleicht gar nicht so witzig. Da sag ich: Moment mal, langsam, langsam, langsam, das ist eine betriebswirtschaftliche Veranstaltung*" (IP 15, 276; 12).

On the one hand, the equity partner has an entrepreneurial interest in its investment. On the other hand, as a member of the club's "*sounding board*", the strategic equity partner is formally committed to act in the best interest of the club. IP 20 (376; 16) admitted that this situation can be "*very difficult*[111]"due to the *differing ambitions* and corresponding differing management approaches between the club and corporate sponsor. However, this concern also reinforces the fundamental aspects of the interrelating concepts of similar *mindsets, management cultures, values (compatibility),* and a mutual *understanding of one's role* as vital preconditions for a strategic equity partnership. Still, an additional shareholding at a club has implications (consequences) for the partnership which are illuminated next.

6.5.5 Having a Say

The sub-category *"having a say"* describes an increased responsibility which results from a shareholding in a football club. While a sponsor is primarily focused on the sporting success of a club, as a strategic equity partner the corporation is part of the club's ownership and, by implication, directly affected by its economic (business) success. Consequently, a shareholder has an interest in the *economic success (extending domain of interest)* of the club in order to ensure the *value retention* of its equity investment.

This sub-category is directly connected to the voting right associated with a binding seat on the club's *"sounding board"* because *"only via the supervisory committee"*[112] (IP 8, 125; 1) the strategic equity partner co-determines the club's strategic issues. IP 15 (281; 29) explains the underlying reasons:

> "The background is that we are just closer and can see earlier if it is economically successful and are able in this way, in terms of the economic development of the club, to exert an influence. Not on the sporting area, but on the economic development because, at the end of the day, it is about our money, our investment [...]".[113]

[111] „*Sehr schwierig*" (IP 20, 376; 16).

[112] „*[..] Nur über das Thema Aufsichtsratssitz*" (IP 8, 125; 1).

[113] „*Hintergrund, wir sind dann näher dran, sehen dann auch schneller und früher, ob das wirtschaftlich erfolgreich ist und können über den Weg, was die wirtschaftliche Entwicklung des Vereins angeht, Einfluss nehmen, nicht auf die sportliche aber die wirtschaftliche Entwicklung, weil es am Ende des Tages um das eigenen Geld geht, um das eigene Investment [...]*" (IP 15, 281; 29).

This statement clearly shows the direct connection between the two concepts of *"having a say"* and *"sounding board"*. Although *"having a say"* indicates a form of influence on the club the term influence is negatively connotated in this research context because it relates to the concept of power and suggests a kind of steering motive of a strategic equity partner, as is illustrated by IP 13 (240; 37):

> "And this influence this is a negative word, I don't think so. I think, if you ask [name of person] he won't say that they take influence in the meaning of power. However, we offer our services".[114]

There is overall agreement in the research field that, as a minority equity partner, *"you are not the top dog, this is clear. You do not have the majority. The club itself possesses [anonymised figure] % and has the say"*[115] (IP 11, 186; 25). While a single seat on the supervisory committee represents (only) one vote of the body, a group of corporate shareholders in the *"sounding board"* has a "bigger" say into the club's issues (IP 22, 392). Corporate equity partners are all economically-driven. Based on their corporate nature they often argue from a similar (economic) perspective. Consequently, the say of economic reasonableness and growth issues is strengthened if a club has several strategic equity partners. Nevertheless, if the stake of one partner entitles the shareholder to get a second seat on the club's *"sounding board"* the influence of this shareholder is increased (correlation to *amount of shares*).

However, due to the mutual *understanding of one's role*, *compatibility*, and *trust* between the club and strategic equity partner *"having a say" "[...] is less a form of influence [...] it is rather a supervising and consulting issue"*[116] (IP 2, 20; 1) which mainly refers to economic advice and growth issues. This advisory function is acknowledged by clubs as a valuable form of support (knowledge transfer). Even though a strategic partner does not aim to influence on sporting decisions (*intervening in sporting decisions*, dimensionalised *not at all/low*), a

[114]*„Und diesen Einfluss, das ist ja so ein negatives Wort, das glaube ich nicht. Ich glaube, wenn du [Name von Person] fragst wird er nicht sage, dass sie Einfluss nehmen in einer Machtform. Aber wir stellen uns zur Verfügung*" (IP 13, 240; 37).

[115]*„Das du da nicht das Große Sagen hast. Das ist auch klar. Du hast keine Majorität. Der Club selber besitzt [anonymisiert] % und hat damit natürlich auch das Sagen*" (IP 11, 186; 25).

[116]*„Ich glaube es ist / wird weniger weniger Einfluss hier, sondern [...] mehr als Beaufsichtigen und Beraten*" (IP 2, 20; 1).

"sounding board" consisting of high-profile individuals (CEOs) can still be challenging for clubs. IP 7 (103; 23) elucidates that *"successful businessmen [..] are used to calling the shots in their company".*[117] While this concern is lessened (or even removed) based on the aforementioned concepts of *understanding of one's role, similar mindsets*, and *trust* there might still be situation in which a strategic partner contemplates using his voting right, according to IP 10 (180; 28): "*And if the question of buying Ronaldo for 120 million Euros arose, I think then we would have to talk about what that means for the whole partnership*".[118] However, as can be abstracted by the statement this only refers to exceptional circumstances, such as an extraordinary high player transfer that could threaten the growth potential of the club.

Besides, *"having a say"* and an *extended domain of interest* a *shareholding* has a multi-faceted symbolic character which is expressed in the sub-category *signifying*.

6.5.6 Signifying

To signify is an active verb which refers *"to make something known; to show"* and *"to have importance or to matter"* (Cambridge dictionary, 2008; 1338), therefore reflecting and underpinning the strategic emphasis (*internally* and *externally*) of the partnership for the club and sponsor. In accordance with the inherent *strategic intent* of the associates, an additional share deal signifies the sponsor's interest in a long-term and sustainable partnership, according to IP 22 (390; 1): *"We are interested in a long-term partnership, we substantiate this with a financial participation and signal enough".*[119] Consequently, *shareholding* signifies the vital status the partner has for its affiliate and adds to the *credibility* of

---

[117] *„Erfolgreiche Unternehmer [..] sind natürlich gewohnt aus ihren Unternehmen zu sagen, wo es lang geht*" (IP 7, 103; 23).

[118] *„Und wenn dann mal das Thema wäre, Ronaldo für 120 Millionen Euro kaufen, ich glaube dann müsste man sich unterhalten, was heißt das denn für das Gesamtkonstrukt*" (IP 10, 180; 28).

[119] *„Wir haben Interesse an einer langfristigen Partnerschaft, die untermauern wir jetzt auch mit einer Finanzbeteiligung und Signal genug*" (IP 22, 390; 1).

the relationship between the partners, with reference to IP 10 (167; 10): *"That means, it is a sort of affirmation to the partnership"*.[120]

Furthermore, acquiring club shares is a form of *signalising exclusivity* to the outside world. Exclusivity has a twofold meaning in this context. A shareholding presents the sponsor as an exclusive partner (status of exclusiveness, form of unique characteristic) of the club in terms of the sponsorship type, therefore underpinning the *"retention factor"*. On the other hand, exclusiveness refers to something valuable (quality of being exclusive). By acquiring club shares, the sponsor signifies the belief in the club's future (financial) success (economic reasonableness). Therefore, a share deal acts as a sign for quality which is beneficial for the club's reputation. The following statement by IP 4 (61; 5) summarises exclusiveness in the form of a signal for quality:

> "Since this is a sign to the outside world that such worldwide corporations are involved and closely linked to football. As a consequence, sponsors join who say: ok, then I can buy an advertising service".[121]

As can be extracted from this statement, *signifying* as an outcome of *shareholding* may encourage other companies to enter into a partnership with the club. This, in turn, serves to boost the club's future success which is beneficial for the strategic equity partner(s), too.

Contrary to this, the signifying effect can also have downsides for both partners in times of trouble (*intensifying problems in times of trouble*) due to the permanent media attention (*being under the public eye*). Although in a strategic equity partnership each partner's business remains largely independent, the fact that the sponsor participates in the ownership of the club and that the top management of both partners are in close dialogue with each other (e.g., via the *"sounding board"*) let the public and media assume that the partner has insights into all critical issues of the associate. IP 15 (279; 28) provides insights into these consequences of an equity deal:

---

[120] „*Das heißt, das ist eben auch ein gewisses Bekenntnis zu der Partnerschaft*" (IP 10, 167; 10).

[121] „*Weil das nach außen hin auch ein Zeichen ist, dass sich solche Weltunternehmen an dem Fußball beteiligen, sich ganz fest mit dem verbinden, dann kommt der ein oder andere Sponsor natürlich auch noch mal dazu. Der sagt ok, dann kann ich hier auch eine Werbeleistung einkaufen*" (IP 4, 61; 5).

"We have to be aware of these issues you buy into these. One is connected with the brand for better or for worse. And if the club not only plays badly but also makes negative headlines one is faced with the whole problem at hand including all the consequences".[122]

The statement illustrates a closer relationship (propinquity) through a shareholding and possible related negative consequences. This can touch on the behaviour of the club and corporate individuals or the partner as a whole and refers generally to image issues. IP 8 (126; 3) exemplifies and talks about the risk *"[...] that the club as a whole, or vital individual actors of the club misbehave in some way which gives rise for questions and rub off on us"*.[123] Other areas relate to the fan base of the club. Fan misbehaviour in the form of e.g., personal hostility or the use of pyrotechnics have a quick negative impact due to the permanent media attention.

Overall, this category outlined the underlying basic requirements *(shareholding essentials)*, processes and strategic considerations *(screening)*, and effects *(having a say, signifying)* of a share deal between a football club and its strategic equity partner, thereby addressing the strategic intent of sponsors. Furthermore, it explains how the brand symbiosis (strategic partnership) is (formally/informally) connected to the shareholding within the sub-category of *managing the dyad*. The conceptual details of the category are illustrated in Figure 6.6 on the next page.

[122] *„Und darüber muss man sich im klaren sein, sowas kauft man sich damit eben auch ein. Sie sind dann auf Gedeih und Verderben mit ihrer Marke / hängen sie dann am Verein. Und wenn der dann nicht nur schlecht spielt, sondern auch negativ in den Schlagzeilen ist, dann haben sie auch das volle Problem auf dem Tisch, mit allen Konsequenzen*" (IP 15, 279; 28).

[123] *„Das ist das Risiko, dass der Verein als Ganzes oder einzelne wichtige Akteure des Vereins sich irgendwo negativ bemerkbar machen, dass das durchaus auch Fragen aufwirft und abfärben kann*" (IP 8, 126; 3).

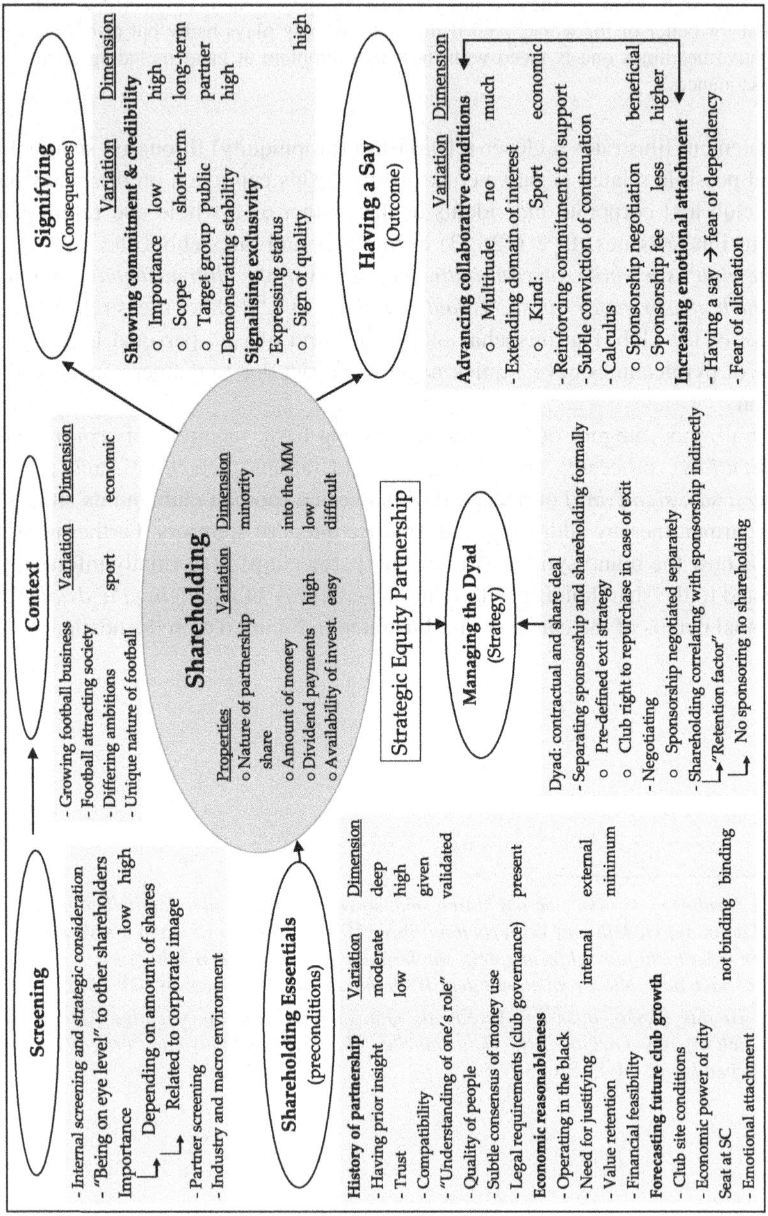

Figure 6.6 Shareholding. (Source: Own Illustration.)

6.5.7 Theoretical Integration

In this subsection, the findings of *shareholding* are discussed against insights from the literature. This discussion will touch on knowledge from equity investments (financial perspective) as well as insights from strategic partnerships as outlined in Table 6.13.

Table 6.13 Contrasting Literature with Shareholding. (Source: Own Illustration)

Empirical concepts from grounded theory	Findings from the literature review
Context Differing ambitions	Maximising sporting success for clubs, clubs operating in economical equilibrium, generating profits for corporations, increasing shareholder value for corporations (Chemnitzer et al., 2015; Amis et al., 1997; Carroll, 1996; Denning, 2011; Jones, 2008; Nagy, 2012; Rudd, 2012; Frick, 2007; Barros & Leach, 2006; Sloane, 1971; Westberg et al., 2012).
Unique nature of the football business	Football clubs not intended to pay dividends (Heijden, 2012; Pinnuck & Potter, 2006; Oediger, 2017b; Prigge & Vöpel, 2014)
	Uncertainty and unpredictability of outcomes (Schade, 2012; Nagy, 2012; Schilhaneck, 2008). Uncertainty, unpredictability, statistical relationship between money and sporting success (Nagy, 2012; Quitzau, 2003; Schade, 2012; Schilhaneck, 2008; Hall et al., 2002; Barajas et al., 2005; Szymanski & Kuypers, 1999; Hovemann & Wieschemann, 2009; Carmichael et al., 2010; Kuypers & Szymanski, 2012)
Country specific rules	Governance structures, 50 + 1 rule, TV distribution (Adam & Hovemann, 2018; Quitzau, 2009, 2003; Nagy, 2012; Szymanski, 2015; Schilhaneck, 2008; Summerer, 2008; Weiler, 2006; Hofmann, 2016; Teevs, 2014)
Contradiction Football is not seen as a risky investment.	Football as a risky investment (Szymanski, 2015; Yueh, 2014; Nagy, 2012; Quitzau, 2003)
Shareholding essentials Having prior insights	Prior relationship as facilitating aspect for equity investments (Parkhe, 1993; Doz, 1996; Reuer et al., 2002)

(continued)

Table 6.13 (continued)

Empirical concepts from grounded theory	Findings from the literature review
History of partnership	**Contrast**: A prior relationship makes companies less likely to opt for equity (Gulati, 1995; Globermann & Nielsen, 2007)
Shareholding builds upon brand symbiosis	A former sponsorship may act as a lever to entering into a strategic equity partnership (Süßmilch, 2004; Adam & Hovemann, 2018).
Extension (divergence) Economic reasonableness Value retention	Increase in shareholder value (Poitras, 2016; Keythman, 2016; VanDuzer et al., 2013; Caselli, 2010)
Need for justifying	Justification of investment towards own stakeholders (e.g., Mintzberg, 1998; Carroll, 1996 Dreher & Ernst, 2016; Adcroft, 2010)
Mutual strategic intent	Partnerships are driven by joint strategic purpose (Todeva & Knoke, 1995; Bleeke and Ernst, 1991)
Contribution to fan view Disposal of amount of shares	-
Number of shareholders	-
Extension Emotional attachment	Findings focus on rational decision-making of equity decisions (e.g., Poitras, 2016; Caselli, 2010; Jones, 2008; Mintzberg, 1998; Carroll, 1996)
Contribution *Managing the dyad*	-
Retention factor	Equity serves as an entry barrier (Welling & Westhoff, 2018; Oediger, 2017b; Prigge & Vöpel, 2014; DePamphilis, 2012; Barringer & Harrison, 2000)
Signifying exclusiveness	Equity verifying a strategic partnership (e.g., Ashelm & Horeni, 2015; Fahy et al., 2004; Liao, 2014; Quimet, 2013; Lin & Darnall, 2014), equity demonstrates worthiness of the investment (Hertzel & Smith, 1993)
Demonstrating stability	Equity indicating long-term stability (e.g., DePamphilis, 2012; Lui et al., 2010; Saxton, 1997; Das & Teng, 2000)
Having a say	An equity partner gets voting and controlling power in return (Liao, 2014; DePamphilis, 2012; Prigge & Vöpel, 2014)

The literature reports on the generally accepted viewpoint that corporations focus on profit maximisation (Chemnitzer et al., 2015; Jones, 2008; Amis et al., 1997; Carroll, 1996) whereas football clubs' primary goal is to win football matches (sporting success) (Acero et al., 2017; Nagy, 2012; Rudd, 2012; Frick, 2007; Barros & Leach, 2006; Sloane, 1971). This basic understanding is clearly reflected in the empirical data and finds expression in the concept of *differing ambitions*.

Those scientists who argue from an investment point of view relate the financial parameters related with a share deal, namely dividend payments, an increase in share value, and availability of money as key investment criteria (Poitras, 2016; Keythman, 2016; Caselli, 2010). In concert with the specific characteristic of the sport (i.e., the uncertainty of results and unpredictability), which have widely been discussed in the academic community (e.g., Schade, 2012; Nagy, 2012; Schilhaneck, 2008; Quitzau, 2003) and are encompassed in the concept of *unique nature of football*, Szymanski (2015), Nagy (2012), and Quitzau (2003) assert that (based on these characteristics) investing in football clubs' shares is a risky investment option. This view contradicts empirical outcomes. Although the primary data evidently illustrate that a shareholding in a football club is financially not the most attractive investment due to its properties of *low dividend payments* and *restricted availability of money* which emanate from the *specific nature of football* clubs (maximising sporting success), they do not assess a share deal as more or less risky than other investments. This essentially depends on their investment (partnership) criteria which are not based on purely financial aspects but rather on a *strategic intent*. This, in turn, conforms with findings from Todeva and Knoke (2005) as well as Bleeke and Ernst (1991) who determined that business partnerships are driven less by companies' retrospective financial logic than by their strategic (joint) purpose. The investment risk is further lessened due to the seat on the supervisory committee of the club which allows an equity partner to have *insights into club management* and therefore an option to co determine the economic development of the club.

Against this, there is accordance that a share deal has to be based on sound financial data due to the need to justify (Bolgar, 2010; Mintzberg, 1998) such investments to the own stake- and shareholders. This conforms with the empirical concept of *need for justifying*. Within the empirical field, justification of a shareholding is primarily based on the growth trend of the football business and on positive forecasts with respect to the club's share performance and club development.

While this development is evaluated via a *screening* process, being part of a growing brand has also been highlighted by Seemann and Schollmeier (2008) as well as Huth et al. (2018) as a motivation for football club share investments. A *growing football business* has widely been determined in terms of e.g., turnover, attendance figures, commercial incomes, and TV revenues by a multitude of scholars such as Adam and Hovemann (2018), Breuer et al. (2018), Boor et al. (2016), and Netzer et al. (2015). Yet, by juxtaposing empirical findings with those of the literature, it becomes evident that the *economic reasonableness* of equity acquisitions is differently classified. Whereas Poitras (2016), Bolgar (2010), and Mintzberg (1998) clearly emphasise the corporation's need to increase shareholder value, the priority of a strategic equity partner, according to the empirical findings, is on *value retention* as financial aspects rather serve as justification than an overall goal.

There is agreement between primary and secondary data that a share deal needs to be based on sound financial data (concepts of *economic reasonableness*). This line of thinking is extended in the empirical domain by adding *emotional attachment* as another requirement for the investment in a football club stake. Although research participants concur with the generally agreed position that business decisions have to be based on rationality (e.g., Dreher & Ernst, 2016; Caselli, 2010; Jones, 2008), since a football club investment is not a direct profit generating investment an *emotional attachment* is consistently mentioned as impacting upon entry into a football club share deal.

Within the *screening* process, further strategic considerations are evaluated with regard to the clubs' main stakeholder groups (especially club members and fans) such as the *amount of shares* to be issued to shareholders. Former studies (e.g., Bauers & Hovemann, 2019a; Bühler, 2017) investigated fan opinion with regard to the 50+1 rule (majority or non-majority shareholdings) only. This study is the first which presents the fans' view in more detail, id est it provides information about fan acceptance and the *amount of shares* to be issued to shareholders. While the empirical findings indirectly verify results from Bauers and Hovemann (2019a), Bühler (2017), and Pilz (2011) that fans want to retain the 50+1 rule, fans do accept minority shareholdings. The present investigation also adds information about fan preference of how disposed shares should be allocated to a number of shareholders. Moreover, the study found that the number of shares has an impact on the fan perception with respect to who is the main commercial partner of the club, thereby verifying primary data from the interviews.

Another requirement for a shareholding at a football club refers to a prior relationship between the club and sponsor. Adam and Hovemann (2018) as well as Süßmilch (2004) remarked that a former sponsorship may act as a lever to entering into a strategic equity partnership. This has also been investigated in the general alliance literature by Parkhe (1993), Doz (1996), Reuer et al. (2002), and

Mitsuhashi (2002) as a supporting issue in the future governance structure of the partnership. The empirical concepts of *history of partnership* and *having prior insights* confirm that a precedent sponsorship is a requirement to entering into a shareholding. This is argued with the prior insights into each other's management processes which ensure that *compatibility* is proven. Moreover, this study has shown the dynamic nature of *trust* which intensifies during the *history of partnership* and appears as a vital requirement for entering into a shareholding. Although Gulati (1995) has shown that a prior relationship between companies act as a proxy for trust Gulati (ibid.) also claimed that the increased level of trust makes companies less likely to opt for equity as a governance form which contrasts to the empirical findings.

A major contribution of the study is the explanation of how the dyad of sponsorship and shareholding is managed *(managing the dyad)*. There are no existing studies which present empirical insights into the management of a strategic equity partnership in the German football business. The sub-category *managing the dyad* not only explains how the sponsorship and shareholding are strategically connected via the *retention factor*, but also provides insights into strategic and contractual issues (e.g., retention factor, fit to overall strategy). Regarding a partnership contract, Hecox (2007) recommended defining a partnership exit strategy beforehand. Although Hecox (ibid.) focuses on strategic alliances in sports in general, this result can be extended to the management of strategic equity partnership as the empirical findings indicate. An exit strategy ensures that in particular the club is still competitive in case of partnership breakdown.

Considering the consequences of a shareholding, the empirical findings (in the form of the sub-category *signifying*) are consistent with existing knowledge that an equity investment verifies the credibility of the partnership, demonstrates stability (e.g., DePamphilis, 2012; Lui et al., 2010; Saxton, 1997; Das & Teng, 2000), and signalises the investment worthiness of the partner (Hertzel & Smith, 1993). Moreover, the sub-category "*having a say*" coincides with an increased responsibility of a shareholder, which has been illustrated in previous works in different contexts by e.g., Liao (2014), DePamphilis (2012), and Prigge and Vöpel (2014). This responsibility is based on an interest to secure the own investment and is empirically expressed with a binding seat in the clubs supervisory committee, which concedes the shareholder a voting right in fundamental club decisions.

6.6 Fear of Loss

6.6.1 Introduction

Fear of loss emerged as a category that embodies the inherent concerns and risks associated with a shareholding in a football club from the perspectives of clubs and club members and fans. However, the category comes across a general concern towards share deals at football clubs in Germany. Hence, *fear of loss* not only focuses on an equity investment with a strategic partner (sponsor) but also touches on the apprehension of share deals with other types of shareholders that emerged in the empirical research area, namely financial investors, Maecenas, and oligarchs *(differentiating shareholders).*

The sub-category shareholding impediments argues from the club perspective and subsumes the club's reasoning for rejecting an equity partnership with regard to various shareholder types. This predominantly refers to the concepts of *fear of dependency* from an external shareholder and *fearing alienation* (of club members and fans). *Considering fan concerns* explains the causes and contextual aspects of the fan's concern against shareholders. "Loss", in this respect, relates to a loss of *tradition, co-determination, identification, independency* (of the club's sporting decisions), and *values.*

The sub-category *fan understanding* illuminates several arguments against (*fan resistance*) and in favour (*fan acceptance*) for the admission of a shareholder in general and addresses the *acceptance* of the four shareholder types from the club member and fan perspective, which can be dimensionalised on the continuum *low/high. Immanent risks* embraces miscellaneous *threatening factors* associated with a share deal at a football club which might lead to partnership breakdown. This implicates the corporate (shareholder) and club perspective.

Furthermore, the sub-category *approaching externally* constitutes a variation in the data by delineating an alternative approach for entering into a shareholding (a share deal which is not based on a prior business partnership). In this specific case, the risk for partnership failure is increased (correlation to *immanent risks*) due to a lack of *shareholding essentials.* This sub-category also addresses club impediments with respect to approaching different shareholder types.

Fear of loss is based on the characteristic (property) *intensity* (of fear) which can differ (*low/high*) according to the club-specific environment and interrelates to a *potential for conflicts* (*low/high*). Moreover, risk can be dimensionalised based on its *likelihood of occurrence* (*low/high*).

6.6.2 Shareholding Impediments and Considering Fan Concerns

A share deal is linked to increased responsibility/influence (correlation to "*having a say*") on the part of the shareholder in the club's issues which can cause a *fear of dependency*. The concept *fear of dependency* (losing autonomy) relates to a fear for intervention of a shareholder into the sporting decisions and can be a reason (*impediment*) for denying a share deal (club view). Simultaneously a *fear of dependency* could arise at club members and fans and could be a reason for *fan resistance* (consequence, correlated to the *idiosyncratic nature of German football*). The concept finds expression in the statement of IP 12 (229; 17): "*Normally it is the case that he who pays for the party determines the music*"[124] which implies that "*clubs become more dependent from their shareholder and their economic resources which are available for the club*"[125] (IP 9, 156; 18). Consequently, a *fear of dependency* consists of a fear to take influence into the decisions in the absent of sporting success. For example, IP 7 (100; 32) explained:

> "If you have no sporting success once or twice you become more dependent. If the partner opens the pockets, he wants to have securities. Then, you become quickly part of a doom loop".[126]

This refers back to the concept of *"understanding of one's role"* (shareholding essential), *trust*, and *having aligned interests*. Based on high trust between the partners, a mutual *understanding of one's role* and aligned interest the *fear of dependency* is *low*. By contrast, if there is a low level of trust, a different role expectation and contrasting goals the *fear of dependency* is accordingly *higher*. The following example illustrates the (possible) intervention of a shareholder (no strategic partner) into the sporting decisions:

---

[124] „*Und in der Regel ist es ja so, der die Party bezahlt bestimmt meistens die Musik*" (IP 12, 229; 17).

[125] „*Die Vereine werden stärker abhängig von ihrem Gesellschafter und den wirtschaftlichen Mittel, die die dann zur Verfügung stellen [..]*" (IP 9, 156; 18).

[126] „*Wenn du ein- zweimal nicht sportlichen Erfolg hast, kommst du auch immer in eine größere Abhängigkeit. Wenn der Partner dann die Taschen aufmacht, dann will er natürlich auch Sicherheiten haben. Also, du kommst sehr schnell in einen Teufelskreis*" (IP 7, 100; 32).

> "Then they wanted, for example, to have [name of coach]. Of course, if he sits on the bench this arouses the attention of 12 cameras. This is a lot more arousal and implications compared to a coach who just arouses two or three cameras. Well, he was considered as a coach because [corporation] wanted him"[127] (IP 5, 79; 15).

This statement illustrates that a shareholder, as a financier of the club and part of the club's ownership, might claim to have a say in the clubs' sporting issues (decisions). Although the 50+1 rule prevents a shareholder to take a controlling influence into the club a certain kind of influence might be gained via the supervisory committee. IP 6 (84; 25) provided insights into the shareholder's considerations:

> "As I said before, they wanted something bigger and participating and having control. And that was the problem, because we did not have the majority but we said: Via the supervisory committee we are able to steer it".[128]

However, a *fear of dependency* mainly relates to shareholders who have no *history of partnership* and who act mainly as a financier of the club instead of a strategic partner who has a sustainable interest into a positive club development. This is confirmed by IP 12 (212; 5), who stated with regards to Chinese investors/oligarchs:

> "Of course, we get requests from potential Chinese investors. However, they have the focus, they want to take over [club] and want to take the control stick in hand and control the operative business".[129]

From the club's perspective, this suspicion predominantly applies to oligarchs but also Maecenas, according to IP 9 (135; 20): *"What is impossible is definitely*

[127]„*Dann wollten die als Beispiel einen Matthäus haben. Aber ist ja klar, wenn der auf der Bank sitz dann halten 12 Kameras drauf. Und das hat natürlich eine viel größere Wirkung als wenn du einen Trainer hast, wo vielleicht nur zwei, drei Kameras draufhalten. Also der war hier mal im Gespräch, weil die Leute von [Unternehmen] den haben wollten*" (IP 5, 79; 15).

[128]„*Die wollten wie gesagt was Größeres machen und mit Beteiligung und Kontrolle haben. Und das war ja auch das Problem, weil wir haben ja nicht die Mehrheit gehabt, aber wir haben gesagt: Durch den Aufsichtsrat können wir das steuern*" (IP 6, 84; 24).

[129]„*Wir kriegen natürlich auch Anfragen von Chinesischen potentiellen Investoren. Die haben aber den Fokus, die wollen [Club] am liebsten übernehmen, sie wollen den Steuerknüppel in die Hand bekommen und die Kontrolle über das operative Geschäft*" (IP 12, 212; 5).

no Maecenas. […] which dominate such a club".[130] While these assessments can differ according to a specific club view both statements provide evidence for the underlying concept *fear of dependency.*

With respect to financial investors a *fear of loss* rather refers to short-termed dividend expectation and the endeavour to increase share value and to exit after a short-term period: *"I don't think that [club] searches for a private equity company which come in and go out tomorrow. Instead, they search for a long-term partnership"*[131] (IP 20, 377; 9). Since a shareholding is a fundamental decision a short-term disposal is not in the interests of the club because *"this is image damaging if one investor after another say good bye after a short period"*[132] (IP 4, 56; 23).

Whereas investor presence has become a modern trend in foreign leagues across Europe (IP 9, 156), in Germany there is a general (fan) concern about shareholder (*debating about investor presence*, context), as IP 2 (16; 5) confirmed: *"Actually, in Germany there is always the discussion about the 50 + 1 rule".*[133] The term "always" indicates the *permanent* nature (property) of the debate and the relevance of the topic in German football. Since German clubs *originate from a non-profit nature* and were established as member associations with a right to co-determination, club members and fans have a sense of belonging to their club which is connected to a claim of ownership *(fans as personification of the club),* according to IP 23 (413; 1):

> "None of these fans want to have a sponsor or maybe a sponsor is ok, but no investor. For fans this is the ultimate no-go because they say the club belongs to us".[134]

---

130 *„Was ausgeschlossen ist, ist ganz klar keinen Mäzenen. […]. Die dann eben so einen Verein dominieren"* (IP 9, 135; 20).

131 *„Ich glaube nicht, dass der [Club] nach einem Private Equity Unternehmen sucht, die dann reingehen und morgen wieder rausgehen. Sondern Sie suchen nach einer langanhaltenden Partnerschaft"* (IP 20, 377; 9).

132 *„Das ist ja auch imageschädigend und sag ich mal für die [Club] gewesen, wenn ein Investor nach dem anderen nach kurzer Zeit verabschiedet"* (IP 4, 56; 23).

133 *„Eigentlich gibt es in Deutschland immer die Diskussion der 50 + 1 Regel"* (IP 2, 16; 5).

134 *„Keiner dieser Fans will eigentlich einen Sponsor oder, einen Sponsor vielleicht gerad noch aber keinen Investor haben. Das ist ja alle für die des Teufels. Weil Sie sagen, der Verein gehört uns"* (IP 23, 413; 1).

If a profit-driven organisation or an individual buys club shares, this "*is extremely difficult for fans. They think the [club] will be sold to someone who has money*"[135] (IP 5, 66; 22). Fans perceive this as *increased commercialisation* and fear a shift in focus of the club towards profit orientation *(increasing focus on money)* which means that "*football loses something from its originality [...]*" (IP 18, 347; 28), therefore countering the club's inherent non-profit status *(loss of tradition, values, and identification)*. This also relates to a "*fear of dependency on an external party, irrespective of where he is from, be it an investor or however you wish to refer to this [...]*"[136] (IP 2, 16; 16).

6.6.3 Fan Understanding and Shareholder Acceptance by Fans

Fan understanding illuminates fan opinion on shareholder presence. The sub-category label is based on the term 'understanding' in order to express that it is about the detailed "*knowledge about a subject*" (Cambridge Dictionary, 2011; 970). Accordingly, *fan understanding* provides insights into arguments upon which fan discussion is based by looking at reasons against (*fan resistance*) and in favour (*fan acceptance*) of the admission of a shareholder. Moreover, consideration of the *degree* of general *acceptance* (*low/high*) allows a differential look into the acceptance of four shareholder types. This enables fan concerns to be better understood and allows these concerns to be addressed more effectively.

The sub-category initially looks at reasons against the admission of a shareholder. The assessment confirms the previous statements of club authorities with regard to the concepts of *loss of tradition, loss co-determination, loss goodwill values, loss of identification, increased commercialisation,* and *fear of influence* as shown in Table 6.14 (n = 1,589) on page 239.

[135] „*Aber das ist bei den Fans ganz, ganz schwierig. Denn dann kommt hoch, der verkauft die [Club] an Irgendjemanden, der Geld hat*" (IP 5, 66; 22).

[136] „*Diese Angst der Abhängigkeit von einem Externen, wo auch immer der herkommt, Investor, wie auch immer man ihn nennen mag [...]*" (IP 2, 16; 16).

Table 6.14 Arguments against Shareholder Admission. (Source: Own Illustration)

What are the arguments against the admission of a shareholder?	Relative frequency in percent %				
Overall: n = 1,589* Club members: n = 991 Non-club members: n = 572	I totally agree	I slightly agree	I slightly disagree	I strongly disagree	No opinion
Avoidance of influence on sporting decisions by a shareholder.					
• Club members	43.3	33.8	10.7	3.6	8.1
• Non-club members	42.5	33,7	11.4	2.6	8.9
• Overall	43.4	33.8	11.0	3.2	8.6
Prevention of increased commercialisation of the Bundesliga.					
• Club members	46.0	29.1	12.5	4.9	6.6
• Non-club members	42.1	27.8	15.4	5.2	8.7
• Overall	45.0	28.8	13.8	5.1	7.4
Decline of fan identification with the club.					
• Club members	40.4	33.5	14.9	6.1	4.5
• Non-club members	29.5	35.8	22.2	6.1	5.8
• Overall	36.6	34.5	17.6	6.2	5.1
Decline of co-determination of fans and club members.					
• Club members	46.5	31.1	11.1	5.9	4.8
• Non-club members	35.7	37.2	13.5	4.5	8.4
• Overall	42.9	33.3	12.0	5.4	6.5
Loss of goodwill values of the club.					
• Club members	44.9	34.3	11.3	4.1	4.6
• Non-club members	35.1	36.9	16.8	4.2	5.9
• Overall	41.6	35.6	13.5	4.1	5.2
Possible loss of the club's tradition due to increased commercialisation of the club.					
• Club members	48.6	30.6	11.4	5.5	3.2
• Non-cub members	43.0	30.8	16.1	5.4	3.8
• Overall	46.8	30.8	13.3	5.5	3.6

* 1.6% (26) non respondents of club member/non-club member

The outcome shows that the concepts upon which the arguments are based are all relevant aspects in the fan perception. Furthermore, the results present a homogeneous picture for all arguments listed. Between 73.9% and 79.2% of the club members and between 65.3% and 76.2% of the non-club members concur with the arguments. Although there is no big difference in the particular ratings between club members and non-club members, the club members regard the arguments slightly higher than the non-club members and consistently opt more often for the extreme category "I totally agree".

It can be assumed that this is based on a higher involvement into the club of club members compared to non-club members. For example, as opposed to non-club members club members have a voting right in the Verein. Yet, the overall difference between the two groups remains low.

With respect to the concern about an *influence on sporting decisions* (overall 77.2%) it can be assumed that the fan's opinion is coined by several practical cases across European football leagues. For example, in Germany investors such as Klaus Michael Kühne (Hamburger SV), Hassan Ismaik (TSV 1860 München), and recently Mikhail Ponomarev (KFC Uerdingen 05) demonstrated that clubs, which are dependent on the financial support from their shareholder, often have to accept investor influence on sport decisions. This in particular refers to decisions about the position of the sport director, coach, and player transfers. In this case, democratic decision-making is limited and the club becomes more dependent on the shareholder's judgements. This could be an explanation that 61.7% of fans refuse that club shares are issued to only one big partner.

Overall, the *avoidance of influence on sporting decisions* (overall 77.2%), the *loss of goodwill values* (77.2%), the *loss of tradition due to increased commercialisation* (77.6%), and the *loss of co-determination* (76.2%) are the highest rated arguments against the admission of a shareholder. This underpins a general *fear of loss* regarding the heteronomy of external investors. It also emphasises that for club members and fans goodwill values and the tradition of the club are vital aspects which justify the idiosyncratic nature of the German football business. Furthermore, these findings provide information on the importance of the retention of the 50 + 1 rule for 94.8% of fans.

The insights about the arguments against shareholder admission shed not only light on fan concerns but could also be a rationale for the related effects (consequences of fan concern) of shareholdings such as *fan resistance*. In some club contexts the intensity of *fan resistance* against equity partners is *very high*, as stated by IP 5 (66, 13): *"I hadn't planned on that but I met with resistance, which is incredible, incredible"*.[137]

High fan resistance can often be observed at the time of a pending deal in which those fans who object to a shareholding try to exert power on club management, with reference to IP 23 (412, 9): *"The ultras have prevented for a long time that it comes to a vote regarding outsourcing"*.[138] This statement indicates the property *intensity* (of *fan resistance*), but also hints at the concept *fans exerting power* which is a concern for the club and shareholder because *fan resistance* (e.g., in the form of fan protests) might have a negative impact on club and partner image. Yet, the intensity (*low/high*) and duration (*temporary/enduring*) of fan discussion as well as the related effects differ according to club-specific circumstances. For instance, there are also clubs at which fan resistance is virtually non-existent, with reference to IP 2 (16; 20): *"There is no discussion at all on this issue, unlike at other clubs"*.[139] Due to the contrasting findings with respect to the property *intensity* (*no* vs. *intensive* fan debates), the sub-category *fan understanding* gives also information on arguments in favour (*fan acceptance*) of the admission of a shareholder. These were derived from existing concepts that represent vital aspects for clubs for entering into a strategic equity partnership (i.e., *networking*, *exchanging knowledge*, income via *one-off payment*, and *signifying*). The club member and fan opinion regarding these concepts are displayed in Table 6.28 (n = 1,589) on page 242.

[137] „*Damit habe ich auch nicht gerechnet, aber da kommt Gegenwind, der ist unglaublich, unglaublich*" (IP 5, 66; 13).

[138] „*[...] echt massive Widerstände gehabt die Ultras haben ja auch lange Zeit verhindert, dass es überhaupt zu einer Abstimmung über einer Ausgliederung kam*" (IP 23, 412; 9).

[139] „*Wir haben überhaupt keine Diskussion bei uns im Club zu diesem Thema, anders als in anderen Clubs*" (IP 2, 16; 20).

Table 6.15 Arguments in Favour of a Shareholder. (Source: Own Illustration)

What are the arguments in favour of a shareholder?	Relative frequencies in percent %				
Overall: n = 1,589* Club members: n = 988 Non-club members: n = 566	I totally agree	I slightly agree	I slightly disagree	I strongly disagree	No opinion
Reinforcement of national competitiveness via additional income					
• Club members	22.9	48.3	14.8	9.0	5.0
• Non-club members	32.0	51.2	9.2	3.9	3.7
• Overall	26.0	49.6	12.8	7.1	12.8
The club benefits from the business network of the shareholder					
• Club members	10.1	43.9	20.5	11.4	14.1
• Non-club members	15.4	43.9	19.6	4.4	16.6
• Overall	12.1	43.9	20.1	8.7	15.2
Reinforcement of international competitiveness via additional income.					
• Club members	20.7	47.6	15.2	10.3	6.2
• Non club members	30.1	48.8	12.3	3.5	5.3
• Overall	24.1	47.9	14.2	7.7	6.1
An equity investment is an expression of attachment to the club.					
• Club members	6.2	23.3	34.3	27.6	8.6
• Non-club members	8.0	28.1	35.2	18.2	10.4
• Overall	6.9	24.9	34.7	24.1	9.4
An equity investment is a signal of trust in a successful club future.					
• Club members	7.5	38.2	27.6	17.6	9.1
• Non-club members	12.1	41.5	25.0	9.9	11.4
• Overall	9.3	39.3	26.5	14.7	10.2
Incorporating a shareholder boosts the expertise of the club.					
• Club members	5.9	23.1	37.7	19.7	13.6
• Non-club members	6.9	23.2	37.3	15.5	17.1
• Overall	6.2	23.3	37.4	17.1	14.9

* 2% (35) non respondents of club member/non-club member

With regard to the overall results, the main arguments in favour of a shareholder are based on the club's reinforced *national* and *international competitiveness* due to additional income related to a share deal (*national competitiveness* overall 75.6% agreement, *international competitiveness* overall 72% agreement). Generally, there is a tendency for club members to rate the arguments in favour of a shareholder slightly (and consistently) lower than the non-club members.

While for the majority of arguments the differences between the two groups is low, concerning the *national* and *international competitiveness* the differences between club members and non-club members becomes more discernible. Club members rated these two aspects more than 10% lower compared to non-club members. Possible reasons for that could be inherent in the voting right and underlying interest in co-determination of club members in the club's issues. As a consequence, club members seem to be more reserved (or even sceptical) regarding shareholder admission as selling equity means giving up voting rights. This interrelates to the former aspect *loss of co-determination* as an argument against the admission of shareholders which is rated higher by club members (77.6%) compared to non-club members (72.9%). Also, club members could be concerned that the club puts the interest of a shareholder into a greater focus than the interest of club members which relates to *a loss of tradition due to an increased commercialisation* as argument against the admission of an equity partner. Similarly, club members rated this argument higher (79.2%) compared to non-club members (73.8%). Irrespective of that, the results from all other arguments in favour of a shareholder admission present a homogenous picture.

Regarding the concept *networking* (*benefit for the club from the shareholder's network*) the majority (overall 56%) of fans anticipate a benefit for the club. In contrast, 28.8% disagree and 15.2% have no opinion on that matter. This outcome indicates a supportive argument in favour of a shareholder although the outcome is not very strong. While for sponsors and clubs a shareholding is an *affirmation* vis-à-vis the partnership, fans appear to see this differently. Overall 58.8% of the fans do not agree that a shareholding is a sign of the attachment of the equity partner to the club (31.8% agree with that argument and 9.4% have no opinion).

Similarly, while *exchanging knowledge* has emerged as a vital concept for clubs in a strategic equity partnership, only 29.5% of fans agree with the idea of a *boost the club's expertise* from entering into a share deal whereas 54.5% disagree. Likewise, there are ambiguous results (48.6% agree, 41.2% disagree) concerning *signifying* (argument *signal of trust in a successful club future*) which represents a split of opinion that does not allow for a definite interpretation. A possible explanation for fan opinion regarding the arguments (concepts) of exchanging knowledge, signifying, and affirmation to the partnership via equity could be that these arguments are mainly based on business (entrepreneurial) and strategic aspects/considerations from equity partners and clubs and need to be seen in the light of the commercial development of football clubs toward economic enterprises.

As already shown, increased commercialisation is regarded critically by the majority of fans. It can be assumed that the commercial development of football clubs accompanied by their interconnectedness with the business world is less transparent for club members and fans as these are predominantly interested in the sporting aspects and take a rather negative stance toward the commercialisation of the sport. Therefore, there might be fans who wonder how a shareholder support the club in the area of e.g., *knowledge transfer,* although *knowledge transfer* is not related to the sporting area but to the business side of the club.

While this information provides valuable insights into arguments against and in favour of the admission of shareholders, there are further features of a shareholder a club considers as significant, id est the partner's image which has to be positive. A *positive image* of a shareholder is equally important for club members and fans as can be abstracted from Figure 6.7 (n = 1,589).

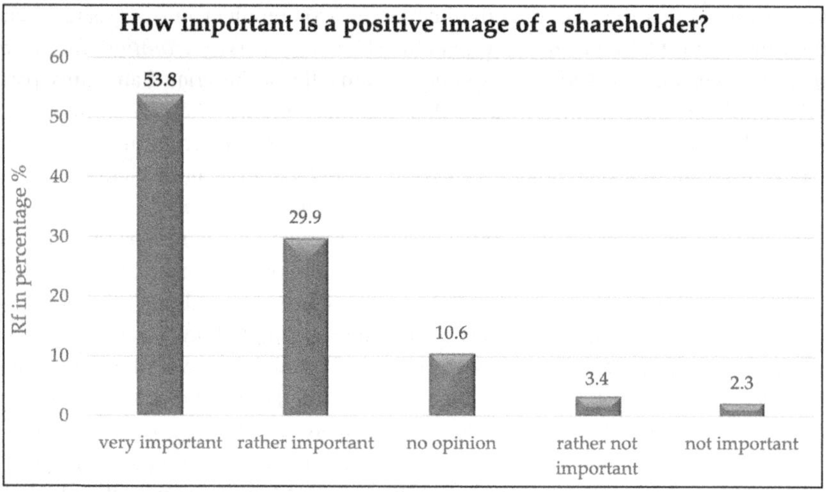

Figure 6.7 Importance of Shareholder Image for Fans. (Source: Own Illustration)

For 83.7% of fans a positive image of a shareholder is an important issue. A differential analysis among club members and non-club members yielded no major differences. It can be assumed that a positive image of a shareholder might be a favourable aspect of club member and fan acceptance as e.g., IP 20 (376; 33) already indicated.

Similar results yielded the aspect about the importance of a *"regional affinity"* of a shareholder. *"Regional affinity"* implies that a shareholder is rooted (in some way, e.g., via its headquarters or a company site) in the same region as the club which might have an impact on fan acceptance as assumed by e.g., IP 7, IP 9, and IP 16. Figure 6.8 sheds light on the importance of a shareholder's *"regional affinity"* to the club (n = 1,589) as illustrated in Figure 6.8:

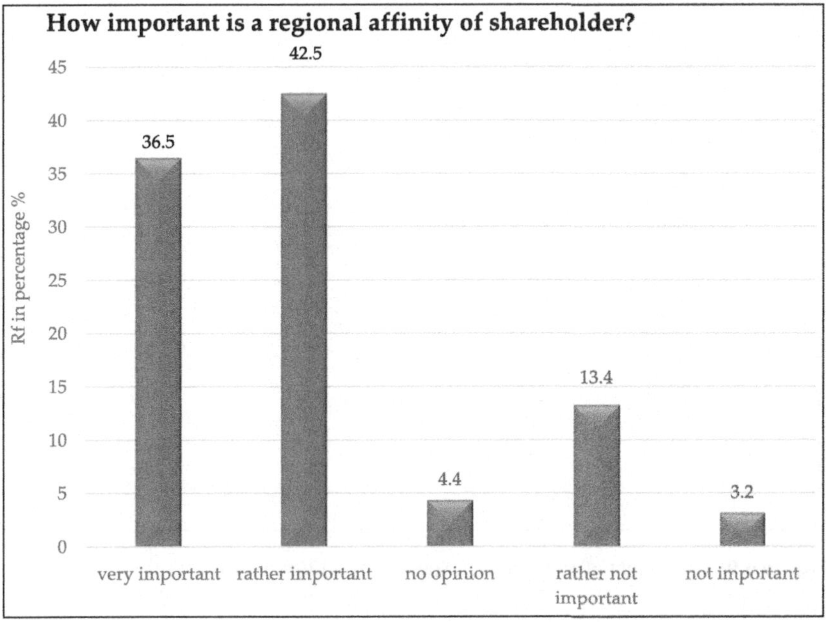

Figure 6.8 Importance of Regional Affinity. (Source: Own Illustration)

Overall, 79% of fans rated *regional affinity* as a crucial aspect. While 4.4% have no opinion on that matter, for 13.4% of fans a regional affinity is less important and for 3.2% not a decisive argument. It can be assumed that a *regional affinity* of a shareholder has a positive impact on fan opinion, thereby confirming the assumption from IP 7, IP 9, and IP 16.

Another argument with reference to the concept *"retention factor"* related to the question *"how important is the option that the club has a priority (right) to repurchase the shares if the shareholder wants to sell his stake?"*. This argument was developed as being in-line with the core category of *securing* since a priority right for repurchase would provide a kind of security (lessen the concern of *loss of control*) that the club retains co-determination in terms of club shares in case of a partnership breakdown. Figure 6.9 clearly indicates preference for a *priority right of repurchase* the shares (n = 1,589) as followed:

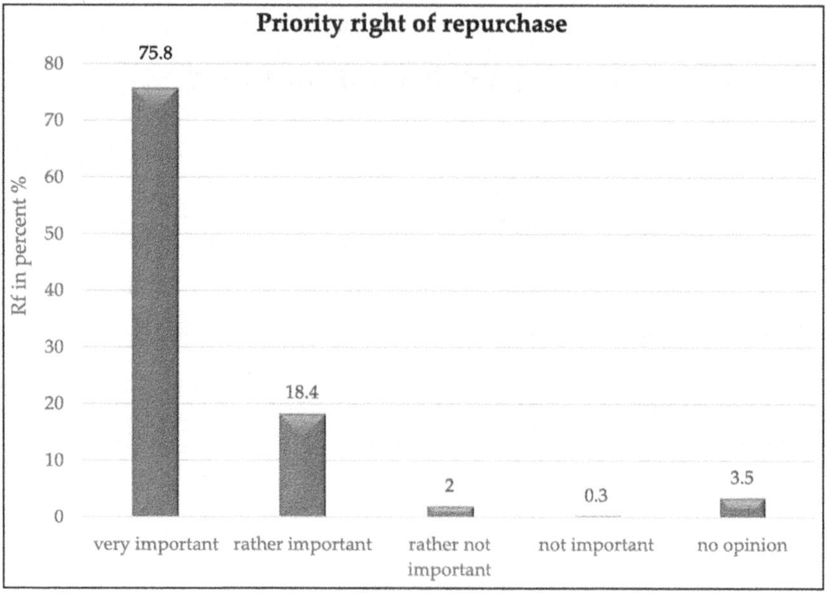

Figure 6.9 Club Right of Repurchase. (Source: Own Illustration)

The bar chart clearly shows that a *priority right of repurchase* is a very important issue (75.8%) for the vast majority of fans (overall 94.2% agreement). This aspect interrelates with the arguments against the admission of a shareholder (e.g., *loss of identity, loss of co-determination*).

While the arguments against a shareholder illustrate a *loss of control*, a *priority right of repurchase* lessens the fear that club shares will be arbitrarily sold on to another shareholder. It seems that a priority clause for repurchase provides club members and fans a sense of security. Consequently, such a clause would secure the club's prevalence in this specific situation. This concept can be related to the argument *decline of co-determination of fans and club members* (against the admission of a shareholder, which is rated by 76.2% of club members and fans) and is an indirect support for this argument. Consequently, this outcome reinforces the significance for the majority of fans for co-determination (to have a say in their club). Since co-determination is traditionally rooted as a right for club members in Germany, the result that the option "blocking minority" is highest rated also underpins the significance of traditional values for club members and fans.

The previous results provided insights to fan opinion towards shareholders in general and illustrated on which arguments the club member and fan opinion is based on. However, the primary data yielded four types of equity partners. There is agreement among the experts that the general fan acceptance of different shareholder types is a crucial aspect for clubs and (potential) co-equity partners. With reference to IP 12 (212; 22): *"Any participation has to be acceptable to fans because the fans are mindful of who has a share in the club"*.[140] This statement indicates that the type of shareholder ("who") has an impact on the *acceptance of fans*. Figure 6.10 (n = 1,589) on page 248 shows the degree of general fan acceptance *("To what degree would you accept the following types of shareholder for your favourite club?")* with regard to the four shareholder types (*differentiating shareholders*) according to five dimensions ranging from *totally accept* to *not accept at all* including a *no opinion* option.

---

[140] „*Und wir müssen auch immer reflektieren, dass muss ja auch fanverträglich sein wen wir denn da mitnehmen. Denn die Fans achten ja schon drauf, wer hier beteiligt ist*" (IP 12, 212; 22).

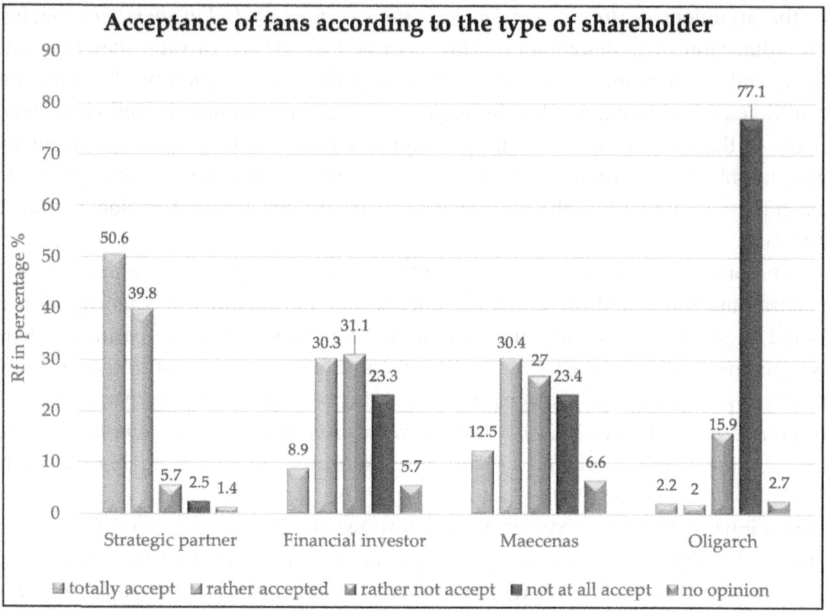

Figure 6.10 Fan Acceptance of Shareholders. (Source: Own Illustration)

Figure 6.10 presents a homogenous picture in regard to each shareholder type. It is clearly shown that a strategic partner is *totally accepted* (50.6%) or *rather accepted* (39.8%) by fans as a club shareholder. Accumulated the vast majority (90.4%) of fans are well disposed towards a strategic partner (well accepted). The 2.5% of fans who do *not accept at all* and the 5.7% who would *rather not accept* a strategic sponsor as a shareholder cannot be categorised to a specific group of fans. In contrast to the strategic partner, an oligarch is generally *not accepted at all* by 77.1% and *rather not accepted* by 15.9%, resulting in overall resistance of 93% to oligarchs. The results regarding financial investors and Maecenas do not allow a definite statement about fan acceptance to be made due to contrasting views.

While around 40% of fans would accept one of these shareholder types, over 50% have reservations (*rather not accept*~30%, *not accept at all*~23%) against these investor types. This information, first and foremost, presents a generic overview about *fan acceptance* towards the four shareholder types. A differential analysis between club members and non-club members as well as between different fan groups, for example those (highly involved) fans who *"try to actively influence the atmosphere in the stadium"* and those fans who *"support the team at away matches",* confirm the results of the overall sample (Appendix VIII). In correlation with the results about the *amount of shares,* 81.9% of fans agree on minority shareholdings of up to 10%. It can be assumed that minority shareholdings with a strategic partner, depending on the *amount of shares* to be issued and the number of shareholders at a club, is largely accepted by club members and fans. It can further be supposed that a minority shareholding with a strategic partner is accepted by fans and consequently hardly arouse fan resistance although this is dependent on the specific club context. Moreover, the aforementioned concepts of a *positive image, regional affinity* and a *priority right for repurchase* of the club impact on fan opinion towards shareholder acceptance in general.

This sub-category sheds light on fan opinion regarding shareholder presence in German football. Arguments for the admission and against the admission of a shareholder are depicted. An increase of national and international competition are the main reasons for the admission of a shareholder. In contrast, fan concerns are predominantly based on five arguments (loss of tradition, values, independency, fear of intervention, increasing commercialisation). A differential view of fans regarding the acceptance of four shareholder types is examined and further aspects (image, regional affinity, priority right of repurchase) that matter to football fans illuminated. While the acceptance of a strategic partner as a club shareholder is high, there is no acceptance of an oligarch. With regard to Maecenas and financial investors there is no uniform fan opinion that allows a definite statement to be made.

6.6.4 Immanent Risks

While it has been shown that a share deal provides a more stable framework for the partnership (*stability*), clubs and sponsors coincide that equity does not save the partnership from potential risks which may lead to collaborative failure or partnership breakdown. The sub-category *immanent risks* addresses the various aspects which may jeopardise the corporate club partnership from continuation. These risks do not exclusively refer to strategic equity partnerships but rather encompass all kinds of business partnerships (i.e., commercial partnership, sponsorships, equity partnerships with other shareholder types) between clubs and corporations. The risks and threatening factors range from inter-partner aspects to industry and macro environmental circumstances.

Immanent risks can basically be dimensionalised based on likelihood of occurrence (*likely/unlikely*). The most likely risks are fundamentally associated to the sub-category *shareholding essentials*. The correlation to *shareholding essentials* refers in particular to the higher ordered concept *compatibility* (i.e., *mindset, partnership culture, aligned interests,* and *understanding of one's role*). *Compatibility* between the partners is difficult to assess without *having prior insights* via a *history of partnership*, according to IP 1 (5; 22): "*I think it was only a year or two later where the partnership broke apart/I think that the incompatibility become obvious [...]*". Without a *history of partnership*, the partners only get a superficial insight into one another which exacerbates figuring out specific characteristics, the idiosyncratic partner context (e.g., club/fan interaction, inter-club setting; decision-making channels in a large corporation) and underlying motives. Additionally, "*it is sometimes forgotten that football clubs are not pure corporations [...]*"[141] (IP 18, 327; 10). This statement indicates the *differing ambitions* between clubs and corporations and hints at the specific role of club members and fans which need to be considered in partnership management.

The difficulty of *compatibility* may even be harder for equity partners from abroad to foresee since these partners might not be familiar with the specific nature of German football (e.g., the 50+1 rule), "*[...] because in other markets, namely England, Italy, Spain the issue of 50+1 does not exist [...]*"[142] (IP 7, 95; 12). With respect to foreign shareholders, close attention needs also to be paid to the *compatibility* of management cultures because "*you are faced with a different cultural environment and you do not know what that means*"[143] (IP 7, 102; 15). By contrast, a *history of partnership* ensures that *compatibility* between the partners can be verified and tested within the scope of *partnership management* (interactions). Accordingly, by entering into an equity partnership without a prior relationship the risk of partnership failure is considerably increased.

[141] „*Und es gerät manchmal in Vergessenheit, dass Fußballvereine eben keine reinen Wirtschaftsvereine sind [...]*" (IP 18, 327; 10).

[142] „*[...], weil natürlich in anderen Märkten sprich England, Italien, Spanien das Thema 50+1 überhaupt nicht vorhanden ist [...]*" (IP 7, 95; 12).

[143] „*[...], weil du natürlich mit einem unterschiedlichen Kulturkreis zu tun hast, wo du einfach nicht weißt, was das dann auch bedeutet*" (IP 7, 102; 15).

Regarding the partnership collaboration a sensitive situation in a strategic equity partnership refers to the renewal of the sponsorship contract (*negotiating*) "*because one has hard economic goals. This is when a partnership is tested*"[144] (IP 12, 228; 5). While a club tries to get the highest possible sponsorship fees, the sponsor, as a profit-driven organisation, is cost-oriented. The inherent risk in this situation is reflected in the following statement by IP 8 (133; 17): "*There were moments following certain discussions that you could not have assumed that things would have ended as they did*".[145] Basically, both parties are focused on making a beneficial deal of their own. Nevertheless, within the scope of a "*brand symbiosis*" the partnership is based on aligned interests, mutual benefits, and trust. Therefore, *negotiating* remains a fair and respectful interaction "*[...], because both know, hey, actually we want to work together, we want to continue together*"[146] (IP 11, 199; 15).

An essential precondition for continued, long-term collaboration (partnership success) is sporting success. Due to the *uncertainty of sporting results* (context) rooted in the specific nature of football *sporting failure* is one of the *most likely* risks from the perspective of the corporate partner. Although a *short-term* failure has no severe damaging effects on the partnership a *consecutive* failure to perform by the club has, first and foremost, a negative impact on the sponsorship (less media attention, decreasing charisma, etc.) and, by implication, on the club's share value (*decrease of share value*). Consequently, the "*fundamental risk is that the club gets relegated, the value goes south and our share is only worth a friction and we waste money up*"[147] (IP 8, 125; 33). An essential component to avoid this is the *quality of people* (*expertise* and *integrity*) as IP 1 (10; 26) underpinned: "*People are what make success*". The *quality of people* is a requirement for *sound club management* which, in turn, is a precondition for sporting success.

[144] „*Weil du ja jetzt harte ökonomische Interessen dann auch hast. Das ist aber dann wo eine Partnerschaft dann getestet wird*" (IP 12, 228; 5).

[145] „*Das war auch schon so ein Moment, wo man in der ein oder anderen Diskussion nicht unbedingt davon ausgehen konnte, dass das am Ende so sein wird, wie es jetzt ist*" (IP 8, 133; 17).

[146] „*[...], weil beide wissen, hey, eigentlich wollen wir miteinander arbeiten, wir wollen miteinander weitermachen*" (IP 11, 199; 15).

[147] „*Naja gut das Risiko fundamental ist natürlich der Club steigt ab, der Wert des Clubs geht in den Keller, unser Anteil ist nur noch ein Bruchteil wert und wir setzten Geld in den Sand*" (IP 8, 125; 33).

Likewise, economic failure by the corporate partner may jeopardise the partnership too, because *"when things get tough for corporations, they look at how to cut costs"* (IP 1, 11; 22) (*cutting costs in times of trouble*). While a football share deal is not a direct profit generating investment (due to *differing ambitions*, non-profit nature of football clubs) and related to high costs (commitment to enlarge the sponsorship permanently, *managing the dyad*), *"the easiest thing is just to say forget it"* (IP 1, 11; 24). However, this refers in particular to equity partnerships which are entered into with corporations whose core business (*corporate mission*) is not sport- or football-related. While for sport-related enterprises football belongs to the own corporate DNA, this does not apply to non-sport businesses.

These may prefer to concentrate on their core business (own DNA) in critical times, according to the maxim: *"Everything which is not core business is out"*[148] (IP 6, 86; 6).

A further threatening factor for a strategic (equity) partnership is reflected in the concept *changing CEO*. The sponsor's CEO occupies a central role when it comes to the decision-making process about a shareholding (as the final decision-maker). Since the CEO is frequently characterised as a person with a personal interest in football (*emotional attachment*) a change of the sponsor's CEO is commonly characterised by the situation that the new leader reconsiders the strategy of the company. This inheres the risk that the corporation switches its (marketing, branding) strategy based on the ideas of the new CEO about the future direction of the business (*business reorientation*). This risk seems to be elevated if the CEO is a person who is not interested in football. IP 22 (390; 6) provides the following insights:

> "Maybe at some point [name of CEO] will no longer be there and then there is someone else who maybe does not care two figs about football and he prefers to go horse riding. You can never know whether the sponsorship strategy will change".[149]

This risk is again reinforced if the core business of the corporate partner is not sport-related (*sponsoring is controversial if non-core business*) based on the

[148]„*Alles, was nicht unser Core Geschäft ist raus*" (IP 6, 86; 6).

[149]„*Aber irgendwann ist vielleicht ein [Person] nicht mehr da und da kommt einer, der hat mit Fußball gar nichts am Hut, sondern der geht lieber zum Reiten. Da weißt du ja nicht, ob irgendwann die Sponsoringstrategie ein bisschen einen anderen Wind kriegt*" (IP 22, 390; 6).

aforementioned reasons. Likewise, *changing CEO* emphasises the need for the club to base a strategic equity partnership on a prior business partnership (*prior insights*) in order to ensure a sustainable interest in the club from the whole partner organisation.

To have the sustainable support from the whole organisation also applies to the concept in which a club enters a shareholding with a subsidiary of a corporation (*equity dealing with subsidiary*). This is based on the background that fundamental decisions such as share acquisitions or expenses above a specific threshold are determined by the parent company or need at least to be verified by it, with reference to IP 20 (369, 6): *"According to specific value limits we have to go to the board [of the parent company] in order to get approval".*[150] By implication, the club needs to ensure that the strategic partnership is supported by all corporate authorities of the partner organisation. The quotation of IP 6 (85; 36) summarises that a dissent between subsidiary and parent company can cause a partnership failure or breakdown: *"[parent company] said we are not allowed. [...]. [parent company] is not signing the contract and we went out of [club]".*[151] While economic failure can result from various causes such as managerial misbehaviour (cross related to *quality of people*) and various industry developments (e.g., increased competition), macro environmental trends (e.g., a global economic downturn) may also be a reason although this likelihood is rather *low*. However, while football has long been the "*top of the town*" even football may lose its attractivity someday due to the ever-changing business environment (*football losing attractivity*). Although this is currently not predictable, the *increasing commercialisation* of the sport is critically seen within the research context. Based on this IP 23 (435; 27) stated:

> "The system has to think about whether money distribution, the resource allocation is really that which will keep football the number one on the emotional scale in the long term".[152]

---

[150] *„Nach bestimmten Wertgrenzen müssen wir dann einfach in das Bord gehen und dort die Freigabe kriegen*" (IP 20, 369; 6).

[151] *„[Mutterkonzern], also die haben gesagt ihr dürft nicht, also [Unternehmen] [...]. [Mutterkonzern] is not signing the contract and we want out of [Club]*" (IP 6, 85; 36).

[152] *„Und deswegen muss irgendwann das System überlegen, ob die Geldverteilung, die Mittelverteilung wirklich die ist, die langfristig den Fußball als Nummer Eins in der emotionalen Skala lässt*" (IP 23, 435; 27).

Of particular concern within the scope of *increasing commercialisation* is the football fan because fans are critical as regards the attractivity of the sport. By comparing the German Bundesliga with the English Premier League, IP 13 (246; 33) determined that the current development of increased ticket prices and a nascent change of audiences in the stadium is *"a first sign, the stadiums are becoming corporate. [...]. The ticket prices are 3, 7, 8, 10 times higher. I don't know. I think this is the biggest challenge for football"*.[153]

The increased commercialisation of German football indeed seems to be of concern for the fans as the survey results indicate. For example, overall 73.8% of fans (survey results) fear increased commercialisation due to equity partnerships. The trend of commercialisation may also lead to a repeal of the 50+1 rule (*expecting repeal of 50+1*) within the next years due to its legal limbo, according to IP 2 (16; 33): *"At some point someone will go to Brussels*[154] *and then it is over"*.[155] Although the concept *expecting repeal of 50+1* clearly emerged in the empirical data, regulative mechanisms against the arbitrariness of individual players (investors, in particular Maecenas and oligarchs) are advocated by sponsors.

While from a club perspective a repeal could be blessing in order to financially catch up with other European clubs as it opens the German market for selling majority shares, the inherent peril from a strategic partner's point of view is that football becomes a *"plaything of the super rich"* (IP 24, 434; 30). This would lessen the attractivity for corporations to engage in commercial or financial partnerships with clubs, according to IP 9 (157; 25):

> "Will it be still attractive to use football if it becomes a plaything of Maecenas? Then the investors will say goodbye and say: pfff, this is someone else's game and they play by different rules, we will find a different product field. Then they go to Formula 1 or somewhere else".[156]

---

[153]„*Und das ist ein erstes Zeichen, dass die Stadien werden Corporate. [...]. Und die Ticketpreise sind 3, 7, 8, 10 Mal höher. Ich weiß es nicht. Ich glaube, da hat der Fußball die größte Herausforderung*" (IP 13, 246; 33).

[154]Brussels is the location of the European Court of Justice.

[155]„*Irgendwann geht irgendjemand nach Brüssel und dann ist das Thema erledigt*" (IP 2, 16; 33).

[156]„*Und ist es dann überhaupt noch so attraktiv, Fußball dafür zu nutzen, wenn das ein Spielball von Mäzen wird? Dann werden die Investoren eher davon verabschieden und sagen: Pfff, nee in dem spielen, da spielen andere mit anderen Regeln, da suchen wir uns ein anderes Produktfeld. Dann gehen wir in die Formel 1 oder wir machen was auch immer*" (IP 9, 157; 25).

This is widely confirmed from the corporate (strategic partner's) perspective, as can be abstracted by IP 15 (285; 25):

> "[...] then I would back out as this would challenge everything, which I have outlined, that brought us together. The only logical thing would be for us to get out. If someone tries to incorporate ideologies or completely different things [...]".[157]

Even though a repeal of the 50+1 rule is likely to change the football business in Germany in some way, it still remains the choice of each club as to how many shares to sell and with what kind of shareholder a partnership is entered into. For a strategic equity partner, who has a strategic interest in the collaboration with the club and who is not interested in dominating the club strategy, regulative mechanisms are perceived as a supportive element.

This part illuminated various kind of risks associated with a partnership with a football club ranging from inter-partner issues to macro environmental factors. The significance to base a club shareholding on a prior business relationship has been underscored. However, a shareholding can also be entered without having a prior relationship. While in this case the risk of failure is increased this procedure is depicted in the sub-category *approaching externally* as a variation in the data.

6.6.5 Approaching Externally

The sub-category *approaching externally* appeared as an alternative approach to enter into a share deal. "Externally" designates that it is about an equity investment without having a prior business relationship to the partner (no history of partnership). *Approaching externally* refers to an *active* (property) search process of how a club approaches a potential shareholder. Consequently, the sub-category is reasoned from a club perspective.

Approaching externally implies a multitude of processes and activities necessary in order to find an adequate partner. Since a football club has normally no experience with a shareholding (M&A) process (IP 23, 414; 14), cooperation with a consultant company (*involving consultancy*), although optional, is a

157 „*[...] dann würde ich aussteigen, weil damit ist all das, was ich ja dargestellt habe, was uns in die Verbindung gebracht hat, würde dann in Frage gestellt. Und dann müssen wir aussteigen konsequenterweise. Wenn da irgendeiner versucht, Ideologien oder völlig andere Dinge einzubringen [...]*" (IP 15, 285; 25).

common practice. The preconditions of the search process are reflected in the concept *preparing an investor approach* and mainly relate to activities which have already been illustrated within the scope of the sub-category "*screening*". Essentially, it is about internal needs, it encompasses the complex issue of club valuation and implies the fundamental decision of which type of shareholder and which attributes and preconditions a potential shareholder must have in order to qualify for an equity investment (*defining strategic equity partner*).

Defining strategic equity partner entails aspects such as size (*financial capacity*), anticipated *compatibility* with own brand (e.g., *image, integrity* of the management) as well as industry and branch origin. Based on these criteria, a database with potential shareholders is created and prioritised according to club-specific issues. For example, these issues can relate to a *regional affinity* of a shareholder, according to IP 20 (377; 33): *"I think it is usual that one starts in the regional area and then extends the radius"*.[158] This focus is based on a club's reasoning to strengthen the mutual regional area of the club and shareholder. Social responsibility may be an aspect for attracting companies to support the club in their region by engaging in an equity partnership. In view of *market penetration* and *positioning abroad,* other clubs may prefer a shareholding with a partner from abroad. However, these preferences depend on a club-specific context.

Yet, the latter option implies a higher risk for alienation between the club and fans since a total of 79% of fans deem a *regional affinity* of a shareholder as an important aspect for acceptance.

Suitable partners are *contacted* with a presentation of the club's facts and figures and the club's strength as well as *attracting factors* (self-portrait). These *attracting factors* are concerted with the aforementioned elements explained as part of the section "*attracting factors*" (5.4.1). However, *"it is essential about saying I am part of a strong growing brand which continues to grow steadily"*[159] (IP 2, 21; 37). In addition to this, regarding a strategic partner (as shareholder type) it is critical to provide rationales for a shareholding. In line with the tenet *"it must be based on content"*[160] (IP 2, 17; 27), a shareholding with a strategic partner requires a *mutual business concept* (a form of business collaboration) which is of joint benefit for the club and strategic partner. However, this concept must to be tailored and adjusted accordingly to specific partner needs (IP 3, 56; 35).

[158]„*Und ich glaube, dass es normal ist, dass man erst mal im regionalen Bereich anfängt und dann den Radius immer größer zieht*" (IP 20, 377; 33).

[159]„*Aber es geht ja vor allem auch darum, dass ich sagen kann, ich bin hier/ ich besitze einen Teil einer extrem starken Marke, die immer weiterwächst*" (IP 2, 21; 37).

[160]„*[...] es müssen Inhalte hinten dranstehen [...]*" (IP 2, 17; 27).

All the facts and figures (including the valuation), attracting factors, and a business concept are part of the *"storyboard"* (printed and electronic documents), which builds the basis for *contacting* the potential shareholder according to their ranking in the list.

Potential shareholders are contacted as part of a *"roadshow"* process, a kind of promotion of the club, in which the club meets potential shareholders and tries to convince these to enter into an equity investment. The *"roadshow"* is often (dimension *yes/no*) accompanied by an image campaign (target group: populace) *"because if the roadshow is not in concert with the opinion of the populace you do not get an investor"*[161] (IP 4, 53; 36). A positive first contact and mutual interest may intensify the dialogue between the parties. Within this step, via myriad conservations both parties try to ascertain *compatibility* on diverse levels (i.e., strategic, cultural, personal, etc.). In order to conclude in a share deal both partners need to be certain that

> "this is someone who has a sustainable, long-term strategic interest. Someone who fits with the culture, mentality and values, who knows what it is all about and isn't just after short-term profits"[162] (IP 7, 95; 33).

However, compatibility in all aspects is difficult to achieve due to the high requirements. Yet, if there is agreement in favour of a deal, intensive negotiations commence on valuation of the club. This process is accompanied by the *screening* of the partners financials in the form of *due diligence* in order to evaluate the viability and financial soundness of the partner. Finally, if all parameters are met shareholding is agreed. Due to the lack of a history of partnership, *approaching externally* still remains a procedure associated with the aforementioned higher risk for failure.

Within the category *fear of loss,* fan opinion has been examined in terms of fan concerns, arguments in favour of a shareholder and fan acceptance. Impediments for clubs to enter into a shareholding and potential risks factors of an equity partnership have been illuminated. Furthermore, the additional strategic option of how to approach a shareholder externally has been explained. Figure 6.11 on the next page summarises the category.

---

[161] *„Weil, wenn diese Roadshow mit der allgemeinen rein öffentlichen Meinung nicht übereinstimmt, dann bekommen sie auch keinen Investor*" (IP 4, 53; 36).

[162] *„Hier ist jemand, der nachhaltig, langfristig strategisches Interesse hat. Der von der Kultur passt, der von der Mentalität passt, der von den Werten passt, der versteht, worauf es ankommt und eben auch nicht eine kurzfristige Renditeerwartung hat*" (IP 7, 95; 33).

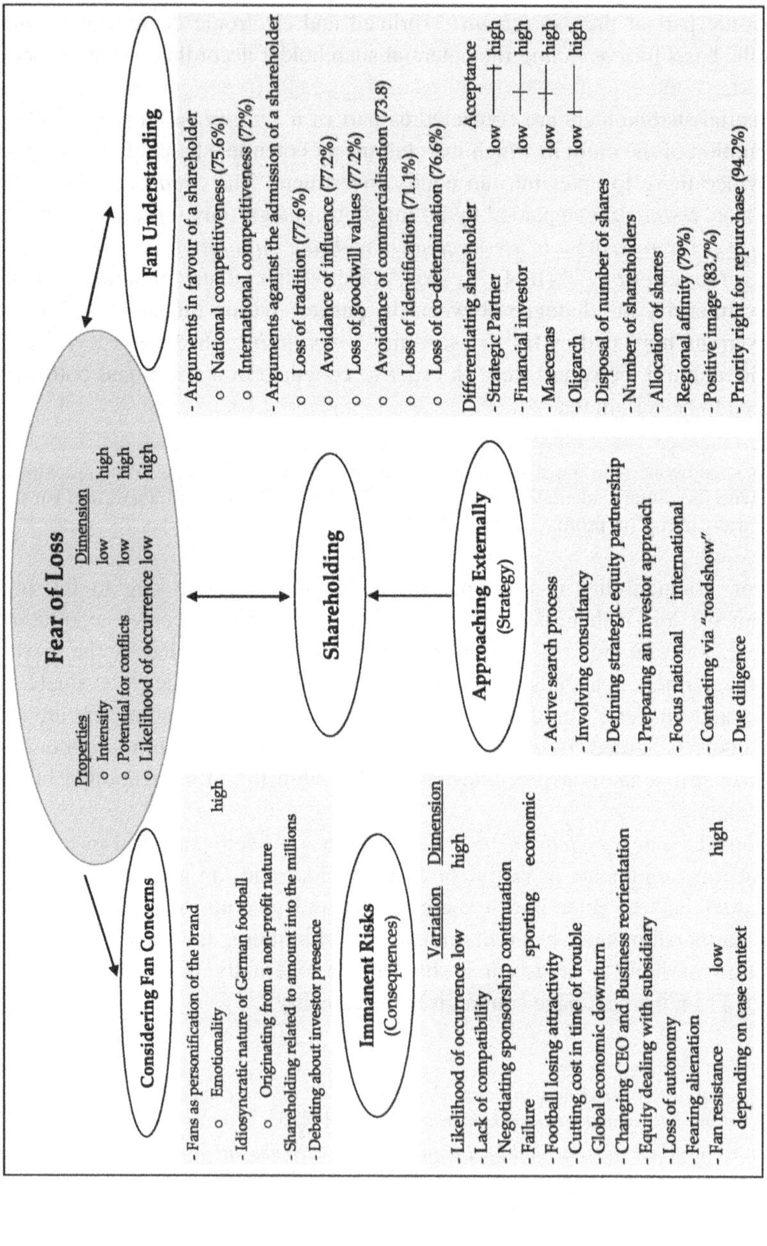

Figure 6.11 Category - Fear of Loss. (Source: Own Illustration)

6.6.6 Theoretical Integration

In this sub-section, the relevant literature is contrasted against the main empirical findings of the category and points of convergence, divergence, and extensions are determined. Table 6.16 presents an overview of existing knowledge and empirical results:

Table 6.16 Contrasting Literature with Fear of Loss. (Source: Own Illustration)

Empirical concepts from grounded theory	Findings from the literature review
Fans as personification of the club	Fans as 'heart of the club', fans as reason for club existence (Bauers & Hovemann, 2019a; Jacobs, 2014; Dierig, 2014b; Herberger et al., 2013; Murphy, 2010).
High emotionality	Fans are very loyal and emotional (Roose & Schäfer, 2017; Adam et al., 2017), 'most loyal customer in the world' (Johnston, 2014)
Idiosyncratic nature of German football system	'Verein' as original governance form, 50+1 rule (Adam et al., 2019; Bauers & Hovemann, 2019b; Hofmann, 2016; Szymanski, 2015; Teevs, 2014; Nagy, 2012; Quitzau, 2009, 2003; Schilhaneck, 2008; Summerer, 2008; Weiler, 2006).
Expecting repeal of 50+1 Debating investor presence	Repeal of 50+1, increasing relevance of equity partnerships (Adam & Hovemann, 2018b; Oediger, 2017a; Boor et al., 2016; Schuster & Unterhitzenberger, 2014; Teevs, 2014; Punte, 2012; Kuper, 2009; Lammert et al., 2009; Summerer, 2008; Weiler, 2006; Metrum, 2004)
Fearing alienation Fan resistance Fear of dependency	Loss of identity associated with selling equity (Cravens et al., 1993), fan concerns (Bauers et al., 2019; Bauers & Hovemann, 2019a; Bühler, 2017; Pilz, 2011), investors ruin the romance of football (Dierig, 2014b), investors as 'corporate raiders' (Ruf & Theweleit, 2018; Steinmann, 2018)
Fans exerting power	Fan protests (Erberich, 2017b; Salzborn, 2017; Wallrodt, 2015)
Contradiction No hostile take-over of strategic partner	Clubs fear restricted decision making due to investor presence (Dierig, 2014b; Bauers et al., 2013)
Extension/contradiction High fan acceptance of strategic partner	General fan concern about investor presence (Bauers & Hovemann, 2019a; Bühler, 2017; Pawlowski, 2013; Pilz, 2011).
Non-acceptance of oligarch Significance of image	Brand personality has positive effects on brand involvement (Tsiotsou et al., 2014)
Regional affinity	Regional affinity is assumed to have a positive impact on fan identification (Schade, 2012; Alexa, 2009)
Contribution Right to repurchase	-

It is commonly accepted in the literature that football clubs operate in a system which is characterised by an intensive link to their club members and fans (Bauers & Hovemann, 2019b; Roose & Schäfer, 2017; Adam et al., 2017; Dierig, 2014b). Johnston (2014) even argues that football fans are the 'most loyal customer in the word' reflecting their high involvement and high emotionality. These insights are verified in the empirical concept of *fans as personification of the club* which explains why clubs and potential shareholders take the fan view into consideration in connection with a share deal. This concept overlaps with the notion of Herberger et al. (2013) who state that fans are 'the heart of the club' and find also support by Bauers and Hovemann (2019a), Jacobs (2014), and Murphy (2010), among others.

While the trend of shareholder presence is omnipresent in the European football business (Adam & Hovemann, 2019c; Boor et al., 2016) there is a permanent discussion about investors in German football. This debate is closely related to the 50+1 rule (Bauers et al., 2019a; Lammert et al., 2009) which has become a relevant aspect in this grounded theory (*debating about investor presence*). Within the industry context, many football theorists (e.g., Hofmann, 2016; Teevs, 2014) are in favour of a repeal of the rule and legal experts such as Punte (2012) and Summerer (2008) have forecasted the rule's termination due to its 'legal limbo'. This is also in line with the opinion of many club authorities and football experts who argue that the rule prevents equal opportunities in the European football business (Schneider, 2018; Lammert et al., 2009). This attitude towards 50+1 is echoed by many of the experts interviewed of whom the majority predict a repeal of the 50+1 rule in the future (*expecting repeal of 50+1*). This, in turn, implies an increased relevance of equity partnerships in German football which is embodied in the concept of *"race of investors"* (in the future).

Similar to the literature the empirical data also identified opposing findings concerning the rule. That means, although the empirical results clearly underpin an expected repeal of 50+1, many strategic equity partners appreciate the rule as it prevents German clubs from becoming a 'plaything' of super rich people and, therefore, the rule protects the significance of (minority) strategic equity partnerships. It is evident that majority shareholdings are not in the interest of a strategic partner because the latter does not desire to dominate the club.

However, this study contributes to existing knowledge by detecting that fans have a differential view in terms of the acceptance of minority shareholdings of different shareholder types. Whereas previous considerations focused on the general term investor (Bauers & Hovemann, 2019a; Bühler, 2017; Pawlowski, 2013; Pilz, 2011) and some authors referred to investors as 'corporate raiders' (Ruf & Theweleit, 2018; Steinmann, 2018), this study adds that fan acceptance differs with respect to four shareholder types. Accordingly, a strategic partner is highly accepted as a club shareholder. In consequence, statements from e.g., Erberich (2017b), Salzborn (2017), and Wallrodt (2015) about fan protests due to a rejection of any kind of investors in German football are empirically not confirmed. Yet, the results ratify fan rejection regarding an oligarch as a club shareholder. The concept *fans exerting power* clearly indicates that fan protests depend on various factors and need to be seen in the light of a club's specific context.

This study found that a *positive image* and a *regional affinity* support the acceptance of a shareholder, therefore connecting to the findings from Schade (2012) and Alexa (2009). Beyond this, a club's *priority right of repurchase* is crucial for fans regarding the admission of a shareholder. However, while an increase in *national* and *international competitiveness* are no reasons for a repeal of the 50+1 rule from the fan perspective (Bauers & Hovemann, 2019a), competitiveness as an argument for the admission of a shareholder is valid for the majority of fans as demonstrated in the present study. Against this, the exclusion of investor *influence on sporting decisions* and the *avoidance of increased commercialisation* as arguments against the admission of a shareholder confirm recent results from Bauers and Hovemann (2019a).

This study also provides supporting evidence for a *loss of identity* and a *loss of values* as relevant arguments against the admission of a shareholder. The latter two aspects have already been investigated by Cravens et al. (1993) in a non-sport setting with regard to equity investments between two corporations.

In the following *securing*, the core category of the theory, is explained which implies the various motives but also impediments to enter into a strategic equity partnership.

6.7 Securing—The Core Category

6.7.1 Introduction

"*Securing*" has emerged as the core category of the research study to which all other categories relate. "*Securing*" explicates the various underlying motives why (why not) and how strategic equity partnerships in German football are entered. The term "*securing*" gains centre stage as an in vivo code which is grounded in diverse contexts in the empirical data and enables the corporate and club perspective to be combined. Consequently, "*securing*" reflects the specificity of the empirical research field.

"*Securing*" constitutes the central building block in the dyad of the sponsorship and shareholding. *Connecting with a symbol* has initially been the reason why corporations partner with a football club. Substantially, a sponsorship leads to continuous revenue streams for clubs and is the foundation for the communication, marketing, and branding strategy of a sponsor. During the *history of partnership* this sponsorship is developed into a "*brand symbiosis*" (strategic partnership) in which both associates incorporate the partner into the own strategic planning. At this stage, synergies are developed which are of mutual benefit for the club and sponsor. Accordingly, the sponsorship in the form of a "*brand symbiosis*" is the heart of the strategic equity partnership. *Connecting with a symbol* and *becoming a brand symbiosis* can therefore be classified as preconditions for the core category. The category *shareholding* serves as a strategy for "*securing*" the existing commercial partnership *("brand symbiosis")* in various ways. While a share deal has additional impact (consequences) on partnership management (i.e., "*having a say*" and *signifying*), these can be conveyed to the consequences of "*securing*" alike.

"*Securing*" originates from the multi-faceted noun security which has a wide range of meanings. The term not only represents security in the sense of "guarantee", "safety", or "protection" (something is not likely to be lost), it also applies in the meaning of "certainty" and "confidence" (the feeling of being confident in a relationship) (Cambridge dictionary, 2008; 1289), therefore expressing another step of *deepening involvement.*

In the context of stock and finance security stands for an investment (buying or selling "shares" or "bonds"), thus representing a specific value (Cambridge dictionary, ibid.) and implying a direct connection to *shareholding* as a strategy. Accordingly, due to its multidimensionality "*securing*" already accomplishes an integration on a semantic layer.

"*Securing*" can be related to Glaser's type family. Types illustrate variations of the whole (Urquhart, 2013). The core category subsumes the five sub-categories

- securing a deepening commitment
- deterring competitors (securing against competitors)
- planning security
- securing competitiveness
- securing regional connectivity and appeal

which vary according to their relevance in a partnership-specific context. Therefore, the motives for entering into a strategic equity partnership can mainly be based on one aspect yet also encompass a combination of motives (hybrid forms) with differing priorities. The central motives of clubs (and also vital for strategic partners) build upon the sub-categories *planning security*, *securing competitiveness*, and *securing a deepening commitment.*

The sub-categories *securing regional connectivity and appeal* as well as *deterring competitors* are argued from the corporate perspective solely. Since these five sub-categories pertain to the same overriding core category, they overlap considerably, and are (partly) interwoven.

6.7.2 Securing a Deepening Commitment

The sub-core category *securing a deepening commitment* puts the collaborative interactions into the focus of the partnership. There is overall agreement that a shareholding (as a strategy) is established because club and sponsor want to *deepen* the partnership and get an even greater benefit from the collaboration. This becomes evident in the next statement:

> "This step was basically an element like many other engagements too, but still to become further entwined in order to collaborate closer and to yield the best results"[163] (IP 8, 120; 12).

"Securing", in this regard, refers to the verb secure in the meaning of to "obtain" or to "get" and indicates the purpose to *deepen* (intensify) the partnership and to yield an added value in the form of improved collaborative conditions via a shareholding. The deepening aspect from a shareholding originates as a commitment in a twofold manner. Commitment is an abstract and ambiguous word and applies in the meaning of "obligation" and "dedication" and also encompasses a *"promise to give your money, energy, and time to support something"* (Cambridge dictionary, 2008; 277).

[163] *„Der Schritt war im Grunde ein Element wie andere Engagements auch, aber halt auch sich noch tiefer zu verwurzeln, um letzten Endes mit dem Partner noch enger zusammenzuarbeiten könne und die besten Ergebnisse erzielen zu können*" (IP 8, 120; 12).

In the meaning of obligation commitment has a normative component and refers back to the concept of *extending domain of interest* (*economic* concern) and *higher responsibility* that a sponsor has upon entering into a shareholding. The financial engagement of a shareholding leads to a *deepening commitment* (obligation) to secure the *value retention* of the investment made. This commitment becomes a central motive for clubs, as IP 12 (209; 12) explained:

> "On the other hand, it is important for us that we bind them to their responsibility by incorporating them as an equity partner. Since they turn the focus onto the other interest, financial stability, because if someone takes a share of a corporation then he wants [...] that the investment is not waste of money".[164]

A shareholding is an equally binding element for the club which results in an on-top commitment for the corporate sponsor, with reference to IP 10 (172; 21): *"So let me make this clear, there is more self-assertion and more win-win situations because it is more binding [...]"*.[165] A *deepening* of the partnership is further grounded in an emotional commitment (dedication). Shareholding leads to a sense of belonging (cohesiveness) between the partners which also adds to closer collaborations. Although emotional attachment occurs as a process of *deepening involvement* over the *history of partnership*, an equity investment is, similar to higher responsibility (obligation), an addition to emotional attachment. IP 11 (198; 26) used a symbolic style by stating: *"And there are a lot of emotional connections [..]. These would have been there either way but I think this was the icing on the cake if I may say so"*.[166]

[164]*„Auf der anderen Seite ist und wichtig, dass wir diese auch in ihrer Verantwortung langfristig binden und das könne wir machen, indem wir sie als Equity Partner an Bord nehmen. Weil sie dann auch / das andere Interesse, nämlich die Finanzstabilität mit in den Fokus nehmen, weil wenn sich jemand an einem Unternehmen beteiligt, dann möchte er [...] auch natürlich, dass das Investment jetzt nicht Verfeuerung von Geld ist*" (IP 12, 209; 12).

[165]*„Und doch bleibe ich bei dem Punkt, dass man mehr Druchsetzungskraft bzw. mehr win-win Situationen schafft, weil es verbindlicher ist [...]*" (IP 10, 172; 21).

[166]*„Und da sind auch viele emotionale Bindungen da [..]. Die wäre vielleicht so auch da, aber ich glaube, das hat halt noch mal die Sahne auf den Kuchen gegeben, wenn ich das so sagen kann*" (IP 11, 198; 26).

Due to this increased bonding and binding (both forms of *commitment* act in concert) associated with an equity investment, the partner organisation is willing to "go the extra mile" (to invest additional effort into the partnership). Although there is already an added value in the light of a *"brand symbiosis"*, by entering into a strategic equity partnership value is again added, according to IP 7 (118; 2): *"These are deepening elements which exceed those of a normal partnership"*.[167] An added value refers to the concept *reinforcing commitment for support* which can be abstracted from the statement by IP 11 (195; 37): *"I believe that, indirectly, if you are a shareholder of the club there is a stronger will to help, to support in order to see the club be successful"*.[168]

This *reinforcing commitment* for support integrates a variety of associated benefits for each partner and the partnership as a whole. For example, it finds expression in support for the partner's activities which are not the primary focus of one's own organisation, as IP 9 (145; 6) elucidates:

> "They benefit from a bigger range of services which the club is willing to perform because they sit at the table, because they are part of the family. Then, you do not have these difficulties of a predefined field this far and no further. Instead you are able to go far beyond".[169]

In specific terms, via a share deal the club and sponsor aim to secure a deepening commitment which is beyond the contractual components of a business partnership. This can also relate to additional collaborative efforts in terms of the internationalisation of one of the partners. In the case of having different target

---

[167] *„Aber das sind schon auch vertiefende Elemente, die über eine normale Partnerschaft hinausgehen"* (IP 7, 118; 2).

[168] *„Ich glaube aber schon, dass, indirekt natürlich, wenn du Anteilseigner bist des Clubs, noch mal ein stärkerer Wille da zu helfen, zu unterstützen und den Club auch erfolgreich zu sehen"* (IP 11, 195; 37).

[169] *„Sie bekommen einfach eine größere Leistungsbreite die der Verein bereit ist mitzumachen, weil die einfach am Tisch sitzen, weil sie Teil der Familie sind. Dann hast du nicht diese Schwierigkeiten, dass du ein definiertes Feld genau hast, und genau bis dahin sind sie bereit die Leistungen zu machen, sondern du kannst ein Vielfaches darüber hinaus gehen"* (IP 9, 145; 6).

markets the affiliate is still willing to support the partner's goals even though this is not their priority. Beyond this, a deepening commitment is reflected in the concept of *equity supporting problem solving*, which becomes evident in the statement from IP 11 (199; 13):

> "But it helps because one has a stronger bond to the club. And I'd say therefore, in case of doubt, it is easier to find solutions because both know: hey, basically we want to continue to collaborate".[170]

This passage also indicates a *subtle conviction of continuation* which links to the sub-core category *"planning security"*. While there are situations of distance (e.g., in negotiation) the shareholding reduces the fear of exiting when the going gets tough, thereby contributing towards *"planning security"* as well as representing a stable partnership *(demonstrating stability)* to the outside world.

The commitment linked with a share deal is expressed by the use of three reoccurring metaphors which appear as a dominant stylistic device in various stages of the empirical data. The allegories "marriage", "family", and "house building" all characterise an obligation and dedication *(deepening commitment)* between the partners. For instance, the quotation from IP 13 (238; 27) illustrates a marriage metaphor as an intensifying effect of a shareholding:

> "It is obvious that the marriage between [company A, own company] and [club] and I guess also between [company B] and [club B] is so deep that/well, you can do a long-term sponsorship without being a shareholder, yet- if you do both then it is stronger still".[171]

[170]„*Aber es hilft dir natürlich, weil du eine deutlich stärkere Bindung und Verbindung zum Club hast. Und ich sage einmal im Zweifelsfall auch dadurch leichter Lösungen findest, weil beide wissen: hey, eigentlich wollen wir miteinander arbeiten, wir wollen miteinander weitermachen*" (IP 11, 199; 13).

[171]„*Es ist klar, dass die Ehe zwischen [Unternehmen A, eigenes Unternehmen] und [Club], und ich schätze auch zwischen [Unternehmen B] und [Club B], liegt ja so tief, dass/ gut du kannst ein langfristiges Sponsoring machen, ohne Eigentümer zu sein. Wenn du beides machst, ist es ja noch stärker*" (IP 13, 238; 27).

This is buttressed by IP 20 (367; 36) who declared: *"Instead we said: for better and for worse we want to maintain the commitment"*.[172] IP 13 (238; 37) also used a comparison by using the diction of "marriage": *"It is like a marriage. There are two parties who [..]/The benefits are to additionally intensify the collaboration"*.[173] Similarly, IP 10 (171; 7) reports that the sponsor *"sees the [club] as family"*[174] and IP 9 (145; 8) used the expression *"part of the family"*.

However, since a strategic equity partnership is more binding and more difficult to exit *securing a deepening commitment* can imply underlying *self-serving benefits* too. This self-serving motive is interrelated to the normative component of commitment. Albeit a self-serving interest appears rather as a hidden-agenda it is still relevant as it allows inspection of the downsides of entering into a strategic equity partnership. Even though the partner is being perceived as "part of the family", IP 10 (182; 20) stresses that the strategic considerations for entering a share deal also imply *"[...] how do I handle it best and what is the numerical effect for us and the greatest effect"*.[175]

A self-serving benefit of the partners crystallises in regard to sponsorship negotiations. Since the partner has committed strategically (formally and emotionally) he might be ready to pay a strategic price *(calculus)* for the sponsorship which is expressed by IP 12 (219; 33):

> "If I agree to connect in the long-term then I am maybe willing earlier on to make an investment in which I perhaps pay more for specific rights, as otherwise required, compared to a third party who has nothing to do with that".[176]

The concept of *calculus* is based on the notion that the shareholding event frequently concurs with the extension of the sponsorship contract. Indeed, following the statement from IP 18 (324; 6), it can be verified that a strategic equity partner

---

[172] *„Sondern wir haben gesagt: In guten und in schlechten Zeiten wollen wir hier das Commitment aufrechterhalten*" (IP 20, 367; 36).

[173] *„Es ist so wie eine Ehe. Es sind zwei Parteien, die [..] / Die Vorteile sind noch enger zusammenzuarbeiten*" (IP 13, 238; 37).

[174] *„Sprich, man sieht den [Club] als Familie*" (IP 10, 171; 7).

[175] *„[...] wie dreh ich es am besten und was ist der nummerische Effekt für uns und die meiste Wirkung*" (IP 10, 182; 20).

[176] *„Wenn ich mich bereit bin, langfristig zu binden, dann bin ich auch vielleicht in einer früheren Zeit, als vielleicht rein wertmäßig notwendig, bereit, ein Investment zu tätigen, in dem ich vielleicht mehr für gewisse Rechte zahle, als vielleicht ein Dritter, der damit sonst nichts zu tun hat*" (IP 12, 219; 33).

might be willing to pay a strategic price for the sponsorship (at the beginning). However, this is coupled with a *calculus* in mind for future benefit in terms of sponsorship fees:

> "At the beginning there is a jump up which would not be absolutely necessary. However, based on the perspective that we can bind [club] in the long-term this pays off quickly".[177]

The concept of *calculus* is reinforced as follows: *"Because we can engage in a successful partnership with [club] based on lower costs"*[178] (IP 18, 346; 18). Likewise, the sponsor might gain a leverage from an equity investment in terms of paying less sponsorship fees due to the long-term direction of a strategic equity partnership. IP 18 (339; 2) honestly admitted that shareholding supported the corporate partner *"[…] that the basic licensing costs, in a European comparison, are fixed at a favourable level"*.[179] This statement hints to the predictability of sponsorship costs which is an indicator for the sub-core category *"planning security"*.

Calculus, nevertheless, remains a subtle concept as the next two quotations illustrate. On the one hand, IP 11 (190; 19) disagree with IP 18 by saying: "*Well, as a shareholder you definitely do not receive any gifts*",[180] which maintains the formally detached handling between shareholding and sponsorship *(managing the dyad)*. However, on the other hand, IP 11 (198; 36) also disclosed: *I am totally convinced, if [club] would exploit the situation and would play [company B] and us off against each other then they would get more*".[181] While this statement

[177] „*Jetzt am Anfang ist erst mal wieder ein Sprung nach oben, hätte man nicht zwingend machen müssen. Aber unter der Perspektive, dass wir den [Club] langfristig binden, lässt sich das sehr schnell amortisieren*" (IP 18, 324; 6).

[178] „*Weil wir dann eben mit geringeren Mittel dann eben doch eine erfolgreiche Partnerschaft mit Borussia Dortmund leben können*" (IP 18, 346; 18).

[179] „*[…], dass das Grundlizenzvolumen auf einem - auf Europäischen Vergleich - günstigem Niveau festgeschrieben wird*" (IP 18, 339; 2).

[180] „*Also es ist definitiv so, dass ihnen als Anteilseigner nichts geschenkt wird*" (IP 11, 190; 19).

[181] „*Ich bin der festen Überzeugung, wenn [Club] die Situation ausnutzen würde und würde [Unternehmen B] und uns gegeneinander ausspielen, dann würden sie mehr kriegen*" (IP 11, 198; 36).

reflects the way of *dealing fairly* by the club it subtly involves a benefit for the corporate partner who has not paid the highest fees because *"[…] they [the club] see that we were the first ones who provided the initial [figure] million"*[182] (IP 11, 198; 21) which hints towards a hidden advantage in terms of sponsorship fees.

Overall, a subliminal benefit *(calculus)* in terms of a favourable bargaining positions for the future sponsorship is implied in *securing a deepening commitment.*

While the deepening commitment clearly emerged as a motive, the normative component (obligation) of commitment can also be a reason for a sponsor to deny a share deal. A shareholding is (implies) an obligation to continually renew (extend) the sponsorship (due to the *"retention factor"*) which can be perceived as a restriction of entrepreneurial flexibility *(retaining flexibility)* because it has a financial impact on the sponsor as a sponsorship permanently ties up a specific (large) corporate budget *(amount into the million).* The concept *retaining flexibility* becomes apparent in the following quotation by IP 14 (256; 10):

> "Why should I bind myself in the long term if I could do so in the medium term because I am not fully aware of how the business will develop. […]. I am just more variable".[183]

Consequently, the associated high costs related with a strategic equity partnership is a main reason for some corporations to reject a shareholding in a twofold manner: due to the aforementioned one-off payment to acquire the club shares and due to the commitment to continuously renew the sponsorship. Similarly, a shareholding could also be an obstacle for clubs since these also commit to the strategic equity partner on the sponsoring side. Accordingly, there is a reduction of sponsorship options (link to *exclusivity*), as reflected below:

> This is, this is something we have to be aware of. If we say we enter this exclusivity which we get paid for appropriately, then it is like that and we have to go this way. Of course, yes. Well, restriction yes if you see it like that"[184] (IP 2, 30; 32).

---

[182] *„[…] die sehen das schon auch, dass wir ihnen die ersten [Zahl] Millionen gegeben haben"* (IP 11, 198; 21).

[183] *„Also warum soll ich mich langfristig binden, wenn ich mich eben lieber mittelfristig binden könnte, weil ich auch nicht hundertprozentig weiß, wie die Geschäftsentwicklung ist. […]. Ich bin da einfach variabler"* (IP 14, 256; 10).

[184] *„Das ist, das ist etwas, darüber müssen wir uns im Klaren sein. Wenn wir sagen, wir gehen diese Exklusivität ein, die, die wir uns auch entsprechend honorieren lassen, dann, dann ist es so und dann müssen wir diesen Weg auch gehen. Klar, ja. Also Einschränkung ja, wenn Sie es so wollen ja"* (IP 2, 30; 32).

However, for clubs this kind of restriction is not perceived negatively since the benefits of a shareholding predominate, e.g., to have *planning security* and to have the security (confidence) of a bond with a loyal partner that allows deeper collaborations.

6.7.3 Securing Competitiveness

Securing competitiveness is based on the *economic* interests (property) of the club and sponsor whereby "competitiveness" relates to the club's competitive position. For a club, a share deal is a strategy for generating income (one-off payment, *sourcing*) in order to enhance its national and international competitive position in the long run which serves their raison d'être *(sporting success)*. Consequently, this motive is of *highest importance* (property) for the club. Although the money cannot be spent (totally) on the squad, because it is predetermined to areas which substantially enhance the club, the payment still has an effect on the club's liquidity and overall spending power. For instance, the equity money enables a club to release bank loans that prevent the payment of interest, according to IP 12 (226; 27):

> "If you are debts of 40, 50 million and you release these you save 5, 6 million on interest and redemption every year which can easily be used for a midfielder, a top midfielder or striker or whatsoever".[185]

This offers financial discretion and allows additional money to be out into the squad. Another example is to invest the money in the infrastructure (e.g., a new youth academy or stadium) which again enables other available money to be spent on improving the team. However, securing the club's *competitiveness* is equally important for the sponsor since a sponsor is dependent on the sporting success of the club in order to benefit from the club's charisma, as IP 17 (310; 14) corroborates: "*[…] One always benefits oneself if the club is strong and develops*

[185]„*Wenn du noch irgendwelche 40, 50 Millionen Kredite mit dir rumschleifst, wenn du die nicht mehr hast, sparst du ja 5, 6 Millionen allein Zins und Tilgung jedes Jahr, die du dann vielleicht für einen guten Mittelfeldspieler oder was auch immer, Topmittelfeldspieler oder Stürmer oder was auch immer einsetzen kannst*" (IP 12, 226; 27).

well economically, has a big reach, good media performance and international appeal".[186] Financing the club becomes especially relevant given the *increasing revenues from international competition.* IP 8 (120; 21) explains that

> "the commitment as a shareholder at [club] was connected with supporting the club in terms of [stadium] acquisition, financing the club, and competitiveness. And for us it was appealing to become part of this as this ensures that the club remains competitive or is competitive at the highest level".[187]

While the economic interest in terms of the share value and share price ranges along the continuum *"not losing money/making money"* the shareholding is subtly based on one's own corporate competitive position. A shareholding secures the competitiveness of the club which is a key component of branding and communication strategy. IP 8 (120; 10) discloses that the share deal *"is ultimately based on a business interest, yes. Everything we do is aimed at selling more products"*.[188] This relates to the sponsor's *corporate mission* (profit-driven) and also sheds light on a growth "ideology" which is required to secure the club's and one's own competitiveness. Consequently, a shareholding is a strategy to secure and push the success of the sponsorship *(supporting own business goals)* by providing the club with additional money (in exchange for shares) and securing its competitiveness. Benefitting from increased club charisma by financially supporting the club becomes a key argument in the reasoning of clubs to convince a strategic partner to enter into a shareholding, with reference to IP 11 (200; 3):

---

[186] „*Weil immer nur wenn man einen starken [Club] hat, der sich wirtschaftlich gut entwickelt, der eine sehr große Reichweite hat, der ja auch Medialisierung baut, internationalisiert, dann profitiert man auch immer, selbst*" (IP 17, 310; 14).

[187] „*Und das Engagement als Anteilseigner war bei [Club] letzten Endes mehr damit verbunden, auch den Club damit zu unterstützen in den Bemühungen, das Thema [Stadionname] oder Arena-Kauf, oder Finanzierung des Clubs, Wettbewerbsfähigkeit. Und für uns war es natürlich attraktiv, da ein Teil dessen zu werden was sichergestellt hat, dass der Club weiterhin wettbewerbsfähig ist oder auf dem höchsten Level wettbewerbsfähig ist*" (IP 8, 120; 21).

[188] „*Also letzten Endes steckt, wie hinter allem bei uns, ein Businessinteresse ja. Wir machen alles, was wir machen letzten Endes, um mehr Produkte zu verkaufen*" (IP 8, 120; 10).

> "Instead we want to compete against Real Madrid and Barcelona and, and, and. And if we have the ability then you [company] have a distinct added value because we have far more presence, we sell more shirts, we increase turnover. Thus, you have far more opportunities. Hence, your money is well invested".[189]

Since securing the club's competitiveness is also in the interest of the sponsor this indirectly verifies that a shareholding is not entered into with the purpose of securing dividend payments.

As the strategic equity partner only benefits from the sponsorship if the club is successful, it does not make sense to take dividends from the club because it means that the club has less money to improve its sporting position. And this would negatively impact on the sponsorship goals (outcomes). The excerpt of Memo 186 in Table 6.17 sheds light on the concept *securing competitiveness* and its link to *paying dividends*:

Table 6.17 Memo 186 - Club Competitiveness and Paying Dividends. (Source: Own Illustration)

Memo 186_Logic of share deal_competitiveness_dividends_12 January 2019
To cut a long story short: a strategic equity partner needs a successful club in order to benefit from the sponsorship. Taking money in the form of dividend payment is money the club needs for enjoying sporting success. Consequently, the strategic equity partner would indirectly weaken its sponsoring outcomes (benefits). Also, a shareholding is an additional financial support for a business partner who is already supported via the sponsorship. This is a kind of *pushing of one's own business interests/strategy*.

[189]„*Sondern wir wollen uns messen mit Real Madrid und Barcelona und, und, und. Und wenn wir dazu in der Lage sind, dann hast du [Unternehmen] auch einen deutlich höheren Mehrwert, weil wir dann natürlich auch viel präsenter sind, wir verkaufen mehr Trikots, wir machen mehr Umsatz. Dadurch hast du auch viel mehr Möglichkeiten. Also ist dein Geld auch gut eingesetzt*" (IP 11, 200; 3).

6.7.4 Securing Regional Connectivity and Appeal

The sub-core category *regional connectivity and appeal* constitutes a corporate motive that puts a regional aspect (*regional scope*, business location) into the focus of the equity investment and integrates two major concepts, namely *employer branding* and *matching social expectations.* An equity investment signifies a sustainable interest (commitment) in the club (*signifying*) and via the shareholding the sponsor aims to generate positive side effects in terms of *employer branding* and *matching social expectations.* The sub-category is based on the condition that the club and strategic equity partner are located in the *same* vicinity (precondition). A corporation, just as a club, acts within the context of its business location and these local conditions (circumstances) have an impact on productivity.

Professional football, with its capacity for *connecting people* (context), is one determining factor for the attractivity and image of a region, according to IP 16 (287; 28): *"And what is evident is that [club] as a Bundesliga team is very important for the image as well as the business location [site]".*[190] With reference to IP 23 (410; 9): *"[...] the attractivity of the region is partly dependent on the sporting success [...]".*[191] This sub-category interacts closely with *securing competitiveness.* Accordingly, via a shareholding the sponsor supports the club's competitiveness in order to secure *regional connectivity and appeal.*

The image and attractivity of the region are eminently crucial for a sponsor in order to be perceived as an attractive employer. The concept *employer branding* has two basic dimensions *(internal/external).* The shareholding assists the sponsor to boost its company profile as an attractive employer in the region (external), regarding IP 21 (378; 11): *"Not only our current employees but also employees we would be keen to attract. That we have a face as [company name], as a corporation".*[192]

The statement illustrates the internal (own staff) and external (potential employees) target group of the strategic equity partner to benefit from an

---

[190] *„Und was natürlich klar ist, ist das [Club] als Bundesligamannschaft ganz wichtig ist auch, für sowohl das Image als auch für den Wirtschaftsstandort [Ort]* " (IP 16, 287; 28).

[191] *„[...] die Attraktivität der Region nun mal auch zum Teil von sportlichen Erfolgen abhängt [...]"* (IP 23, 410; 9).

[192] *„Nicht nur unseren jetzigen Arbeitnehmern, sondern auch Arbeitnehmern, die wir tendenziell für uns haben wollen. Das wir auch ein Gesicht haben als [Firma], als Konzern"* (IP 21, 368; 11).

attractive location. Specifically, a shareholding substantiates the corporate identity as an employer who commits to the region by deepening its partnership (cross connection to *securing a deepening commitment*) with the club and therefore secures a *regional connectivity and appeal*. However, due to the close vicinity between the corporation and club, support of the club is also perceived as a kind of *social obligation*. Hence, the concept *employer branding* interrelates to the concept *matching social expectations*. While IP 23 (410; 30), talks about *"a commitment for the attractivity of the region and the support for the many employees who care about the club"*,[193] IP 5 (78; 36) concurs by emphasising that the motivation to substantially support the club is based on providing *"their employees an element of home, this is their club, this is our thing"*.[194] Consequently, as a large corporation in the region the sponsor wants to meet the expectations *"[...] from the fans, the employees but also the region, to commit ourselves as an attractive employer"*[195] (IP 22, 397; 6). A strategic equity partnership is *"insofar a perfect platform right on your doorstep*[196]*"* (IP 22, 398; 15) in order to demonstrate *"good corporate citizenship"*.

Additionally, a strategic equity partnership increases the likelihood of sporting success which strengthens the charisma of the club. A charismatic, successful club makes the region more attractive. This helps the corporation to appeal to employees from out-of-town. IP 16 (287; 31) clearly stressed that a shareholding, therefore, is *"also an investment into our own strength when we are committed to [the club]"*[197] which relates to the concept of *pushing one's own business*. To summarise, a successful club essentially impacts on the domains *"image, in the range of prestige, corporate social responsibility, in the range of corporate citizenship"*[198] (IP 22, 39; 30).

[193] *„[...], dass zur Attraktivität der Region und Unterstützung der vielen Mitarbeiter, die den [Club] unterstützen, dient [...]"* (IP 23, 410; 30).

[194] *„[...] die Mitarbeiter haben dort auch eine gewisse Heimat, das ist unser Verein, das ist unser Ding"* (IP 5, 78; 36).

[195] *„[...], weil das erwarten dann zum einen die Fans, die Mitarbeiter, auch die Region, dass man sich da als attraktiver Arbeitgeber auch engagiert"* (IP 22, 397; 6).

[196] *„Und insofern sage ich mal ist das für uns direkt vor der Haustür eine perfekte Plattform"* (IP 22, 398; 15).

[197] *„Das ist ein bisschen ein Invest in die eigene Stärke, wenn wir uns da engagieren"* (IP 16, 287; 31).

[198] *„Ich sag mal im Bereich Image, im Bereich Prestige, gesellschaftliche Verantwortung, im Bereich Corporate Citizenship"* (IP 22, 391; 30).

6.7.5 Deterring Competitors

This sub-category needs to be seen within the specific context of an intensified competitive environment in which a sponsor operates. This particularly refers to companies whose core business is sport or football related, for example sports equipment companies, car manufacturers, and also media companies.

Due to the high *attractivity of football in society* associated with *high media attention* football clubs become the priority of sport-focused corporations for *connecting with a symbol* (enter into commercial partnership) in order to achieve their communication and branding goals. The increasing *charisma of clubs* to attract large audiences and the *high status of football in society* lead to a *fight for symbols* among corporations to partner with the "most attractive" (charismatic) football clubs. The label "most attractive" basically refers to those clubs with high *international charisma* and chiefly pertains to a few top clubs which permanently fight to qualify for European competitions (in particular the UEFA Champions League). For instance, in the sports equipment industry there is a tendency that the leading kit companies pursue a strategy of only sponsoring a few top clubs within each European top league. In line with the motto: *"[...] we withdraw and we build/we build lighthouses. Just one or two clubs per league but no more than that"*[199] (IP 9, 145; 24). However, irrespective of the corporate industry, a *fight for symbols* chiefly refers to "top clubs". These can be identified based on their high brand value which, as illustrated previously, interrelates to the club's turnover. Accordingly, highly attractive clubs are commonly those with the highest turnover within a football league.

In an intense corporate competitive environment, the *fight for symbols* is expressed by the effort of companies to enter into a sponsorship with one of those clubs. That means the club receives financially attractive sponsorship offerings from potential partners while the current sponsor is faced with the situation of having to defend (and renew) the current contract by putting in more money in order to comply with attractive sponsorship proposals from rivals, according to IP 22 (388; 30): *"And then it happened that the rival in [location] woke up and made an offer which was pretty attractive".*[200] Although enterprises know

[199] *„Nee, wir ziehen uns zurück und wir machen uns / Leuchttürme bauen wir uns. Jeweils ein oder zwei Vereine pro Liga aber mehr machen wir gar nicht mehr"* (IP 9, 145; 24).

[200] *„Und dann war es doch soweit, dass halt auch der Wettbewerber in [Ort] aufgewacht ist und dort mit gegen angeboten, auch ziemlich attraktiv unterwegs war"* (IP 22, 388; 30).

about the contract duration of clubs and their current sponsors (i.a., due to the *transparency* created by the media) and there is also normally a "*window of opportunity*[201]" included in sponsorship contracts, potential sponsors do not accept these contractual limits (*not accepting limits*) due to *changing business values*. Consequently, current club sponsors are increasingly faced with (financially attractive) sponsorship offerings by other companies, as illustrated by IP 11 (188; 21): *"They repeatedly come and make an offer even though [company B] is in and, and, and"*.[202]

This *fight for symbols* is even reinforced for clubs who are resident in a *business location* in which many large enterprises are domiciled *(high economic power)* because these companies are able to afford a main sponsorship. Additionally, football clubs in the native region allow a partnership to be utilised to pursue corporate responsibility objectives *(regional connectivity)*. The high economic power of the business location, in turn, is a promoting factor for clubs (a factor for the club's economic capabilities/potential) that facilitates the opportunity to enter into attractive business partnerships and move into strategic equity partnerships.

The need to secure the existing sponsorship with a top club is further conditioned by *changing business values* on the club side. Despite a long-term existing partnership, this relational value is no longer valued as in the past due to an *increased focus on money*. Within the context of *increased international competition* among football clubs and the *idiosyncratic nature of the German football system* (i.e., 50+1 and TV revenue distribution) other European clubs have access to further and higher revenues streams. Due to the *correlation between revenues and money* on sporting success, German clubs tend to favour the highest bidding sponsorship offerings in order to keep pace with international competition (cross connection to *securing competitiveness*). IP 11 (138; 33) commented: *"You know, nowadays bonds in sports do not matter as much as they did in the past"*.[203] Based on this, the sponsor tries to secure the existing partnership *("brand symbiosis")*

[201]A window of opportunity regulates a specific timeframe in which a club is allowed to negotiate with other companies for the respective sponsorship area (IP 11, 202).

[202]„*Die kommen immer wieder an und haben Angebote gemacht, obwohl [Unternehmen B] noch drin ist und, und, und*" (IP 11, 188; 21).

[203]„*Das wissen Sie auch, dass Bindungen heute im Sport bei weitem nicht mehr so viel zählen wie früher*" (IP 11, 188; 33).

with the club via a shareholding, with reference to IP 18 (339; 25): *"Yes, securing the brand partnership, this was the issue"*.[204] *"Securing"* is a form of *deterring competitors* which is achieved via the connected *"retention factor"* that acts as an obstacle for potential sponsors. Since the shareholding is connected to the sponsorship (*managing the dyad*) a potential partner or the club has to rebuy the shares from the strategic equity partner which is associated with considerable costs. *"Securing"* is further supported by the aforementioned *signifying effect* of a share deal (signifying a stronger bond, *demonstrating stability*). Consequently, a share deal can be perceived as a *"preventative measure"* for deterring competitors, as IP 11 (202; 25) reported: *"It is definitely more difficult for us to enter [club], if [corporation] has an equity because you need to pay off. [...]. It is certainly a kind of preventative measure"*.[205]

This *deterring* is expressed in the following statement by IP 22 (396; 20): *"I have described it previously as a thick nail which we drove into the wall in order to deter others [smile]"*.[206] The style used here is characterised by vigour and determination which expresses the emphasis of the partnership for the sponsor. The use of the metaphor "house building" is also a stylistic device that proves a higher stability achieved from shareholding. The excerpt from Memo 162 (Table 6.18) on page 278 provides an insight into the in-depth analysis about the diction utilised regarding *deterring competitors*.

[204] *„Ja, Absicherung der Markenpartnerschaft, das war das Thema"* (IP 18, 339; 25).

[205] *„Aber es ist definitiv schwieriger für uns bei [Club] jetzt rein zu gehen, wenn [Unternehmen] ein Equity hat, weil das musst du erst raus kaufen. [...] Also, ist schon so eine Art Präventivmaßnahme auch [..]"* (IP 11, 202; 25).

[206] *„Ich habe es vorhin beschrieben, das war ein dicker Nagel, den wir in die Wand gehauen haben, damit andere Abstand nehmen [schmunzeln]"* (IP 22, 396; 20).

Table 6.18 Memo 162 - Building a House. (Own Illustration)

Memo 162_ House building_stability_under the surface_02 September 2018
The metaphor of "house building" seems to express a certain stability for the club (*demonstrating stability*). While IP 22 talks about "*driving a nail into the wall*" IP 8 (120; 29) uses the formulation of "*stronger foundation*" and "*to develop deeper roots in the partnership*" (IP 8, 120; 13). It is more stable to build a house on a strong foundation than a house on sand. This is underpinned by IP 15 (183; 30): "*Essentially, this [the shareholding] substantiates and stabilises the sponsoring on the one hand*". Consequently, the partnership is less likely to fail, less vulnerable to any attacks or offerings from other corporations (continuation character, not to lose the partner). IP 18 (336; 8) compares a main sponsorship with a property which is rented in contrast to a shareholder who owns the property: "*I am the main sponsor [...] but I am just a logo on the chest. I am just a property. And to rent the property as such does not mean that I can already start harvesting the fruits of my labour*"[a]. → Equity as a claim of ownership. This statement indicates an intensified relationship in order to benefit more effectively from the partnership. The "house building" metaphor can be cross connected to the "marriage" metaphor. A marriage is also a more stable relationship which makes it more difficult to exit from the partner.

[a] *„Ich bin zwar der Hauptsponsor, [...] ich bin am liebsten auf der Brust, aber ich bin halt nur ein Logo auf der Brust. Ich bin eben nur ein Grundstück. Und das Grundstück alleine zu pachten heißt noch nicht, dass ich schon Früchte ernte"* (IP 18, 336; 9).

The metaphors "house building" and "marriage" are commonly actions that are directed towards the long term. Accordingly, an additional shareholding as a sponsor underpins the long-term direction of the partnership and offers "*planning security*", too.

6.7.6 Planning Security

The sub-core category "*planning security*" is a mutual motive of the club and corporate partner. For corporations this entails the security for long-term business planning, namely a certainty that enables them to base their marketing and branding strategy on the club in the long term. For clubs, "*planning security*" refers to reliable and predictable revenue streams. By implication, "*planning security"* implies a reduction of uncertainties which is crucial for sponsors *"[...] because you do not want as [company] that they permanently go shopping somewhere else"*[207] (IP 11, 202; 13). This statement links to the concept of *differing business values* since it embodies that the club is looking for other partners who might be willing to pay more for the sponsorship rights compared to the current sponsor. Thus, the link between *"planning security"* and *deterring competitors* becomes apparent and refers to the aforementioned concept of *demonstrating stability*. Accordingly, in this research context *"planning security"* can be defined as "reliability", "predictability", "certainty", and a "reduction of uncertainties" for the future, as can be abstracted by the statement of IP 9 (143; 29):

> "They could have done only the stadium name, but this is always/then I have a contract for the next 5 years and then I do not know what will happen. In this way it is cast in stone. [..] And thereby I can secure it".[208]

Likewise, reducing uncertainties is crucial for clubs. By entering into a strategic equity partnership, the club reduces uncertainties and increases *"planning security"* for the future independent of sporting results. This *"planning security"* is eminently significant due to the volatile nature of the football business (i.e., *uncertainty* and *unpredictability*). According to IP 12 (209; 7), arguing from a club perspective: *"For us it is of course important to have this sustainable predictability regarding revenue streams"*.[209] The quotation clearly shows that *"planning security"* for clubs refers to reliable, predictable, and continuous income streams which are generated via the sponsorship partnership.

Due to the indirect connection of sponsorship and shareholding *(managing the dyad, retention factor)*, the club can be secure (confident) that the sponsor is interested in a long-term partnership. Although a sponsorship contract needs to be extended after a certain time there is still a *subtle conviction of continuation* due to the commitment made via the *shareholding*. Consequently, for clubs *"planning security"* is a certainty to be supported (and financially equipped) by a loyal strategic sponsor. This allows for long-term sustainable club development to

---

[207] *„[...], weil du willst nicht als [Unternehmen], dass die permanent irgendwo anders shoppen gehen*" (IP 11, 202; 13).

[208] *„Sie hätten nur den Stadionnamen machen können, ja klar. Aber da ist es natürlich immer / dann habe ich einen Vertrag über 5 Jahre und dann weiß ich nicht, was passiert. Und so ist es in Stein gemeißelt. [..] Und das kann ich dadurch absichern*" (IP 9, 143; 29).

[209] *„Für uns ist wichtig natürlich, dass wir diese nachhaltige Planbarkeit auf der Erlösseite haben*" (IP 12, 209; 7).

occur which is of mutual interest for the club and strategic equity partner (strategic intent of the *"brand symbiosis"*).

Furthermore, *"planning security"* refers to the certainty of both partners to benefit from the existing *"brand symbiosis"* in the long run. For corporations, this long-term character is even required in order to benefit most effectively from a *"brand symbiosis"*, according to IP 17 (317; 2):

> "There are completely diverse business concepts and nothing is safe. And one tries at least to secure some assets for the long term, simply in order to benefit from the whole story which is related to the partnership/when one invests in [anonymised word]. This just does not pay off if it is not pursued for a certain length of time".[210]

A certainty for long-term business planning applies for clubs too, as IP 18 (323; 38) explained: *"Still, this long-term predictability is an advantage for [club]. One does not need to worry about searching for a new lead sponsor"*.[211] Due to the financial commitment of the sponsor on an equity basis, the club can be certain that the sponsor has a strategic interest *(strategic intent)* and is willing to extend the sponsoring contract in the future (cross reference to *securing a deepening commitment*). Searching for a new main sponsor can be especially challenging for clubs that do not belong to the top clubs. While a top club is perceived as a symbol which *"preferably everyone will possess who can afford it*[212]*"* (IP 11, 189; 26), non-top clubs face difficulties in finding sponsors who are ready to afford the money associated with a high-priced main sponsorship. This situation is even worse for clubs who are located in an economically underdeveloped area (low *economic power of city*).

The core category *securing* explained the underlying motives for clubs and sponsors to enter into a strategic equity partnership. The motives are classified into five sub-categories *(securing a deepening commitment, securing competitiveness, securing regional connectivity and appeal, deterring competitors*, and *planning security)* which are interrelated but have a different focus. Figure 6.12 on page 281 presents a conclusive overview of how the main sub-categories and concepts of *"securing"* are correlated.

---

[210] *„Es gibt völlig unterschiedliche Geschäftsmodelle, und da ist nichts mehr sicher. Und man versucht dann zumindest ein paar Assets sich langfristig zu sichern, um einfach die ganze Story, die man damit macht /, wenn man in den [anonymisiertes Wort] investieren, dann lohnt sich das nicht, so lang man das nicht eine gewisse Zeit macht und aufbaut"* (IP 17, 317; 2).

[211] *„Trotzdem hat das für [Club] den Vorteil gehabt langfristig Berechenbarkeit. Also man muss sich nicht Gedanken machen, sich einen neuen Hauptsponsor suchen zu müssen"* (IP 18, 323; 38).

[212] *„[...] am liebsten jeder haben, der es bezahlen kann"* (IP 11, 189; 26).

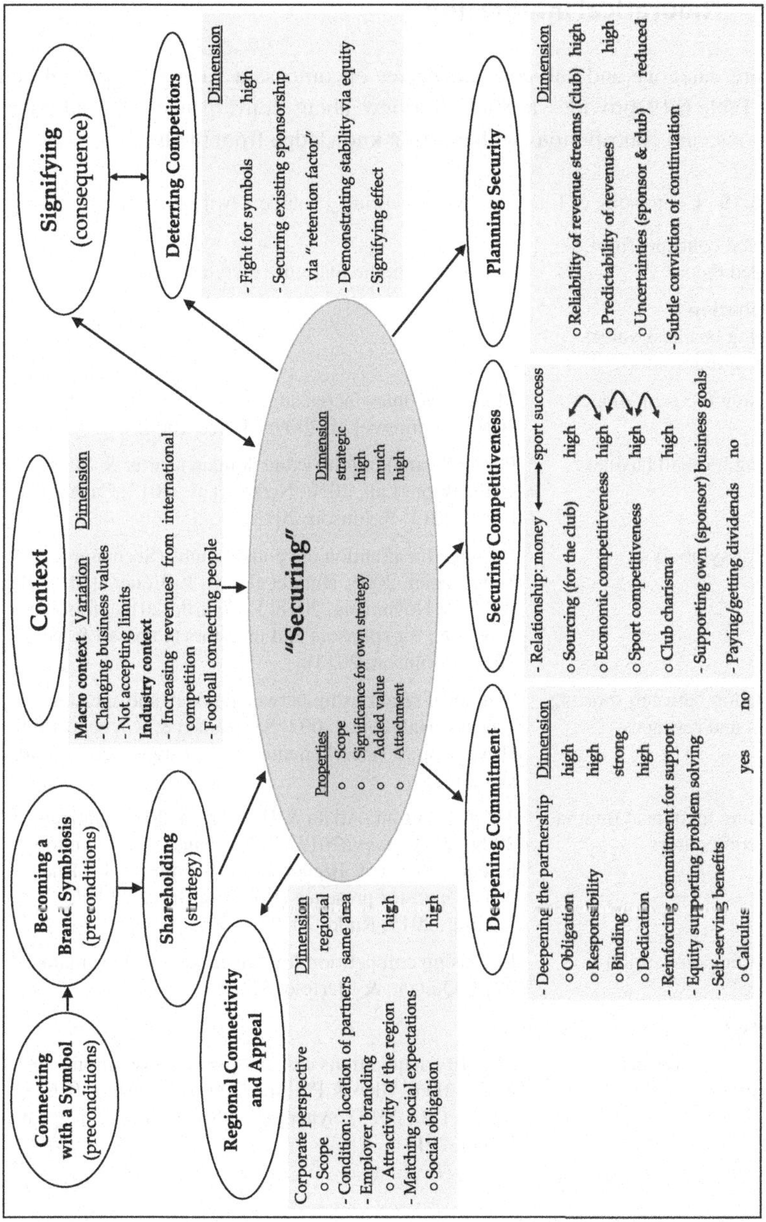

Figure 6.12 Securing - The Core Category. (Source: Own Illustration)

6.7.7 Theoretical Integration

The core category and sub-core categories encompass a variety of critical concepts. Table 6.19 provides a brief overview about convergence, contradictions, extensions, and contributions with existing knowledge from the literature.

Table 6.19 Contrasting of Literature with Securing. (Source: Own Illustration)

Empirical concepts from grounded theory	Findings from the literature review
Contribution Changing business values Not accepting limits	-
Increasing focus on money	Money becomes increasingly significant (Boor et al., 2016; Lammert et al.,2009; Müller, 2008)
Growing football business	Football extending its value domain (Sarter & Mies, 2017; Boor et al., 2016; Netzer et al., 2015; Capasso & Rossi, 2013; Robinson, 2013)
Fight for symbols	High media attention of football clubs (Seemann & Schollmeier, 2008; Huth et al., 2018; Breuer et al., 2018; Adam & Hovemann, 2018; Rosentritt, 2016), football appealing for sponsors and investors (Capasso & Rossi, 2013; Robinson, 2013)
Correlation between sporting success and revenues	Statistical relationship between money and sporting success (Hall et al., 2002; Szymanski & Kuypers, 1999; Hovemann & Wieschemann, 2009; Kuypers & Szymanski, 2012)
Increasing income at international competitors	TV distribution (Adam & Hovemann, 2018; Quitzau, 2009, 2003; Nagy, 2012), TV-revenues in foreign top leagues (Rohde & Breuer, 2017, Schmitt, 2015; Rudd, 2012), investor presence (Rohde & Breuer, 2017; Schmitt, 2015; Rudd, 2012)
Increasing competition	Increasing competition for player talent (McNamara, 2013; Quitzau & Merfeld, 2016)
Extension	
Securing a deepening commitment	Minority acquisitions ease cooperation conditions (Fee et al., 2006; Allen & Phillips, 2000). Intensifies (Chemnitzer et al., 2015); synergies in 'other forms (Prigge & Vöpel, 2014)

(continued)

Table 6.19 (continued)

Empirical concepts from grounded theory	Findings from the literature review
Self-serving benefits Negotiating	Related cost to acquiring control (Grossmann & Hart, 1986; Hart & Moore, 1990; Hart, 1995). 'Holdup' problem' (Quimet, 2013). 'Post-formation bargaining costs' (Krishnaswami et al., 2012)
Securing competitiveness	A shareholding makes a club wealthier (Rudd, 2012; Carmichael et al., 2010; Kuper, 2009)
Paying dividends	Paying dividends is not a strategic intent of clubs (Rudd, 2012; Barros & Leach, 2006)
Extension	
Deterring competitors	Equity as entry barrier for competitors (DePamphilis, 2012; Barringer & Harrison, 2000), safeguarding (Welling & Westhoff, 2018; Oediger, 2017b; Prigge & Vöpel, 2014).
Planning security	Equity emphasises long-term contribution (Ashelm & Horeni, 2015; Prigge & Vöpel, 2014; Fahy et al., 2004)
Contribution Securing regional connectivity	-

With regard to the industry context, the various empirical concepts conform with existing knowledge. Many authors report on the better pecuniary means of foreign clubs compared to German ones. Rosentritt (2016) and Wöckener and Tenbusch (2016) reported on TV revenues in foreign leagues, Boor et al. (2016), Rohde and Breuer (2017), and Plumley et al. (2017) examined the financial advantages of clubs based on cash injections from investors which intensifies a competitive advantage vis-à-vis German clubs. While this is reflected in the concept of *increased money for international competition* this contextual aspect correlates to the motive *securing competitiveness* as a shareholding improves the spending power and liquidity for German clubs. Empirical findings concur with existing knowledge about a correlation between revenues und sporting success. Consequently, *securing competitiveness* as a primary motive of the club to sell equity stakes, accords to insights from the literature (Rudd, 2012; Carmichael et al., 2010; Kuper, 2009).

The empirical finding highlighting a *deepening commitment* verifies previous studies from the alliance literature. Fee et al. (2006) and Allen and Phillips (2000) detected improved cooperative conditions for both partners from entering into a minority equity partnership. With respect to the football literature, Welling and Westhoff (2018) and Chemnitzer et al. (2015) stated that a share deal intensifies an existing sponsorship and Prigge and Vöpel (2014) assumed 'advantages in other forms'. Yet, the empirical findings extend the assumptions of Welling and Westhoff (2018), Chemnitzer et al. (2015), as well as Prigge and Vöpel (op. cit.) by describing additional synergies and explaining how and why these come into effect. The improvement in collaborative conditions occurs due to higher responsibility and obligation to retain the value of one's own investment and due to an increased dedication to the partner which implies an increased emotional attachment.

The vital role of emotional attachment has already been highlighted by scholars such as Kahuni et al. (2009) and Tsiotsou et al. (2014) in co-branding partnerships, although not with respect to equity partnerships. The results from the present research extend this line of thinking by detecting an increase of *emotional attachment* as an essential element for entering into a shareholding because a share deal acts as a commitment in the meaning of dedication (sense of belonging).

With regard to the normative component of *securing a deepening commitment* a matter of academic debate is the impact of additional shares on the continuation of the contractual partnership. Grossmann and Hart (1986), Hart and Moore (1990), Hart (1995), and Quimet (2013) discovered implications on bargaining power if the value of partnership-specific assets depends on continued trade between the partners. Krishnaswami et al. (2012) found evidence that equity alleviates 'post-formation bargaining costs' that occur if the contrast in negotiating power is high. An impact on sponsorship contract negotiations is empirically determined in this study too and even serves as a subtle motive for some sponsors and clubs to enter into a share deal.

While an employer branding and social responsibility approach is widely investigated in the marketing literature by e.g., Hermanns (1997),

Walzel and Schubert (2018), and Plewa et al. (2016) the sub-core category *securing regional connectivity and appeal* widens this motive to include strategic equity partnerships. The concept of *football attracting society* substantiates the great appeal of football to people and to corporations (Statista, 2016; Boor et al., 2016; Capasso & Rossi, 2013; Rudd, 2012). Yet, the empirical findings complement to the existing knowledge with respect to the macro context in form of the concept *changing business values* which includes the codes of *not accepting limits* and an *increasing focus on money.* While an increasing focus on money is mirrored in the literature by e.g., Boor et al. (2016), Lammert et al., (2009) and Müller (2008), *changing business values* and *not accepting limits* are not explicitly investigated in the literature. Even though change is an omnipresent phenomenon, not only in the business world but in society in general (Mazodier & Quester, 2014; Abimbola & Vallaster, 2007; Cousens et al., 2006; Ernst & Bamford, 2005), the literature does not explicitly refer to a change in business values in the formation of football club partnerships. Consequently, this study contributes by incorporating *differing business value* and *not accepting limits* as two changes in business society which impact on corporate football club partnerships.

The sub-core category *deterring competitors* ratifies insights from the literature. For example, in the football related literature Welling and Westhoff (2018) as well as Oediger (2017b) concur by assuming that equity is a form of "safeguarding" the sponsorship against competitors and future sponsorship income. These motives have already been examined in a strategic alliance context by Barringer and Harrison (2000) as well as DePamphilis (2012) who found that equity acts as an entry barrier for competitors and reinforces exclusivity respectively. Yet, Fiedler (2017) remarks that exclusivity is usually part of any main sponsorship deals in the football business too. While this study accords to Fiedler's (2017) argument regarding the exclusivity of main sponsorships, the focus on money is taking centre stage and the significance of long-term existing ties to sponsors is fading *(change in business values)*. Hence, this GT explains the need for additional security (via a shareholding) for strategic partnerships with *changing business values* and an *increased fight for symbols*.

A multitude of scholars (e.g., Ashelm & Horeni, 2015; Prigge & Vöpel, 2014; Fahy et al., 2004) have discovered that equity underpins the long-term contribution of a business partnership which corresponds to the empirical finding of *"planning security"*. Welling and Westhoff (2018) relate their main assumption of safeguarding to the protection of future income from sponsorship revenues for the club. This is empirically confirmed in this study.

6.8 The Substantive Theory

The rigorous process of analysis of empirical data, the meticulous development of the categories, sub-categories and concepts, as well as the explanation of how these interrelate and build upon each other culminate in the emergence of "A Management Theory of Strategic Equity Partnerships" as illustrated in Figure 6.13 on the next page.

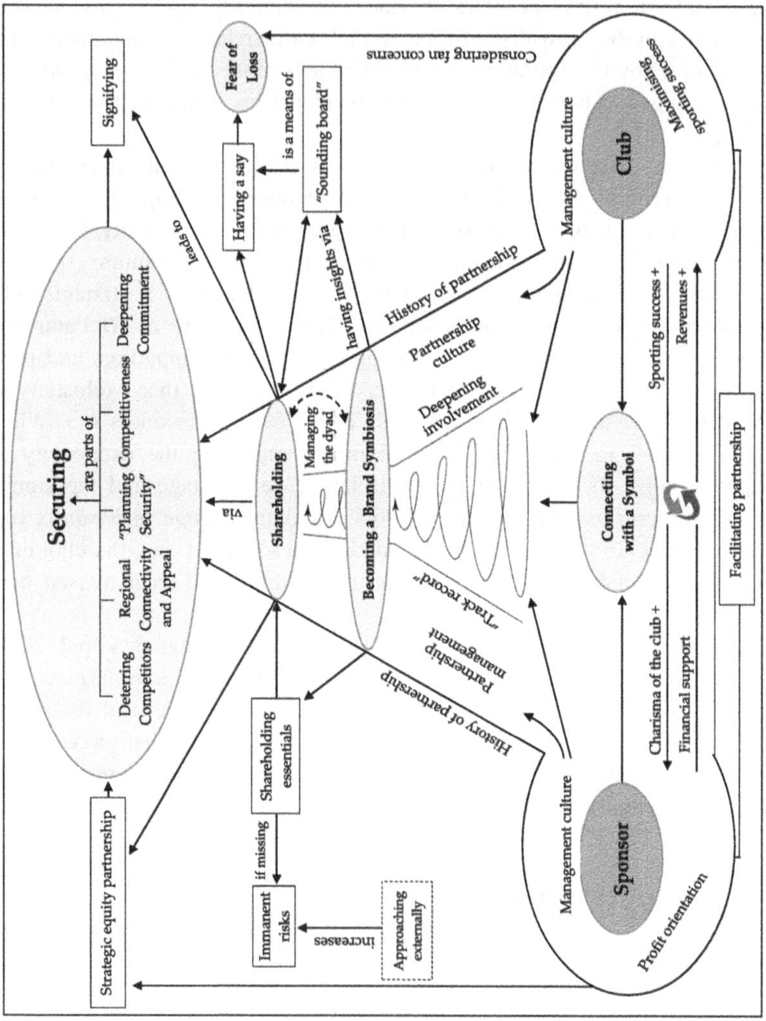

Figure 6.13 "A Management Theory of Strategic Equity Partnerships". (Source: Own Illustration)

The model is to be interpreted bottom-up. The two main actors in the field, a sponsor and a football club, are located on opposite sides in order to demonstrate that they are run under different criteria *(differing ambitions).* This also aims to highlight that both the sponsor and club keep a large part of their business independent of the other.

The ellipses represent the major categories of the theory, namely *connecting with a symbol, becoming a brand symbiosis, shareholding, fear of loss,* and *securing* (the core category). The squares are important categories which mainly act as sub-categories in the form of basic requirements (preconditions) and success factors, strategies, or consequences for the major categories. The circular, symbiotic process of alignment which leads to a *deepening involvement* between the club and sponsor is represented by the helix.

The partnership starts with *connecting with a symbol*, a commercial, exchange partnership between a sponsor (corporate partner) and a club (both shaded in dark grey) in which the sponsor provides money in exchange for commercial rights. This category involves the sub-categories *attracting factors* (factors which attract corporate partners) and *basic requirements*, hence connecting to research sub-question 1 (critical success factors). This contractual partnership develops over time (*history of partnership*). Via each parties' *partnership management,* which reflects how the club and sponsor bring the partnership to life, the parties recognise the value of the collaboration (e.g., via a *"track record"*). Additionally, through permanent interactions, the club and sponsor experience a mutual understanding about their business conduct (*partnership management*, same *partnership culture, understanding of one's role*). Over the course of the *history of partnership* there is a *deepening involvement*, a process in which the club and sponsor become closer (attachment) and build *trust*. These concepts are mutually dependent (which is illustrated by the helix) and lead to the category of *becoming a brand symbiosis*. This category expresses that the sponsorship has developed from a former mere exchange relationship towards a strategic sponsorship (strategic partnership). The helix is inspired by the sponsoring hierarchy German football clubs.

Although the sponsorship has already become a *"brand symbiosis"* the category *shareholding* serves to further deepen the partnership and transforms a strategic partner/sponsor into a strategic equity partner of the club. For this to occur, some fundamental basic requirements need to be met. These are depicted via the sub-category *shareholding essentials*, linking to SQ 1 (critical success factors). *Shareholding essentials* are *screened* before deal making and entail further strategic considerations (e.g., interdependencies with other stakeholder groups), thereby linking to SQ 3 (strategic intent) and SQ 6 (fan opinion).

Shareholding, as a phenomenon, has several consequences which are embodied by the sub-categories *signifying* (a signal effect) and *having a say* and expresses a long-term commitment to the partner, thereby correlating to SQ 7 (added value) and SQ 3 (strategic intent). By increasing the level of abstraction *shareholding* proves to be a strategy for *securing*, the core category of the study. *Securing* is expressed via its five sub-categories *deepening commitment, competitiveness, regional connectivity and appeal, deterring competitors*, and *"planning security"*. These sub-categories subsume the various motives (causes) and answer the research question why clubs and corporate sponsors enter into a strategic equity partnership but also address why sponsors do not enter into a strategic equity partnership (SQ 2, impediments). Furthermore, the sub-core categories address SQ 7 (added value).

The category *managing the dyad* is a 'connector' category between *becoming a brand symbiosis* and *shareholding*. In other words, the category explains how the strategic equity partnership is managed and how the sponsorship and the shareholding are related, thereby answering the research sub-question *how* a strategic equity partnership is managed (SQ 4 and SQ 3 respectively). Since the shareholding and the sponsorship are formally not linked, they are still related informally which is why this relationship is depicted via a doted, vice versa arrow.

Fear of loss is mainly connected to the fan and club (member) perspective. It comprises fan and club concerns in connection with an equity partnership, therefore referring to SQ 2, SQ 5, and SQ 6 (impediments, evaluation of four type of equity partners, and justification of fan opinion respectively). *Fear of loss* also addresses the *immanent risks* for the club and sponsor which are related with a strategic equity partnership and might lead to partnership failure or breakdown. Accordingly, the sub-category *immanent risks* also implies the corporate perspective.

The sub-category *approaching externally* is framed in a dotted line in order to highlight that this is a variation of the theory allowing to improve the depth of the study (Strauss & Corbin, 1998). It largely denotes a strategic equity partnership which is not derived from a prior commercial partnership.

Since this model is a 'snapshot' of a process during the *history of partnership* it has to be taken into account that some categories and sub-categories are e.g., consequences of a category (phenomenon), but can turn (from a different perspective) into basic requirements for another concept/category in the next step. Likewise, consequences can turn into strategies or causes during the process. For instance, the category of *becoming a brand symbiosis* appears to be a basic requirement (*shareholding essentials*) and success factor for entering into a *shareholding,* therefore relating to SQ 1. *Shareholding*, in turn, is (becomes) a strategy for *securing* (the core category) the sponsorship partnership, which refers to the research question (why).

The array of the main categories of *signifying* (shareholding as a sign to competitors and the public to show commitment to the club), *"having a say"*, and *"sounding board"* does not imply that the categories only refer to the sponsor or the club. They are, rather, arranged with the research question and sub-questions in mind and refer to the partnership as a whole. For example, *"sounding board"* refers to the supervisory committee of the club in which the corporate partner has a seat, at the latest if a shareholding is entered.

Although some categories refer directly to specific research sub-questions, this dissertation is a theory developing process in which, not only individual categories and concepts, but the theory as a whole refers to the research question and sub-questions.

6.9 Introduction of New Terms

6.9.1 Introduction

Based on the empirical findings presented above and in line with the study's main goal of theory generation the preliminary definition of "strategic partnership" and "strategic equity partnership" (Sect. 3.3.1) is revisited in this part. Accordingly, both terms are defined as applied and understood in the football business in Germany and are combined with elements of definitions discussed previously.

6.9.2 Defining Strategic Partnership

A strategic partnership in the football business can be defined as follows:

> *A strategic partnership is a contractual business partnership between a club and corporation (a sponsor) with the aim of developing each partner's brand in the long-term. By orchestrating complementary resources and incorporating the partner into own strategic planning, the club and sponsor are able to generate business opportunities beyond contractually defined contents and develop synergies which each partner could not attain on their own.*

A strategic partnership is not a static state. A real strategic partnership develops over time and requires ongoing effort and commitment from the associates. That means the partnership goes beyond a mere exchange of money and rights (transactional cost perspective) and realises the relational value for both partners. This relational value creates business opportunities and synergies which suggest additional collaborative activities. This can refer, for example, to mutual efforts concerning the establishment of an international marketing strategy (penetrating international markets). Business opportunities can also be directed to merchandising activities e.g., in the form of establishing a store abroad, building up football clinics and junior football camps around the world. In the era of digitalisation there are several other opportunities for a mutual business concept, such as developing a club TV channel or a mobile app. Moreover, synergies can arise out of knowledge exchange in diverse areas, including marketing, legal, or strategic issues.

6.9.3 Defining Strategic Equity Partnership

Hitherto, the existence of equity in strategic partnerships has predominantly been seen as a specific partnership characteristic or a form of partnership governance. This study establishes the dyad of sponsorship and shareholding at a football club as a strategic equity partnership and clearly emphasises that this dyad, although formally separated, is treated and managed as a partnership in its entirety. Yet, this study has clearly shown that an additional shareholding of a sponsor at a club is a conscious move which is based on various motives and strategic considerations and has several implications for the partnership for both associates. Consequently, a delimitation of a purely contractual strategic partnership and a strategic equity partnership is proposed in order to make these implications (of equity) visible.

Since "strategic equity partnership" is not yet an established term in the scientific community this is an endeavor to provide an initially valid definition of the term in the context of football partnerships. Consequently, this definition captures the specificity of the given research setting. The definition builds upon the former definition of a strategic partnership, but is enhanced by the equity perspective. A strategic equity partnership is defined as follows:

A strategic equity partnership is a dyad of a (contractual) strategic partnership between a club and corporate partner in which the corporate partner holds an additional minority equity stake in the club. Both partners make a very long-term commitment in order to sustainably and mutually develop each partner's brand via *equity. Equity leads to a securing of the existing strategic partnership in various ways.*

The main elements of the definition are specified below:

- Minority equity stake: this is an equity share of up to 49%.
- Commit/commitment: this refers to dedication (emotional component) and obligation.
- Very long-term: this expresses the intended time horizon which exceeds 10 years. Indeed, a time frame of more than 15 years is envisaged.
- Securing the existing strategic partnership in various ways: this refers to the five components of securing (competitiveness, deepening commitment, deterring competitors, regional connectivity and appeal, planning security). Not all components (e.g., regional connectivity) refer to every strategic equity partnership. The priority depends on a partnership-specific context.
- Corporate partner: this is a profit-driven organisation which has a commercial strategic partnership with the club. This commercial partnership is most often a sponsorship but can also relate to other commercial partnerships such as right distribution.

As the introductory part of this Chapter has indicated, the contractual partnership between a club and corporation is not limited to sponsorships but is also open to other forms of commercial partnership (e.g., partnerships with right distributors). However, the predominant forms of strategic equity partnership are those partnerships with a sponsor. This specific form of strategic equity partnership can also be designated as a "strategic equity sponsorship". This term directly refers to the specific form of contractual partnership, namely a sponsorship. However, the general and more abstract term refers to strategic equity partnership.

6.10 Summary of Empirical Findings

This Chapter has outlined the emergent grounded theory "A Management Theory of Strategic Equity Partnerships". The development and formation of strategic equity partnerships from three different perspectives (clubs, corporate partners, and fans) is illuminated via the integration of the major categories of the study *connecting with a symbol*, *becoming a brand symbiosis*, *shareholding*, *fear of loss*, and *securing*. The interrelationships between the various constructs were situated in the specific research context and the placement of categories within the study's specific paradigm is explained and graphically illustrated on a categorical basis. While the emergent theory is explicated bottom-up the integration of representative quotations from expert interviews and survey data assisted the presentation of categories and concepts and supported the development of the storyline, thereby providing a chain of evidence for category development.

The integration of original memo abstracts delivered insights into the interpretation and made in-depth analysis visible. Furthermore, the inclusion of information from document analysis added to category saturation. By comparing and contrasting the empirical findings with insights from the related literature on a categorical level, theoretical integration of the conceptual elements was achieved. The use of tables within the scope of theoretical integration allowed similarities, contradictions, and extensions to be discovered at a glance and highlighted the significance and originality of the present research.

The specific research context of football partnerships, which consists of various conditions and circumstances in the *macro, industry*, and *case-specific context*, has been initially outlined. The empirical research context is largely in accord with insights from the literature. However, the role of *changing business values (increasing focus on money)* is explicitly mentioned in the empirical data and appeared as a pivotal aspect in the emergence of strategic partnerships in the football business.

The category *connecting with a symbol* addressed the realisation *(attracting factors, causes, basic requirements, and facilitating partnership)* of a sponsorship between a club and corporation. While the *permanent high media attention* and the *charisma* of the brands are the main attracting factors for entering into a sponsorship, for clubs sponsorships are expedient for generating income while corporations use sponsorships for brand building (awareness, image improve, emotionalisation) and employer branding. The basic requirements are essentially *compatibility* (the same *goals*, *business values*, *image*, and *management cultures*) and *trust* and it has been shown that personal relationships act as a *"door opener"* for entering into business partnerships. While the concept *personal relationships* is vital in the grounded theory the literature places much less significance on this in the formation of sponsorships. Moreover, the theory extends existing knowledge by emphasising that *emotional attachment* and *CEO passion* for football are facilitating aspects for entering into football sponsorships.

Becoming a brand symbiosis explained the transition (progress) from an initial sponsorship towards a strategic partnership. Based on positive *interactions* (positive *partnership management*) during the *history of partnership* and the achievement of a "*track record*", the associates recognise a value-adding cooperation in which both partners collaborate closely. This leads to a *deepening involvement* (*formal* and *emotional attachment*) and the establishment of a trustful partnership. As a consequence, the partner is incorporated into the strategy of the associate and the partnership starts to create synergies for both the club and sponsor that go beyond stipulated content *(brand symbiosis)*. The status of being a strategic partner is often associated with a seat on the club's *"sounding board"* (supervisory committee) which assumes a multidimensional role in the partnership management. It not only acts as a consulting and supervising body, but also as a supportive tool in terms of the club's strategic decision making and is used for informal partnership management. Furthermore, a seat in the SC is frequently a preliminary step in the establishment of a strategic equity partnership. Since a seat in the club's sounding board is often occupied by the sponsor's CEO, it has a *signifying* effect in public as this symbolises the high level of expertise of the club's management body. The fundamental precondition for sitting on the club's SC is an *"understanding of one's role"*. That means the sponsor, as a member of the sounding board, focuses on supervising and advising the economic and growth development of the club and does not intervene in the sporting decisions.

The vital role of the club's sounding board extends current findings on interlocking directorates by highlighting the *sounding board* as a vehicle for informal partnership management and as a tool for *deepening involvement*. This study also underpins the fact that knowledge transfer within the network of partners (sponsors and shareholders) from various leading industries can create synergy effects for the club and for each partner within the sounding board, too.

The category *shareholding* elucidated the success factors *(shareholding essentials)*, processes *(screening)*, and consequences *(having a say, signifying)* of a share deal between the club and sponsor and revealed how the sponsorship and shareholding are strategically interrelated and managed *(managing the dyad)* although both partnership forms are formally and legally unrelated. It is illustrated that, from a financial perspective, a share deal at a football club is not a lucrative investment due to the difficulty of reselling the shares and the *differing ambitions* between clubs (sporting success) and corporations (profit). A shareholding is rather entered into on the basis of a *strategic intent* of the partners.

Nevertheless, the sound financial situation of the club and sponsor, which is determined via a *screening* process (due diligence), is a crucial requirement for realising a share deal *(economic reasonableness, financial feasibility)*. While an increase in shareholder value is a fundamental investment criterion in the economy, investments in a football club share need to comply with the tenet *value retention* (and economic reasonableness). Whereas the rational decision making of share acquisitions is postulated in the literature in the context of football an *emotional attachment* to the club appears to be an accompanying requirement in favour for a shareholding. Beyond this, the empirical findings explain how the dyad of sponsorship and shareholding is managed and how the retention factor act as a strategic means in the partnership, something which has not been the case in the literature up to now.

The *screening* process also entails internal aspects (e.g., need, fit to own strategy) and an evaluation of industry and macro environmental developments. With regards to the own strategy, there are three options for share allocation (one partner or several partners who hold different/same *amount of shares*). While these options differ in a club-specific context, the majority of club members and fans prefer to issue shares to several equity partners. Some strategic partners put less emphasis on the *amount of shares* unless it is a significant stake (at least 5%), others aim to hold a superior stake compared to co-shareholders in order to be perceived as the number one partner of the club. Indeed, the survey results confirm that fans determine who the main partner of the club is based on the *amount of shares*.

Due to the progress character of a strategic equity partnership a former sponsorship relationship is perceived as another fundamental requirement to entering into a shareholding as only via a *history of partnership, compatibility* and an *"understanding of one's role"* between the associates can be assured. Moreover, *trust* (which predominantly refers to the *quality of people*) among the partners appeared essential. Although a contractual sponsorship and a shareholding are legally and formally unrelated, *managing the dyad* shed light on how the strategic equity partnership is managed. Both partnership forms are strategically interrelated via the *retention factor*.

While a seat in the club's sounding board becomes mandatory in a strategic equity partnership, a shareholding acts as a *stabilising factor* for the whole partnership. In addition, there is a shifting interest (*sporting* and *economic success*) on the sponsors side since the sponsor is part of the ownership structure and has a say in the club (*having a say*), too. A shareholding has, furthermore, a symbolic character as it signalises exclusivity (*signalising exclusivity*) and the positive future development of the club and also act as affirmation of the partnership. However, this can have negative consequences too, as it *intensifies problems in times of trouble* since the close relationship implies, in the perception of the media, that the strategic partner is always up to date about all issues of the club.

Regarding the theoretical integration the empirical data contradict the literature that football is seen as a risky investment option. Football is rather seen as the growth market number one which is of public interest irrespective of the economic cycle. Also, the argument that a prior business relationship makes organisations less likely to opt for equity is refuted in this research context. A prior sponsorship is seen as a success factor for entering into an additional share deal.

The category *fear of loss* illuminated the effects of a shareholding within the composition of various stakeholder groups of the club, in particular the opinion of club members and fans. Arguments against the admission of a shareholder are *avoidance of influence on sporting decisions, prevention of increased commercialisation, decline of fan identification, decline of co-determination, loss of goodwill values, possible loss of the club's tradition due to increased commercialisation.* Against this, the *increase in national* and *international competitiveness* are the two main arguments in favour of a shareholder. While the literature reports on the general resistance of fans against investors, this study showed that fans hold distinct views on the four equity partner types, of which a strategic partner (sponsor) is largely accepted by fans. In contrast, an oligarch is not accepted while with regards to financial investors and Maecenas no definite fan opinion could be determined due to contrasting views.

This study contributed to the literature by establishing that a *priority right for repurchase* is important in fan opinion and confirmed the assumption that a *positive image* of a shareholder and a *regional affinity* are crucial aspects for an investor from the perspective of club members and fans. While it could be derived that the vast majority of fans are in favour of the retention of the 50+1 rule, 81.9% are open to minority equity partnerships, of which more than half accept the disposal of up to 24.9% of club shares.

This category also elucidated the *impediments* of a share deal from the club's perspective *(fearing alienation, fear of dependency)* and shed light on *immanent risks* of strategic equity partnerships. This, notably refers to a lack of *shareholding essentials* such as no compatibility and no prior relationship, but also to the idiosyncratic nature of German football (50+1) which is difficult to comprehend in particular for foreign investors. Besides, the uncertainty of sporting success *(consecutive sporting failure)* appeared to be a main threatening factor because sporting success is a precondition for sponsorship outcomes and the value retention of shares.

The sub-category *approaching externally* described an alternative strategy of how to enter into a share deal without having a prior relationship with the partner. While *immanent risks* are increased, potential shareholders are addressed via a *story board* and a *roadshow process.* In case of an intense mutual interest a detailed *screening* process is performed followed by negotiations for deal-making.

Securing emerged as the core category of the study. Five sub-core categories were identified *(securing a deepening commitment, deterring competitors, planning security, securing competitiveness, securing regional connectivity and appeal)* which constitute the dyadic motives as to why strategic equity partnerships in the German football business are entered into. It is shown that these sub-categories are interdependent and vary according to their emphasis and the specific partnership context. Yet, *securing regional connectivity and appeal* as well as *deterring competitors* are corporate motives solely.

Securing as classified by *deterring competitors* serves the purpose of protecting the existing *"brand symbiosis"* against competitors (deterring other companies that want to supersede the current sponsorship) thereby empirically confirm the "safeguarding" motive proposed by Welling and Westhoff (2018). The *"retention factor"* act as an obstacle for other corporations to form a partnership with the club. *Planning security* is a mutual motive of the sponsor and club. The sponsor wants to have planning certainty and not to be permanently challenged by other corporate offerings from rivals. The club needs security for reliable and predictable revenue streams for the future.

Securing competitiveness is an economically driven motive. With an equity investment the club receives a large one-off payment to secure its competitiveness on the national and international football competition stage. This is equally a goal of the corporate partner since he is, in terms of sponsorship outcomes, dependent on the sporting success of the club. *Securing regional connectivity and appeal* refers to the corporate perspective and correlates to *securing the competitiveness* of the club. However, the focus of supporting the club is to secure the attractiveness of the native region and to pursue image effects in order to be perceived as an attractive employer. Furthermore, the support of the club is seen as a social obligation to demonstrate regional connectivity (social responsibility). While it has already been proven that sponsorships act as a tool for employer branding and to show social responsibility this study extends this line of thinking to minority equity partnerships.

In the context of *securing a deepening commitment* shareholding is a strategy to secure collaborative benefits in the long run and, by implication, intensifies the partnership (a kind of coalescing, becoming closer). Due to the shareholding the formal interests are extended (financial interest) which implies a commitment to support (commitment for value retention). A shareholding also leads to an added emotional attachment (dedication, sense of belonging) which encourage participation to "go the extra mile". *Securing a deepening commitment* merely extends the theoretical studies from Prigge and Vöpel (2014) and Welling and Westhoff (2018) by explicating how this form of securing occurs and how this deepening happens.

The last part of this Chapter presents a new definition of strategic partnership as applied in the German football business. It also introduced and defined the new term strategic equity partnership and strategic equity sponsoring to the academic community.

Management Implications and Recommendations

7

7.1 Introduction

The preceding Chapter illustrated the emergence of this grounded theory and discussed the findings against existing knowledge from the literature. This Chapter presents the theoretical and practical management implications which are derived from the study's findings. The novelty of the study and its contributions are underpinned. In line with the study's practical research objective recommendations for action are given. Finally, research limitations are acknowledged and an outlook for future research is suggested.

7.2 Research Implications and Contributions

7.2.1 Implications for Theory on the Football Investor Literature

First and foremost, equity partnerships between sponsors and football clubs in Germany have only been descriptively investigated in the past (Welling & Westhof, 2018; Oediger, 2017b; Prigge & Vöpel, 2014). This study significantly contributes to the field of equity partnerships in football as it is the first of its kind to explore strategic equity partnerships in the German football business empirically. The findings from this study support the motive of safeguarding proposed by Welling and Westhoff (2018) with the core category securing (sub-core category deterring competitors). Yet, this grounded theory expands on this by conceptually explaining how securing against competitors takes place (retention factor), exposing further motives which could be classified under the core category of securing

T. Duffner, *Strategic Equity Partnerships in Professional Football*, Event- und Impaktforschung, https://doi.org/10.1007/978-3-658-31301-2_7

and also explaining how the dyad of sponsorship and shareholding are connected and managed as claimed by the overall purpose of the study. Providing first-hand insights into the topic allowed details about components of the shareholder contract to be uncovered. This not only enhances a better understanding of strategic equity partnerships in the football business, but may also provide a sound basis for discussion regarding investors in football in general.

Furthermore, this study meets the call for research made by Farrelly (2010) who suggested thoroughly investigating sponsor-property partnerships and how these develop into strategic partnerships. The study also introduces the retention factor which contributes to the literature as this dimension have not been identified beforehand.

Next, the term strategic equity partnership has previously not been defined in the literature. Although the existence of equity in contractual partnerships has been examined by many scholars (e.g., Lin & Darnall, 2014; Quimet, 2013; Lowensberg et al., 2010) in a non-sport setting, who found that equity enhances the credibility and stability of the partnership or that equity is used as a financial investment to yield returns, no study endeavoured to define the term strategic equity partnership to date. Likewise, in the football literature share deals are mainly related to the general term investor (Ruf & Theweleit, 2018; Leister, 2017; Heun, 2016) or strategic partner (Laskin, 2018; Oediger, 2017b). However, this research underpinned the significance of considering the dyad of sponsorship and shareholding at a football club as a holistic and integral partnership in terms of its strategic intent and daily management. The present study found profound evidence that, upon entering into a strategic equity partnership, the dyad is perceived as a whole and the exit of either the sponsorship or a repeal as a shareholder implies the termination of the whole partnership.

In light of a missing classification, the study offers a definition of strategic equity partnership that puts the dyad of contractual partnership and shareholding in one term and explains its informal bond. The definition of the term makes an original contribution to the literature and the field of business partnerships as it supports the conceptualisation of investors and strategic partnership types in the football business and introduces strategic equity partner(ship) as an idiosyncratic type (form) of corporate club partnership. It may not be imperative that clubs and organisations decide upon the definition, but that one is needed is clear from this study. Presenting a definition of strategic equity partnership not only encourages future discussion, but the definition could also be used as a reference point for subsequent studies. Even though the definition emerged out of the specific field of football partnerships, valuable insights from large enterprises and different industries are involved. Therefore, the definition could contribute to critical debates in other research contexts too, and may be adopted or even adapted. Beyond this, the study proposes the classification of the term strategic equity sponsoring as a unique form of strategic equity partnership which indicates the specific form of the contractual partnership, a sponsorship, in the dyad with the shareholding.

7.2.2 Implications Resulting from the Nature of the Research

In line with the call for research by Beamish et al. (2016) and Bell et al. (2006) to investigate strategic partnerships from various participant perspectives, this grounded theory presents an integrated approach and investigates strategic equity partnerships from three different viewpoints, namely those of the main actors in the field: clubs, sponsors, as well as club members and football fans. While the majority of sponsorship and strategic partnership studies examine the issue from a unilateral perspective, only a few scholars such as Chadwick (2004), Farrell and Quester (2005), Bühler (2006), Hecox (2007), and Morgan et al. (2014) concentrated on a joint perspective of both partners. However, the integration of three (participant) perspective is exclusive for this research hitherto. Additionally, the corporate perspective even encompasses the sponsorship and shareholder view. Therefore, this study contributes insights into managing sponsorship relationships, shareholding, and fan discussion about investor presence in football.

This paper further complies with the request made by Jiang et al. (2008) and Bell et al. (2006) to base strategic partnership research on a clear working definition (which type of alliance is the focus?), by explicitly indicating the type of partnership under investigation, namely corporate sponsors which buy additional club shares in the German football business. Hence, the study meets the requirement of conceptual clarity.

7.2.3 Strategic Partnership as a Business Building Strategy

In football, equity partnerships with sponsors have mainly been addressed from a financial viewpoint within the discussion about investors presence and how this affects the competitiveness of clubs (e.g., Rohde & Breuer, 2017; Plumley et al., 2017) and as a general means to finance football clubs (Welling & Westhof, 2018; Oediger, 2017b; Dworak, 2010). Only a few (e.g., Welling & Westhoff, 2018; Chemnitzer at al., 2015; Prigge & Vöpel, 2014) have attempted to also anticipate strategic benefits (further synergies) from share deals with a variety of different club investors.

This study, in contrast, is the first to address the topic holistically by illuminating financial, strategic, but also operational aspects and processes. A variety of categories and concepts give an inclusive picture of strategic equity partnerships as a central part of strategy and specific part of operations. While Szymanski (2015), Quitzau (2013), and Nagy (2012) contend that the acquisition of football club stakes is a risky investment due to the sport's specific characteristics, this study opposes by demonstrating that a shareholding is not perceived as a risky investment, but rather as a business building activity that allows the existing sponsorship to be deepened for both the club and sponsor.

In this respect, this research makes another contribution to theory. Most studies which have investigated football sponsorship as a business building activity (e.g., Oettgen, 2008; Süßmilch, 2004) have concentrated on the perspective of the sponsor. Only a few scholars (e.g., Schade, 2012; Alexa, 2009; Bühler, 2006) have investigated the opportunity of sponsorships to be used as a brand building tool for the sponsee (i.e., clubs), too. While these findings are supported in this dissertation, this grounded theory extends this line of thought by stating that a mutual branding effect is even intensified via an additional shareholding. This might have practical implications for club managers to concentrate on building the club brand with the aid of their main sponsors.

The present study conformed with the request of Cornwell (2008) and Farrelly (2010) to investigate relational dynamics in sport sponsorships. While Morgan et al. (2014) added insights from the general sport context, this dissertation contributes to the literature as it offers new empirical data about relational dynamics of football sponsorships and its potential to develop into strategic (equity) partnerships. This research provides further evidence to the fact that entering into a strategic equity partnership is a business building activity for sponsors which is directed towards the achievement of long-term strategic goals. Direct financial goals are not the focus of the strategic equity partner. This challenges the view that investors need to yield financial returns as put forward by Keythman (2016), Poitras (2016), and VanDuzer et al. (2013). This study rather argues that an equity investment does not need to yield direct financial returns in the form of dividend payments, therefore supporting findings from von der Heijden (2012) and Pinnuck and Potter (2006). Others such as Oediger (2017b) and Prigge and Vöpel (2014) argue that club shareholders are focused on an increase in the club's share value. This grounded theory underpins that an increase in share value is indeed a desired outcome but not a necessity. Instead, value retention is essential. Yet, a return needs to be achieved but via an increase in relational value, the deepening of the partnership, and in the form of securing in various ways (five sub-core categories).

Furthermore, this study provides an insight into the reality of corporate decision making. Although rational decision making is stated as required by participants, which conforms with the generally accepted notion presented by many scholars (e.g., Poitras, 2016; Caselli, 2010; Jones, 2008; Mintzberg, 1998; Carroll, 1996), this research highlights the importance of an emotional attachment as an integral aspect of sponsors to invest in a football club stake. This reinforces the specificity of managing football partnerships and opens the discussion about the influence of an emotional component in sport management.

This grounded theory further adds to existing studies in the alliance literature (Parmigiani & Santos, 2011; Cobbs, 2011; Lui et al., 2010) and sponsorship literature (Nufer & Bühler, 2011, Farrelly & Quester, 2005b) regarding the vital role of trust in the management of strategic partnerships. While the findings confirm the central role of trust for partnership management and relationship development, this paper elaborates trust as a static component which acts as a precondition for entering into sponsorships and as a dynamic component which intensifies during the history of partnership, therefore anchoring trust as an active process rather than leaving it as a static concept.

There has been very little consideration of the vital role of a club's supervisory committee in the management of strategic partnerships. The study provides valuable insights into the strategic role of the SC as it extends its original function as a supervisory tool which is also used for informal business conduct between the club and its partner sitting on the board.

7.2.4 Implications on Investor Fan Debate in German Football

A further unique characteristic of this study refers to the approach of integrating the club member and fan perspective into the theory. The fan view not only adds a third perspective on the subject, but this is the first fan inquiry which took different shareholder types into account. Previous fan research from Bauers and Hovemann (2019a), Bühler (2017), Pawlowski (2013), and Pilz (2011) concentrated on the 50+1 rule and investor acceptance but did not differentiate between various shareholder types. These studies agree that fans want to retain the 50+1 rule and also found that investors are generally not accepted by football fans.

While the empirical findings confirm the fan perspective on the retention of the 50+1 rule, this study contradicts the notion of general resistance of investor presence in German football by fans. Instead, this research found that football fans have a differential view on the acceptance of four shareholders types and made the valuable contribution that a strategic partner is well accepted by football fans. Additionally, and for the first time, this paper makes an original contribution as it sheds light on the differential view among football fans as to the amount of shares fans will accept to be issued to shareholders. Therefore, it extends existing fan research by establishing that fans accept minority shareholdings. Those investigations that focused on the 50+1 rule took only the decision of repeal or retention of the rule into consideration, which implies the acceptance or non-acceptance of majority shares (50+1) or not.

Beyond this, the study confirmed results from Schade (2012) and Alexa (2009) by relating the image and regional affinity of a shareholder to the club. Both aspects seem to have a positive impact on shareholder acceptance by fans. The findings also ratify the results from Bauers and Hovemann (2019a) who found that the arguments for the retention of the 50+1 rule are mainly based on the maintenance of co-determination, exclusion of heteronomy, avoidance of increased commercialisation, and retaining the club's tradition and goodwill values. It is also discovered that for the majority of fans enhanced national and international competitiveness are the main reasons for the admission of a shareholder at their favourite club. While Bauers and Hovemann (2019a) found that an enhanced competitiveness is no argument for the repeal of the 50+1 rule, it seems at least to be an argument for the admission of a minority shareholder. Therefore, the study's findings offer new impetus to the permanent discussion about investor presence in German football and should be the starting point for a differential consideration of the fan perspective. These insights also allow the needs of football fans to be more effectively observed. This is crucial as fans (as prosumers) are a fundamental part for the attractiveness of the football business.

7.2.5 Implications on Theoretical Perspectives

This grounded theory is informed by a variety of theoretical perspectives. The study has demonstrated that reducing football partnerships to a single theoretical framework ignores the complexity of business partnerships. Hence, the findings confirm those studies of Lowensberg (2010), Nufer and Bühler (2011), Demir and Söderman (2015), and Barringer and Harrison (2000) which state that a single theoretical framework is not sufficient to understand business alliances.

A purely transactional view is criticised as the study evidently supports relational value in football club partnerships. It is shown that football sponsorship is a relational construct that—by taking a long-term view—has the capacity to be developed into a strategic partnership and strategic equity partnership. It is demonstrated that relational elements (compatibility, trust, understanding of one's role), Network Theory (football partnerships as a proper strategy and endeavor for business networking), Resource-Based Theory (brand building, image, and money) and elements from Knowledge-Based Theory (transfer of know-how) add to the theoretical understanding of strategic partnerships in football. Furthermore, Resource Dependency (Hillman et al., 2009) and Theory of Property Rights, as postulated by Adam and Hovemann (2018), contribute towards a better understanding of the football specific context (club dependency on money) and the critical relationship between the club and the club's fans.

7.2.6 Practical Implication for Managing Football Sponsorships

Finally, this research offers further practical implications for sport clubs, sponsors, and strategic equity partners. In a strategic equity partnership, the club partnership is part of the sponsor's strategy and thus impacts on the sponsor's business success. The theory can help managers to avoid pitfalls in the creation and management of strategic equity partnerships by indicating vital preconditions and critical success factors. Hence, this grounded theory provides valuable information to go through the process of sponsorship development towards a strategic (equity) partnership more successfully.

The sub-category securing a deepening commitment also suggests areas of added value of an additional share deal, therefore illustrating incentives/rationales why an equity investment into a football club can make sense for sponsors. Moreover, for corporations which intend to enter into a football sponsorship this grounded theory provides a framework for orientation on relevant goals associated with different sponsorship types. This might support strategic decision making.

While former studies (e.g., Welling & Westhoff, 2018; Chemnitzer et al., 2015; Prigge & Vöpel, 2014) on equity partnerships in German football neglect to take the downsides of the management of strategic equity partnerships into account, this grounded theory contributes to an enhanced practical understanding by addressing the drawbacks and potential risk factors of strategic equity partnerships. Knowing the (potential) pitfalls enables these to be avoided and supports better management of strategic equity partnerships.

7.3 Recommendations for Action

This grounded theory not only aims to generate theory, but also to provide recommendations for action for managing football partnerships, therefore contributing to managerial practice. These recommendations are directed at those people working in the specific field under study, namely those responsible at football clubs and their sponsors. The following recommendations may also be of interest for managers from corporations which intend to enter into a partnership with a football club.

This study has clearly demonstrated that football sponsorships have the capacity to be developed into strategic partnerships and, furthermore, into strategic equity partnerships. In order to achieve this, clubs and sponsors need to have the awareness that football sponsorships have the potential to exceed purely exchange relationship between money and rights. This requires viewing sponsorships as a business building strategy which demands mutual effort by both parties that goes beyond contractually defined issues. Since clubs provide a commercial service, they need to have a partnership-like approach in managing sponsorships. Treating the sponsor as a partner in an honest, fair, and trustful way becomes key to the successful management of sponsorships and fosters an open and positive collaborative environment.

Clubs are further advised to incorporate their main sponsors into the club's strategy and actively ask for advice and support. Corporations often possess a lot of economic expertise and management experience as well as a different way of thinking which could enrich and support strategic decision making. While clubs can benefit from the know-how of the sponsor, demanding further support also demonstrates that the sponsor is a vital affiliate instead of merely a source of income. Such an exchange increases the quality of relationship, is likely to deepen the collaboration with positive effects on a long-term business partnership, and may also lead to a know-how transfer for the sponsor. A permanent information flow, regular updating of and communication with the partner is a first good starting point. This could be done via personalised weekly e-mail updates, regular sponsorship meetings, or workshops.

Since sponsors often have an emotional attachment to the club they sponsor, many even want to help the club. Although sponsors are recommended to offer additional support too (which is beneficial for their own sake), this should be bound to economic issues and not interfere with sport decisions. It also appears necessary for sponsors to understand the idiosyncrasies of the football business (e.g., emphasis of money, focus on sporting success, being under the permanent public eye, critical role of fans). A basic understanding not only facilitates understanding and traceability of club decisions, but also assists in ensuring a cooperation between equals. Therefore, sponsors should accumulate football business specific knowledge. Furthermore, managers on both sides of the alliance should be cognisant of the strength of inter-personal relationships between those responsible for managing the partnership on a daily basis. Hence, getting feedback from sponsors on daily collaboration is crucial. If there is no compatibility between those responsible for daily management, the club should adjust their personnel accordingly.

However, there might be corporations which enter into a sponsorship with rather short-term (transaction focused) objectives in mind and want to use the club as an advertising platform instead of building up a long-lasting partnership. While this can be beneficial for clubs and sponsors too, it reinforces the need for clubs to know the partner's goals because a purely transactional sponsorship does not require an extensive relational orientation.

As evidenced in this study, a strong club brand and its charisma are essential for attracting corporate partners and investors. Therefore, it is recommended that clubs actively engage in brand building and establish a positive brand image. Brand strength and a positive image also facilitate clubs who are in search of an equity partner externally. Again, sponsors can help in this process as large corporations often have a lot of M&A know-how.

Since equity partnerships require to be based on sound financial club management, clubs should try at least to operate in the black and not make consecutive losses as this has a negative impact on image and lessens the attractivity of the club for potential investors. By implication, the club management should not only consist of football experts but include people with a high degree of economic expertise, too.

The study has clearly shown that a shareholding decision is fundamental for clubs because a share deal is irreversible. Consequently, a shareholding with a sponsor should be based on strategic considerations instead of being a financial option (only). The need to enter into a share deal with a trusting partner who has the same fundamental understanding of how to develop the club and the partnership in the future is highlighted. This requires an equity partnership to be based on a prior business partnership which can act as a test phase for intensive collaborative actions. A history of partnership should provide both partners with the certainty of mutual trust and compatibility and also ensures that the partnership is backed by the whole organisation instead of only the CEO.

Since this study supports existing findings that sponsorship is a tool for business networking, this should be supported by clubs by proactively connecting (club) sponsors to one another. For example, regular sponsoring events on a monthly basis, marketing workshops or "get-to-know events" when a new partner is gained could be an appropriate vehicle to further support networking among partners and to provide a platform for exchange. Collaborations may be intensified by inviting the main club sponsors within the scope of training camps in the summer and winter preparation phase.

Moreover, concrete measures are suggested for preparing a shareholding. Clubs are advised to negotiate an exit strategy before reaching a deal. This should include a priority right for repurchase as this ensures the club has a final say about what happens with the shares in case of partnership breakdown. The priority right for repurchase should be openly communicated to fans because this may increase fan acceptance. For sponsors, the shareholding contract should include a retention factor which secures the partnership against competitors who want to sponsor the club.

Clubs are also counseled to impose an internal club rule to restrict the share issue to 24.9% and to implement this into the club constitution. Active and open communication to club members and fans must, once again, be ensured. This allows the admission of strategic equity partners, but also secures that the club retains its independence in terms of decision making as the issue of additional shares calls for a change in the club constitution, which (normally) requires a two-third majority. Another guideline for shareholder composition is to incorporate several shareholders instead of only one big equity partner who holds all issued stakes. Various shareholders contribute different expertise and networks. In addition, a distribution of shares between several investors prevents the impression that one big partner wants to dominate the club. While the amount of shares merely depends on a mutual understanding of how much money the sponsor wants to invest, a minimum of 5% stake is recommended in order to show a strategic commitment.

This grounded theory provides guidelines and suggestions on how to approach an equity partner externally. The results from the fan survey suggest that clubs who intend to externally enter into a share deal should take the investor's image into account. Also, a shareholder with a regional affinity seems to be more accepted by fans.

Last but not least, the study emphasised the crucial role of personal relationships as a facilitating factor for entering into football partnerships. By implication, clubs should attempt to build and foster a network of informal relationships with representatives of local and regional companies as this could be a door opener for future sponsorships. For example, the club's visibility at social events could promote public relations and personal contacts to boost the club's standing as a potential business partner.

7.4 Research Limitations

Within the evaluation of research quality (Section 5.5), research design limitations were addressed previously. This part discusses further research limitations with regard to the research findings.

Overall, this study faces the common limitations of qualitative research. Even though the significance of qualitative studies in the management discipline is illustrated, qualitative studies are difficult to conduct because the main part focuses on listening, watching, interviewing, and logical inferring and making sense of complex situations, practices, concepts, and their relationships. Since interpretations are not exact replications of data but the analyst's impression of that data, qualitative research still persists a critical effort as *"it can open minds, bring another's experience to life, and explain that which we might not otherwise understand"* (Corbin & Strauss, 2015; 66).

As findings are co-created by research participants and the researcher, the author acknowledges that interpretations are temporally restricted—in a binary way. First, interpretations are actually provisional. Their nature considers continuous elaboration and partial negation. Every analyst should accept that there are restrictions to what can be explored based on access to the field, amount of analytical experience, and degree of personal reserves. Likewise, theories are restricted in time: humans living in certain periods, informed by societies, and current ideas and trends. Hence, as change on various levels is omnipresent, this influences the validity of theories and their affiliation to contemporary reality (Strauss & Corbin, 1998). To address the academic call for neutrality and impartiality, the researcher endeavoured to provide the reader the opportunity to follow and understand the researcher's reasoning process by explaining the ontological and epistemological stance. Moreover, the author has planned the research design systematically with regard to the research paradigm, methodology, applied methods, and logic of thinking.

With regard to subjectivity, the study is about the subjective interpretation of data in a field in which the researcher is passionate. This passion could be perceived as encouraging to providing valuable research outcomes, but could also distort results if the researcher unconsciously proves his assumptions (preconceptions). In order to avoid that the research outcomes do not just become reflections of the researcher's preconceived ideas and thoughts, the researcher incorporated a reflexive part into memos and documents his preconceptions before entering the empirical data collection (Section 5.4.2) which refer to Steinke's (2010) criterion of 'reflective subjectivity'. This process, in phenomenology studies known as 'bracketing', encourages entering of the participants world with an open mind (Savage, 2005). Referring to Shenton (2004), reflection also supports evaluation of the project as it develops towards final outcomes. Nevertheless, it cannot be claimed that the study is entirely free from the bias of preconceptions.

Furthermore, the study findings rely on subjectivity on the part of the experts because the expert (interviewee) has to reconstruct situations, contexts, routines, and practices which are incorporated in the answers. This is often accompanied by "*systematic knowledge about subjective experience*" (Bryman, 1999; 55). However, grounded theory provides systematic and concrete mechanisms for data collection and analysis, which offers direction and, if rigorously applied, secure the development of a valid theory (Fendt & Sachs, 2008). By the use of constant comparative method, categories and concepts are systematically identified in the data. These categories are then clarified and elaborated in subsequent interviews within the frame of theoretical sampling. Hence, the data analysis procedure in itself can basically be seen as a process of repeated triangulation and review, which addresses the issue of the internal validity of the study (Denzin & Lincoln, 1985). Still, theoretical sampling may produce a biased sample (Kolb, 2012). Hence, outcomes pertain largely to the football-related context.

Regarding the chosen distribution channels of the online survey a bias (for external validity) could have emerged if a group of people had more opportunities to participate than others (Esterby-Smith et al., 2006). For example, the distribution via the SVW Twitter channel could have ensured better visibility of the survey link for subscribers of the channel. As there is no information about how participants were informed about the link, this remains unknown. Several distribution channels were used (e.g., e-mail to all fan representatives and fan projects) but it cannot be guaranteed that all fan representatives forwarded the link to their members as agreed. Certainly, football fans with no access to the internet had no opportunity to participate. Overall, a biased sample could not entirely be excluded. Still, the target group was reached, which is supported by the survey's sample characteristic. Nevertheless, fans from the 2nd Bundesliga and the 3rd Liga are underrepresented in the fan survey. Therefore, the fan perspective stems mainly from fans of 1st Bundesliga clubs.

Finally, although the purpose of a grounded theory study is not to represent the world, but to represent a theory which is grounded in the data, the results lack statistical reliability (Fisher, 2010). Even with careful selection of relevant participants (and cases), it is not presumed that the study findings apply across different industry sectors, as strategic equity partnerships are complex phenomena which require an idiosyncratic consideration of specific contexts (Bell et al., 2006). However, future research may yield evidence that the emergent theory will also apply in other (sport-related) contexts.

7.5 Future Research

This study raises a multitude of prospects for future research, both in terms of theory validation and theory development. Further research will indeed be necessary to elaborate the novel findings of this study. First, this research could be expanded to integrate an increased number of cases of corporate football partnerships from lower leagues (the 2nd Bundesliga and the 3rd Liga) as this would enrich the study with perspectives and motives of corporation which engage in strategic equity partnerships on a smaller scale. In addition, broadening and empirically testing this GT in other corporate football partnerships could validate the findings.

Next, this study focused on equity partnerships with corporate sponsors. Consequently, very little can be derived of the nature of equity partnerships with other shareholder types, namely Maecenas, oligarch and financial investors. Hence, this study could be extended to get first-hand information about motives, goals, success factors, and collaborations with those shareholder types. This would also allow the comparison and testing of different understandings of strategic partnerships in various club contexts.

Future research may enhance the findings by testing the theory within other sport-related contexts such as ice hockey, basketball, or handball.

In basketball, sponsors also arise as club name sponsors which inheres a very strong connection. An additional shareholding might have similar effects on the partnership as presented in this study.

This grounded theory clearly emphasised that the club brand is a main attracting factor for corporations to enter into a partnership and it is shown that sponsorships are a vital tool for clubs to build their brand. Also, the brand value is the reference for club valuation. By implication, future research could provide practical implications on how clubs can make use of a sponsor's support in brand building. Although the phenomenon of strategic equity partnership relates to German football, future studies could spotlight which aspects impede main sponsors in other European leagues from entering into strategic equity partnerships. This could provide a future outlook for German clubs on what could happen if the 50+1 rule was abolished in the future as expected by many football and legal experts (e.g., Hofmann, 2016; Teevs, 2014; Punte, 2012; Summerer, 2008).

Since football fans, in their role as prosumers, occupy a vital role in the football business, consideration of fan opinion appears crucial from a sport economic perspective. Although this fan survey was directed at fans from the 1st Bundesliga, 2nd Bundesliga and the 3rd Liga, the majority of fans in this survey support a club from the 1st Bundesliga. Studies that also encompass the opinion of fans from second and third tier clubs would present a more complete picture. In addition, since football fans are of a heterogenous nature, future research can build upon the approach of this fan survey by differentiating between four types of shareholders and spotlighting the view of specific fan groups by the use of a cluster analysis. This could yield interesting insights, for example, whether the opinion of fans relate to a specific club situation (existence of shareholder or not, which type of shareholder). If future research builds upon the distinction of various shareholder types, this would enhance an understanding of the fan opinion and allow measures for acceptance to be developed relating to specific shareholder types.

Research Summary 8

8.1 Introduction

In the previous Chapter theoretical and practical implications were provided and recommendations for action were presented. It has clearly been outlined that the study makes a variety of valuable contributions to theory and practice. Research limitations were discussed and an avenue for future research in the field of strategic partnerships is suggested. This Chapter briefly summarises the study by responding to the research question and sub-questions. The study's key findings are condensed and the dissertation concludes with a final statement.

This dissertation aimed at exploring the development of corporate football sponsorships in German football towards strategic equity partnerships and enhancing an understanding about the motives and value generating processes from the perspectives of clubs, sponsors, and football fans. Due to the increasing appearance of this partnership form in German football, its significance on club and corporate strategy, and since there is no empirical research on the issue hitherto, the study's goal was to generate theory from the specific field of football partnerships and to provide practical recommendations for managing such partnerships via the use of grounded theory methodology.

The international competition between football clubs in Europe, a statistically proven relationship between money and sporting success, the opportunity for foreign clubs to generate additional money via majority shareholdings, and the competitive advantage of foreign leagues with regard to TV revenues explain the need for German clubs to enter into strategic equity partnerships. Yet, football clubs (maximising sporting success) and corporate sponsors (maximising profit) have contrasting (overriding) goals. Corporations also need to justify their investments to their own share- and stakeholders. This led to the central research question: *Why*

T. Duffner, *Strategic Equity Partnerships in Professional Football*, Event- und Impaktforschung, https://doi.org/10.1007/978-3-658-31301-2_8

do football clubs and corporations establish strategic equity partnerships? Besides, seven research sub-questions were deemed to be of major significance to address the central research question and to support theory development with regard to the central phenomenon of the study: strategic equity partnerships in German football.

8.2 Key Findings and Review of the Research Questions

This grounded theory is based on four main categories (*connecting with a symbol, becoming a brand symbiosis, shareholding, fear of loss*) and the core category *securing* which subsumes five sub-core categories (*competitiveness, deepening commitment, regional connectivity and appeal, deterring competitors,* and *planning security*). Table 8.1 presents a brief overview of where and how the research question and sub-questions have been answered in theory and practice. However, it should be considered that this dissertation is a theory developing process in which, not only individual categories and concepts, but the theory as a whole refers to the research question and sub-questions.

Table 8.1 Answer of Research Question and Sub-Questions. (Source: Own Illustration)

Research question Motives (why)	Section 2.3 addressed general motives for entering into strategic partnerships, e.g., access to distinct resources and brand building. Motives for equity investments refer to dividend payments and an increase of share value. Empirically, the key motives are explained in the core category *securing* and find expression in five sub-categories (*competitiveness, regional connectivity, deterring competitors, deepening commitment, planning security*)
SQ 1 Critical success factors (what)	Section 2.4 discussed the critical success factors for strategic partnerships as presented in the literature, in particular the fit-construct, trust, and commitment Empirically, the concept *growing football business* and in the sub-category *attracting factors* (*charisma* of the brand) explained the main attracting factors. The sub-category *preconditions* refers to *compatibility, trust, quality of people*, and *economic feasibility*. Requirements for a strategic equity partnership were added in the sub-category *shareholding essentials* in the form of *having prior insights, understanding of one's role, economic reasonableness* and *emotional attachment*

(continued)

Table 8.1 (continued)

Research question Motives (why)	Section 2.3 addressed general motives for entering into strategic partnerships, e.g., access to distinct resources and brand building. Motives for equity investments refer to dividend payments and an increase of share value. Empirically, the key motives are explained in the core category *securing* and find expression in five sub-categories (*competitiveness, regional connectivity, deterring competitors, deepening commitment, planning security*)
SQ 2 Impediments (what)	Section 3.3 addressed the clubs' and fans' fear of dependency from investors as a main concern Impediments are empirically uncovered in the category *fear of loss* and finds expression in the concept of *retaining flexibility*
SQ 3 Strategic intent (how)	The strategic intent is addressed throughout the whole theory, in detail in the category *becoming a brand symbiosis, shareholding* and in the core category *securing*. A shareholding is a further commitment to the long-term direction of the partnership and enhances its credibility and stability
SQ 4 Processes (how)	Various partnership processes are explained throughout the theory, e.g., *partnership management, screening, and deepening involvement. Shareholding* represents a strategy for *securing*. The sub-category *managing the dyad* and "*sounding board*" provided further insights and explained interrelationships between the sponsorship and shareholding
SQ 5 Club member and fan's view (how)	A strategic partner is well accepted by 90.4% of fans. As opposed to this, an oligarch is not accepted by 93%. A Maecenas is not accepted by 50.4% while 42.9% of fans would accept this shareholder type. A financial investor is not accepted by 54.4% while 39.2% of fans would accept it. Overall, there is no significant difference between the evaluation of club members and non-club members (fans). The fans base their arguments against shareholder mainly on: fear of influence on sporting decisions (77.1%), increased commercialisation (75.1%), loss of identification (73.9%), loss of co-determination (77.6%), loss of goodwill values (79.2%), and loss of tradition 79.2%). The arguments in favour of a shareholder are: increase of national (75.6%) and international (72%) competitiveness

(continued)

Table 8.1 (continued)

Research question Motives (why)	Section 2.3 addressed general motives for entering into strategic partnerships, e.g., access to distinct resources and brand building. Motives for equity investments refer to dividend payments and an increase of share value. Empirically, the key motives are explained in the core category *securing* and find expression in five sub-categories (*competitiveness, regional connectivity, deterring competitors, deepening commitment, planning security*)
SQ 6 Fan opinion on the attributes of an equity partner (how)	A positive image of an equity partner is a vital issue for 83.7% of fans. Similarly, 79% of fans demand a regional affinity of an equity partner. 94.2% of fans rate "a priority right of repurchase" as a crucial aspect. With regard to the amount of shares, 24.9% of fans agree on selling shares up to 10%, 43.6% of fans agree on up to 24.9%, and 13.4% of fans agree on the disposal of up to 49.9% Overall 75.5% of fans seem to prefer the allocation of shares to be allocated among several shareholders based on the argument (61.7%) that the influence of only one shareholder would be too big
SQ 7 Added value (what)	Chapter 2 and 3 highlighted the added value (better information flow, stability, honest conduct and to curb opportunistic behaviour) of strategic equity partnerships as presented in the general management field The main empirical insights are found in the category *shareholding* and the core category *securing*. Equity deepens the partnership, advances collaborative conditions, facilitates problem solving, and provides stability for the partnership as an exit is exacerbated via equity.

To address the research question and sub-questions appropriately the current state of the general strategic alliance, sport-related sponsorship, and football specific partnership literature were reviewed. Theory development was mainly based on 24 expert interviews with club and corporate managers at top management level as the main data collection method. A quantitative online survey (n = 1,589) complemented the emergent theory with the perspective of club members and football fans on the topic. Document analysis supported the whole theory generating process. The central findings of the study are the following:

Motives (research question)
The motives find expression in the core category *securing* and its five sub-categories which are prioritised differently according to the specific corporate club context. While *securing competitiveness*, *deepening commitment*, and "*planning security*" refer to clubs and sponsors, *securing regional connectivity and appeal* as well as "*deterring competitors*" are motives from the sponsor's perspective.

Clubs are, to a large extent, financially motivated. The money generated via a shareholding serves their overall goal of retaining a competitive sporting edge which is beneficial for the sponsor and sponsorship outcome too, due to the higher media reach and increased club charisma. With regard to *securing a deepening commitment* and "*planning security*", the partnership intention is focused on internal and inter-partner aspects. Since a sponsor's stake is difficult to sell and due to an increased commitment associated with an equity investment, a shareholding provides security and certainty for long-term business planning and collaboration. Moreover, a shareholding is entered since equity deepens the partnership and enhances collaborative conditions.

Against this, with a focus on *regional connectivity and appeal*, the arguments are predominantly put forward on the *signifying* effect of a shareholding and shifts towards social responsibility. A successful club positively affects regional attractivity which, in turn, appeals to employees and fosters a connection to the home region of the sponsor. A shareholding is, furthermore, entered to secure the partnership against competitors ("*deterring competitors*"). This deterring is achieved via the *retention factor*. A potential sponsor would have to supersede the equity stake from the current sponsor in order to occupy the sponsorship which is an obstacle due to heavy costs.

Overall, an additional share deal is based on a multitude of strategic considerations and is another step of deepening involvement between the club and sponsor.

Critical success factors (SQ 1)
The high popularity of football, its financial impact for society, the sport's capacity to evoke people's emotions, and the high media coverage and reach are key factors for corporations to engage in football partnerships. Strong evidence is provided that the *charisma of the club's brand* is critical in attracting sponsors. In particular those clubs with a strong charismatic brand are attractive for share deals. Since football is seen as a lucrative market which is expected to grow in the next years, becoming part of a strong growing brand is the main attracting factor for sponsors to buy club shares. Partnering a reputable sponsor brand is also

appealing for clubs as this is a sign of exclusivity and may attract further commercial partners who see the opportunity for business networking within the pool of club sponsors. It can be concluded that football as a sport is not only appealing for people but also for corporations to engage in commercial partnerships. This impact is maximised by a charismatic brand with a positive image.

The concept of *compatibility* is a basic requirement for entering into partnerships with football clubs. However, in order to develop a sponsorship into a strategic (equity) partnership, the compatibility of various aspects such as goals, management culture, and mindsets needs to be proven over a certain period of collaboration. Therefore, a prior insight via a sponsorship is a preliminary step to enter into a shareholding. Furthermore, both partners must adequately comprehend each other's dynamic expectations and objectives to maintain successful relations. An *understanding of one's role* becomes especially fundamental for clubs as a precondition to selling club shares. Likewise, *trust* between the partners is pivotal for entering into a sponsorship and becomes essential for entering and managing a strategic equity partnership. Without trust a football sponsorship cannot develop into a strategic equity partnership. While economic reasonableness is undoubtedly critical for a share acquisition, a shareholding at a football club is not a direct profit generating investment. Hence, an emotional attachment to the club appeared as a precondition for sponsors to invest in a football club stake.

The conclusion that can be drawn with regard to the critical success factors is that becoming a strategic equity partner is not a straight-line process. The requirements for entering into an additional share deal are high and relational and strategic elements have a significant impact on partnership success and progress.

Impediments (SQ 2)

The reasons for sponsors to not enter into a shareholding relate mainly to the concept of retaining flexibility. A shareholding in a 1st Bundesliga club equates to a multi-million-euro investment and a commitment to repeatedly extend the sponsorship contract. This ties up a specific share of the annual corporate budget in the long term which may restrict entrepreneurial flexibility. Corporations also require that clubs have a solid financial basis and that club management acts in an economically reasonable manner. If this is not the case, a shareholding is unlikely to be realised.

An aspect from the club perspective is that, by giving up ownership, clubs face the fear of restricted decision-making and investor influence in sporting decisions. Likewise, club members and fans have the same concerns and further assume investors will exploit the club for their business interests which may lead to a loss of identity. Fan resistance against investors is therefore another impediment for clubs who fear an alienation from their fans in case of selling shares. However, as the survey results show a shareholding of a sponsor is neither perceived as a hostile take-over by clubs nor by football fans.

Overall, a shareholding at a football club is a strategic move with wide-ranging implications for clubs, sponsors, and fans. Consequently, a share deal at a football club needs to be in line with the overall strategic intent of the partnering organisations.

Strategic intent (SQ 3)

As evidenced in this study, a shareholding affects the strategic intent of the sponsor and club by emphasising the long-term interest and strategic direction of the partnership. Evidence is given that a minimum stake of 5% is required to express a strategic commitment. A shareholding not only enhances the credibility of the partnership but also constitutes a more stable structure for cooperation.

Furthermore, the sponsorship is strategically related to the shareholding due to consistency in the communication and branding strategy of the sponsor. Although a shareholding is not a direct profit generating issue for the sponsor the club partnership is of high strategic and relational value (from a corporate perspective) and therefore secured with a shareholding. Due to the financial support of the sponsor via a shareholding the sponsor supports a vital part of its own marketing and branding strategy (the club partnership) and hence indirectly bolsters sponsorship outcomes. This is justified as the shares act as counter value, are expected to increase in value, and also through a seat in the club's supervisory committee.

For clubs, a share deal enhances the financial capabilities and hence serves the overall goal of winning football matches as there is a proven relationship between money and sporting success. In addition to this, a shareholding with a strategic partner improves know-how, provides security for long-term planning, and the partnership signalises exclusivity which fosters further business partnerships.

It can be concluded that a corporate club partnership is a business building activity for both partners which serves to drive forward one's own organisation.

Processes (SQ 4)

This grounded theory clearly emphasises the dynamic nature of football sponsorships which develops over time (process character) and explains the underlying mechanisms and procedures towards the development of a strategic equity partnership. It is evident that the greater the level of mutual support and relational effort, the more positive the sponsorship and collaborative appraisal. Consequently, the sponsorship proceeds towards a brand symbiosis in which club and sponsor start to see the mutual synergies of the collaboration.

The sub-category *managing the dyad* provides minutiae insights that the sponsorship and shareholding are formally separated (separated contracts) but informally and strategically connected. The *retention factor* (a contractual item) for sponsors ensures that, in case of a sponsorship breakdown, either the club or the new sponsor has to buy the equity stake from the leaving partner. Since this is linked to a high amount of money the *retention factor* acts as an obstacle for competitors to supersede the strategic equity partner as a club sponsor. *Managing the dyad* further explicates that the shareholding may impact on bargaining (to pay less or to get more) in sponsorship negotiations, which even becomes a subtle motive in some cases. However, in the daily operations the dyad of sponsorship and shareholding is managed as a whole. The category *sounding board* explicitly details the strategic function of the club's supervisory committee and its significance for the management of the partnership. The supervisory board is not only a tool for exchanging ideas, the mutual planning of strategic issues, and informal partnership management, it also serves as justification for the sponsor towards the partner's share- and stakeholder as a seat on the board ensures a deep insight into the club.

Managing a strategic equity partnership requires a strategic, long-term, and holistic approach in which the club and sponsor need to mutually contribute in order to yield joint objectives.

Fan opinion on four types of equity partners (SQ 5)

Although there is an ongoing debate about equity partnerships in German football which is predominantly related to the discussion about the repeal or retention of the 50+1 rule, football fans have distinct views on different shareholder types and in terms of the amount of club shares which may be sold. While fans are in favour of the retention of the 50+1 rule (96%), the majority of fans (84%) still agree on minority shareholdings at their favourite club. In this respect, a strategic partner (sponsor) is highly accepted (90.4%) by fans whereas the acceptance of financial investors and Maecenas yielded ambiguous results. In contrast, an oligarch is not accepted at all by 90% of fans.

Attributes of fan opinion (SQ 6)

A rejection of shareholder admission is predominantly based on the negative impact in terms of *influence on sporting decisions, fan identification, commercialisation, co-determination, goodwill values*, and *tradition of the club*. These arguments are homogenously rated as important aspects against shareholder admission by club members (between 73.9% and 79.2%) and non-club members (between 65.3% and 76.2%).

For the majority of football fans, an *increase in national* (75.6%) and *international* (72%) *competitiveness* due to additional income from the share deal are the main factors for the admission of a club shareholder. In this respect, there is no difference between the ratings of club members and non-club members. A *positive image* (83.7%) and the *regional affinity* (79%) of a (potential) shareholder are further important features for club members and fans. Additionally, a *club's priority right for repurchase* was found to be of major significance (94.2%).

Added value (SQ 7)
Value is added to the sponsorship when both partners start to integrate the associate into their own strategic planning and to pool complementary resources in order to achieve mutual strategic goals. Indeed, equity adds value to the strategic sponsorship although this added value is sometimes difficult for outsiders to grasp. Compared to a purely contractual sponsorship, an additional shareholding is a dedication and obligation on top of the partnership which leads to higher mutual involvement (sense of belonging) between the parties.

This motivates those involved to put additional effort into partnership management and to "go the extra mile" which, in turn, allows better collaborative conditions and more relational value to be achieved. This added value can differ with regard to the specific corporate club context, e.g., in terms of internationalisation and market development by getting support to enter new markets which are not the priority market of the partner. A shareholding can also positively affect inter-partner issues such as easier problem solving. Moreover, the added value can become visible in rough times since equity implies a more stable partnership which the club and sponsor want to maintain in the long term.

Unexpected findings
This grounded theory also uncovered an unexpected finding. The absence of an agreed definition of the term strategic equity partner(ship) appears to be a hindrance to meaningful discussion. This study presents a first attempt to integrate a definition of strategic equity partnership in the discussion in German football.

8.3 Concluding Statement

This Chapter concludes the study by illustrating how the grounded theory addressed the research question and sub-questions. "Strategic Equity Partnerships between Sponsors and Football Clubs in the German Bundesliga: A Grounded Theory about Motives, Success Factors, Processes, and Effects Generated by Corporate and Club Expert Interviews and a Fan Survey" contributes to the limited understanding among theorists regarding the formation process, the dynamics, and evolution of strategic equity partnerships in German football and the factors that determine its success.

In line with the study's purpose, theory was developed within the specific field of strategic equity partnerships in football for the first time. The dynamic nature of this grounded theory complies with the "dynamic understanding" of theories put forward by Corbin and Strauss (1998) in which a theory reconstructs the sequence of a variety of actions. Managerial and theoretical implications are provided and practical recommendations are offered that support an understanding about complex interactions among clubs, their sponsors, and club members and fans in the establishment and management of football partnerships.

At the core of the theory, each section presented new empirical insights to increase and deepen the understanding of the underlying motives and mechanics of the corporate club partnership. This study has clearly shown how the added value of an additional share deal is created that benefits both the club and sponsor. In addition to that, the study findings showed that fan resistance lost relevance with regard to minority equity partnerships with corporate sponsors. This reinforces the incentive for sponsors and football clubs to either buy or sell football club shares.

Yet, although theoretical implications were illustrated and recommendations for action were made, it is not given that these apply in every partnership environment regarding partnership complexity. Adding to the complexity, strategies are not equally successful across club and corporate contexts. Therefore, the theory generated in this dissertation should be seen as the first step in investigating various forms of shareholdings in football clubs.

However, just as football club share acquisitions will continue to be a considerable strategic choice for football clubs in Europe in the future (Boor et al., 2016), so will the competitive reality of the football business encourage German clubs to team up with corporate sponsors to enter into strategic equity partnerships.

Bibliography

Aaker, D., A., (1996). *Building Strong Brands*. New York: Free Press.

Aaker, D., A., (1997). Dimensions of Brand Personality. *Journal of Marketing Research*, 34, S. 347–356.

Abimbola, T., & Vallaster, C., (2007). Brand, Organisational Identity and Reputation in SMEs: An Overview. *Qualitative Market Research: An International Journal*, IV (10), S. 341–348.

Acero, I., Serrano, R., & Dimitropoulos, P., (2017). Ownership Structure and Financial Performance in European Football. *Corporate Governance: The International Journal of Business in Society*, 17 (3), S. 511–523.

Adam, S., Bauers, S., B., & Hovemann, G., (2019). Inevitable Need for Change – Identifying and Removing Barriers to Supporter Participation in German Professional Football. *Sport in Society*, DOI: https://doi.org/10.1080/17430437.2019.1596082.

Adam, S., & Hovemann, G., (2018). Auswirkung der Corporate Governance auf die Internationalisierung im deutschen professionellen Fußball. In Breuer, M., Druker, K., & Grotz, M., (editors). *Internationalisierung im Profisport*. Sciamus: Sport und Management 1/2018, S. 89-107.

Adam, S., Lammert J., & Hovemann, G., (2017). Status quo und potenzielle Einflussfaktoren der Club Corporate Governance im deutschen professionellen Fußball. In Hovemann, G., & Lammert J., (editors). *Sport im Spannungsfeld unterschiedlicher Sektoren*, 18, Schorndorf: Hofmann, S. 43-67.

Advidera (20. December 2018). *Retweet* [online]. Available at: https://www.advidera.com/glossar/retweet/.

Ahonen, M., (2008). Branding: Does it even exists among SMEs? *16th Nordic Conference on Small Business Research*, Tallin.

Alchian, A., A., & Demsetz, H., (1972). Production, Information Costs, and Economic Organisation. *American Economic Review*, *72*, S. 777-795.

Aldiabat, K., M., (2011). Philosophical Roots of Classical Grounded theory: Its Foundation in Symbolic Interactionism. *The Qualitative Report*, 16 (4), S. 1063-1080.

Alexa, F., (2009). *Markenpersönlichkeit von Fußballvereinen – Eine empirische Untersuchung*. 1st Edition. Göttingen: Cuvillier-Verlag.

T. Duffner, *Strategic Equity Partnerships in Professional Football*, Event- und Impaktforschung, https://doi.org/10.1007/978-3-658-31301-2

Allen, J., W., & Phillips, G., M., (2000). Corporate Equity Ownership, Strategic Alliances, and Product Market Relationships. *The Journal of Finance*, 15 (6), S. 2791- 2816.

Amis, J., P., N., & Slack, T., (1997). Achieving a Sustainable Competitive Advantage: A Resource-Based View of Sport Sponsorship. *Journal of Sport Management*, 11 (1), S. 80-96.

Amis, J., P., N., Slack, T., & Berrett, T., (1999). Sport Sponsorship as Distinctive Competence. *European Journal of Marketing*, 33, S. 250–272.

Anderson, E., & Weitz, B., (1992). The Use of Pledges to Build and Sustain Commitment in Distribution Channels. *Journal of Marketing Research*, 29, S. 18-34.

Ansoff, I., H., (1965). *Corporate Strategy*. New York: McGraw-Hill Inc.

Argyris, C., & Schön, D., A., (1978). *Organisational Learning: A Theory of Action Perspective*. Reading, MA: Addison-Wesley.

Ashelm, M., (25 November 2011). Mäzenatentum als Auslaufmodell [online]. *FAZ*, available at: https://www.faz.net/aktuell/sport/fussball/financial-fairplay-maezenatentum-als-auslaufmodell-14901.html. [accessed: 04/06/2017].

Ashelm, M., & Horeni, M., (04 March 2015). Die Klubs der starken Männer [online]. *FAZ*, available at: https://www.faz.net/aktuell/sport/fussball/vfl-wolfsburg-gegen-leipzig-duell-der-starken-maenner-13461571.html. [accessed: 04/06/2017].

Aulakh, P., Kotabe, M., & Sahay, A., (1996). Trust and Performance in Cross-Border Marketing Partnerships: A Behavioural Approach. *Journal of International Business Studies*, 27 (5), S. 1005–1032.

Bähring, K., Hauff, S., Sossdorf, M., & Thommes, K., (2008). Methodologische Grundlagen und Besonderheiten der qualitativen Befragung von Experten in Unternehmen. *Die Unternehmung*, 62 (1), S. 89-111.

Baker, M., & Wurgler, J., (2002). Market Timing and Capital Structure. *The Journal of Finance,* 57 (1), S. 1-32.

Barajas, A., Fernández-Jardón, C., & Crolley, L., (2005). Does Sports Performance Influence Revenues and Economic Results in Spanish football? *SSRN Electronic Journal*. https://doi.org/10.2139/ssrn.986365, S. 1-19.

Barber, B., (1983). *The Logic and Limits of Trust*. New Brunswick, New York: Rutgers University Press.

Barney, J., B., (1986). Strategic Factor Markets: Expectations, Luck, and Business Strategy. *Management Science*, 32 (10), S. 1231-1241.

Barney, J., B., (1991). Firm Resources and Sustained Competitive Advantage. *Journal of Management*, 17 (1), S. 99-120.

Barney, J., B., Ketchen, J., & Wright, M., (2011). The Future of Resource-Based Theory. Revitalization or Decline? *Journal of Management*, 37 (5), S. 1299-315.

Barringer, B., R., & Harrison, J., S., (2000). Walking a Tightrope: Creating Value Through Interorganisational Relationships. *Journal of Management*, 26 (3), S. 367-403.

Bauers, S., B., & Hovemann, G., (2019a). Regulation von beherrschendem Einfluss im deutschen Profifuß-ball – Eine empirische Vergleichsanalyse von Faninteressen der Jahre 2011 und 2017. In *Sport und Gesellschaft*.

Bauers, S., B., & Hovemann, G., (2019b). Stakeholderorientierte Perspektiven in der sportpolitischen Diskussion von beherrschendem Einfluss im deutschen Profifußball – Empirische Ergebnisse einer Befragung von Investoren und Investorinnen zur 50+1-Regel und deren Zukunft. In *Fußball und Gesellschaft*.

Bauers, S., B., & Hovemann, G., (2019c): The Regulation of Investors‘ Influence in German Professional Football – An Analysis of the ‚50+1 Rule‘ and Its Future from the Perspective of Potential Investors. In *German Journal of Exercise and Sport Research.*

Bauers, S., B., Lammert, J., Faix, A., & Hovemann, G., (2019d). Club Members in German Professional Football and Their Attitude towards the ‚50+1 Rule‘ – A Stakeholder-Oriented Analysis. In *Soccer and Society,* https://doi.org/10.1080/14660970.2019.15977 17.

Bauers, S., B., Lammert, J., & Hovemann, G., (2015). Beherrschender Einfluss von Investoren im deutschen Profifußball – Eine Bestandsaufnahme und Analyse bestehender Umgehungen der 50+1-Regel. In: *Sciamus – Sport und Management*, 6 (3), S. 1-17.

Bauers, S., B., Lammert, J., & Hovemann, G., (2013). Regulation von beherrschendem Einfluss im deutschen Profi-Fußball – Eine empirische Analyse der Interessen von Fußballklubs. In: *Leipziger Sportwissenschaftliche Beiträge*, 54 (2), S. 77-106.

Baumgarth, C., (2003). *Wirkungen des Co-Brandings.* Wiesbaden: Deutscher Universitäts Verlag.

Beamish, P., W., (1987). Joint Ventures in LDCs: Partner Selection and Performance. *Management International Review*, 27 (1), S. 23–37.

Becker, J., (23 April 2013). Hoeneß-Steueraffäre: Jetzt redet Adidas [online]. *The Horizon,* available at: https://www.horizont.net/marketing/nachrichten/-Hoeness-Steueraffaere-Jetzt-redet-Adidas-114216 [accessed: 13/12/2018].

Beech, J., (2010). Finance in the Football Industry. In Hamil, S., Cadwick, S., (editors). *Managing Football – An international Perspective*. Oxford: Routledge, S. 119-149.

Bell, J., Den Ouden, B., & Ziggers, G., W., (2006). Dynamics of Cooperation: At the Brink of Irrelevance. *Journal of Management Studies*, 43 (7), S. 1607-1619.

Bergkvist, L., & Rossiter, J., R., (2009). Tailor-Made Single-Item Measures of Doubly Concrete Constructs. *International Journal of Advertising*, 28 (4), S. 607–621.

Barnard, M., Boor, S., Winn, C., Wood, C., & Wray, I., (2019). World in Motion. In Jones, D., & Green, M., (editors). *Annual Review of Football Finance 2019.* Manchester: Deloitte Sport Business Group.

Berrett, T., & Slack, T., (1999). Corporate Sponsorship and Organisational Strategy: Bridging the Gap. *International Journal of Sports Marketing & Sponsorship*, 1, S. 261-277.

Bhaskar, R., (2010). *Reclaiming Reality: A Critical Introduction to Contemporary Philosophy – Classical Texts in Critical Realism.* London: Routledge.

Birks., M., & Mills, J., (2015). *Grounded Theory – a Practical Guide.* 2nd Edition. London: Sage.

Birks, M., Mills, J., Francis, K., & Chapman, Y., (2009). A Thousand Words Paint a Picture: The Use of Storyline in Grounded Theory Research. *Journal of Research in Nursing*, 14 (5), S. 405-417.

Biggam, J., (2011). *Succeeding with your Master's Dissertation.* 2nd Edition. Berkshire: McGraw Hill, Open University Press.

Bleeke, J., & Ernst, D., (1991). The Way to Win in Cross-Border Alliances. *Harvard Business Review*. November-December 1991.

Blumer, H., (1969). *Symbolic Interactionism; Perspective and Method.* Englewood Cliffs: Prentice-Hall.

Bodet, G., & Chanavat, N., (2010). Building global football brand equity. *Asia Pacific Journal of Marketing and Logistics*, 22 (1), S. 55-66.

Bogner, A., Littig, B., & Menz, W., (2009). *Interviewing Experts*. Hampshire: Palgrave McMillan.

Böhm, A., (2000). Theoretisches Codieren. In Flick, U., von Kardorff, E., & Steinke, I., (editors). *Qualitative Forschung, Ein Handbuch*, S. 475-485.

Bolgar, C., (2010). Teams Try to Find Their Formulas Through Mergers, Acquisitions, Outsourcing [online]. *The Wall Street Journal*, available at: http://online.wsj.com/ad/article/businessoffootball-acquisition.html. [accessed: 06/10/2015].

Bollen, K., A., (1989). *Structural Equations with Latent Variables*. New York: Wiley.

Boor, S., Green, M., Hanson, C., Shaffer, A., Thorpe, A., & Winn, C., (2016). *Annual Review of Football Finance 2016*. Reboot: Deloitte Sports Business Group.

Bowen, G., A., (2009). Supporting a Grounded Theory with an Audit Trail: An Illustration. *International Journal of Social Research Methodology*, 12 (4), S. 305-316.

Boyce, C., & Neale, P., (2006). Conducting in-depth Interviews: A Guide for Designing and Conducting in-depth Interviews for Evaluation Input. *Pathfinder International Tool Series, Monitoring and Evaluation*, 2.

Bradford, A., (2015). What is a Scientific Theory? [online]. *LiveScience*, available at: http://www.livescience.com/21491-what-is-a-scientific-theory-definition-of-theory.html. [accessed: 24/11/2016].

Breuer, C., & Hovemann, G., (2006). *Finanzierung von Sportstätten: Perspektiven der Sportvereine und Kommunen*. 5th Edition. Köln: Institut für Sportökonomie und Sportmanagement.

Breuer, M., Druker, K., & Grotz, M., (2018). Internationalisierung im Sport – ein Weg ohne Wiederkehr? In Breuer, M., Druker, K., & Grotz, M., (editors). *Internationalisierung im Profisport*, Sciamus: Sport und Management 1/2018, S. 1-3.

Birkinshaw, J., (2001). Making Sense of Knowledge Management. *Ivey Business Journal*, 65 (4), S. 32–36.

Brookes, S., (2016). *The Selfless Leader: A Compass for Collective Leadership*. London: Palgrave.

Brouthers, K., D., Brouthers, L., E., & Wilkinson, T., J., (1997). Strategic Alliances: Choose Your Partners. In Lloyd, B., (editor). *Creating Value through Acquisitions, Demergers, Buyouts and Alliances*. Kidlington: Pergamon/Elsevier Science.

Brown, P., A., (2008). A Review of the Literature on Case Study Research. *Canadian Journal for New Scholars in Education*, 1 (1), S. 1-14.

Bryman, A., (2006). Integrating Quantitative and Qualitative Research: How is it Done? *Qualitative Research*, 6 (1), S. 97-113.

Büch, M.-P., & Frick, B., (1999). Sportökonomie: Erkenntnisinteresse, Fragestellungen und praktische Relevanz. In Matschke, M., Sieben, G., & Schildbach, T., (editors). *Betriebswirtschaftliche Forschung und Praxis*, Berlin/Herne, S. 109-123.

Bühler, A., (2017). *Situationsanalyse Profifußball 2017*. Berlin: FC Play Fair.

Burger, A., Ulbrich, P., & Ahlenmeyer, N., (2010). *Beteiligungscontrolling*. 2nd Edition. München: Oldenbourg Verlag.

Burmann, C., & Nitschke, A., (2005). Profilierung von Marken mit Sponsoring und Events. In Meffert, H., Burmann, C., & Koers, M., (editors). *Markenmanagement – Identitätsorientierte Markenführung und praktische Umsetzung*, 2nd Edition. Wiesbaden: Gabler, S. 388-409.

Burmann, C., Jost-Benz, M., & Riley, N., (2009). Towards an Identity-Based Brand Equity Model. *Journal of Business Research*, 62, S. 390-397.

Business Dictionary (2019). Strategic Alliance [online]. *Business Dictionary*, available at: http://www.businessdictionary.com/definition/strategic-allance.html#ixzz2nxWd6Suv.

Calman, L., (2006). What is Grounded Theory? The University of Manchester, School of Nursing, Midwifery and Social Work. In Calman, L., (editor). *Patients' Views of Nurse Competence*. Nurse Education Today, 26, S. 719-725.

Cambridge Dictionary (2008). *Cambridge Advanced Learner's Dictionary*. 3rd Edition. Cambridge: University Press, S. 1040.

Cambridge Dictionary (2011). *Cambridge Business English Dictionary*. Cambridge: University Press.

Cambridge Dictionary (2011). *Cambridge Advanced Learner's Dictionary*. 2nd Edition. Cambridge: University Press, S. 970.

Cambridge Dictionary (2019). Meaning of Commercialisation in English [online]. *Cambridge Dictionary*, available at: https://dictionary.cambridge.org/dictionary/english/commercialization [accessed: 09/02/2019].

Capasso, A., & Rossi, M., (2013). Systemic Value and Corporate Governance. Exploring the Case of Professional Football Teams. *Business Systems Review*, 2 (2). S. 216-237.

Capon C., (2008). *Understanding Strategic Management*. Harlow: Pearson Education Ltd.

Caselli, S., (2010). *Private Equity and Venture Capital in Europe: Markets, Techniques, and Deals*. Oxford: Elsevier Ltd.

Chadwick, S., (2007). Is Sponsorship still Sponsorship? *International Journal of Sports Marketing & Sponsorship*, 21 (4), S. 287.

Chalip, L., (2006). Toward a Distinctive Sport Management Discipline. *Journal of Sport Management*, 2006 (20), S. 1-21.

Chamberlain-Salaun, J., Mills, J., & Usher, K., (2013). *Linking Symbolic Interactionism and Grounded Theory Methods in a Research Design: From Corbin and Strauss' Assumption to Action*. Sage Open. July-September, 2013, S. 1-10.

Chandler, A., D., (1962). *Strategy and Structure. Chapters in the History of the American Industrial Enterprise*. Cambridge: MIT Press.

Charmaz, K., (2006). *Constructing Grounded Theory: A Practical Guide Through Qualitative Analysis*. London: Sage.

Charmaz, K., (2016). A Personal Journey with Grounded Theory Methodology. *Qualitative Social Research*, 17 (1), S. 1-27.

Chemnitzer, F., Lwißlw, N., & Quitzau, J., (2015). *Finanzierung im Profifußball. Anleihen, Investoren, Mäzene & Co*. Berenberg: Wirtschaftstrends.

Cheng, P., S., & Stotlar, D., K., (1999). Successful Sponsorship: A Marriage between Sport and Corporations for the Next Millennium. *The Cyber-Journal of Sport Marketing*, 3 (3), S. 1-9.

Chien, P., M., Cornwell, B., T., & Pappu, R., (2011). Sponsorship Portfolio as a Brand-Image Creation Strategy. *Journal of Business Research*, 64, S. 142–149.

Christoffersen, J., (2013). A Review of Antecedents of International Strategic Alliance Performance: Synthesized Evidence and new Directions for Core Constructs. *International Journal of Management Reviews*, 15, S. 66-85.

Churchill, G., A., (1979). A Paradigm for Developing Better Measures of Marketing Constructs. *Journal of Marketing Research*, 16, February, S. 64-73.

Civichino, A., (2010). Inside Out or Outside In? CMA Magazine, July/August. In Day, G., & Moorman, C., (editors). *Strategy from the Outside In: Profiting from Customer Value*. New York: McGraw-Hill.

Cliffe, S., J., & Motion, J., (2005). Building Contemporary Brands: A Sponsorship-Based Strategy. *Journal of Business Research*, 58, S. 1068-1077.

Cobianchi, T., T., (1994). *Relationships among Strategic Alliance Factors and Strategic Alliance Success.* Thesis (DBA), San Diego: United States International University, College of Business Administration.

Cobbs, J., (2011). Legal Battles for Sponsorship Exclusivity: The Cases of the World Cup and NASCAR. *Sport Management Review*, 14, S. 287-298.

Cohen, L., & Manion, L., (2007). *Research Methods in Education.* 6th Edition. Abingdon: Routledge.

Contractor, F., J., & Lorange, P., (1988). Why Should Firms Cooperate? The Strategy and Economics Basis for Cooperative Ventures. In Contractor F., J., & Lorange P., (editors). *Cooperative Strategies in International Business.* San Francisco: New Lexington Press, S. 3–30.

Contractor, F., J., & Reuer, J., J., (2014). Structuring and Governing Alliances: New Directions for Research. *Global Strategy Journal*, 4, S. 241-256.

Cooper, J., N., Grenier, R., & Macauley, C., (2017). Autoethnography as a Critical Approach in Sport Management: Current Applications and Directions for Future Research. *Sport Management Review*, 20 (1), S. 43-54.

Coote, L., V., & Cornwell, T., B., (2004). Employee Identification with Sponsorship Programs: A Conceptual Framework of Antecedents and Outcomes. *American Marketing Association, Winter Educators' Conference Proceedings*, 2004 (15), S. 305-306.

Corbin, J., & Strauß, A., (1990). Grounded Theory Research: Procedures, Canons and Evaluative Criteria. *Qualitative Sociology*, 13 (1), S. 3-22.

Cornwell, T., B., (1995). Sponsorship-Linked Marketing Development. *Sport Marketing Quarterly*, 4 (4), S. 13–24.

Cornwell, T., B., Weeks, C., S., & Roy, D., P., (2005). Sponsorship-Linked Marketing: Opening the Black Box. *Journal of Advertising*, 34 (2), S. 21–42.

Cornwell, T., B., Roy, D., P., & Steinard, E., A., (2001). Exploring Managers' Perceptions of the Impact of Sponsorship on Brand Equity. *Journal of Advertising*, 30 (2), S. 41–51.

Costa, C., A., (2005). The Status and Future of Sport Management: A Delphi Study. *Journal of Sport Management*, 19, S. 117-142.

Cousens, L., Babiak, K., & Cheri, L., (2006). Beyond Sponsorship: Re-Framing Corporate-Sport Relationships. *Sport Management Review*, 9, S. 1-23.

Cravens, D., W., & Piercy, N., F., (2003). *Marketing*. 9th Edition. Boston: McGraw Hill.

Cravens, D., W., Shipp, S., H., & Cravens, K., S., (1993). Analysis of Interorganisational Relationships, Strategic Alliance Formation and Strategic Alliance Effectiveness. *Journal of Strategic Marketing*, 1, S. 55-70.

Creswell, J., W., & Plano Clark, V., L., (2011). *Designing and Conducting Mixed Methods Research*. 2nd Edition. CA: Sage.

Creswell, J., W., (2007). *Research Design: Qualitative and Quantitative Approaches*. 2nd Edition. Thousand Oaks. CA: Sage.

Creswell, J., W., (2009). *Research Design - Qualitative, Quantitative, and Mixed Methods Approaches*. 3rd Edition. London: Sage.

Christ, T., W., (2013). The Worldview Matrix as a Strategy when Designing Mixed Methods Research. *International Journal of Multiple Research Apporaches*, 7 (1), S. 110-18.

Cullen, J., B., Johnson, J., L., & Sakano, T., (2000). Success Through Commitment and Trust: The Soft Side of Strategic Alliance Management. *Journal of World Business*, 35 (3), S. 223-40.

Culpan, R., (2002). *Global Business Alliances: Theory and Practice*. Westport CT: Greenwood Publ. Group Inc.

Dacin, M., T., Oliver, C., & Roy, J.-P., (2007). The Legitimacy of Strategic Alliances: An institutional perspective. *Strategic Management Journal,* 28, S. 169-187.

Daellenbach, K., Davies, J., & Ashill, N., (2006). Understanding Sponsorship and Sponsorship Relationships – Multiple Frames and Multiple Perspectives. *International Journal Non-profit Volunt. Sect. Mark,* 11, S. 73-87.

Dana, L., P., (2011). *World Encyclopaedia of Entrepreneurship*. Cheltenham: Edward Elgar Publishing Ltd.

Danermark, B., (2002). *Explaining Society: Critical Realism in the Social Sciences*. London: Routledge.

Darke, P., Shanks, G., & Broadbent, M., (1998). Successfully Completing Case Study Research: Combining Rigour, Relevance and Pragmatism. *Information Systems Journal*, 8 (1), S. 273-289.

Das, T., K., & Kumar, R., (2007). Learning Dynamics in the Alliance Development Process. *Management Decision*, 45 (4), S. 684-707.

Das, T., K., & Teng, B., S., (2000). A Resource-Based Theory of Strategic Alliances. *Journal of Management*, 26 (1), S. 31–61.

Das, T., K., & Teng, B., S., (2001). Trust, Control, and Risk in Strategic Alliances: An Integrated Framework. *Organisation Studies*, 22 (2), S. 251–283.

Das, T., K., & Teng, B., S., (2003). Partner Analysis and Alliance Performance. *Scandinavian Journal of Management*, 19, S. 279–308.

Das, T., K., & Teng, B., S., (1998). between Trust and Control: Developing Confidence in Partner Cooperation in Alliances. *Academy of Management Review,* 23 (3), S. 491–512.

Davies, J., Daellenbach, K., & Ashill, J., N., (2008). Value in a Multiple Perspective View of Sports Sponsorships. *International Journal of Sport Management and Marketing*, 3 (3), S. 184-202.

Davies, M., & Prince, M., (1999). Examining the Longevity of New Agency Accounts. *Journal of Advertising*, 28 (4), S. 75–89.

Davis, G., B., Clyde, P., A., & Detmar, S., W., (2012). *Writing the Doctoral Dissertation*. 3rd Edition. New York: Barron's Educational Series, Inc.

De Chernatony, L., & McDonald, M., (2003). *Creating Powerful Brands*. 3rd Edition. Oxford: Butterworth Heinemann.

Demir, R., & Söderman, S., (2015). Strategic Sponsoring in Professional Sport: A Review and Conceptualization. *European Sport Management Quarterly*, 15 (3), S. 271-300.

Denning, S., (2011). The Goal of Corporations to Make Money [online]. *Forbes*, available at: http://www.forbes.com/sites/stevedenning/2011/09/26/is-the-goal-of-a-corporation-to-make-money/#2b348a957658. [accessed: 23/01/2016].

Denzin, N., K., & Lincoln, Y., S., (2005). *The Sage Handbook of Qualitative Research*. 3rd Edition. Thousand Oaks, CA: Sage.

DePamphilis, M., D., (2012). *Mergers, Acquisitions, and Other Restructuring Activities*. 6th Edition. San Diego: Elsevier.

DFB (2013). Satzung [online]. *DFB*, available at:// www.dfb.de/uploads/media/satzung.pdf [accessed at: 03/02/2016].

Dey, I., (1999). *Grounding Grounded Theory Guidelines for Qualitative Inquiry*. San Diego: Academic Press.

DFB (23 December 2018). *Mitglieder-Statistik 2018* [online]. DFB, available at: https://www.dfb.de/verbandsstruktur/mitglieder/.

DFL (2019). *Wirtschaftsreport 2019*. Frankfurt/Main: DFL Deutsche Fußball Liga GmbH.

Diamantopoulos, A., Sarstedt, M., Fuchs, C., Wilczynski, P., & Kaiser S., (2012). Guidelines for Choosing between Multi-Item and Single-Item Scales for Construct Measurement: A Predictive Validity Perspective. *Journal of the Acad. Mark. Science,* 40, S. 434-449.

Die Welt (22 January 2015). Warum Platz Drei Erfreulich ist für den FC Bayer [online]. *Die Welt*, available at: http://www.welt.de/sport/fussball/ bundesliga/fc-bayern-muenchen/article136640172/Warum-Platz-drei-erfreulich-ist-fuer-den-FC-Bayern.html. [accessed: 27/06/2016].

Dierig, C., (20 August 2014a). Finanzinvestoren krallen sich deutsche Profiklubs [online]. Die Welt, available at: https://www.welt.de/wirtschaft/article131408548/Finanzinvestoren-krallen-sich-deutsche-Profiklubs.html. [accessed: 04/02/2016].

Dierig, C., (27 February 2014b). Das große Geld und die Angst der Fußball-Romantiker [online]. *Die Welt*, available at: http://www.welt.de/wirtschaft/article125236764/Das-grosse-Geld-und-die-Angst-der-Fussball-Romantiker.html. [accessed: 04/02/2016].

Dietl, H., M., & Weingaertner, C., (2011). The Effect of Professional Football Clubs' Legal Structure on Sponsoring Revenue. *Journal of Sponsorship*, 4 (4), S. 377-392.

Dietl, H., M., & Franck, E., (2007). Governance Failure and Financial Crisis in German Football. *Journal of Sports Economics*, 8 (6), S. 662–669.

Dörnemann, J., (2002). Controlling im Profi-Sport: Ausgangssituation, Bedarf und konzeptioneller Überblick. In von Galli, A., Gömmel, R., Holzhäuser, W., Straub W., (editors). *Sportmanagement – Grundlagen der unternehmerischen Führung im Sport aus Betriebswirtschaftslehre, Steuern und Recht für den Sportmanager*. München: Vahlen, S. 129–167.

Douma, M., U., Bilderbeek, J., Idenburg, P., J., & Looise, J., K., (2000). Strategic Alliances – Managing the Dynamics of Fit. *Long Range Planning*, 33 (4), S. 579-598.

Dowd, K., (16 June 2016). *Not just for kicks: PE gaze turns toward European Football* [online]. Available at: http://pitchbook.com/news/articles/not-just-for-kicks-pe-gaze-turns-toward-european-football. [accessed: 16/06/2016].

Doz, Y., L., (1996). The Evolution of Cooperation in Strategic Alliances: Initial Conditions or Learning Processes? *Strategic Management Journal,* 17, S. 55–83.

Dreher, M., & Ernst, D., (2016). *Mergers & Acquisitions*. 2nd Edition. Stuttgart: UTB GmbH.

Dresing, T., & Pehl, T., (2015). *Praxisbuch Interview, Transkription & Analyse. Anleitungen und Regelsysteme für qualitativ Forschende* [online]. 6th Edition. Marburg, available at: www.audiotranskription.de/praxisbuch. [accessed: 02/02/2017].

Drucker, P., F., (1998). *Peter Drucker on the Profession of Management*. Boston: Harvard Business Review Press.

Dudovski, J., (2018). *The Ultimate Guide to Writing a Dissertation in Business Studies: A Step-by-Step Assistence*. E-book: Research-Methodologies.net.

Duff, A., (31 January 2014). Buyout Firm KKR Invests in Top Berlin Soccer Club Hertha [online]. *Bloomberg*, available at: http://www.bloomberg.com/news/articles/2014-01-31/kkr-invests-in-top-berlin-soccer-club-to-provide-quantum-leap- [accessed: 01/10/2016].

Dussauge, P., & Garrette, B., (1999). *Cooperative Strategy: Competing Successfully Through Strategic Alliances*. West Sussex: John Wiley & Sons Ltd.

Dworak, A., (2010). *Finanzierung für Fußballunternehmen – Erfolgreiche Wege der Kapitalbeschaffung*. Berlin: Erich Schmidt Verlag.

Dyer, J., H., & Singh, H., (1998). The Relational View: Cooperative Strategy and Sources of Interorganisational Competitive Advantage. *Academy of Management Review*, 23 (4), S. 660–679.

Egan, J., (2007). *Marketing Communications*. London: Thomason Learning.

Eisenhardt, K., M., & Schoonhoven, C., B., (1996). Resource-Based View of Strategic Alliance Formation: Strategic and Social Effects in Entrepreneurial Firms. *Organisation Science*, 7, S. 136–150.

Eisenhardt, K., M., (1989). Building Theory from Case Study Research. *Academy of Management Review*, 14 (4), S. 532–550.

Elfenbein, D., W., (2017). Property Rights Theory and the Governance of Strategic Alliances. In Mesquita, L., F., Ragozzino, R., & Reuer, J., J., (editor). *Collaborative Strategy*. Cheltenham: Edward Elgar, S. 107-113.

Elmuti, D., & Kathawala, Y., (2001). An Overview of Strategic Alliances. *Management Decisions*, 39 (3), S. 205-218.

Emery, R., & Weed, M., (2006). Fighting for Survival? The Financial Management of Football Clubs Outside the ‚Top Flight' in England. *Managing Leisure,* 11 (1), S. 1-21.

Erberich, M., (07 March 2017a). Aus Fans wurden Kunden [online]. *Die Zeit*, available at: https://www.zeit.de/sport/2017-03/fc-arsenal-champions-league-fc-bayern-england-fans-stimmung/komplettansicht [accessed: 15/09/2018].

Erberich, M., (28 March 2017b). Der Aufstand der Fußballfans [online]. *FAZ*, available at: http://www.faz.net/aktuell/sport/fussball/debatte-um-investoren-im-fussball-am-beispiel-england-14939805.html. [accessed: 04/05/2018].

Ernst, D., & Bamford, J., (2005). Your Alliances are too Stable. *Harvard Business Review*, June 2005, S. 1-9.

Esterby-Smith, M., Thorp, R., & Jackson, P., R., (2015). *Management and Business Research*. 5th Edition. London: Sage.

Esterby-Smith, M., Thorpe, R. & Lowe, A., (2006). *Management Research- An Introduction*. 2nd Edition. London: Sage.

Evan, W., M., (1965). Toward a Theory of Inter-Organizational Relations. *Management Science*, 11 (10), S. 217-230.

Fahy, J., Farrelly, F., & Quester, P., (2004). Competitive Advantage through Sponsorship. *European Journal of Marketing*, 38 (8), S. 1013–1030.

Farrelly, F., & Quester, P., (2003). The Effect of Market Orientation on Trust and Commitment. The Case of the Sponsorship Business-to-Business Relationship. *European Journal of Marketing,* 37 (3/4), S. 530 – 553.

Farrelly, F., & Quester, P., (2005a). Investigating Large-Scale Sponsorship Relationships as Co-Marketing Alliances. *Business Horizons*, 48 (1), S. 55 – 62.

Farrelly, F., & Quester, P., (2005b). Examining Important Relationship Quality Constructs of the Focal Sponsorship Exchange. *Industrial Marketing Management*, 34 (2), S. 211 – 219.

Farrelly, F., (2010). Not Playing the Game: Why Sport Sponsorship Relationships Break Down. *Journal of Sport Management*, 24, S. 319-337.

Faulkner, D., O., (1995). *International Strategic Alliances: Co-operating to Compete*. Maidenhead: McGraw-Hill.

FAZ (24 April 2015). Internationale Sponsoren meiden die Bundesliga [online]. *FAZ*, available at: https://www.faz.net/aktuell/wirtschaft/schneller-schlau/grafik-des-tages-internationale-sponsoren-meiden-die-bundesliga-13556977.html. [accessed: 28/07/2018].

FCB (20 November 2018). *Geschäftsjahr 2017/2018: Erneut Rekordumsatz für den FC Bayern München* [online]. FC Bayern München Website, available at: https://fcbayern.com/de/news/2018/11/pressemitteilung-geschaeftsjahr-2017-2018-erneut-rekordumsatz-fuer-den-fc-bayern-muenchen.

Fee, C., Hadlock, C., & Thomas, S., (2006). Corporate Equity Ownership and the Governance of Product Market Relationships. *Journal of Finance*, 61, S. 1217-1251.

Fendt, J., & Sachs, W., (2008). Grounded Theory Method in Management Research. *Organisational Research Methods*, 11 (3), S. 430-455.

Ferreira, M., P., Storopoli, J., E., & Serra, F., R., (2014). Two Decades of Research on Strategic Alliances: Analysis of Citations, Co-Citations and Themes Researched. *RAC, Rio de Janeiro*, 18 (6), S. 109-133.

Fiedler, D., (2017). *Sportsponsoring und Arbeitsrecht – Arbeitsrechtliche Selbstvermarktungsgrenzen*. Wiesbaden: Springer Gabler.

FIFA (16 December 2015). FIFA Fußball-WM 2014: 3,2 Milliarden Zuschauer, 1 Milliarde beim Finale [online]. *FIFA*, available at: http://de.fifa.com/worldcup/news/y=2015/m=12/news=fifa-fussball-wm-2014tm-3-2-milliarden-zuschauer-1-milliarde-beim-fina-2745551.html. [accessed: 01/10/2016].

Fischer, S., (04 February 2018). Bayern einholen mit Geld aus China [online]. *Süddeutsche Zeitung*, available at: https://www.sueddeutsche.de/sport/-in-der-bundesliga-bayern-einholen-mit-geld-aus-china-1.3852591#redirectedFromLandingpage.

Fisher, C., (2010). *Researching and Writing a Dissertation: An Essential Guide for Business Students*. 3rd Edition. Harlow: Prentice Hall.

Foddy, W., (1995). *Constructing Questions for Interviews and Questionnaires*. Cambridge: Cambridge University Press.

Forbes, (10 October 2016a). #103 Klaus Michael Kühne [online]. *Forbes*, available at: http://www.forbes.com/profile/klaus-michael-kuehne/.

Forbes, (10 October 2016b). #24 Dietmar Hopp & Family [online]. *Forbes*, available at: http://www.forbes.com/profile/dietmar-hopp/

Fordyce, T., (14 December 2005). Ten Years Ago, this Friday, the European Court of Justice Passed a Ruling that Presaged a revolution in European Football [online]. *BBC Sport*, available at: http://news.bbc.co.uk/sport2/hi/football/4528732.stm [accessed: 03/02/2017].

Fort, R., & Quirk, J., (1995). Cross-Subsidization, Incentives, and Outcomes in Professional Team Sports Leagues. *Journal of Economic Literature*, 33 (3), S. 1265-1299.

Franck, E., (1995). *Die ökonomischen Institutionen der Teamsportindustrie: Eine Organisationsbetrachtung*. Wiesbaden: Gabler.

Franck, E., (2010a). Private Firm, Public Corporation or Member's Association Governance Structures in European Football. *International Journal of Sport Finance*, 5 (2), S. 108–127.

Franck, E., (2010b). Zombierennen und Patenonkel – Warum deutsche Fußballklubs in der Champions League regelmäßig den Kürzeren ziehen. *ZFBF Sonderheft*, 62 (10), S. 1–13.

Franck, E., & Lang, M., (2014). A theoretical analysis of the influence of money injections on risk taking in football clubs. *Scottish Journal of Political Economy*, 61 (4), S. 430–454.

Franke, N., (2000). Marketingwissenschaft: Eine Empirische Positionsbestimmung. In Backhaus, K., (editor). *Deutschsprachige Marketingforschung: Bestandsaufnahme und Perspektiven*, Stuttgart, S. 409-444.

Franke, N., (2002). *Realtheorie des Marketings: Gestalt und Erkenntnis*. Tübingen: Mor Siebeck.

Franzen, A., (2014). Antwortskalen in standardisierten Befragungen. In Baur, N., & Blasius, J., (editors). *Handbuch Methoden der empirischen Sozialforschung*. Wiesbaden: Springer, S. 701-712.

Fraser-Sampson, G., (2011). *Alternative Assets – Investments for a Post-Crisis World.* Southerngate: John Wiley & Sons Ltd.

Frick, B., (2007). The Football Players' Labor Market: Empirical Evidence from the Major European Leagues. *Scotish Journal of Political Economy*, 54 (3), S. 422-446.

Frick, B., (2005). "... und Geld schießt eben doch tore". Die Voraussetzungen sportlichen und wirtschaftlichen Erfolges in der Fußball-Bundesliga. *Sportwissenschaft*, 35, S. 250–70.

Frick, B. (2006). Salary Determination and the Pay-Performance Relationship in Professional Soccer: Evidence from Germany. In Rodriguez, P., Kesenne S., & Garcia, J., (editors). *Sports Economics After Fifty Years: Essays in Honour of Simon Rottenberg*. Oviedo: Ediciones de la Universidad de Oviedo, S. 125-46.

Gabler, J., (2009). *Ultrakulturen und Rechtsextremismus: Fußballfans in Deutschland und Italien*. Köln: PapyRossa Verlag.

Geh, E., Z., (2011). Understanding Strategic Alliances from the Effectual Entrepreneurial Firm's Perspective - An Organisation Theory Perspective. *SAM Advanced Management Journal*, 76 (4), S. 27.

Gephart, R., P., (2004). Qualitative Research and the Academy of Management Journal. *Academy of Management Journal*, 47, S. 454-462.

Gerke, W., (2002). *Börsen Lexikon*. 2nd Edition. Wiesbaden: Betriebswirtschaftlicher Verlag Dr. Th. Gabler GmbH.

Geylani, T., Inman, J., J., & Hofstede, F., T., (2008). Image Reinforcement or Impairment: The Effects of Co-Branding on Attribute Uncertainty. *Marketing Science*, 27 (4), S. 730-744.

Giles, T., King, L., de Lacey, S., (2013). The Timing of the Literature Review in Grounded Theory Research: An Open Mind versus an Empty Head. *ANS Adv. Nursing Science*, 36 (2), S. 29-40.

Giulianotti, R., (2002). Supporters, Followers, Fans, and Flaneurs – A Taxonomy of Spectator Identities in Football. *Journal of Sport and Social Issues*, 26 (1), S. 25-46.

Glaser, B., G., (2002). Conceptualization: On Theory and Theorizing Using Grounded Theory. *International Journal of Qualitative Methods*, 1 (2). Article 3, doi.org/https://doi.org/10.1177/160940690200100203.

Glaser, B., G., (2012). Stop. Write! Writing Grounded Theory. *Grounded Theory Review, an International Journal*, 1 (11).

Glaser, B., G., (1992). *Basics of Grounded Theory Analysis*. Mill Valley, CA: Sociology Press.

Glaser, B., G., (2005). *The Grounded Theory Perspective III: Theoretical Coding*. Mill Valley, CA: Sociology Press.

Gläser, J., & Grit, L., (2004). *Experteninterviews und Qualitative Inhaltsanalyse*. Wiesbaden: VS Verlag für Sozialwissenschaften.

Glover, S., I., & Wassermann, C., M., (2003). *Partnerships, Joint Ventures & Strategic Alliances*. New York: Law Journal Press.

Glück, O., (2018). Absolute und relative Häufigkeit [online]. *Welt der BWL*, available at: https://welt-der-bwl.de/Absolute-und-relative-H%C3%A4ufigkeit [accessed: 23/12/2018].

Golden-Biddle, K., & Locke, K., (1993). Appealing Work: An Investigation of how Ethnographic Texts Convince. *Organization Science*, 4 (4), S. 595-616.

Gomes, E., Barnes, B., R., & Mahmood, T., (2016). A 22 Year of Strategic Alliance Research in the Leading Management Journals. *International Business Review*, 25 (2016), S. 15-27.

Goulding, C., (1999). *Grounded Theory: Some Reflections on Paradigm, Procedures and Misconceptions*. Working Paper Series June, 1999. UK: University of Wolverhampton.

Grant, R., M., (1991). The Resource-Based Theory of Competitive Advantage: Implications for Strategy Formulation. *California Management Review*, 33 (3), S. 114-35.

Gravier, J., Randall, W., S., & Strutton, D., (2008). Investigating the Role of Knowledge in Alliance Performance. *Journal of Knowledge Management*, 12 (4), S. 117-130.

Gray D., E., (2009). *Doing Research in the Real World*. 2nd Edition. California: Thousand Oaks, Sage Publications.

Greene, J., (2006). Toward a Methodology of Mixed Methods Social Inquiry. *Research in the School*, 1 (13), S. 93-98.

Gregson, J., (05 April 2015). Running a Team is Becoming a ‚Science' for Academia and the Corporate World [online]. *Wall Street Journal*, available at: http://online.wsj.com/ad/article/businessoffootball-management.html.

Groscurth, S., (2005). Strategische Partner im Fußball [online]. *Sponsors*, available at: http://www.sponsors.de/strategische-partner-im-fussball. [accessed: 06/06/2016].

Grossman, S., & Hart, O., (1986). The Costs and Benefits of Ownership: A Theory of Lateral and Vertical Integration. *Journal of Political Economy*, 94, p. 691-719.

Grundy, T., (1998). Strategy, Value and Change in the Football Industry. *Strategic Change*, 7, p. 127-138.

Guercini, S., (2014). New Qualitative Research Methodologies in Management, *Management Decision*, 52 (4) p. 662 – 674.

Gulati, R., (1995). Does Familiarity Breed Trust? The Implications of Repeated Ties for Contractual Choice in Alliances. *Academy of Management Journal*, 38 (1), p. 85–112.

Gupta, A., K., & Govindarajan, V., (2000). Knowledge Flows within Multinational Corporations. *Strategic Management Journal*, 21 (4), p. 473–496.

Hall, S., G., & Zimbalist, A., (2002). Testing Causality between Team Performance and Payroll. The Cases of Major League Baseball and English Soccer. *Journal of Sports Economics,* 3 (2), p. 149-168.

Hallberg, L., R., M., (2010). Some Thoughts About the Literature Review in Grounded Theory Studies. *International Journal of Qualitative Health Well-being*, 5 (3), p. 1.

Hamel, G., (1991). Competition for Competence and Inter-Partner Learning with International Strategic Alliances. *Strategic Management Journal,* 12, p. 83–103.

Hammersley, M., (1992). Deconstructing the Qualitative-Quantitative Divide. In Brannen, J., (editor). *Mixing Methods: Qualitative and Quantitative Research*. Aldershot: Ashgate Publishing Company, p. 39-55.

Handelsblatt (09 July 2016). Geldregen für Deutsche Profi-Clubs [online]. *Handelsblatt*, available at: http://www.handelsblatt.com/sport/fussball/neuer-tv-vertrag-der-dfl-geldregen-fuer-die-deutschen-profi-klubs/13711882.html.

Harrigan, K., R., (1988). Joint Ventures and Competitive Strategy. *Strategic Management Journal,* 9 (2), p. 141-158.

Harrison, J., S., (1997). Alternatives to Merger–Joint Ventures and Other Strategies. In Lloyd, B., (editor). *Creating Value through Acquisitions, Demergers, Buyouts and Alliances*. Kidlington: Pergamon/Elsevier Science.

Harrison, J., S., Hitt, M., A., Hoskinson, R., E., & Ireland, R., D., (2001). Resource Complementarity in Business Combinations: Extending the Logic to Organisational Alliances. *Journal of Management*, 27 (6), p. 679–690.

Hart, O., (1995). *Firms, Contracts and Financial Structure*. Oxford: Oxford University Press.

Hart, O., & Moore, J., (1990). Property Rights and the Nature of the Firm. *Journal of Political Economy*, 98, p. 1119-1158.

Hatch, M., J., & Schultz, M., (2001). Are the Strategic Stars Aligned for Your Corporate Brand? *Harvard Business Review*, 2 (79), p. 128-134.

Hau, L., N., & Evangelista, F., (2007). Acquiring tacit and explicit marketing knowledge from foreign partners in IJVs. *Journal of Business Research*, 60, p. 1152– 1165.

Hecox, M., G., (2007). Strategic Alliances in the Sport Industry: A Case Review of Reebok International and the NFL. In Pitts, B., G., (editor). *Sport Marketing in the New Millennium: Selected Papers from the Third Annual Conference of the Sport Marketing Association. Morgantown*, WV: Fitness Information Technology.

Heermann, P., W., (2011). Fast alle Fragen zur rechtlichen Zulässigkeit der 50+1-Regelung bleiben offen. *Causa Sport,* 8 (4), p. 339-343.

Heier, S., (05 April 2011). Fan-Hass auf Uli Hoeneß – zwei Kritikpunkte und viel Unterstützung für den Bayern-Präsidenten [online]. *Goal*, available at: https://www.goal.com/de/news/3642/hintergrund/2011/04/05/2426957/fan-hass-auf-uli-hoene%C3%9F-zwei-kritikpunkte-und-viel-unterst%C3%BCtzung- [accessed: 13/12/2018].

Hemme, F., Morais, D., G., Bowers, M., T., & Todd, J., S., (2017). Extending Sport-Based Entrepreneurship through Phenomenological Inquiry. *Sport Management Review*, 20 (1), p. 92-104.

Hennart, J., (1988). A Transaction Costs Theory of Equity Joint Ventures. *Strategic Management Journal*, 9, p. 361–374.

Henseler, J., Wilson, B., Gotz, O., & Hautvast, C., (2007). Investigating the moderating role of fit on sports sponsorship and brand equity. *International Journal of Sports Marketing & Sponsorship*, 8 (4), p. 321-329.

Herberger, T., Oehler, A., Wedlich, F., (2016). Finanzierungsentscheidungen von Fußballunternehmen im Spannungsfeld verschiedener Fangruppen. *Betriebswirtschaftliche Forschung und Praxis,* 5, p. 495-525.

Herdtstück, M., (16 October 2018). Hertha BSC will KKR herauskaufen [online]. *Finance Magazine*, available at: https://www.finance-magazin.de/deals/private-equity-private-debt/hertha-bsc-will-kkr-herauskaufen-2026121/ [accessed: 22/11/2018].

Hermanns, A., (1997). *Sponsoring*. 2nd Edition. München: Vahlen.

Hertzel, M., & Smith, R., L., (1993). Market Discounts and Shareholder Gains for Placing Equity Privately. *Journal of Finance*, 48, p. 459-485.

Heselmann, E., (29 March 2018). 30 Millionen winken in der Champions League [online]. *Ruhr Nachrichten*, availbale at: https://www.ruhrnachrichten.de/Sport/Schalke/30-Millionen-Euro-winkenin-der-Champions-League-1270490.html. [accessed: 14/10/2018].

Hess, A., (11 December 2015). What the Evolution of Kit Sponsors tells Us about the Premier League [online]. *Vice Sports*, available at: https://sports.vice.com/en_ca/article/kbdebv/what-the-evolution-of-kit-sponsors-tells-us-about-the-premier-league [accessed: 11/09/2018].

Heun, V., (2016). *Assetklasse Fußball: Chancen und Risiken für Investoren im Fußball.* Norderstedt: BoD.

Hey, A., (22 July 2016). Wolfs Take Over Means 25 of Top English Clubs Now Have A Foreign Owner [online]. *Daily Mail*, available at: https://www.dailymail.co.uk/sport/football/article-3703138/Wolves-25th-club-England-s-two-tiers-foreign-owner-majority-shareholder.html.

Hickman, T., M., Lawrence, K., E., & Ward, J., C., (2005). A Social Identities Perspective on the Effects of Corporate Sponsorship on Employees. *Sport Marketing Quarterly*, 14, p. 148-157.

Hills, M., (2002). *Fan Cultures*. New York: Routledge.

Hirsch, M., (30 May 2018). Fußball: Fünf Topligen Europas bei TV-Einnahmen über Milliardengrenze [online]. *Der Standard*, available at: https://www.derstandard.de/story/2000080689918/fussball-fuenf-topligen-europas-bei-tv-einnahmen-ueber-milliardengrenze.

Hirschman, A., O., (1970). *Exit, Voice and Loyalty. Responses to Declines in Firms, Organisations, and States*. Cambridge, MA: Harvard University Press.

Hitt, M., A., Bierman, L., Uhlenbruck, K., & Shimizu, K., (2006). The Importance of Resources in the Internationalization of Professional Service Firms. The Good, the Bad, and the Ugly. *Academy of Management Journal*, 49 (6), p. 1137–1157.

Hitt, M., A., Ireland, R., D., & Hoskisson, R., E., (1996). *Strategic Management: Competitiveness and Globalization*. 2nd Edition. Minneapolis/St. Paul: West Publishing.

Holloway, I., (2008). *A-Z of Qualitative Research in Healthcare*. 2nd Edition. Oxford: Blackwell.

Holt, M., (2009). UEFA, Governance, and the Control of Club Competition in European Football. *Birkbeck Sport Business Centre*, 2 (1), p. 1-191.

Holton, J., (2009). Qualitative Tussles in Undertaking a Grounded Theory Study. *The Grounded Theory Review*, 8 (3), p. 37-50.

Hosmer, L., T., (1995). Trust: The Connecting Link between Organisational Theory and Philosophical Ethics. *Academy of Management Review*, 20, p. 379–403.

Hovemann, G., & Schubert, M., (2006). Finanzen im Fußball: Zur wirtschaftlichen Lage und den Perspektiven des Profi-Fußballs in Deutschland. *f.i.t.-Magazin*, 11 (1), p. 34-40.

Hovemann, G., & Wieschemann, C., (2009). Regulierung von Investitionen in der Fußball-Bundesliga. Eine Diskussion des Streitstandes. *Zeitschrift für Sport und Recht*, 16 (5), p. 234-240.

Hovemann, G., (2009). Finanzierung im Sport. In Breuer, C., & Thiel, A., (editors). *Handbuch Sportmanagement - Beiträge zur Lehre und Forschung im Sport*. 2nd Edition. Schorndorf: Hofmann, p. 224-235.

Hovemann, G., and Wieschemann, C. (2009). Regulierung von Investitionen in der Fußball-Bundesliga. Eine Diskussion des Streitstandes. *Zeitschrift für Sport und Recht, 16* (5), p. 234–240.

Hovemann, G., Lammert, J., Richter, F., & Hallmann, K., (2010). Defizite der aktuellen UEFA-Regulation zur Identifikation von beherrschendem Einfluss gegenüber Profi-Fußballclubs. *Betriebswirtschaftliche Forschung und Praxis*, 62 (4), p. 447-461.

Hufnagel, J., (2011). *Private Equity-Aktivitäten in der Sportbranche - Bestandsaufnahme und Analyse*. Dissertation. Köln: Deutsche Sporthochschule Köln.

Huth, C., Hähnlein, J., & Kurscheidt, M., (2018). Internationale Zielmarktauswahl im Profifußball: Ein Scoring-Modell zur Deutschen Fußball Liga. In Breuer, M., Druker, K., & Grotz, M., (editors). Internationalisierung im Profisport, *Sciamus: Sport und Management*, 1/2018, p. 32-48.

IEG (International Event Group), (2008). Dealing with data: how properties can collect audience information sponsors require. *IEG Sponsorship Report*, 21 (27). Chicago: IEG.

IEG (International Event Group), (2011). Sponsorship Spending: 2010 Proves Better than Expected; Bigger Gains Set for 2011. *IEG Sponsorship Report*, available at: http://www.sponsorship.com/ieg/files/fc/fcbe683b-d2a8-4f0b-9b35-121a86ab3a2b.pdf.

Inkpen, A., C., & Beamish, P., W., (1997). Knowledge, Bargaining Power, and the Instability of International Joint Ventures. *Academy of Management Review*, 22 (1), p. 177–202.

Inkpen, A., C., (1998). Learning and Knowledge Acquisition Through International Strategic Alliances. *Academy of Management Executive*, 12 (4), p. 69–80.

Inskip, I., (2004). Corporate Branding for Small to Medium-Sized Businesses - A Missed Opportunity or an Indulgence. *Journal of Brand Management*, 11, p. 358-365.

Institut für Demoskopie Allensbach (01 December 2017a). Umfrage nach Häufigkeit des Besuchs von Sportveranstaltungen bei Fußball-Fans. In Statista (editor), *Dossier – Fußball-Fans in Deutschland*, (p. 23), availabel at: https://de.statista.com/download/MTUx-MjM4MjgxOSMjNjE5MT YjIzQ2NjY5IyMxIyNwZGYjI1N0dWR5.

Institut für Demoskopie Allensbach (01 December 2017b). Umfrage in Deutschland zum Geschlecht der Fuß-ball-Fans 2017. In Statista (editor). *Dossier – Fußball-Fans in Deutschland* (p. 7), available at: https://de.statista.com/download/MTUxMjM4Mjgx-OSMjNjE5M TYjIzQ2NjY5Iy MxIyNwZGYjI1N0dWR5.

Institut für Demoskopie Allensbach (01 December 2017c). Fußball-Fans der Bundesliga in Deutschland nach Alter im Vergleich mit der Bevölkerung im Jahr 2017. In Statista (editor). *Dossier – Fußball-Fans in Deutschland* (p. 8), available at: https://de.sta-tista.

com/download/MTUxMjM4MjgxOSMjNjE5MTYjIzQ2NjY5IyMxIyNwZGYjI1N0dWR5.

Institut für Demoskopie Allensbach (01 December 2017d). Fußball-Fans der Bundesliga in Deutschland nach Alter im Vergleich mit der Bevölkerung im Jahr 2017. In Statista (editor). *Dossier – Fußball-Fans in Deutschland* (p. 8), available at: https://de.statista.com/download/MTUxMjM4MjgxOSMjNjE5MTYjIzQ2NjY5IyMxIyNwZGYjI1N0dWR5.

Ireland, D., R., Hitt, M., A., & Vaidyanath, D., (2002). Alliance Management as a Source of Competitive Advantage. *Journal of Management*, 28 (3), p. 413-446.

Jacobs, H., (08 August 2014). Fanproteste gegen RB Leipzig verschärfen sich [online]. *Abendblatt*, available at: http://www.abendblatt.de/sport/fussball/article131011240/Fanprotest-gegen-RB-Leipzig-verschaerft-sich.html. [accessed: 03/03/2016].

Jamshed, S., (2014). Qualitative Research Method-Interviewing and Observation. *Journal of Basic and Clinical Pharmacy*, 5 (4), p. 87-88.

Jiang, M., S., & Menguc, B., (2012). Brand as Credible Commitment in Embedded Licensing: A Transaction Cost Perspective. *International Marketing Review*, 29, p. 134–150.

Jiang, X., & Li, Y., (2009). An Empirical Investigation of Knowledge Management and Innovative Performance: The Case of Alliances. *Research Policy,* 38, p. 358–368.

Jiang, X., Li, Y., & Gao, S., (2008). The Stability of Strategic Alliances: Characteristics, Factors and Stages. *Journal of International Management*, 14, p. 173-189.

Johnson, B., R., Onwuegbuzie, A., J., & Turner, L., A., (2007). Toward a Definition of Mixed Methods Research. *Journal of Mixed Methods Research*, 1 (2), p. 112-133.

Johnson, G., Scholes, K., & Whittington, R., (2011). *Exploring Corporate Strategy*. 9th Edition. Harlow: Pearson Education Limited.

Johnston, C., (22 August 2014). Football is Nothing Without Fans [online]. *Open University*, available at: http://www.open.edu/openlearn/football-league-clubs/football-nothing-without-fans-jock-stein [accessed: 27/09/2018].

Jolly, D., (2002). Alliance Strategy: Linking Motives with Benefits. *European Business Forum*, 9, p. 47-50.

Jones, D., (2008). *Annual Review of Football Finance 2008*. Manchester: Deloitte & Touch LLP.

Jones, D., (2011). *Annual Review of Football Finance 2010*. Manchester: Deloitte & Touch LLP.

Joshi, A., Kale, S., Chandel, S., & Pal, D., K., (2015). Likert Scale: Explored and Explained. *British Journal of Applied Science & Technology*, 7 (4), p. 396-403.

Kahuni, A., T., Rowley, J., & Binsardi, A., (2009). Guilty by Association: Image Spill-over in Corporate Co-Branding. *Corporation Reputation Review*, 12 (1), p. 52-63.

Kale, P., & Singh, H., (2009). Managing Strategic Alliances: What Do we Know Now, and Where Do we Go from Here? *Academy of Management Perspectives*, 23, p. 45–62.

Kale, P., Singh, H., & Perlmutter, H., (2000). Learning and Protection of Proprietary Assets in Strategic Alliances: Building Relational Capital. *Strategic Management Journal*, 21 (3), p. 217–237.

Kaplan, J., (2002). Partners in Outsourcing. *Network World*, 19 (11), p. 41.

Kamp, C., (19 February 2015). Ein Signal aus dem hohen Norden [online]. *Frankfurter Allgemeine Zeitung*, available at: http://www.faz.net/aktuell/sport/fussball/bundesliga/

kommerzialisierung-ein-signal-aus-dem-hohen-norden-13436288.html. [accessed: 03/03/2016].

Kanealy, J., J., (2008). Management Research and Grounded Theory: A Review of Grounded Theory Building Approach in Organisational and Management Research. *International Journal of Grounded Theory Review*, 2 (7), available at: http://groundedtheoryreview.com/2008/06/28/1004/.

Kapferer, J., N., (1998). *The New Strategic Brand Management: Creating and Sustaining Brand Equity Long Term*. 2nd Edition. London: Kogan Page.

Kapferer, J., N., (2012). *The New Strategic Brand Management: Creating and Sustaining Brand Equity Long Term*. 5th Edition. London: Kogan Page.

Keller, C., (2006). *Corporate Finance im Profifußball: Erfolgsfaktoren, Strategien und Instrumente für die Finanzierung von Fußballunternehmen*. Dissertation. Stuttgart: Ibidem Verlag.

Kelly, S., (2008). Understanding the Role of the Football Manager in Britain and Ireland: A Weberian Approach. *European Sport Management Quarterly*, 8 (4), p. 399-419.

Kern, M., (2007). *Besonderheiten der Unternehmensfinanzierung und Investitionseffizienz im professionellen Fußball*. Schriftenreihe Sportökonomie in Forschung und Praxis. 3rd Edition. Hamburg: Dr. Kovac.

Keythman, B., (08 October 2016). Advantage & Disadvantage of Equity Capital [online]. *Small Business*, available at: http://smallbusiness.chron.com/advantage-disadvantage-equity-capital-58005.html.

Kicker (22 May 2018). 50+1: Kind reaktiviert Übernahmepläne für Hannover 96 [online]. *Kicker Sportmagazin*, available at: http://www.kicker.de/news/fussball/bundesliga/vereine/724371/artikel_502b1_kind-reaktiviert-uebernahmeplaene-fuer-hannover-96.html.

Kim, C., & Inkpen, A., C., (2005). Cross-Border R&D Alliances, Absorptive Capacity and Technology Learning. *Journal of International Management,* 11 (3), p. 313–329.

Klein, J., (11 November 2008). Traditionsverein? Ein Definitionsversuch [online]. *Leuchtturm-fcs*, available at: http://leuchtturm-fcs.blogspot.de/2008/11/traditionsverein-ein-definitionsversuch.html.

Knips, B., (29 Juli 2014). Werder vertraut Wiesenhof, weil das so sein muss [online]. *Die Kreiszeitung*, available at: https://www.kreiszeitung.de/werder-bremen/werder-vertraut-wiesenhof-weil-sein-muss-2455687.html.

Knox, S., & Bickerton, D., (2003). The Six Conventions of Corporate Branding. *European Journal of Marketing*, 37 (7/8), p. 998-1016.

Kohli, A., K., & Jaworski, B., J., (1990). Market Orientation: The Construct, Research Propositions, and Managerial Implications. *Journal of Marketing*, 54 (2), p. 1–18.

Kolb, S., M., (2012). Grounded Theory and the Constant Comparative Method: Valid Research Strategies for Education. *Journal of Emerging Trends in Educational Research and Policy Studies*, 3 (1). p. 83-86.

Kollmann, T., Karczewski, M., & Dölken, T. (2010). *Faninvestor 2.0 – Modelle – Faninvestoren – Meinungen – Ergebnisse einer Onlineumfrage*. Essen: Universität Duisburg-Essen.

Kotler, P., & Keller, K., L., (2009). *Marketing Management*. 13th edition. New Jersey: Pearson Education Ltd.

Koza, M., & Lewin, A., (2000). Managing Partnerships and Strategic Alliances: Raising the Odds of Success. *European Management Journal*, 18 (2), p. 146-151.

König, T., (2002). *Fankultur: Eine soziologische Studie am Beispiel des Fußballfans*. Münster: LIT.

Krishnaswami, S., Pablo E., & Venkat S., R., (2012). When is Equity More than Just Financing? Evidence from Strategic Alliances [online]. *Midwest Finance Association 2013, Annual Meeting Paper*, doi.org/https://doi.org/10.2139/ssrn.2154659.

Krosnick, J., A., (1999). Survey Research. *Annual Review of Psychology*, 50, p. 537-567.

Kuhn, T., S., (1962). The Structure of Scientific Revolutions. 1st Edition. CA: University of Chicago Press.

Kuypers, S., & Szymanski, S., (2012). *Soccernomics*. London: Hapersport.

Lammert, J., Bauers, S., B., & Hovemann, G., (2018). Die 50+1-Regel im deutschen Profifußball – Eine qualitative Evaluation von Lösungsvorschlägen zur Herstellung des regulatorischen Sollzustandes. *Sciamus – Sport und Management*, 9 (2), p. 21-45.

Lammert, J., Hovemann, G., Wieschemann, C., & Richter, F., (2009). The Tension between Financial Interests and Prevention of a Controlling Influence in German Professional Football – Needs and Recommendations for a Modification of the Existing Regulation. *Sport and Society*, 6 (3), p. 203-233.

Lane, P., J., & Lubatkin, M., (1998). Relative Absorptive Capacity and Interorganisational Learning. *Strategic Management Journal*, 19 (5), p. 461–477.

Lane, P., J., Salk, J., E., & Lyles, M., A., (2001). Absorptive Capacity, Learning, and Performance in International Joint Ventures. *Strategic Management Journal*, 22, p. 1139–1161.

Lange, J., (2011). Qualen auf dem Hühnerhof. *Süddeutsche Zeitung*, 2 September, p. 2.

Laskin, A., V., (2018). *The Handbook of Financial Communication and Investor Relations*. New Delhi: John Wiley & Sons, Inc.

Lavie, D., & Rosenkopf, L., (2006). Balancing exploration and exploitation in alliance formation. *Academy of Management Journal*, 49 (4), p. 797–818.

Lavinsky, D., (02 April 2013). Does Your Business Have Strategic Partners? Why not? [online]. *Forbes*, available at: https://www.forbes.com/sites/davelavinsky/2013/04/02/does-your-business-have-strategic-partners-why-not/. [accessed 06/10/2018].

Lawrence, P., R., & Lorsch, J., W., (1967). *Organisation and Environment*. Cambridge: Harvard University Press.

Legewie, H., & Schervier-Legewie, B., (2004). Forschung ist harte Arbeit, es ist immer ein Stück Leiden damit verbunden. Deshalb muss es auf der anderen Seite Spaß machen. Anselm Strauss im Interview mit Legewie, H., & Schervier-Legewie, B., [90 Absätze]. *Forum Qualitative Social Research, 5* (3), Art. 22.

Lei, D., Solcum, J., W., & Pitts, R., A., (1997). Building Cooperative Advantage: Managing Strategic Alliances to Promote organisational learning. *Journal of World Business*, 32 (3), S. 203-224.

Leidecker, J., & Bruno, A., (1984). Identifying and Using Critical Success Factors. *Long Range Planning*, 17 (1), S. 23-32.

Leister, R., (30 August 2017). Welchen dieser 3 Typen von Investoren im Fußball bevorzugst Du? [online]. *Fußballwirtschaft*, available at: https://fussballwirtschaft.de/investoren-im-fussball [accessed: 19/09/2017].

Lerner J., Shane H., & Tsai, A., (2003). Do Equity Financing Cycles Matter? Evidence from Biotechnology Alliances. *Journal of Financial Economics*, 67, S. 411-446.

Levers, M.-J., D., (2013). *Philosophical Paradigms, Grounded Theory, and Perspectives on Emergence*. Sage Open, October-December 2013, S. 1-6.

Liao, R., C., (2014). What Drives Corporate Minority Acquisitions Around the World? The Case for Financial Constraints. *Journal of Corporate Finance*, 26 (C), S. 78-95.

Lin, B., & Darling, J., (1999). An Analysis of the Formulation of Strategic Alliances: A Focus on the Pharmaceutical Industry. *Industrial Management & Data Systems,* 3, S. 121-127.

Lin, H., & Darnall, N., (2014). Strategic Alliance Formation and Structural Configuration. *Journal of Business Ethics*, 127 (3), S. 549-564.

Lin, Z., Yang, H., & Arya, B. (2009). Alliance Partners and Firm Performance: Resource Complementary and Status Association. *Strategic Management Journal*, 30, S. 921–940.

Lincoln, Y., S., & Guba, E., G., (1985). *Naturalistic Inquiry*. Newbury Park: Sage.

Locke, K., (2003). *Grounded Theory in Management Research*. London: Sage.

Locke, K., (2011). Field Research Practice in Management and Organisation Studies: Reclaiming its Tradition of discovery. *Academy of Management Annals*, 5, S. 613-652.

Locke, K., (2015). Pragmatic Reflection on a Conversation About Grounded Theory in Management and Organisation Studies. *Organisational Research Methods*, 18 (4), S. 1-8.

Löffler, M., (2009). Methodensammlung zu Auswertung klinischer und epidemiologischer Daten. *IMISE-Reports*, Nr. 2/2007. Universität Leipzig: Institut für Medizinische Informatik, Statistik und Epidemiologie.

Loonam, J., (2014). Towards a Grounded Theory Methodology: Reflections for Management Scholars. *Irish Journal of Management*, 33 (1), S. 49-72.

Lorange, P., & Ross, J., (1991). Analytical Steps in Formation of Strategic Alliances. *Journal of Organisational Change Management*, 4 (1), S. 60-72.

Lorange, P., & Ross, J., (1993). *Strategic Alliances. Formation, Implementation and Evolution.* Cambridge: Blackwell Pub.

Lorentzen, P., Fraval, T., M., & Paine, J., (2016). Qualitative Investigation of Theoretical Models: The Value of Process Tracing. *Journal of Theoretical Politics,* 29, S. 1-25.

Lowensberg, D., A., (2010). "A “New” View on “Traditional” Strategic Alliances‘ Formation Paradigms. *Management Decision*, 48 (7), S. 1090 – 1102.

Luck, L., Jackson, D. & Usher, K., (2006). Case Study: A Bridge Across the Paradigms. *Nursing Inquiry*, 2 (13), S. 103-109.

Lucks, K., & Meckl, R., (2015). *International Mergers & Acquisitions*. Wiesbaden: Springer Gabler.

Lui, C., L., Pervez, N., Ghauri, B., Rudolf, R., & Sinkovics, C., (2010). Understanding the Impact of Relational Capital and Organisational Learning on Alliance Outcomes. *Journal of World Business*, 45, S. 237–249.

Lund, R., & Gryser, S., A., (2016). More Effective Sports Sponsorships – Combining and Integrating Key Resources and Capabilities of International Sports Events and their Major Sponsors. *Harvard Business School. Working Paper*, 16 (139), S. 1-37.

Luo, Y., (1997). Partner Selection and Venturing Success: The Case of Joint Ventures with Firms in the People’s Republic of China. *Organisation Science*, 8, S. 648–662.

Lyles, M., A., & Salk, J., E., (1996). Knowledge Acquisition from Foreign Parents in International Joint Ventures: An Empirical Examination in the Hungarian Context. *Journal of International Business Studies*, 27 (5), S. 877–903.

Madrigal, R., (2001). Social Identity Effects in a Belief-Attitude-Intentions Hierarchy: Implications for Corporate Sponsorship. *Psychology & Marketing*, 18 (2), S. 145–165.

Mahony, D., F., & Pitts, B., G., (1998). Research Outlets in Sport Marketing: The Need for Increased Specialization. *Journal of Sport Management*, 12 (4), S. 259-272.

Maital, S., Prakhya, S., & Seshadri, D., V., R., (2008). Bridging the Chasm between Management Education, Research, and Practice: Moving Towards the ‚Grounded Theory' Approach. *Vikalpa*, 33 (1), S. 1-18.

Mangold, G., W., & Mills, J., S., (2007). The Employee Brand: Is Yours an All-Star. *Business Horizons*, 5 (50), S. 423-433.

Marcus, A., A., (2016). *Management Strategy: Achieving Sustained Competitive Advantage*. 3rd Edition. New York: McGraw Hill.

Marsden, P., (2002). Brand Positioning: Meme's the Word. *Marketing Intelligence & Planning,* 5 (20), S. 307-3012.

Mazloomi K., H., & Jolly, D., R., (2006). Knowledge Transfer in Alliances: Determinant Factors. *Journal of Knowledge Management*, 12 (1), S. 37-50.

Mazodier, M., & Quester, P., (2014). The Role of Sponsorship Fit for Changing Brand affect: A Latent Growth Modelling Approach. *International Journal of Research in Marketing*, 31, S. 16-29.

Mäläska, M., Saraniemi, S., & Tähtinen, J., (2011). Network Actors' Participation in B2B SME Branding. *Industrial Marketing Management,* 7 (40), S. 1144-1152.

McAllister, D., J., & Ferrell, L., (2002). The Role of Strategic Philanthropy in Marketing Strategy. *European Journal of Marketing*, 36, S. 689–705.

McAllister, D., J., (1995). Affect- and cCgnition-Based Trust as Foundations for Interpersonal Cooperation in Organisations. *Academy of Management Journal,* 38, S. 24–59.

McNamara, P., Peck, S., I., & Sasson, A., (2011). Competing Business Models, Value Creation and Appropriation in English Football. *Long Range Planning*, 46, S. 475-487.

McPhail, C., & Rexroat, C., (1979). The Divergent Methodological Perspectives of Social Behaviourism and Symbolic Interactionism. *American Sociological Review*, 44 (3), S. 449-467.

McQuerrey, L., (09 December 2018). The Disadvantages of Forming Business Alliances. *Chron*, available at: http://smallbusiness.chron.com/disadvantages-forming-business-alliances-73390.html.

Meenaghan, T., & Shipley, D., (1999). Media Effecting Sponsorship. *European Journal of Marketing*, 33 (3/4), S. 328 – 347.

Meenaghan, T., (1991). The Role of Sponsorship in the Marketing Communications mix. *International Journal of Advertising*, 10 (1), S. 35–47.

Meenaghan, T., (1998). Current Developments and Future Directions in Sonsorship. *International Journal of Advertising*, 17 (1), S. 3–28.

Meenaghan, T., (2001a). Sponsorship and Advertising: A Comparison of Consumer Perceptions. *Psychology & Marketing*, 18 (2), S. 191–215.

Meenaghan, T., (2001b). Understanding Sponsorship Effects. *Psychology & Marketing*, 18 (2), S. 95–122.

Meffert, H., & Bierwirth, A., (2005). Corporate Branding – Führung der Unternehmensmarke im Spannungsfeld unterschiedlicher Zielgruppen. In Meffert, H., Burmann, C., & Koers, M., (editors). *Markenmanagement – Identitätsorientierte Markenführung und praktische Umsetzung*. 2nd Edition. Wiesbaden: Gabler, S. 73- 114.

Meier, M., (2011). Knowledge Management in Strategic Alliances: A Review of Empirical Evidence. *International Journal of Management Reviews*, 13, S. 1–23.

Merkel, U., (2012). Football Fans and Clubs in Germany: Conflicts, Crises and Compromises. *Soccer & Society,* 13 (3), S. 359–376.

Mertens, D., M., (1998). *Research Methods in Education and Psychology: Integrating Diversity with Quantitative & Qualitative Approaches*. London: Sage.

Metrum (2004). *Financing the Game: Die Kapitalmarktfähigkeit von Profifußballclubs aus Investorensicht*. München: Metrum Management Beratung GmbH.

Meuser, M., & Nagel, U., (1991). ExpertInneninterviews: Vielfach erprobt, wenig bedacht. In Garz, D., & Kraimer, K., (editors). *Qualitativ-empirische Sozialforschung: Konzepte, Methoden, Analysen*. Opladen: Westdeutscher Verlag, S. 441-471.

Mey, G., & Mruck, K., (2007). Grounded Theory Methodologie - Bemerkungen zu einem prominenten Forschungsstil. *Historical Social Research*, 19, S. 11-39.

Mills, M., B., & Huberman, M., A., (1994). *Qualitative Data Analysis: A Sourcebook of New Methods*. 2nd Edition. Newbury Park: Sage.

Mills, R., E., & Snow, C., C., (1994). *Fit Failure, and the Hall of Fame: How Companies Succeed and Fail*. New York: The Free Press.

Mintzberg, H., Ahlstrand, B., & Lampel, J., (1998). *Strategy Safari – A Guided Tour Through the Wilds of Strategic Management*. New York: The Fre Press.

Mitchie, J., & Oughton, C., (2005). The Corporate Governance of Professional Football Clubs in England. *Corporate Governance: An International Review*, 13 (4), S. 517-531.

Mitsuhashi, H., (2003). Effects of the Social Origins of Alliances on Alliance Performance. *Organization Studies*, 24 (2), S. 321-339.

Moorman, C., Zaltman, G., & Deshpande R., (1992). Relationships between Providers and Users of Market Research: The Dynamics of Trust Within and between Organisations. *Journal of Marketing Research*, 29, S. 314–328.

Morgan, A., Adair, D., Taylor, T., & Hermens, A., (2014). Sport Sponsorship Alliances: Relationship Management for Shared Value. *Sport, Business and Management: An International Journal*, 4, S. 270–283.

Motion, J., Leitch, S., & Brodie, R., J., (2003). Equity in Corporate Co-Branding. The Case of Adidas and the All Blacks. *European Journal of Marketing*, 37 (7/8), S. 1080-1094.

Müller, F., (20 September 2008). Befreit die Liga von der Vereinsmeierei [online]. *Die Zeit*, available at http://www.zeit.de/online/2008/48/bundesliga-investorenfreiheit-dfl-contra. [accessed: 03/03/2016].

Murphy, N., (2018). Markenrelevante Erfolgsfaktoren zur Erschließung des US-amerikanischen Markets. In Breuer, M., Druker, K., & Grotz, M., (editors). Internationalisierung im Profisport, *Sciamus: Sport und Management,* 1/2018, S. 49-70.

Murphy, R., (2010). Playing Fair in the Boardroom: An Examination of the Corporate Structures of European Football Clubs. *Michigan State Journal of International Law*, 19 (2), S. 409-448.

Murray, J., Y., & Kotabe, M., (2005). Performance Implications of Strategic Fit between Alliance Attributes and Alliance Forms. *Journal of Business Research*, 58 (11), S. 1525-1533.

Nagy, Z., I., (2011). The Unique Features of the Financing of Professional Football. *Public Finance Quarterly*, 4, S. 539-552.

Nagy, Z., I., (2012). Modern Forms of Business in Professional Football. *Law and Economics Review*, 2, S. 1-20.

Nagy, Z., I., (2013). The Role of Legal Forms in Professional Football. *Acta Polytechnica Hungarica*, 10 (4), S. 209-227.

Nauright, J., & Ramfjord, J., (2011). Who Owns England's Game? American Professional Sporting Influences and Foreign Ownership in the Premier League. In Hassan, D., & Hamil, S., (editors). *Who Owns football*? London: Routledge, S. 86-99.

NDR (24 March 2018). Vor 45 Jahren: Hirsch Revolution in Braunschweig [online]. *NDR*, available at: https://www.ndr.de/sport/fussball/50_jahre_bundesliga/Eintarcht-Braunschweig-Jaegermeister-Trikotwerbung-Hirsch,braunschweig2433.html. [accessed: 09/08/2018].

Neale, W., C., (1964). The Peculiar Economics of Professional Sports. *The Quarterly Journal of Economics*, 78, S. 1-14.

Netzer, T., Behrenbeck, K., Ecker, T., Gatzer, S., Reimig, S., Strojny, P., & Tacke, T., (2015). *Wachstumsmotor Bundesliga. Die ökonomische Bedeutung des professionellen Fußballs in Deutschland – Ergebnisse 2015*. McKinsey & Company, Inc.

Nicholas, J., Mastracchio, J., R., & Zunitch, V., M., (2002). Difference between Mergers and Acquisitions. *Journal of Accountancy*, November, S. 38-71.

Nielsen Sports (02 November 2018). Sponsor-Trend 2018 [online]. *Nielsen*, available at: https://nielsensports.com/de/sponsor-trend-2018/.

Nielsen, B., B., & Gudergan, S., (2012). Exploration and Exploitation Fit and Performance in International Strategic Alliances. *International Business Review*, 21, S. 558-574.

N-TV (03 March 2004). *Die reichsten Fußball-Clubs* [online]. Available at:
http://www.n-tv.de/sport/Die-reichsten-Fussball-Clubs-article94398.html [accessed: 27/06/2016].

Nufer, G., & Bühler, A., (2011). Relevant Factors for Successful Relationships between Professional Sporting Organisations and their Sponsors. *Journal of Physical and Sports Management*, 2 (3), S. 26-31.

Nufer, G., (2018). Lessons from Sports: What Corporate Managers Can Learn from International Professional Sports. In Breuer, M., Druker, K., & Grotz, M., (editors). Internationalisierung im Profisport. *Sciamus: Sport und Management*, 1/2018, S. 132-146.

O'Reilly, N., & Horning, D., L., (2013). Leveraging Sponsorship: The Activation Ratio. *Sport Management Review*, 16, S. 424-437.

Oediger, F., (10 February 2017a). Spielplatz der Milliardäre – die größten Fußball-Investoren [online]. *Manager Magazine*, availble at: https://www.manager-magazin.de/unternehmen/artikel/europaeischer-fussball-spielplatz-der-milliardaere-a-1133884-2.html [accessed: 30/06/2017].

Oediger, F., (20 May 2017b). Diese Investoren drängen in die Bundesliga [online]. *Manager Magazine*, available at: http://www.manager-magazin.de/unternehmen/artikel/fussball-investoren-perspektiven-in-der-bundesliga-a-1146279.html. [accessed: 30/06/2017].

Oesterle, M.-J., (1999). Fiktionen der Internationalisierungsforschung – Stand und Perspektiven einer realitätsorientierten Theoriebildung. In Engelhard, J., & Oechsler, W., A., (editors). *Internationales Management: Auswirkungen globaler Veränderungen auf Wettbewerb, Unternehmensstrategie und Märkte*. Wiesbaden: Gabler, S. 219-245.

Oettgen, N., (2008). *Integriertes Marketing für professionelle Fußballvereine: Eine Analyse der Anspruchsgruppenorientierung in der deutschen Fußballbundesliga*. Frankfurt: Peter Lang GmbH, Internationaler Verlag der Wissenschaft.

Olejniczak, M., & Aicher, J., (2010). Conceptual Framework of Sponsorship's Relationship with Components of Organisational Culture. *International Journal of Sport Management Recreation & Tourism*, 6, S. 18-36.

Oliver, C., (1990). Determinants of Interorganisational Relationships: Integration and Future Directions. *The Academy of Management Review*, 15 (2), S. 241-265.

Olkkonen, R., T., (2001). Case Study: The Network Approach to International Sport Sponsorship Arrangement. *Journal of Business and Industrial Marketing*, 16, S. 309–327.

Olkkonen, R., T., Tikkanen, H., & Alajoutsijärvi, K., (2000). Sponsorship as Relationships and Networks Implications for Research. Corporate Communications: *An International Journal*, 5 (1), S. 12–18.

Olson, E., L., & Thjomoe, H., M., (2009). Sponsorship Effect Metric: Assessing the Financial Value of Sponsoring by Comparisons to Television Advertising. *Journal of the Academy of Marketing Science*, 37 (4), S. 504–515.

Ong, B., K., (2012). Grounded Theory Method (GTM) and the Abductive Research Strategy (ARS): A Critical Analysis of their Differences. *International Journal of Social Research Methodology*, 15 (5), S. 417-432.

Parkhe, A., (1991). Interfirm Diversity, Organisational Learning, and Longevity in Global Strategic Alliances. *Journal of International Business Studies*, 22 (4), S. 579–601.

Parkhe, A., (1993). Strategic Alliance Structuring: A Game Theoretic and Transaction Cost Examination of Interfirm Cooperation. *Academy of Management Journal,* 36 (4), S. 794-829.

Parmigiani, A., & Rivera-Santos, M., (2011). Clearing a Path Through the Forest: A Meta-Review of Interorganisational Relationships. *Journal of Management,* 37 (4), S. 1108–1136.

Paul, C., & Teevs, C., (03 August 2015). Investoren in der Bundesliga: Bis nichts mehr bleibt [online]. *Spiegel Sport*, available at http://www.spiegel.de/sport/fussball/fussball-bundesliga-so-gehen-die-klubs-mit-investoren-um-a-1042220.html. [accessed: 16/06/2016].

Pawlowski, T., (2013). *Wettbewerbsintensität im Profifußball – Eine Empirische Untersuchung zur Bedeutung für die Zuschauer*. Wiesbaden: Springer Gabler.

Pcmag (16 December 2018). *Encyclopaedia: Definition of Cookie* [online]. Available at: https://www.pcmag.com/encyclopedia/term/40334/cookie.

Pekar, P., & Allio, R., (1994). Making Alliances Work – Guidelines for Success. In Lloyd, B., (editor). *Long Range Planning,* 27 (4), S. 54-65.

Pekar, P., & Margulis, M., (2003). Equity Alliances Take Centre Stage. *Business Strategy Review*, 14 (2), S. 50-62.

Pepels, W., (2001). *Kommunikations-Management: Marketing-Kommunikation vom Briefing bis zur Realisation.* Stuttgart: Schaffer-Poeschel Verlag.

Parrish, R., (2003). *Sports Law and Policy in the European Union*. Manchester: Manchester University Press.

Pfeiffer, S., Hovemann, A., Herpel, P., (2007). *Bälle, Tore und Finanzen IV*. Ernst & Young AG.

Pilot Group (2005). *Sponsors Visions 2005*. Hamburg: Pilot Checkpoint GmbH.

Pilz, G., A., (2011). *Zusammenfassung der Einstellungen der Faninitiativen und Interessengemeinschaften der organisierten Fußballfans zur 50+1 – Regel und gutachterliche Stellungnahme zu den Einstellungen*. Hannover: University of Hannover.

Pinnuck, M., & Potter, B., (2006). Impact of On-Field Success on the Off-Field Financial Performance of All Football Clubs. *Accounting and Finance*, 46, S. 499-517.

Pisano, G., P., (1989). Using Equity Participation to Support Exchange: Evidence from the Biotechnology Industry. *Journal of Law, Economics, and Organisation*, 5 (1), S. 109–126.

Plewa, C., Carrillat, F., Mazodier, M., & Quester, P., (2016). Which Sport Sponsorships Most Impact Sponsor CSR Image? *European Journal of Marketing*, 50 (5/6), S. 796-815.

Plumley, D., Wilson, R., & Ramchandani, G., (2017). Towards a Model for Measuring Holistic Performance of Professional Football Clubs. *Soccer & Society*, 18 (1), S. 16–29.

Poitras, G., (2016). *Equity Capital: From Ancient Partnership to Modern Exchange Traded Funds*. New York: Routledge.

Pons, F., & Richelieu, A., (2008). *The Internationalization of Football Team Brands: The Specific Case of Chivas (Mexico and USA)*. Book of Abstracts. 16th European Management Conference "Management at the Heart of Sport". S. 495-497. GSM mbH.

Pope, N., (1998). Overview of current Sponsorship Thought. *The Cyber Journal of Sport Marketing*, 2 (1), S. 1-7.

Porter, M., E., & Kramer, M., R., (2002). The Competitive Advantage of Corporate Philanthropy. *Harvard Business Review*, 80 (12), S. 56–69.

Porter, M., E., (1979). How Competitive Forces Shape Strategy. *Harvard Business Review*, 57 (2), S. 137-45.

Porter, M., E., (1991). Towards a Dynamic Theory of Strategy. *Strategic Management Journal*, 12 (2), S. 95-117.

Post, F., & Druker, K., (2018). Eine Untersuchung zum Internationalisierungsstand der Bundesliga 2015/2016. In Breuer, M., Druker, K., & Grotz, M., (editors). Internationalisierung im Profisport, *Sciamus*: *Sport und Management*, 1/2018, S. 4-31.

Pötschke, M., (2009). Potentiale von Online-Befragungen: Erfahrungen aus der Hochschulforschung. In Jacob, N., Schoen, H., & Zerback, T., (editor). *Sozialforschung im Internet*. Wiesbaden: Springer, S. 75-89.

Prahalad, C., K., & Hamel, G., (1994). Competing for the Future. *Harvard Business Review*, 72 (4), S. 122-128.

Pramschüfer, M., (16 June 2016). Fällt die 50+1 Regelung? [online]. *Fußball*, available at: http://www.fussball.news/faellt-die-50plus1-regelung/.

Pratt, S., F., (2016). Pragmatism as Ontology, not (just) Epistemology: Exploring the Full Horizon of Pragmatism as an Approach to IR Theory. *International Studies Review*, 10, S. 1 -20.

Prigge, S., & Vöpel, H., (2014). *Investoren und Mäzene im Fußball- Eine Typologie Externer Kapitalgeber*. Hamburgisches Weltwirtschaftsinstitut, Standpunkt: 20. Februar 2014. Sportökonomik.

Pryziborski, A., & Wohlrab-Sahr, M., (2014). *Qualitative Sozialforschung*. 4th Edition. München: Oldenbourg Wissenschaftsverlag.

Quester, P., & Thompson, B., (2001). Advertising and Promotion Leverage on Arts Sponsorship Effectiveness. *Journal of Advertising Research*, 41 (1), S. 33–47.

Quimet, P., P., (2013). What Motivates Minority Acquisitions? The Trade-Offs between a Partial Equity Stake and Complete Integration. *Review of Financial Studies*, 26 (4), S. 1021-1049.

Quitzau, J., & Merfeld, T., (27 January 2016). *Auf dem Weg zu amerikanischen Verhältnissen – Wirtschaftliche Trends im Profifußball* [online]. Berenberg Bank, available at: http://fussball-oekonomie.de/wp-content/uploads/2016/04/Wirtschaftliche-TrendsLigasport_USA-vs-Europa-final.pdf. [accessed 09/08/2018].

Quitzau, J., (2003). Erfolgsfaktor Zufall im Profifußball: Quantifizierung mit Hilfe informationseffizienter Wettmärkte. *Diskussionspapier*, 20, September 2003.

Quitzau, J., (2009). Fußball als Markt. *Die Zeit*, 1. September 2009.

Quitzau, J., (22 December 2014). Wehe, wenn der Investor kommt [online]. *Capital*, available at: https://www.capital.de/wirtschaft-politik/wehe-wenn-der-investor-kommt-3172. [accessed: 08/08/2018].

Radhakrishna, R., B., (2007). Tips for Developing and Testing Questionnaires/Instruments. *Extension Journal*, 45 (1), S. 710-714.

Rehm, H., (18 March 2018). Die Bundesliga ist international nur zweitklassig [online]. *Manager Magazin*, available at: http://www.manager-magazin.de/unternehmen/artikel/bundesliga-international-suche-nach-anschluss-a-1197681.html. [accessed: 05/09/2018].

Reich, H., (07 December 2007). Management by Publikumsliebling [online]. *Manager Magazin*, available at: http://www.manager-magazin.de/unternehmen/karriere/a-521569-2.html. [accessed: 25/09/2016].

Renard, N., & Sitz, L., (2011). Maximising Sponsorship Opportunities: A Brand Model Approach. *Journal of Product & Brand Management*, 20 (2), S. 121-129.

Rentz, I., (17 December 2015). Wie der US-Sportartikler Capelli in Europa Fuß fassen will [online]. *Horizont*, available at: https://www.horizont.net/marketing/nachrichten/Capelli-Group-US-Sportartikler-will-in-Europa Fuss-fassen---und-steigt-beim-MSV-Duisburg-ein-137992. [accessed: 03/07/2018].

Reuer, J., J., Zollo, M., & Singh, H., (2002). Post-Formation Dynamics in Strategic Alliances. *Strategic Management Journal*, 23 (2), S. 135–151.

Richter, F., (31 May 2019). Zuschauermagnet Bundesliga [online]. *Statista*, available at: https://de.statista.com/infografik/12546/zuschauerschnitt-in-europas-fussballligen/. [accessed: 03/09/2019].

Rindfleisch, A., & Moorman, C., (2001). The Acquisition and Utilization of Information in New Product aAliances: A Strength-of-Ties Perspective. *Journal of Marketing*, 65, S. 1–18.

Ring, P., S., & Van De Ven, A., (1994). Developmental Processes of Cooperative Interorganisational Relationships. *Academy of Management Review*, 19, S. 90-118.

Ring, P., S., (1996). Fragile and Resilient Trust and Their Roles in Economic Exchange. *Business & Society*, 35, S. 148–175.

Ring, P., S., (2000). The three T's of Alliance Creation: Task, Team and Time. *European Management Journal*, 18 (2), S. 152-163.

Ritchie, J., Lewis, J., McNaughton N., C., & Ormston, R., (2013). *Qualitative Research Practice: A Guide for Social Science Students and Researchers*. London: Sage.

Ritter, J., & Peitsmeier, H., (24 April 2018). Keine Rückendeckung von Sponsoren [online]. *Frankfurter Allgemeine Zeitung*, available at: https://www.faz.net/aktuell/wirtschaft/uli-hoeness-keine-rueckendeckung-von-sponsoren-12160815.html. [accessed: 13.12.2018].

Ritter, T., (1999). The Networking Company: Antecedents for Coping with Relationships and Networks Effectively. *Industrial Marketing Management*, 28 (5), S. 467–479.

Robbins, S., P., (1997). *Organisational Behaviour: Concepts, Controversies and Applications*. 6th Edition. Englewood Cliffs, New York: Prentice-Hall.

Robinson, T., (26 May 2013). Companies Continue to Score with Football Sponsorship [online]. *Financial Times*, available at: https://next.ft.com/content/2182ce9e-c5e5-11e2-99d1-00144feab7de. [accessed: 19/04/2015].

Robson, C., (2002). *Real World Research*. 2nd Edition. Oxford: Blackwell.

Rohde, M., & Breuer, C., (2017). The Market for Football Club Investors: A Review of the Theory and Empirical Evidence from Professional European Football. *European Sport Management Quarterly*, 17 (3), S. 265-289.

Rohr, S., (13 November 2018). Hertha zahlt US-Investor KKR 71,2 Millionen Euro [online]. *Kicker Sportmagazin*, available at: http://www.kicker.de/news/fussball/bundesliga/startseite/736005/artikel_hertha-zahlt-us-investor-kkr-712-millionen-euro.html. [accessed: 18/11.2018].

Roose, J., & Schäfer, M., S., (2017). Fans und Partizipation. In Roose, J., Schäfer, M., S., & Schmidt-Lux, T., (editors). *Fans – Soziologische Perspektiven*. Wiesbaden: Springer, S. 319–342.

Rosentritt, M., (11 November 2016). Darf's noch ein Stück Retorte sein? [online]. *11 Freunde, Magazin für Fußballkultur*, available at: https://www.11freunde.de/artikel/wie-wird-das-tv-geld-verteilt. [accessed: 04/09/2018].

Rosentritt, M., (13 April 2013). Top oder Hopp [online]. *Tagesspiegel*, available at: https://www.tagesspiegel.de/sport/maezene-im-deutschen-fussball-top-oder-hopp/8054280.html. [accessed: 06/09/2018].

Rossiter, J., R., (2002). The C-OAR-SE Procedure for Scale Development in Marketing. *International Journal of Research in Marketing*, 19 (4), S. 305–335.

Roy, P., (2009). Private-Equity-Investments im Fußball: Situation, Modelle und Zukunftsperspektiven der Eigenkapitalversorgung durch Finanzinvestoren. In Dietl., H., Franck, E., & Kempf, H., (editors). *Fußball: Ökonomie einer Leidenschaft*. Münster: Hofmann Verlag, S. 141-152.

Ruda, W., & Klug, F., (2010). *Sport-Sponsoring: An den Beispielen: FIFA Fußball-WM 2006TM in Deutschland und FIFA Fußball-WM 2010 in Südafrika*. München: Oldenbourg: De Gruyter.

Ruf C., & Theweleit, D., (04 March 2018). Kindische Vorstellungen [online]. *TAZ*, available at: http://www.taz.de/!5485600/.

Russo, M., & Cesarini, M., (2017). Strategic Alliance Success Factors: A Literature Review on Alliance Lifecycle. *International Journal of Business Administration*, 3, S. 1-10.

Rust, R., T., & Zahoric, A., J., (1993). Customer Satisfaction, Customer Retention, and Market Share. *Journal of Retailing,* 69 (2), S. 193-215.

Sahay, B., S., & Maini, A., (2002). Supply Chain: A Shift from Transactional to Collaborative Partnerships Decisions. *Indian Institute of Management Calcutta*, 29 (2), S. 67-88.

Saldana, J., (2013). *The Coding Manual for Qualitative Researchers*. 2nd Edition. London: Sage.

Salz, J., Steinkirchner, P., Mersch, T., & Merx, S., (14 August 2015). Der Fußball würde von einer Öffnung von Investoren profitieren [online]. *Wirtschaftwoche*, available at: http://www.wiwo.de/unternehmen/dienstleister/bundesliga-der-fussball-wuerde-von-einer-oeffnung-fuer-investoren-profitieren/12180774.html. [accessed 15/12/2015].

Salzborn, C., (2017). *Phänomen Shitstorm: Herausforderungen für die Onlinekommunikation von Unternehmen*. Baden-Baden: Tectum Verlag.

Sam, P., M., Batty, R., & Dea, R., G., (2005). A Transaction Cost Approach to Sport Sponsorship. *Sport Management Review*, 8 (1), S. 1-17.

Sandler, D., M., & Shani, D., (1993). Sponsorship and the Olympic Games: the Consumer Perspective. *Sport Marketing Quarterly,* 2 (3), S. 38-43.

Sankaran, S., Kouzim, A., & Hase, S., (2005). Learning from Alliances. *The International Journal of Knowledge, Culture, and Change Management: Annual Review*, doi.org/https://doi.org/10.18848/1447-9524/cgp.

Santala, M., & Parvinen, P., (2007). From Strategic Fit to Customer Fit. *Management Decision*, 45 (3), S. 582-601.

Sarkar, A., N., & Singh, J., (2005). New Paradigm in Evolving Brand Management Strategy. *Journal of Management Research,* 2 (5), S. 80-90.

Sarter, A., & Mies, J., (26 January 2017). Zwölfter Umsatzrekord in Folge - Fußball Bundesliga schwimmt im Geld [online]. *N-TV*, available at: https://www.n-tv.de/sport/fussball/Fussball-Bundesliga-schwimmt-im-Geld-article19653842.html.

Saunders, M., Lewis, P., & Thornhill, A., (2009). *Research Methods for Business Students*. 5th Edition. Harlow: Pearson Education Ltd.

Savage, S., (24 February 2005). Case and Grounded Theory as Qualitative Research Methods [online]. *Red Orbit*, available at http://www.redorbit.com/news/science/130594/case_and_grounded_theory_as_qualitative_research_methods/. [accessed: 25/05/2016].

Saxton, T., (1997). The Effects of Partner and Relationship Characteristics on Alliance Outcomes. *Academy of Management Journal*, 40 (2), 443 – 459.

Sayer, A., (2000). *Realism and Social Science*. London: Sage.

Schade, M., (2012). Identitätsbasierte Markenführung professioneller Sportvereine. Dissertation. In Burmann, C., & Kirchgeorg, M., (editors). *Innovatives Markenmanagement*, 32. Gaebler.

Schmitt, T., (02 December 2015). Ohrfeigen für Rummenigge und Schweinchen Schlau [online]. *Handelsblatt*, available: https://www.handelsblatt.com/sport/fussball/streit-um-tv-milliarden-vertagt-ohrfeigen-fuer-rummenigge-und-schweinchen-schlau/12670260-all.html. [accessed: 05/09/2018].

Schmitt, T., (10 May 2017). Bundesliga kriecht im Ausland hinterher [online]. *Handelsblatt*, available at: https://www.handelsblatt.com/sport/fussball/fussball-sponsoren-und-facebook-bundesliga-kriecht-im-ausland-hinterher/19781414.html?ticket=ST-813582-bGObDKl76ljeBezOgOnv-ap3. [accessed: 11/09/2018].

Schmitt, T., (12 November 2016a). Bundesliga knackt Marke von drei Milliarden Euro [online]. *Handelsblatt*, available at: http://www.handelsblatt.com/sport/fussball/umsatz-rekord-im-fussball-bundesliga-knackt-marke-von-drei-milliarden-euro/14856184.html.

Schmitt, T., (16 February 2016b). Warum Jürgen Klopp eine Gefahr ist. *Handelsblatt*, available at: https://www.handelsblatt.com/sport/fussball/premier-league-gegen-bundesliga-warum-juergen-klopp-eine-gefahr-ist/12976788-all.html.

Schneider, M., (08 March 2018). Der deutsche Fußball ringt um seine heilige Regel [online]. *Süddeutsche Zeitung*, available at: https://www.sueddeutsche.de/sport/-der-deutsche-fussball-ringt-um-seine-heilige-regel-1.3897612. [accessed: 12/02/2019].

Schnell, R., Hill, P., & Esser, E., (2008). *Methoden der empirischen Sozialforschung*. 8th Edition, München: Oldenbourg Verlag.

Schurch, L., S., (2015). *Seducing Engagement: A Classic Grounded Theory Study of Virtual Leadership*. College of Education: Walden Dissertations and Doctoral Studies.

Schürmann, L., (22 May 2015). Warum diese Männer Millionen in den Fußball stecken [online]. *Manager Magazin*, available at: http://www.manager-magazin.de/unternehmen/artikel/die-maezene-der-bundesliga-a-1035129.html. [accessed: 01/10/2016].

Schurr, P., H., (2007). Buyer-Seller Relationship Development Episodes: Theories and Methods. *Journal of Business and Industrial Marketing*, 22 (3), S. 161 – 170.

Schuster, F., & Unterhitzenberger, C., (2014). *Bälle, Tore und Finanzen VI*. Ernst & Young Real Estate GmbH.

Schwier, J., & Fritsch, O., (2003). *Fußball, Fans und das Internet*. Baltmannsweiler: Schneider-Verlag Hohengehren.

Seemann, D., & Schollmeier, A., (2008). Fußball – Ein Interessantes Feld für Private Equity? *Venture Capital Magazin*, 6 (7/8), S. 18–19.

Selm, M., Jankowski, N., W., (2006). Conducting Online Surveys. *Quality & Quantity,* 40, S. 436–456.

Sener, I., & Karapoltagil, A., A., (2015). Rules of the Game: Strategy in Football Industry. *Procedia – Social and Behavioural Science*, 207 (2015), S. 10–19.

Setzen, K., M., (1999). Gruppen im Sport. In Schäfers, B., (editor). *Einführung in die Gruppensoziologie: Geschichte, Theorien, Analysen*. Wiesbaden: Springer, S. 269–287.

Seydel, M., (2005). Sportsponsoring in der Praxis: am Beispiel T-COM und FC Bayern München. In Schewe, G., & Rohlmann, P., (editors). *Sportmarketing*. Schondorf Verlag, S. 53–66.

Shalin, D., N., (1990). The Pragmatic Origins of Symbolic Interactionism and The Crisis of Classical Science. *Studies in Symbolic Interaction*, 12, S. 223–251.

Shank, M., D., (1999). *Sports Marketing. A Strategic Perspective*. Upper Saddle River. New York: Prentice-Hall.

Shenton, A., K., (2004). Strategies for Ensuring Trustworthiness in Qualitative Research Projects. *Education for Information, 22* (2), S. 63–75.

Simonin, B., & Ruth, J., A., (1998). Is a Company Known by the Company It Keeps? Assessing the Spillover Effects of Brand Alliances on Consumer Brand Attitudes. *Journal of Marketing Research*, 35 (1), S. 30–42.

Sluyts, K., Matthyssens, P., Martens, R., & Streukens, S., (2011). Building Capabilities to Manage Strategic Alliances. *Industrial Marketing Management*, 40 (6), S. 875–886.

Smith, A., C., & Stewart, B., (2010). The Special Features of Sport: A Critical Revisit. *Sport Management Review*, 13 (1), S. 1–13.

Söderman, S., & Dolles, H., (2010). Sponsoring the Beijing Olympic Games: Patterns of Sponsor Advertising. *Asia Pacific Journal of Marketing and Logistics*, 22 (1), S. 8–24.

Sotiriadou, P., & Shilbury, D., (2008). Using Grounded Theory in Sport Management Research. *International Journal of Sport Management and Marketing*, 4 (1/2), S. 125–146.

Spekman, R., E., (1988). Strategic Supplier Selection: Toward an Understanding of Long-Term Buyer and Seller Relationships. *Business Horizons*, 31, S. 75–81.

Spekman, R., E., Forbes, T., M., Isabella, L., A., & MacAvoy, T., C., (1998). Alliance Management: A View from the Past and a Look to the Future. *Journal of Management Studies*, 35 (6), S. 747–772.

Spekman, R., E., Isabella, L., A., & MacAvoy, T., C., (2000). *Alliance Competence: Maximizing the Value of Your Partnerships*. New York: John Wiley.

Spender, J., C., (1996). Making knowledge the basis of a dynamic theory of the firm. *Strategic Management Journal*, 17, S. 45–62.

Sportfive (2007). *Fußballstudie 2007: Märkte, Events, Vereine, Medien, Marken*. In Sportfive GmbH (editor). Hamburg 2007.

Sportspromedia (20 April 2011). Adidas and Bayern Munich Renew Kit Deal for Eight Years [online]. available at: http://www.sportspromedia.com/news/adidas_and_bayern_munich_renew_kit_deal_for_eight_years. [accessed: 05/02/2016].

Stadionwelt (26 February 2018). Stadien: Bundesliga im Naming Right weit vorne [online]. *Stadionwelt*, available at: https://www.stadionwelt.de/sw_stadien/index.php?-head=Stadien-Bundesliga-im-Naming-Right-weit-vorne&folder=sites&site=news_detail&news_id=1756. [accessed: 10/09/2018].

Statista (02 May 2015). Gesamtumsatz des europäischen Fußballmarktes von 2006/07 bis 2012/13 (in Milliarden Euro) [online]. *Statista*, available at: http://de.statista.com/statistik/daten/studie/198723/umfrage/umsatz-des-europaeischen-fussballmarktes-seit-2006/. [accessed: 02/05/2015].

Statista (2017). Market Size of the European Professional Football Market from 2006/07 to 2016/17 (in Billion Euros) [online]. *Statista*, available at https://www.statista.com/statistics/261223/european-soccer-market-total-revenue/. [accessed: 23/11/2017].

Statista (23 December 2018). Fußball-Fans der Bundesliga in Deutschland nach Häufigkeit des Besuchs einer Sportveranstaltung im Vergleich mit der Bevölkerung im Jahr 2018 [online]. *Statista*, available at: https://de.statista.com/statistik/daten/studie/729201/umfrage/fussball-fans-in-deutschland-nach-haeufigkeit-des-besuchs-einer-sportveranstaltung/. [accessed: 27/11/2018].

Steinke, I., (1999). *Kriterien qualitativer Forschung. Ansätze zur Bewertung qualitativ-empirischer Sozialforschung*. Weinheim: Juventa.

Steinke, I., (2010). Gütekriterien qualitativer Forschung. In Flick, U., von Kardorff, E., & Steinke, I., (editors). *Qualitative Forschung*. Ein Handbuch. 9th Edition. Reinbek: Rowohlt, S. 319–331.

Steinmann, T., (18 November 2018). Hertha und die „Heuschrecke" [online]. *Capital - Wirtschaft ist Gesellschaft*, available at: https://www.capital.de/wirtschaft-politik/fussball-investoren-kkr-hertha-und-die-heuschrecke?article_onepage=true.

Stotlar, D., K., (2004). Sponsorship Evaluation: Moving from Theory to Practice. *Sport Marketing Quarterly*, 13 (1), S. 61–64.

Strauss, A., L., & Corbin, J., M., (1990). *Basics of Qualitative Research: Grounded Theory Procedures and Techniques*. Newbury Park, CA: Sage.

Strauss, A., L., & Corbin, J., M., (1998). *Basics of Qualitative Research: Techniques and Procedures for Developing Grounded Theory*. 2nd Edition. Thousand Oaks: Sage.

Stride, A., Fitzgerald, H., F., & Allison, W., (2017). A Narrative Approach: The Possibilities for Sport Management. *Sport Management Review*, 20 (1), S. 33–42.

Strübing, J., (2018). Grounded Theory: Methodische und Methodologische Grundlagen. In Pentzhold, C., Bischof, A., & Heise, N., (editors). *Praxis Grounded Theory*. Wiesbaden: Springer Fachmedien, S. 27–52.

Summerer, T., (2008). Investoren für die Bundesliga. *Zeitschrift für Sport und Recht*, 15 (6), S. 234–241.

Süßmilch, I., (2004). Alternative Finanzierungsmöglichkeiten. In Süßmilch, I., & Elter, V., C., (editors). *FC Euro AG – Fußball und Finanzen*. 4th Edition. WGZ-Bank und KPMG.

Szymanski, S., & Kuypers, T., (1999). *Winners and Loosers: The Business Strategy of Football*. London: Penguin.

Szymanski, S., & Smith, R., (1997). The English Football Industry: Profit, Performance and Industrial Structure. *International Review of Applied Economics*, 11, S. 135–153.

Szymanski, S., (2001). Income Inequality, Competitive Balance and the Attractiveness of Team Sports: Some Evidence and a Natural Experiment from English Soccer. *The Economic Journal*, 111 (469), S. 69–84.

Szymanski, S., (2007). Incentives and Competitive Balance in Team Sports. *European Sport Management Quarterly*, 3 (1), S. 11.30.

Szymanski, S., (2010). The Financial Crisis and English Football: The Dog That Will Not Bark. *International Journal of Sport Finance, 5* (1), S. 28–40.

Tauber, A., (05 November 2013). Das Dilemma der Bayern-Sponsoren im Fall Hoeneß [online]. *Die Welt*, available at https://www.welt.de/wirtschaft/article121578036/Das-Dilemma-der-Bayern-Sponsoren-im-Fall-Hoeness.html. [accessed: 13/12.2018].

Teece, D., J., (1998). Research Directions for Knowledge Management. *California Management Review*, 40 (3), S. 289–92.

Teece, D., Pisano, G., & Shuen, A., (1997). Dynamic Capabilities and Strategic Management. *Strategic Management Journal*, 18 (7), S. 509 – 533.

Teevs, C., (2014). 50+1 Regel: Bahn frei für die Fußballinvestoren [online]. *Spiegel*, available at: http://www.spiegel.de/sport/fussball/bundesliga-kommentar-der-unsinn-der-50-1-regel-a-1009280.html. [accessed: 15/01/2016].

Teddlie, C., & Tashakkori, A., (2006). A General Typology of Research Designs Featuring Mixed Methods. *Research in the School,* 1 (13), S. 12–28.

Teichmann, K., (2006). Strategie und Erfolge von Fußballunternehmen. Dissertation. Kiel: Deutscher Universitätsverlag.

Theobald, A., (2007). Zur Gestaltung von Online-Fragebögen. In Welker, M., & Wenzel, O., (editors). *Online-Forschung*. Köln: von Halem, S. 103–118.

Thompson, P., & Speed, R., (2000). Determinants of Sports Sponsorship Response. *Journal of the Academy of Marketing Science*, 28 (2), S. 226–238.

Todeva, E., & Knoke, D., (2005). Strategic Alliances and Models of Collaboration. *Management Decision*, 43 (1), S. 123–48.

Tome, M., (2003) *Ausländer in der Fußball Bundesliga.* Mainz: Volkskunde in Rheinland-Pfalz.

Tourangeau, R., C., & Mick P., C., (2007). Colour, Labels and Interpretive Heuristics for Response Scales. *Public Opinion Quarterly*, 71, S. 91–112.

Trendel, O., & Warlop, L., (2007). Positive Implicit Memory Effects for Event Incongruent Sponsorship. *Advances in Consumer Research*, 34, S. 102–103.

Truschkat, I., Kaiser, M., & Reinartz, V., (2005). Forschen nach Rezept? Anregungen zum praktischen Umgang mit der Grounded Theory in Qualifikationsarbeiten. *Forum: Qualitative Sozialforschung*, 6 (2), S. 1–24.

Tsang, E., W., K., (2000). Transaction Cost and Resource Based Explanations of Joint Ventures: A Comparison and Synthesis. *Organisation Studies*, 21, S. 215–242.

Tsang, E., W., K., Nguyen, D., T., & Eramilli, M., K., (2004). Knowledge Acquisition and Performance of International Joint Ventures in the Transition Economy of Vietnam. *Journal of International Marketing*, 12, S. 82–103.

Tsiotsou, R., H., Kostas, A., & Cornwell, B., T., (2014). Using Evaluative Conditioning to Explain Corporate Co-Branding in the Context of Sport Sponsorship. *International Journal of Advertising*, 33 (2), S. 295–327.

UEFA (2017). *Club Licensing Benchmarking Report: Financial Year 2017*. Geneva: Financial Sustainability and Research Division/UEFA Intelligence Centre.

UEFA (01 October 2016). Financial Fair Play [online]. *UEFA*, available at http://www.uefa.org/protecting-the-game/club-licensing-and-financial-fair-play/.

UEFA (2012). *The European Club Footballing Landscape. Club Licensing Benchmarking Report Financial Year 2010.* Nyon: UEFA.

Urde, M., (2009). Uncovering the Corporate Brand's Core Values. *Management Decision*, 4 (47), S. 616–638.

Urriolagoitia, L., & Planellas, M., (2007). Sponsorship Relationships as Strategic Alliances: A Life Cycle Model Approach. *Business Horizons*, 50, S. 157–166.

Urquhart, C., (2013). *Grounded Theory for Qualitative Research: A Practical Guide*. London: Sage.

Uzzi, B., (1997). Social Structure and Competition in Interfirm Networks: The Paradox of Embeddedness. *Administrative Science Quarterly*, 42, S. 35–67.

Van der Heijden, L., (2012). *Does HRM Matter for Professional Soccer Organisations*? University of Twente: School of Management and Governance.

Varey, R., J., (1995). A Model of Internal Marketing for Building and Sustaining a Competitive Service Advantage. *Journal of Marketing Management*, 11, S. 41–54.

Vergauwen, P., Roberts, H., & Vandemaele, S., (2010). Business Alliance & Partnership Performance and its Value Drivers: An Intellectual Capital Approach. *Review of Business and Economics,* 55, S. 249–274.

Vidal, C., (2008). What is a Worldview? In van Belle, H., & van der Veken, J., (editors). *Nieuwheid Denken. De Wetenschappen en het Creatieve Aspect van de Werkelijkheid.* Leuven: In Press, S. 1–14.

Von Loh, S., (24 November 2018). C-level [online]. *Sven von Loh Entrepreneurial Partner,* available at: https://svenvonloh.de/wissenswertes/c-level.

Von Overloop, P., (2015*). Internationalisierung professioneller Fußballclubs*. Wiesbaden: Springer Gabler.

Vöpel, H., (2009). Wettbewerb und Regulierung in der Fußball-Bundesliga. *Wirtschaftswissenschaftliches Studium*, 38 (12), S. 629–634.

Wahyuni, D., (2012). The Research Design Maze: Understanding Paradigms, Cases, Methods and Methodologies. *Journal of Applied Management Accounting Research,* 1 (10), S. 69–80.

Walliser, B., (2003). An International Review of Sponsorship Research: Extension and Update. *International Journal of Advertising,* 22 (1), S. 5–40.

Wallrodt, L., (27 November 2015). Das dilettantische PR-Manöver von Werder Bremen [online]. *Die Welt,* available at: http://www.welt.de/sport/fussball/bundesliga/werder-bremen/article149347148/Das-dilettantische-PR-Manoever-von-Werder-Bremen.html. [accessed: 15/12/2015].

Walsh, A., J., & Giulianotti, R., (2001). This Sporting Mammon: A Normative Critique of the Commodification of Sport. *Journal of the Philosophy of Sport*, 28 (1), S. 53–77.

Walzel, S., & Schubert, M., (2018). *Sport, Corporate Social Responsibility and Sponsoring*. Berlin, Heidelberg: Springer.

Warren, R., (1967). The Interorganizational Field as Focus for Investigation. *Administrative Science Quarterly*, 12, S. 396–419.

Weed, M., (2009). Research Quality Considerations for Grounded Theory Research in Sport & Exercise Psychology. *Psychology of Sport and Exercise*, 10, S. 502–510.

Weiber, R., & Mühlhaus, D., (2010). *Strukturgleichungsmodellierung – Eine anwendungsorientierte Einführung in die Kausalanalyse mit Hilfe von AMOS, Smart-PLS und SPSS*. Berlin: Springer.

Weiler, S., (2006). *Mehrfachbeteiligungen an Sportkapitalgesellschaften: Verbote von "Multi-Club Shareholding" und deren Grenzen aus der Sicht europäischen Rechts unter besonderer Berücksichtigung des Profifußballs in Deutschland*. Berlin: Duncker & Humboldt.

Welling, M., & Westhoff, M., (19 April 2018). Diese Investorentypen gibt es im Sport [online]. *Sponsors*, available at: https://www.sponsors.de/diese-investorentypen-gibt-es-im-sport# [accessed: 28/04/2018].

Welling, M., (2005). Markenführung im professionellen Ligasport. In Meffert, H., Burmann, C., & Koers, M., (editors). *Markenmanagement – Identitätsorientierte Markenführung und praktische Umsetzung*. 2nd Edition. Wiesbaden: Gabler, S. 37 - 72.

Wernerfelt, B., (1984). A Resource-Based View of the Firm. *Strategic Management Journal*, 5 (2), S. 171–180.

Westberg, K., Stavros, C., A., & Wilson, B., (2011). The Impact of Degenerative Episodes on the Sponsorship B2B Relationship: Implications for Brand Management. *Industrial Marketing Management*, 40, S. 603-611.

Whitney, J., D., (1993). Bidding till Bankrupt: Destructive Competition in Professional Team Sport. *Economic Inquiry,* 31, S. 100-115.

Wilkesmann, U., (2014). Geld schießt Tore – Zur sozialen Ungleichheit im Fußball. In Behnke, C., Lengersdorf, D., & Scholz, S., (editors). *Wissen – Methode – Geschlecht: Erfassen des fraglos Gegebenen*. Wiesbaden: Springer, S. 107-124.

Will, A., (23 November 2015). Unterscheidung: Mäzen, Spender, Sponsor [online]. *Sportmarketing*, available at: http://www.sportmarketing-sponsoring.biz/blog/sponsoring/unterscheidung-maezen-spender-sponsor/.

Williams, C., (2007). Research Methods. *Journal of Business & Economic Research*, 3 (5), S. 1-8.

Williamson, O., (1991). Comparative Economic Organisation: The Analysis of Discreet Structural Alternatives. *Administrative Science Quarterly*, 36, S. 269–296.

Wilson, R., Plumley, D., & Ramchandani, G., (2013). The Relationship between Ownership Structure and Club Performance of Football Clubs in the English Premier League. *Sport, Business and Management*, 3 (1), S. 19–36.

White, B., (2000). *Dissertation Skills for Business and Management Students*. London: Thomson Learning.

Wöckener, L., & Tenbusch, R., (01 April 2016). So werden die TV Millionen in Europa verteilt [online]. *Die Welt*, available at: https://www.welt.de/sport/fussball/bundesliga/article153701973/So-werden-die-TV-Milliarden-in-Europa-verteilt.html. [accessed: 04/09/2018].

Woisetschläger, D., Backhaus, Dreisbach, J., & Schnöring, M., (2015). *Sponsoringstudie 2015 – Die Sponsoringpotenziale in der Fußball-Bundesliga*. Technische Universität Braunschweig.

Woisetschläger, D., M., & Michaelis, M., (2012). Sponsorship Congruence and Brand Image. *European Journal of Marketing*, 46 (3/4), S. 509 – 523.

Woisetschläger, D., M., Backhaus, C., Dreisbach, J., & Schnöring, M., (2014). *Fußballstudie 2014 – die Markenlandschaft der Fußballbundesliga*. Technische Universität Braunschweig.

Woisetschläger, D., M., Backhaus, C., Evanschitzky, H., & Michaelis, M., (2010). Determinants of Sponsorship Fit: A Multilevel Analysis. In Campbell, M., C., Inman, J., & Pieters, R., (editors). *Duluth Advances in Consumer Research*, 37, MN: Association for Consumer Research, S. 548-549.

Wolcott, H., E., (1992). Posturing in Qualitative Research. In LeCompte, M., D., Millroy, W., L., & Preissle, J., (editors). *The Handbook of Qualitative Research in Education*. San Diego, CA: Academic Press. S. 3-52.

Wolf, T., (07 December 2012). Von Stadion Namen und Tradition [online]. *NDR*, available at: https://www.ndr.de/sport/fussball/50_jahre_bundesliga/Von-Stadionnamen-und-Tradition,arenen103.html. [accessed: 10/09/2018].

Wong, A., & Sohal, A., (2002). An Examination of the Relationship between Trust, Commitment and Relationship Quality. *International Journal of Retail and Distribution Management*, 30 (1), S. 34-50.

Woo, K., & Ennew, C., T., (2004). Business-to-Business Relationship Quality. *European Journal of Marketing*, 38 (9/10), S. 1252-1271.

Woodside, A., G., & Wilson, E., J., (2003). Case Study Research Methods for Theory Building. *Journal of Business & Industrial Marketing*, 18 (6/7), S. 493–508.

Yin, R., K., (2014). *Case Study Research: Design and Methods*. 5th Edition. CA: Sage.

Yueh, L., (2014). Why on Earth Buy a Football Club? [online]. *BBC*, available at: http://www.bbc.com/news/business-26365955. [accessed: 15/02/2016].

Zagnoli, P., & Radicchi, E., (2010). The Football Fan Community as a Determinant Stakeholder in Value Co-Creation. *Physical Culture and Sport Studies and Research*, 50 (1), S. 79-99.

Zu Knyphausen-Aufseß, D., (Juni 2009). Leitfaden für die Anfertigung wissenschaftlicher Arbeiten [online]. *Technische Universität Berlin: Fachgebiet Strategische Führung und Globales Management*. Available at: https://www.strategie.tu-berlin.de/fileadmin/fg94/Download/Leitfaden_wissenschaftliches_Arbeiten.pdf [accessed: 08/01/2019].

Williamson, O. E. (1991): Comparative Economic Organization: The Analysis of Discrete Structural Alternatives, Administrative Science Quarterly, 36, S. 269-296.
Wilson, R./Plumley, D./Ramchandani, G. (2013): The Relationship between Ownership Structure and Club Performance of Football Clubs in the English Premier League, Sport, Business and Management, 3 (1), S. 19-36.
[illegible]
[illegible]
[illegible]
[illegible]
[illegible]
[illegible]

The manufacturer's authorised representative in the EU is Springer Nature Customer Service Centre GmbH, Europaplatz 3, 69115 Heidelberg, Germany. If you have any concerns regarding our products, please contact ProductSafety@springernature.com

Printed and bound by CPI Group (UK) Ltd, Croydon, CR0 4YY
30/09/2026
02225601-0006